Forecasting Retirement Needs
and Retirement Wealth

Pension Research Council Publications

A list of current PRC publications appears at the back of this volume.

Forecasting Retirement Needs and Retirement Wealth

Edited by Olivia S. Mitchell,
P. Brett Hammond, and Anna M. Rappaport

Pension Research Council
The Wharton School of the University of Pennsylvania

PENN

University of Pennsylvania Press

Philadelphia

10 9 8 7 6 5 4 3 2 1

Published by
University of Pennsylvania Press
Philadelphia, Pennsylvania 19104-4011

Library of Congress Cataloging-in-Publication Data
Forecasting retirement needs and retirement wealth / edited by
    Olivia S. Mitchell, P. Brett Hammond, and Anna M. Rappaport.
        p.   cm.   "Pension Research Council Publications"
        Includes bibliographical references and index.
        ISBN 0-8122-3529-0 (alk. paper)
        1. Retirement income — United States — Planning.   I. Mitchell,
    Olivia S.   II. Hammond, P. Brett.   III. Rappaport, Anna M.
    HG179.F577   1999
    332.024′01. — dc21
                                                            99-41733
                                                            CIP

Contents

Preface

Economic security in retirement is a topic about which more people are now worrying than at any other time in human history. Global population aging and weaknesses plaguing financial institutions threaten our hopes for wellbeing in old age. Indeed the very meaning of retirement itself may now be called into question, as humanity confronts three or even more decades of life after the age of 65. This book offers guidance to those seeking answers to several compelling questions. What are retirement needs, and how should we think about how much to save for old age? What is retirement becoming, especially in an era of downsizing and early retirement windows? What assets should we hold prior to, and then throughout, the retirement period? How should we invest our pension capital, and how can education influence 401(k) plan saving? How important are employer-provided pensions and social security in protecting retirees against old-age poverty, and what special problems do minorities and women face? How do health shocks and the death of a spouse affect wellbeing at older ages, and how do these influence retirement?

Several empirical surveys have recently been developed with which researchers can begin to address these questions. The Health and Retirement Study (HRS) is the source of interesting new insights for many chapters in this volume, and we are proud to collaborate with this important project, which makes it possible to link information on health, retirement, pensions, and social security for the first time. In addition, contributors to this volume have obtained invaluable information from a wide range of other sources, including employer surveys and federal government databases. These rich datasources will open new vistas for researchers in the retirement arena for years to come.

As with all Pension Research Council volumes, our book seeks a broad and inquisitive readership. For this reason we have collected the views of a fine, interdisciplinary group of academics, benefits consultants, lawyers, policymakers, and actuaries. Their cross-cutting analysis should interest both U.S. residents and experts from other countries as we work to shape reliable old-age systems to meet the challenges of the new millennium.

In preparation of this volume I have enjoyed the cooperation as coeditors of Brett Hammond and Anna Rappaport. Research and publication support was afforded by the U.S. Department of Labor, the Penn Aging Research Center, and particularly the Financial Institutions Center at the Wharton School under the guidance of Anthony Santomero. Our Institutional Members always provide excellent intellectual and financial assistance, and our Senior Partners are particularly helpful in shaping our research agenda. We also gratefully acknowledge continuing support from the Wharton School.

Introduction

Retirement is a twentieth-century institution. Earlier, most people died before reaching retirement, but those who did not worked until severe disability forced them on the mercy of family and charity. Work and home were often one place, and a role was found for older family members. Even during the first half of the twentieth century, as public and private pensions were developed with government, union, and corporate support, many people eligible for a pension passed away before or shortly after retirement. By contrast, today more people than ever before attain retirement age due to increased longevity and earlier retirements, and many elderly live well into their 70s, 80s, and even beyond. Retirement has spread beyond the exclusive purview of the rich to include the vast majority of the older population.

This growth in retirement can be partly attributed to demography, but it is mainly due to the institutions of private and public pensions, systems that provided a secure and generous stream of income on which millions have grown to depend in old age. Many older people today face the future with high hopes for a better and longer retirement period.

Despite the successes of pension programs, however, huge challenges loom. For many, security in old age now seems riskier than expected even a decade or two ago. Global population aging trends are prompting developed nations to consider major changes to previously popular pay-as-you-go social security systems. Increased reliance on defined contribution plans raises questions of how well individuals are managing their assets intended for retirement, but sometimes spent in advance of that time. In addition, weakened financial institutions in some countries worry pension policymakers confronting proposals to privatize public pensions. In the face of these changes, it is easy to understand why the very meaning of retirement is now being examined more closely.

This book offers new perspectives on how to support the growing group of older citizens for three, and possibly even four, decades of life in retirement. We draw these perspectives from the most recent and relevant research,

investigating several of the most compelling questions facing people anticipating retirement during the next century.

The discussion begins by asking whether the meaning and process of
retirement is changing in this era of downsizing and early retirement windows. We show that new paths to retirement are emerging, paths that involve
"bridge" jobs and gradual transitions through various labor market states.
Equally important, we explore the related, and knotty, problems of determining or characterizing what resources people need during retirement
and how to encourage people to think about how much to save for old age.

These issues take on greater urgency as a growing proportion of people's
future retirement income will come from accumulated assets managed by
individuals rather than by employers, and a smaller proportion flows from
defined benefit pensions that define a specific retirement benefit. For this
reason, we investigate what assets people should consider holding before
they retire, and how investment portfolios might be best structured during
retirement. In the course of the discussion, we note how important it is to
understand the prominent role of employer-provided pensions and social
security. These institutions have played a central role in the past, by protecting retirees against old-age poverty. Particular problems facing minorities
and women in old age are also highlighted, along with the growing importance of health shocks, divorce, or the death of a spouse at older ages. In
addition, there is reason to worry that some people formulate inaccurate
expectations regarding their need for retirement income, perhaps based on
inaccurate expectations regarding what the family will provide in old age.
Each of these factors can profoundly affect older persons' work and retirement patterns, and in turn their financial wellbeing.

These and several others we cover here are serious issues that retirees will
face as the population ages in the United States and abroad. We believe they
are deserving of attention now for two reasons. One is because of the long
lead time between action and outcome in public and private pension policy.
The second is that we are now better equipped to analyze these issues, due to
the development of invaluable new datasets recently released for use by
retirement researchers. Most prominent among these is the Health and
Retirement Study (HRS), a nationally representative survey of people initially aged 51–61. Previously, analysts wishing to track older people as they
moved into older age and retirement in the United States had no recent
high-quality databases, being forced to rely instead on somewhat outdated
and often unrepresentative surveys to draw policy conclusions.

By contrast, the HRS began to be collected with an initial interview in 1992,
in which over 12,000 participants were recruited to the study. This large and
nationally representative group generously agreed to be re-interviewed every
two years thereafter, a structure that has generated an ongoing, and longitudinal, study of incalculable value. Retirement researchers now have a
priceless source of economic, psychological, sociological, health, and other

information about a wide cross-section of the population, devised specifically for the purpose of studying retirement and health transitions in the older population.

This volume is the first to feature analyses and insights on retirement preparedness using the HRS. Below we describe in greater detail aspects of this wonderful new data source, along with many of the rich opportunities for research that it affords.

In this introductory chapter we preview several of the key old-age economic security issues raised in this volume, issues engendered by recent movements in the U.S. retirement marketplace along with anticipated future developments. We begin with a look at how the concept of retirement is evolving, and then go on to assess how well — or how poorly — people are planning for their retirement years. Next we highlight several challenges to a secure retirement, focusing on how the unexpected — in the form of corporate downsizing and early retirement windows, for example — can influence the opportunities open to the older worker. More persistent challenges confront older women and minorities in old age, as well as widows, who often experience sharp decreases in their standard of living after the death of a spouse. Finally, we examine how health shocks, and the expenditures associated with poor health, can undermine older people's economic security. The discussion concludes with a brief overview of an exciting new dataset that has recently become available to researchers studying retirement needs and retirement wellbeing.

Looking Ahead to Retirement

Even today, many people's conception of retirement is one where a full-time employee remains with a life-long employer until his or her 65th birthday and then exits the labor force completely, suddenly, and permanently. If this was ever a useful model, it is no longer the standard, as pointed out by Joseph Quinn's interesting description of retirement paths in the HRS. That is, many older people follow unconventional tracks, some working forever, some gradually winding down on the same jobs, and some finding a "bridge" job to move into at older ages.

One explanation for these gradual labor market withdrawal patterns is that people may reach retirement age with inadequate saving, and find that they must remain employed to make ends meet. The extent of retirement saving shortfalls is examined from two different vantage points, by Mark Warshawsky and John Ameriks, and by James Moore and Olivia Mitchell. Though these authors use different technologies to derive what people "should be" saving, both studies conclude that the typical American household falls far short of its mark, lacking sufficient assets to live comfortably in retirement. For example, in the HRS file, the median 56-year old household head would have to boost saving by an additional 16 percent of annual gross income, if the family is to have enough to live on after retirement. People at the bottom of the wealth distribution (prior to retirement) face far worse prospects, with saving shortfalls amounting to an insurmountable one-third of annual income. For many in this latter group, social security represents virtually their only form of retirement income.

Why do we fall so far short, and what can be done about it? Several factors are identified by Mitchell, Moore, and John Phillips as reasons why older Americans have insufficient saving. For instance, people reporting themselves in very poor health save less than do people in good health. This may be quite a reasonable finding if the very ill have higher than average health-care costs, and they may also expect to die sooner than average. The authors also find that people who have a long planning horizon and those with a more positive outlook on life are better savers than people who have a shorter horizon or who are depressed. This study is one of the first exploring factors influencing saving shortfalls, and it will spur additional research on this fascinating topic.

Related work by Robert Clark, Gordon Goodfellow, Sylvester Schieber, and Drew Warwick offers exciting new information on what employers can do to encourage retirement saving, particularly in the environment of a 401(k) pension plan. Drawing on a unique dataset of employer pension plans covering some 234,000 workers, the authors explore models of employee decision to participate in a company pension, and what fraction of salary to devote to the plan if the worker is covered. The detailed data permit more in-depth investigation of 401(k) investment decisions than was previously possible, and they reveal substantial differences in men's and women's investment patterns. Perhaps surprisingly, there is no evidence that women invest more conservatively than men. Further, women's propensity to participate in a pension plan is more sensitive to age and income than is men's.

Facing the Challenges of Retirement

Beyond analyses of the "typical" or average employee, many policymakers are concerned about the special problems faced in retirement by particular socioeconomic and demographic groups, such as minorities, older women, and widows. Here several useful studies exploit new datasets, including the Health and Retirement Study (HRS), that have recently been made available (the HRS is discussed more below).

In their analysis, Phillip Levine, Mitchell, and Moore conclude that older women on the verge of retirement are projected to have less income when retired than their male counterparts. Reasons that older women are more vulnerable include the fact that they are in worse health than men; they had weaker labor force attachment over their lifetimes; and they spend more time caring for other family members. The chapter reports that differences in health and labor market history explain most of the differences in projected wellbeing in retirement, with labor market histories dominating for whites and nonmarried persons. On this basis it appears reasonable to project a narrowing of future differences in economic wellbeing between men and women.

Related research by Robert Willis and David Weir, and by Marjorie Honig, devotes further attention to the situation of women and minorities in retirement. To the extent that both groups experience lower wages and have fewer years of employment than white men, consequent pension benefits will be lower and widowhood could leave them devastated. Using the HRS data, which enable researchers to focus especially on minorities, these authors show just how vulnerable to poverty many older minority workers will be. For example, minorities more than white men face the need to cut consumption as they move into retirement. To some, these facts will reinforce the key importance of a social insurance safety net in retirement. Others might take away a different policy implication, namely, that time spent away from the job market has negative consequences for later life that reach beyond wages alone.

Early retirement windows are one way that corporations seek to use incentives to induce workers to leave, and Charles Brown takes advantage of the HRS to explore who takes the windows, who does not, and why. He finds that only one third of window offers are accepted; furthermore, among those who accept the offers, most do not withdraw completely from the workforce but rather find employment in another demanding job.

A different kind of shock — namely illness — worries many older people as they move into retirement, but few have a very clear idea of what risks they bear, and what the likely costs of treatment might be. To this end, Anna Rappaport's analysis supplies a useful compendium of the major health costs and utilization patterns by age, and it should update concerned readers on the possible shape of healthcare risk with age. How health shocks affect retirement behavior is the topic of the research by Deborah Dwyer and Jianting Hu. Their analysis explores the question of how retirement expectations mesh with (or diverge from) reality, and how poor health forces people to change their retirement plans. As expected, declining health and acute health problems are more likely to elicit changes in retirement plans than chronic, long-term problems. They also show that the effect of health shocks on people's retirement plans is as important as the effects of economic variables.

Methodological and Data Issues in Retirement Research

The empirical studies in this volume share a reliance on new data sets focused specifically on people who are retired or preparing for retirement. Many of these studies use the Health and Retirement Study, a novel dataset developed at the Institute for Social Research (ISR) at the University of

TABLE 1: Estimated Sample Sizes by Cohort

| | | Longitudinal Interviews | | | | Baseline Interviews | |
| | | HRS Wave 4 | | AHEAD Wave 3 | | CODA | War Babies |
Birth Cohort	Total	Living	Deceased	Living	Deceased	Living	Living
1890–1923	6,317	108	9	5,249	948		3
1924–1930	3,833	821	53	588	27	2,324	20
1931–1941	8,398	8,057	194	75	4		68
1942–1947	3,055	1,099	9	21			1,926
1948+	916	430	2	10		17	457
Total	22,519	10,515	267	5,943	979	2,341	2,474

Source: ISR (1999).

Michigan. First fielded in 1992, this survey of 12,000 older Americans is "the most extensive, complex, and complete data collection effort ever under-taken on a nationally representative cohort of aging people" (ISR 1997). The study was devised by collaborative teams of economists, psychologists, sociologists, medical experts, and other scientists, and funded by several agencies, including the National Institute on Aging (NIA), the Social Security Administration (SSA), the U.S. Department of Labor (DOL) and the U.S. Department of Health and Human Services (HHS).

One reason that the HRS is so valuable to retirement researchers is that it was designed to be longitudinal, and as of this writing four waves have been fielded (1992, 1994, 1996, and 1998). Each time, the survey has gathered extensive information on wealth, health, family structure, and some fascinating questions about people's expectations regarding their own future health, longevity, and resources.[1] A companion study called the Assets and Health Dynamics of the Oldest Old (AHEAD) study, gathers similar data on approximately 8,200 persons born prior to 1924, first surveyed in 1993 when they were age 70 and older along with their spouses (see Soldo, et al. 1997). In addition, people who grew up during the Great Depression (born 1924–1930) and people born during and just after World War II (1942–1947) were also included to ensure that the ongoing panel would be representative of the entire U.S. population age 50 and over. The front runner baby boomers, termed "Early Boomers" (born 1948–53), will be added in 2004, and "Middle Boomers" (born 1954–59) are scheduled to enter the study in 2010 (ISR 1997). Sample sizes for the baseline and longitudinal samples for HRS and AHEAD appear in Table 1. In the future, researchers will be able to compare behavior across cohorts to determine how behavior is changing in ways of interest to policymakers and researchers.

Another reason that the HRS is so valuable for retirement research is that the respondent questionnaires have been linked with various other valuable files. Specifically, data were gathered from employers regarding the pension and health insurance plans provided at the workers' place of business,[2] and we have also obtained data on respondents' earnings and benefits histories from the Social Security Administration[3] (both subject to respondents' consent). These files afford the researcher an invaluable addition to knowledge about retirees' social security and pension benefits, and are described by Mitchell, Jan Olson, and Thomas Steinmeier in one study, and also in a companion study by Alan Gustman, Mitchell, Andrew Samwick, and Steinmeier.

Conclusion

As we move into the twenty-first century, many new retirement-related opportunities and risks confront individuals, employers, and policymakers. Opportunities include the exciting prospects of living longer, living healthier, and living a more productive life than ever before. But the risks are also huge, including the challenge of setting an income adequacy goal and then saving enough for retirement, investing wisely in a time of financial turmoil, and planning carefully for a long period of time in retirement.

The work presented in this research volume will spur future analysts to investigate additional questions. For example, retirement ages under social security and pension programs are currently changing, and the impact of these changes can be evaluated as additional data on retirement patterns are collected. Further, new information on people attaining their 50s in different periods will permit invaluable comparisons of how retirement age changes affect behavior before the transition, during it, and afterward.

There are no easy answers to the problems and questions facing us as we experience population age shifts and the consequent pressures on old-age support systems. However we are fortunate in having the new HRS data, as well as new databases from corporate pension sponsors and providers, that offer the opportunity for analysts to devise and test exciting new theories and applications in the years to come. Much talent, effort, and resources have been devoted to developing these data thus far, along with the time and energy of thousands of cooperative respondents. The research we offer here, drawing from this rich source of information on health, wealth, and retirement in America, will help us make better decisions and better policy, as policymakers, practitioners, and eventually retirees in the twenty-first century.

Notes

1. See, e.g., Smith (1995); Wallace and Herzog (1995); and Soldo and Hill (1995).
2. ISR will make available to researchers under restricted conditions a computer software program to compute pension benefits as well as a pension wealth file. Interested analysts should visit the ISR web page at www.umich.edu/~hrswww for more information, or see Mitchell, Olson, and Steinmeier (this volume).

3. Social security restricted data are also described as in note 2; see also Gustman, Mitchell, Samwick, and Steinmeier (this volume).

References

Brown, Charles. "Early Retirement Windows." This volume.

Burkhauser, Richard V. and Paul Gertler. 1995. "The Health and Retirement Study, Data Quality and Early Results." *Journal of Human Resources* 30 (Supplement).

Clark, Robert L., Gordon P. Goodfellow, Sylvester J. Schieber, and Drew Warwick. "Making the Most of 401 (k) Plans: Who's Choosing What and Why?" This volume.

Dwyer, Debra Sabatini and Jiangting Hu. "Retirement Expectations and Realizations: The Role of Health Shocks and Economic Factors." This volume.

Gustman, Alan L., Olivia S. Mitchell, Andrew A. Samwick, and Thomas L. Steinmeier. "Evaluating Pension Entitlements." This volume.

Gustman, Alan L., Olivia S. Mitchell, and Thomas L. Steinmeier. 1995. "Retirement Measures in the Health and Retirement Study." *Journal of Human Resources* 30 (Supplement): S57–83.

Honig, Marjorie. "Minorities Face Retirement: Worklife Disparities Repeated?" This volume.

Institute for Social Research (ISR). 1999. Competing Renewal for Years 11–16 of the Cooperative Agreements with the National Institute on Aging for the HRS/AHEAD Study. University of Michigan, Ann Arbor, March.

Juster, F. Thomas and Richard Suzman. 1995. "An Overview of the Health and Retirement Study." *Journal of Human Resources* 30 (Supplement): S7–56.

Levine, Phillip B., Olivia S. Mitchell, and James F. Moore. "Women on the Verge of Retirement: Predictors of Retiree Wellbeing." This volume.

Mitchell, Olivia S., James F. Moore, and John W. Phillips. "Explaining Retirement Saving Shortfalls." This volume.

Mitchell, Olivia S., Jan Olson, and Thomas L. Steinmeier. "Social Security Earnings and Projected Benefits." This volume.

Moore, James F. and Olivia S. Mitchell. "Projected Retirement Wealth and Saving Adequacy." This volume.

Myers, George C., ed. 1997. "Asset and Health Dynamics Among the Oldest Old (AHEAD): Initial Results from the Longitudinal Study." *Journals of Gerontology* Ser. B, *Psychological and Social Sciences* 52B, Special Issue (May).

Quinn, Joseph F. "New Paths to Retirement." This volume.

Rappaport, Anna M. "Planning for Health Care Needs in Retirement." This volume.

Smith, James P. 1995. "Racial and Ethnic Differences in Wealth in the Health and Retirement Study." *Journal of Human Resources* 30 (Supplement): S158–83.

Soldo, Beth J. and Martha Hill. 1995. "Family Structure and Transfer Measures in the Health and Retirement Study." *Journal of Human Resources* 30 (Supplement): S108–37.

Soldo, Beth J., Michael Hurd, Willard L. Rodgers, and Robert B. Wallace. 1997. "Asset and Health Dynamics of the Oldest Old: An Overview of the AHEAD Study." *Journals of Gerontology*, Ser. B, *Psychological and Social Sciences* 52B, Special Issue (May): 1–20.

Wallace, Robert B. and A. Regula Herzog. 1995. "Overview of the Health Measures in the Health and Retirement Study." *Journal of Human Resources* 30 (Supplement): S84–107.

Warshawsky, Mark J. and John Ameriks. "How Prepared Are Americans for Retirement?" This volume.

Weir, David R. and Robert J. Willis. "Prospects for Widow Poverty." This volume.
Willis, Robert J. 1997. "Theory Confronts Data: How the HRS Is Shaped by the Economics of Aging and How the Economics of Aging Will Be Shaped by the HRS." Paper presented at the 1997 Conference on Economics of Aging, International Health, and Retirement Studies, Amsterdam.

Part I
Looking Ahead
to Retirement

Chapter 1
New Paths to Retirement

Joseph F. Quinn

One of the most important and intriguing phenomena in the United States labor markets was the post-World War II early retirement trend: the fact that older men left the labor force earlier and earlier with each succeeding cohort. In 1950, 72 percent of all 65-year-old men were in the labor force, either employed or actively looking for work. As shown in Table 1, this percentage fell steadily over the next three and a half decades, reaching about 30 percent by 1985, a decline of well over half. Even larger percentage declines were observed for men over age 65: from 58 to 20 percent for those age 68, from 50 to 16 percent age 70, and from 39 to 15 percent for those age 72. The decline was also unmistakable for those age 62, although it did not begin until the 1960s when the earliest age of entitlement for social security old-age benefits was lowered for men from 65 to 62. Significant declines also occurred below the age of social security eligibility: from 85 to 71 percent at age 60, and from 91 to 84 percent at age 55.

Economists and others have devoted considerable effort to trying to explain these large declines in older men's labor force attachment. Analysts point to the increasing wealth of subsequent cohorts of Americans, and to the fact that leisure (at the margin, at least) is a normal good. Thus earlier retirement has been interpreted as one of the ways that Americans chose to "spend" their increased wealth. Other experts focused more specifically on the social security program, whose increased coverage and generosity over time bestowed large windfall gains on past cohorts of retirees. Economists also examined the details of social security's benefit calculation rules, and demonstrated that many Americans faced substantial financial penalties if they remained in the labor force too long: certainly beyond age 65, and for some, even earlier (Quadagno and Quinn 1997). Benefits forgone because of continued work were never fully made up later.

Employer policies reinforced these downward trends in men's labor force participation. Mandatory retirement rules, which once covered about half of all American workers, forced departure from the firm (although not

TABLE 1: Male Labor Force Participation Rates (%) by Age, 1950–1997

				Age			
Year	55	60	62	65	68	70	72
1950	90.6	84.7	81.2	71.7	57.7	49.8	39.3
1960	92.8	85.9	79.8	56.8	42.0	37.2	28.0
1970	91.8	83.9	73.8	49.9	37.7	30.1	24.8
1975	87.6	76.9	64.4	39.4	23.7	23.7	22.6
1980	84.9	74.0	56.8	35.2	24.1	21.3	17.0
1985	83.7	71.0	50.9	30.5	20.5	15.9	14.9
1990	85.3	70.5	52.5	31.9	23.4	17.1	16.4
1995	81.1	68.9	51.3	33.5	22.4	20.6	16.0
1997	83.4	68.3	52.6	32.4	22.4	21.7	17.3

Source: Burkhauser and Quinn (1997: table 1), updated by the author as in republished data supplied by BLS.

from the labor force), usually at age 65. Defined benefit employer pensions, which were the dominant form of coverage for those participating in pension plans in prior decades, often contained the same type of work disincentives that social security did. Those who stayed on the job too long could expect lower lifetime benefits (higher benefits per year, but for fewer years, and not enough higher to compensate for the benefits initially forgone) than those received by people who left earlier. These three factors, mandatory retirement, the financial incentives imbedded in social security and many employer pension rules, and increasing levels of wealth, combined to induce older Americans out of the labor force at earlier and earlier ages. Evidence suggests that most of these retirements were voluntary: given the options they faced, most workers chose to leave their jobs when they did.[1]

The End of an Era?

This trend in older men's labor market attachment came to an end in the mid-1980s. Indeed, men's participation rates stopped declining and have actually increased in recent years. Figure 1 shows actual labor force participation rates for men age 60 to 64 (traditionally, earlier retirement years) as well as age 65 to 69 (traditional retirement years), along with a linear extrapolation of the trend line between 1964 and 1985.[2] Evidently the postwar early retirement trend came to an abrupt halt in the mid-1980s, and many more older men are working today than the pre-1986 trend would have suggested.[3]

Labor force trends for older American women differ from those of men in one regard, but are similar in another. Since World War II, married women have entered the job market in increasing numbers, so older women's market attachment did not exhibit the dramatic declines that men's

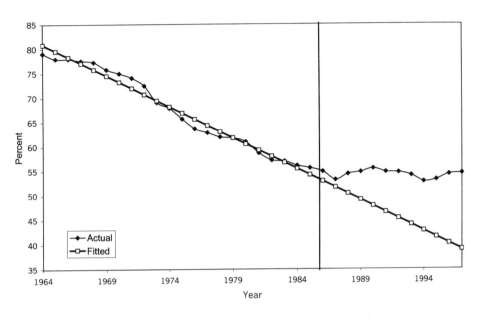

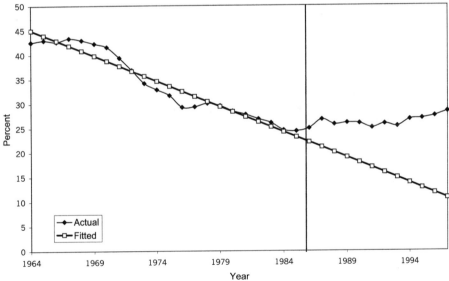

Figure 1. Labor force participation rates for men (%): ages 60–64 (top) and 65–69 (bottom). Source: USBLS (various years) and author's calculations.

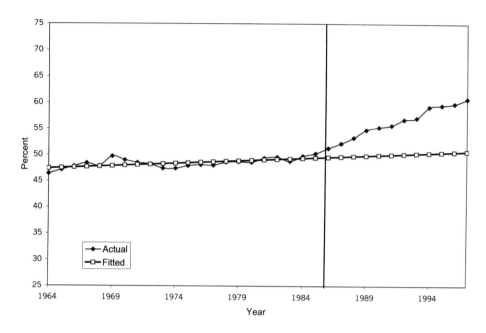

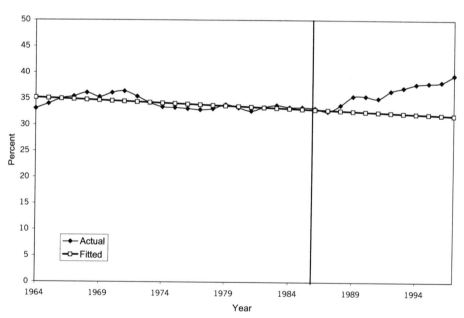

Figure 2. Labor force participation rates for women (%): ages 55–59 (top) and 60–64 (bottom). Source: USBLS (various years) and author's calculations.

rates did through the mid-1980s. Participation rates for younger women rose substantially, with smaller increases at ages 55 to 59 and small declines at ages 60 and over. After 1985, women's pattern grew similar to that of men, as seen in Figure 2. For both age groups shown (ages 55–59 and 60–64), women's labor force participation rates since 1985 have risen above what the pre-1986 trend would have suggested. The same is true, although less dramatically, for women aged 65–69 and 70 or over. The similarity of the break points in the male and female time series is striking. It is clear that something is very different today from what it was a decade and a half ago.

These changes are consistent with important policy initiatives that increased work opportunities available to older workers and altered the relative attractiveness of work and retirement. As a result, the era of earlier and earlier retirement appears to be over, at least for the near term.

What changes occurred to make the American labor market more encouraging (or at least less discouraging) toward work at older ages? First, mandatory retirement has virtually been eliminated in the United States. In the private sector, the earliest allowable age of mandatory retirement was boosted from 65 to 70 in 1978; it was then outlawed entirely in 1986 for the vast majority of American workers. This action created more flexibility for those who wanted to work beyond the mandatory retirement age, and it also sent an important message to society about the appropriate age to retire.[4]

In addition, social security rules have changed several times and continue to do so in ways that make work more attractive.[5] The amount of income a recipient can earn before losing social security benefits has been indexed to wage growth since 1975, and higher exempt amounts were introduced in 1978 for those aged 65–71. The age at which the earnings test no longer applied, permitting recipients to earn any amount without loss of benefits, was lowered from 72 to 70 in 1983, and in 1990, the benefit loss for each dollar earned over the exempt amount was cut from 50 to 33 cents for recipients aged 65–69. Congress then legislated a set of increases in the exempt amount for recipients aged 65–69 far in excess of the rate of wage growth in 1996, and by 2002 workers receiving social security will be able to earn up to $30,000 per year without losing benefits due to the earnings test.

Social security rule changes are also altering the financial rewards for those who delay benefit receipt past the normal retirement age, currently age 65. Within the system, the delayed retirement credit is defined as the increase in subsequent benefits enjoyed by a potential recipient who delays benefit receipt by one year. This credit was increased from 1 percent per year of delay to 3 percent in 1977, and it is now being increased further from three to 8 percent (by 2010) per year of delay. Eight percent is close to an actuarially fair adjustment for the average worker, which means that the present discounted value of expected social security benefits will no longer decline because of work beyond age 65.[6] Instead of penalizing work at older ages, social security is now becoming more age-neutral. Another important change will also phase in soon. The normal age of eligibility for social security benefits—the age at which one receives 100 percent of one's Primary Insurance Amount—has been age 65 since the creation of the program 60 years ago. Between the years 2003 and 2008, however, the normal retirement age will be increased from 65 to 66, and then raised further to age 67 between 2021 and 2026. These changes are almost identical to across-the-board benefit cuts, but they will also send an important societal message about the appropriate age for retirement.[7]

Important changes are also occurring in private sector inducements to retire. There has been a movement away from defined benefit toward defined contribution pension plans.[8] As defined benefit plans decline in relative importance, so does their ability to discourage work and encourage retirement. Defined contribution plans, in contrast, have none of the age-specific work disincentives that defined benefit plans often contain; by their very nature they are age-neutral.

A counter-argument to our "end of an era" conjecture is that the observed reversal in the early retirement trend may only be a temporary hiatus in the long-run decline in retirement ages—a decline made inevitable by the increasing wealth of the nation and the desire of older Americans to stop working. This argument suggests that once the social security rule changes mentioned above are in force, older Americans' labor force participation rates will resume their longtime decline. Buttressing this view is the fact that the American economy has been very strong over the last decade. The national unemployment rate fell from about 10 percent in 1983 to near 5 percent in 1989, and, following a brief recession in the early 1990s, has fallen below 5 percent. Such a prosperous job market creates employment options for older workers who want to remain employed. Therefore part of what appears to be a new labor market trend could actually be the result of strong, but *cyclical*, labor demand. If so, the long-run participation rate declines may resume when the economy falters.[9]

Macroeconomic effects are undoubtedly important, but deeper changes are also at work. There is a new attitude toward work late in life, encouraged by public policy initiatives, shifts from manufacturing to less arduous service occupations, and the realization that many 62-year-olds today can anticipate two or more decades of healthy activity ahead. Although many may not want to continue full time on their career jobs, many older people do want to remain active in the labor market, perhaps part-time, perhaps self-employed, and perhaps in an entirely new line of work.

Survey evidence supports this view that many older Americans want to work more. The Commonwealth Fund sponsored a survey of 3,500 older Americans, men aged 55–64 and women aged 50–59. Of those no longer employed, between 14 and 25 percent suggested that they would have preferred to work if a suitable job were available (McNaught, Barth, and Henderson 1989). Though far from a majority of the retirees, this percentage did represent between 1 and 2 million potential workers. Among those still employed, Quinn and Burkhauser (1994) found that a minority — another million people — said that they expected to stop working before they really wanted to. One interpretation of this response is that these individuals expected to stop given the financial incentives that they faced (from social security and employer pensions), but they would have wanted to continue working in the absence of these work disincentives.

Using data from the Health and Retirement Study, Gustman, Mitchell, and Steinmeier (1995) report that many older Americans face hours constraints on their jobs. Among full-time workers aged 51–61 in 1992, 15 percent said that they would like to work more hours than they did, but could not, as did about 20 percent of part-time workers. Similar numbers of full-time workers (but many fewer part-timers) said they would like to work fewer hours than they currently did.

How Do Older Americans Leave the Labor Force?

The retirement patterns of American workers are much more complicated and varied than is often suggested by the stereotypical view of retirement as a one-step transition directly from a career job to complete labor force withdrawal.[10] Although the one-step pattern is still common, many older Americans retire gradually and in stages, utilizing so-called "bridge jobs" on the way out.[11] Hence we believe that retirement is most fruitfully understood as a process, rather than a single event. These insights are fruitfully examined using the Health and Retirement Study (Quinn 1997b). In previous research, I have analyzed the 1992 and 1994 waves of the HRS; here, we add to the analysis the third wave of data from 1996, when primary respondents were age 55–65. Therefore a reasonable number of the respondents had crossed the important age 62 threshold.[12]

The word "retirement" means different things to different people: some equate the term with total labor withdrawal, while others would include people still working but who had cut back significantly on hours worked late in life. Others deem retirement to be coincident with the receipt of retirement benefits from social security or an employer pension, regardless of labor force status, while still others use responses to subjective questionnaire items; that is, the retired are those who call themselves retired. Here we examine a different issue — the process by which older Americans leave their full-time career jobs. As noted above, some move out of the labor force directly from a full-time job. For these people, the timing of retirement is relatively well-defined. But as we will see, others exit more gradually, utilizing transition or bridge jobs on the way out. In what follows, we study the older American population to ask several questions: What is a bridge job?

How important are bridge jobs to older Americans today? Do these jobs tend to be full-time or part-time? How do they compare to workers' career jobs? How important is self-employment in this process?

Retirement Patterns in the 1990s

Since we focus on the transition from work, the analysis sample excludes people without work experience after age 49. Consequently, our HRS analysis sample consists of about 8,000 individuals who appear in each of the first three waves of the HRS. In some of the analysis, we restrict this sample further to concentrate on those for whom we can identify a career job, defined as a full-time job that lasted or is expected to last for at least 10 years. The subsample includes about 5,800 respondents, with 3,600 men and 2,200 women. At the time of the 1996 HRS survey, 38 percent of the respondents were no longer working (36 percent of the men and 40 percent of the women; see Table 2.)[13] By utilizing the longitudinal nature of the survey data, we can look back in time and ask how these people moved out of employment. The other 62 percent were still working — some still on full-time career jobs (and we will have to wait to see how they retire) and others on bridge jobs, often as part of the retirement process.

The evidence shows that employment rates declined over time as the HRS respondents aged. In 1994, just two years earlier, 70 percent of this sample had been working, and in 1992, nearly 80 percent had been employed. Each subsequent wave of the HRS provides more insight into how people retire, since more respondents have left the labor force each time. The effect of age can also be seen in Figure 3, which shows HRS employment rates in 1996 by age and gender. Employment declined monotonically with age for both men and women, and there are noticeable drops at ages 62 and 65, the ages

TABLE 2: Employment Status of HRS Respondents (%) with Work Experience After Age 49

	Men	*Women*	*Total*
1996			
Employed	64	60	62
Not employed	36	40	38
1994			
Employed	71	70	70
Not employed	29	30	30
1992			
Employed	79	79	79
Not employed	21	21	21

Source: Author's calculations.

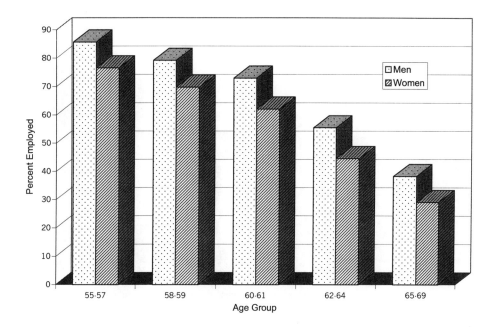

Figure 3. HRS employment status by age and gender, 1996. Source: Author's calculations.

of eligibility for early (actuarially reduced) and normal social security benefits as well as for some employer pensions.

Figures 4 and 5 show part-time and self-employment patterns by gender and age. The fraction of workers employed part-time rises with age (Figure 4), with dramatic jumps at ages 62 and 65, and the rate is generally higher for women than for men. The proportion of self-employed men also rises with age, with a noticeable jump at age 62, and it is higher for men than for women (Figure 5). For the working women in our sample, there is little change in the percentage self-employed below age 62, but the rate rises for those 62 and older.

A look back: how did the respondents get where they are? The labor market status of our HRS sample in 1996 is detailed in Figure 6. We differentiate between those still on a career job in 1996 (full-time, and of at least 10 years duration) and those on a bridge job (either part-time, or less than 10 years tenure), and then look back in time to identify their transition paths.[14] In 1996, 40 percent of the men were still working on career jobs (Figure 6a). We will have to follow this group through subsequent waves of the HRS to see how and when they retire. Thirty-six percent were not working at all (as noted in Table 2), and nearly a quarter (23 percent) were working on what

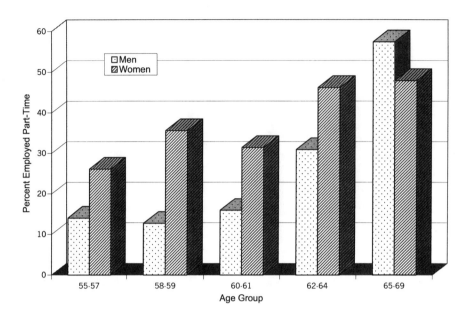

Figure 4. HRS part-time employment status by age and gender, 1996. Source: Author's calculations.

we define as a bridge job.[15] Two-thirds of these bridge jobs were part-time; the remaining third were full-time jobs that we anticipate will end with under 10 years duration.

How did the 36 percent of the male sample that had already stopped working by 1996 leave the labor market? As seen in Figure 6, nearly two-thirds left directly from a full-time career job (the stereotypical retirement pattern), while about 30 percent last worked on a bridge job before leaving the labor force. About half of these bridge jobs were part-time, and the other half were full-time, but with less than 10 years tenure. Nearly a quarter of the HRS men were working on bridge jobs in 1996. Of those for whom we had good data, we find that about two-thirds of the people held full-time career jobs prior to their bridge jobs, and they appear to be utilizing bridge jobs on the way out of the labor force.

The experiences of the HRS women were somewhat different from those of the men, mainly because bridge jobs appear to be more important (Figure 6). Slightly more of the women had stopped working by 1996 (40 versus 36 percent, despite the fact that the women are, on average, a bit younger), and of those still at work, a higher proportion of the women were still working on bridge jobs (43 versus 36 percent).[16] An even higher proportion of the women's bridge jobs were part-time rather than short-duration in nature (80 versus 65 percent). Of the women not working in 1996, nearly 60

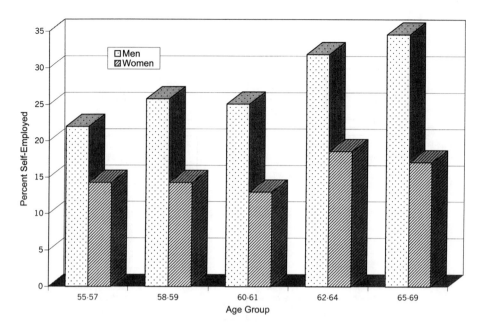

Figure 5. HRS self-employment status by age and gender, 1996. Source: Author's calculations.

percent of those with good data on their last job last worked on a bridge job, compared to only about 30 percent of the non-employed men. Again, women's bridge jobs were more likely to have been part-time rather than short duration.

In other words, the HRS reveals a considerable amount of bridge job activity among older Americans in the 1990s. Of those no longer employed, nearly half (about 30 percent of the men and nearly 60 percent of the women) last worked on a bridge job. Among those still working, between 36 percent (of the men) and 43 percent (of the women) were employed on a bridge job. These numbers will change as people age, because some with fewer than 10 years tenure in 1996 will work more or fewer years than we expected, and because we do not know how those still on full-time career jobs will exit. To estimate a lower bound on the importance of bridge job activity, we could assume that *none* of those still working on full-time career jobs in 1996 would use a bridge job on the way out. In this case, about one-third of the men and nearly one-half of the women will change jobs between their last career job and complete labor force withdrawal.[17] To determine how our results vary with the definition of a career job, we also experimented with requiring only eight or five years' duration, although the latter seems a bit short to be defined as a "career" job. Table 3 shows, for each of

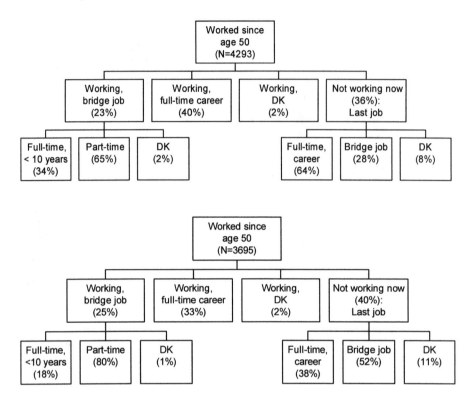

Figure 6. 1996 job status of HRS respondents with work experience since age 50: men (top) and women (bottom). DK means respondent responded "don't know" to relevant HRS question. Source: Author's calculations.

the three tenure definitions, the fraction working on a bridge job in 1996, the fraction of those not working in 1996 whose last job was a bridge job, and our lower bound estimate of the extent of bridge job activity (assuming that none of those still working on a career job will utilize a bridge job on the way out). The qualitative conclusions remain unchanged though specific definitions do make a difference. When we drop the tenure definition for a career job from 10 to eight years, the difference in the extent of bridge job activity is modest, on the order of five percent (Table 3). When we drop the definition to five years, the number of bridge jobs drops about 20 percent. But even under this strict definition, our lower bound estimates suggest that between a quarter (of the men) and 40 percent (of the women) — compared to one third to half under the 10-year definition — pass through a bridge job late in life. Bridge job activity is thus seen to be an important part of the labor force withdrawal process in America.

TABLE 3: Bridge Job Activity of HRS Respondents (%) with Three Definitions of Full-Time Career Job

Full Time Career Job Requires	Percent Working on a Bridge Job, 1966[a]		Percent Not Working Whose Last Job Was a Bridge Job[b]		Lower Bound of Bridge Job Activity[c]	
	Men	Women	Men	Women	Men	Women
10 years tenure	23	25	30	58	34	49
8 years tenure	21	24	29	55	32	46
5 years tenure	17	22	25	48	27	41

Source: Author's calculations.
Notes:
[a] From Fig. 6 for 10 years or more tenure, and analogous figures using tenure greater than or equal to 8 or 5 years.
[b] For those not employed, bridge / (bridge + full-time career) on last job; see Fig. 6 for 10 year tenure figures.
[c] People (currently working on bridge job) plus (not working and last job was a bridge job) as a percent of all those with work experience since age 50. We ignore the DKs, and assume that none of those currently working on a full-time career job utilize a bridge job on the way out.

A look forward: how did those with career jobs leave them? Thus far, we have implicitly assumed that a part-time or a short duration job late in someone's work career indicates gradual or partial retirement. This might not be true for some workers whose job histories consist of a series of part-time or shortduration jobs. Therefore, we conducted additional analysis on just the subsample for whom we could identify a full-time career job. For these workers, a bridge job would represent a change in behavior. For each individual with work experience after age 49, we searched the HRS survey response to identify some prior career job.[18] If we did find one, we then proceeded forward in time to see how (if at all) the individual left that career job. HRS information on the current, last (for those no longer working), and prior jobs revealed a career job for most of the men (84 percent) and for 60 percent of the women analyzed above.[19]

Retirement transitions for men and women where we can identify a full-time career job appear in Figure 7. About 44 percent of these men were still working on their full-time career jobs, about 28 percent moved out of employment directly from their career jobs, and a quarter moved to a bridge job.[20] (Most of them were still on this bridge job in 1996; some had subsequently moved out of employment altogether.) Of those who had already left their full-time career jobs and for whom we have good data, nearly half (47 percent) moved to a bridge job rather than directly out of employment. Transition data for career women tell a similar story (Figure 7b). Of those who had left their career jobs by 1996, about half (49 percent) moved next to a bridge job rather than directly out of employment. In general, exit

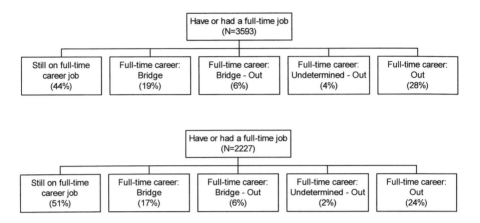

Figure 7. Job transitions of HRS respondents with a full-time career job: men (top) and women (bottom). Source: Author's calculations.

patterns of career men and women look more similar than do those of all men and women in general.

Prior research suggests that self-employed and wage-and-salary workers leave their career jobs in different ways, and that crossovers between classes of worker are common late in life (Quinn, Burkhauser, and Myers 1991). The HRS data confirm both of these surmises. Of the wage and salary workers, 46 percent was still on career jobs in 1996, 37 percent was not working (some of whom had moved to and then out of a bridge job in the interim), and 16 percent was employed on a post-career bridge job (Figure 8). Of those who had left their career jobs by 1996, nearly half (44 percent) moved to bridge jobs. Of those who did move to a bridge job (whether still on it or not in 1996), nearly two-thirds moved from full-time to part-time status and nearly a quarter moved from the wage-and-salary world to self-employment. This is one of the reasons why self-employment is more prevalent among older workers than it is among the labor force in general. For some older Americans, self-employment provides the means for gradual retirement, with additional flexibility with respect to hours and type of work.

By contrast, among those who were self-employed in their career jobs, 77 percent was still working in 1996, compared to only 62 percent of the wage-and-salary workers (Figure 8). The majority of the employed was still on career jobs, but some had switched to bridge jobs. Of those who had switched, more than half (54 percent) moved from full-time to part-time status, and about a third switched from self-employment to wage-and-salary work. Although the proportion of self-employed job switchers moving to a wage and salary job is higher than the reverse, there is still a net increase in the

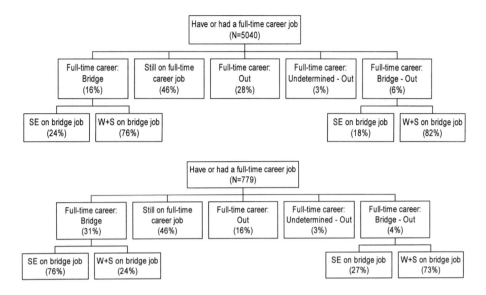

Figure 8. Job transitions of HRS career wage and salary workers with a full-time career job: wage and salary workers (W+S) (top); self-employed workers (SE) (bottom). Source: Author's calculations.

number of self-employed, because of the much larger number of career wage-and-salary workers.

Comparisons Between Career Jobs and Bridge Jobs

We next follow the transitions of those career employees who moved to bridge jobs, and we ask how the two jobs compare.[21] About 60 percent of the bridge jobs involved part-time work, whereas all the career jobs, by definition, were full-time. Table 4 categorizes the jobs by white collar/blue collar status and by skill level. About three-quarters of those who switched to a bridge job stayed in the same job category, and for those who switched categories there was a net movement down the socioeconomic ladder. About 70 percent of those who switched moved down the scale, and only 30 percent moved up. The largest increase occurred among those in blue-collar jobs without high skill requirements, which increased from 13 percent of the career jobs to 21 percent of the bridge jobs.

Slippage can also be seen in Table 5, which tabulates workers' hourly wage rates on both career and bridge jobs. Only about one-third of these workers earned less than $10 per hour on their career jobs, but 60 percent did on their post-career jobs, mostly in the $5 to $10 per hour category. At the

TABLE 4: Occupational Status of HRS Respondents Moving from Career to Bridge
Jobs (%)

Subsequent Bridge Job	Initial Full-Time Career Job				
	White Collar Highly Skilled	White Collar Other	Blue Collar Highly Skilled	Blue Collar Other	Total
White collar, highly skilled	79	15	9	6	41
White collar, other	6	67	4	1	14
Blue collar, highly skilled	8	9	64	11	24
Blue collar, other	7	6	23	82	21
Total	45	15	27	13	100

Source: Author's calculations.

TABLE 5: Wage Rate of HRS Respondents Moving from Career to Bridge Jobs (%)

Subsequent Bridge Job Wage Rate ($/hour)	Initial Full-Time Career Job Wage Rate ($/hour)						
	0–5	5–10	10–15	15–20	20–30	30+	Total
0–5	51	19	14	15	1	4	18
5–10	26	64	44	34	34	24	43
10–15	16	12	27	19	15	8	18
15–20	1	3	9	2	6	8	8
20–30	3	1	3	7	25	24	7
30+	1	2	2	6	9	32	6
Total	9	26	28	17	14	6	100

Source: Author's calculations.

upper end of the spectrum, 20 percent of these workers earned over $20 per hour in career employment, but only 13 percent did on their bridge jobs. Overall, only about one-third of these job switchers stayed in the same wage category in Table 5. Of those who did not stay in the same status/skill cell, three quarters moved down at least one wage rate category, while only one-quarter moved up.

Conclusion

We present evidence suggesting that the post-war trend toward earlier retirement for men has come to a halt. Many more older Americans are working today than the pre-1986 trends would have suggested. Explanations for this change in trend include the elimination of mandatory retirement, changes in the work incentives imbedded in social security rules, the steady increase in the importance of defined-contribution pension programs, and the strength of the American economy over most of the past decade.

We also explored the complex and numerous paths to retirement revealed in the Health and Retirement Study. Bridge jobs are emphasized, which are part-time or short-duration jobs between career employment and complete labor force withdrawal. Our research shows that many older Americans do retire gradually, often using part-time jobs or stints of self-employment on the way out. Exit routes from career employment are many and varied, and the traditional one-step retirement pattern is no longer the norm it once was. These transitional stages in the retirement process will probably grow more important through time as the nation ages, and as the large baby-boom cohorts contemplate how and when to leave the world of work.

The author thanks the Retirement Research Foundation, the Employee Benefit Research Institute, and the W. E. Upjohn Institute for Employment Research for research support, Kevin Cahill for excellent research assistance, and Olivia Mitchell for helpful comments on an earlier draft.

Notes

1. The financial incentives imbedded in social security and many defined-benefit pension rules created pay cuts for older workers. Total annual compensation includes both the paycheck and any changes in social security and pension wealth (the present value of future benefits) that accrue during that year of work. Many pension systems are set up so that after some age, these present values begin to decline. At this point, the annual "accruals" become negative, and one's compensation (the paycheck *minus* the loss in retirement wealth) declines. Faced with these implicit pay cuts, many workers chose to retire. Under these circumstances, the distinction between voluntary and involuntary retirement is a fuzzy one. See Quinn (1991) for a discussion of these issues.

2. The trends are based on simple linear regressions with a constant and a time trend. Figures 1 and 2 are updated from Quinn (1997a).

3. To estimate the magnitude of this change, Burkhauser and Quinn (1997: table 2) multiplied the difference between the actual 1996 participation rates and rates predicted by the pre-1986 extrapolations by the population figures for men at these ages. The results indicate that an additional 1.4 million men age 60–69 were working in 1996.

4. The net effect of the elimination of mandatory retirement on retirement patterns was probably small, since financial incentives to retire remained in many public and private pension schemes. Burkhauser and Quinn (1983) estimated that at least half of what looked like a mandatory retirement effect was actually due to the simultaneous financial incentives.

5. The changes outlined in the next several paragraphs can be found in the Social Security Administration's *Annual Statistical Supplement to the Social Security Bulletin* (1996), tables 2.A20, 2.A29.

6. Inadequate delayed retirement credits meant that benefits forgone because of continued work were never fully made up via higher benefits in the future. This loss

in social security wealth was the "pay cut" mentioned earlier. Of course, a delayed retirement credit that is actuarially fair *on average* will not be so for individual workers with different life expectancies.

7. Waiting longer for a given benefit is the same as getting a smaller benefit at any given age. Imagine an upward sloping line showing the relationship between age of initial receipt (on the horizontal axis) and monthly benefit (on the vertical axis.) A benefit cut would lower the line; a benefit delay would move it to the right. Although these two changes are indistinguishable, they can have very different interpretations. Describing the change as a benefit cut makes it appear that the benefit was too high, an opinion with which many recipients and elderly advocates would disagree. Describing the change as a benefit delay makes it sound like the amount was correct, but the age was wrong, a view which resonates with many more people, given the increases in life expectancy Americans have enjoyed. Despite the different interpretations, however, the policies are nearly identical.

8. The proportion of employer pension plan participants whose primary coverage is in a defined-contribution plan increased from 13 to 30 percent between 1975 and 1985, and then to 42 percent in 1992. Including secondary plans, which are nearly all defined-contribution, the proportion of participants in defined-contribution plans doubled from 26 to 52 percent between 1975 and 1993, and then rose slightly to 53 percent (estimate) by 1997 (Olsen and VanDerhei 1997, table 2).

9. Peter Diamond has pointed out (in private correspondence) that labor force participation rates for older American men were also very flat in the late 1960s, when the economy was very strong and the unemployment rate was on its way to a postwar low of 3.5 percent. When the economy sagged in the 1970s, participation rates began to tumble, as one can see in Figure 1 (especially for ages 65 to 69.) The next recession may cast some light on this debate.

10. See Quinn, Burkhauser, and Myers (1990) for a more extensive discussion of this point.

11. In this research, we define a "career job" as a full-time job of at least 10 years tenure. A "bridge job," therefore, can be a part-time job of any length or a full-time job of less than 10 years duration.

12. See Juster and Suzman (1995) along with other papers in the same volume for an overview of the Health and Retirement Study.

13. Employment rates for this HRS subsample are not comparable to labor force participation rates published by the Bureau of Labor Statistics, because we have eliminated those individuals with no worker experience after age 49, and are looking at employment rather than labor force participation, which includes those not employed and actively searching for work. Since the HRS oversamples blacks and Hispanics, sample weights are provided so that the estimates will better represent population percentages. All percentages used in this paper are weighted.

14. For those still working in 1996, the concept of job duration is a fluid one. Some full-time workers were on jobs with less than 10 years duration in 1996, but will probably have more than 10 years tenure by the time they leave. Therefore, what appears to be a "bridge job" by our definition might prove to be a "10-year or more" career job when it is over. Rather than classify all jobs with less than 10 years duration in 1996 as bridge jobs, as though all these workers were just about to leave, we assume here that full-time workers younger than 62 remain on their current jobs until age 62 and those still employed after age 62 remain until age 65. There is no need for any such assumption for those working part time (the majority of those on bridge jobs), since we consider part-time jobs to be bridge jobs no matter what the duration. We then classify the 1996 jobs as either "career" or "bridge" depending on their (assumed) eventual tenure.

15. A small percentage (2 percent) of these men and women were known to be bworking, but missing data prevented us from discerning whether they were employed on full-time career jobs.

16. These are the ratios of those on a bridge job to those on a bridge or a full-time career job. Those whose career or bridge job status cannot be determined are ignored in these calculations.

17. These estimates add those on bridge jobs in 1996, plus those who already left the labor market via a bridge job.

18. We return to the original definition here — more than 1600 hours per year, and 10 or more years duration.

19. In defining this subsample of career workers, we do not have to assume that workers remain on their current jobs until age 62 or age 65. For those who leave these career jobs by 1996, we can calculate the actual tenure at transition to define the job one leaves as either career or bridge. On the other hand, for those who take another job when they leave their career jobs, we do assume they remain on the post-career job until age 62 (or age 65 for those already 62 or older) when deciding to describe it as a bridge job or as another career job.

20. A small number moved out of employment via an intermediate job, but data deficiencies prevent us from determining whether the intervening job was a bridge job or another career job.

21. Tables 4 and 5 contain very preliminary data. The early-release version of Wave 3 is missing data on occupational status and wage rates, so the comparisons in these tables are based on those career workers who switched to a bridge job by 1994 (Wave 2).

References

Burkhauser, Richard V. and Joseph F. Quinn. 1983. "Is Mandatory Retirement Overrated? Evidence from the 1970s." *Journal of Human Resources* (Summer): 337–58.

———. 1997. "Implementing Pro-Work Policies for Older Americans in the Twenty-First Century." In *Preparing for the Baby-Boomers: The Role of Employment.* U.S. Senate Special Committee on Aging, Serial No. 105-7. Washington, D.C., July: 60–83.

Gustman, Alan L., Olivia S. Mitchell, and Thomas L. Steinmeier. 1995. "Retirement Measures in the Health and Retirement Study." *Journal of Human Resources* 30 (Supplement): S57–83.

Juster, F. Thomas and Richard Suzman. 1995. "An Overview of the Health and Retirement Study." *Journal of Human Resources* 30 (Supplement): S7–56.

McNaught, William, Michael Barth, and Peter Henderson. 1989. "The Human Resource Potential of Americans over 50." *Human Resource Management* 50: 455–73.

Olsen, Kelly and Jack L. VanDerhei. 1997. "Defined Contribution Plan Dominance Grows Across Sectors and Employer Sizes, While Mega Defined Benefit Plans Remain Strong." Employee Benefit Research Institute Special Report 190. Washington, D.C.: Employee Benefit Research Institute, October.

Quadagno, Jill and Joseph F. Quinn. 1997. "Does Social Security Discourage Work?" In Eric Kingson and James Schulz, eds., *Social Security in the 21st Century.* New York: Oxford University Press: 127–46.

Quinn, Joseph F. 1991. "The Nature of Retirement: Survey and Econometric Evidence." In Alicia H. Munnell, ed., *Retirement and Public Policy.* Ames, Iowa: Kendall-Hunt: 115–37.

———. 1997a. "Retirement Trends and Patterns in the 1990s: The End of an Era?" *Public Policy and Aging Report* 8, 3: 10–14.

———. 1997b. "The Role of Bridge Jobs in the Retirement Patterns of Older Americans." In Philip deJong and Theodore Marmor, eds., *Social Policy and the Labour Market*. Aldershot: Ashgate Publishing: 91–116.

Quinn, Joseph F. and Richard V. Burkhauser. 1994. "Public Policy and the Plans and Preferences of Older Americans." *Journal of Aging and Social Policy* 6, 3: 5–20.

Quinn, Joseph F., Richard V. Burkhauser, and Daniel A. Myers. 1990. *Passing the Torch: The Influence of Economic Incentives on Work and Retirement*. Kalamazoo, Mich.: W. E. Upjohn Institute for Employment Research.

Social Security Administration. 1996. *Annual Statistical Supplement to the Social Security Bulletin*. Washington, D.C.: U.S. Government Printing Office.

U.S. Bureau of Labor Statistics (USBLS). Various years. *Employment and Earnings*. Washington, D.C.: U.S. Government Printing Office.

Chapter 2
How Prepared Are Americans for Retirement?

Mark J. Warshawsky and John Ameriks

In this era emphasizing individual economic responsibility, policymakers and the media often pose a question that many of us ask ourselves: "Will current workers retire in comfort?" This chapter takes a practical approach to answering this question, one that might be adopted by an intelligent layperson using currently available financial planning tools. Specifically, we use as our assessment model a publicly available software package known as the Quicken Financial Planner (QFP), manufactured by the Intuit Corporation. We pass through the Planner a recent nationally representative survey of Americans known as the Survey of Consumer Finances, a study that contains extensive data on household financial and economic status. The objective is to assess the preparedness of the American public for retirement. In the process, we also comment on usefulness of the QFP as a modeling tool. Finally, we suggest ways to help researchers produce better surveys of household economic status so as to improve the value-added of research to policy and practice.

We begin the discussion with a review of the economics literature on workers' preparedness for retirement. Next, we describe the range of publicly available retirement and financial planning software and provide a detailed overview of the Quicken Financial Planner, highlighting its comprehensiveness but also noting its limitations. We implement the model using data from the Survey of Consumer Finances (SCF) and provide results from the empirical analysis. The discussion concludes with a summary of key results, accompanied by suggestions for improvements in financial planning software and the design of surveys.

Previous Studies

Whether the baby boom generation is preparing adequately for retirement was analyzed by Bernheim (1992), who set up a complex liquidity-constrained lifetime utility maximization problem assuming certainty and perfect foresight.[1] In his model, inputs include (a) assumed data such as rates of mortality, time preference, and intertemporal substitution; (b) environmental factors such as social security, tax structures, and macroeconomic conditions; and (c) household characteristics. Household characteristics include those imputed (e.g., age-earnings profiles, family composition, and pension income), and those taken from a database on American households fielded by Merrill Lynch in early 1992. That survey obtained information on household demographic and economic characteristics as well as financial and nonfinancial assets, home equity and other real estate, pension coverage, and debt. Bernheim estimated age-wealth profiles using these data, and on the presumption that birth cohorts behave similarly at different ages, and forecast how wealth is likely to accumulate in the future for the baby boom generation. His evaluation then compared observed asset accumulation paths with those predicted by his economic model, which he summarized in an "index of saving adequacy." Bernheim concluded that the typical American household would have to triple its rate of asset accumulation to finance retirement. Married couples and low-income households were found to be holding more adequate assets than singles and high-income households; he attributed this result to the redistributive effects of social security.

A follow-up study by Bernheim and Scholz (1993) used a similar simulation approach but instead used the 1983 and 1986 Surveys of Consumer Finances to derive actual asset paths. This study concluded that actual asset trajectories were well below target trajectories in families where the head of household had not completed college. By contrast, actual and desired trajectories matched up well in households who had completed college; the main reason appeared to be that the latter were more likely to be covered by a pension plan.

Taking a different tack, the Congressional Budget Office (1993) examined the question of how well baby boomers were preparing for retirement by comparing households aged 25–44 in 1989 with households at the same point in their life cycle in the early 1960s. Boomer households proved to have more real income and a higher ratio of wealth to income than their parents' generation. Furthermore, the CBO found that people ages 55–74 in 1989 were relatively well off, and baby boomers were anticipated to have higher real retirement incomes than their retired parents. These results have been interpreted to mean that baby boomers can expect a comfortable retirement.

In a recent critical review of this literature, Gale (1997) found fault with all approaches. Regarding the CBO study, he pointed out that concluding that current workers will do well in retirement requires making some questionable assumptions. One is that the current generation of elderly is doing well, a second is that boomers will face the same prosperous economic conditions from now until retirement that their parents did, and a third is that boomers will be content to fare as well in retirement as did today's retirees. The last presumption, in particular, is debatable, as it is likely that boomers will aim for retiree living standards comparable to their own working years, rather than the living standard of today's retirees.

Regarding the Bernheim research, Gale noted that Bernheim's model did not use retirement needs to judge the adequacy of retirement saving using households' entire asset stock. Rather, he examines the ratio of "other assets" to the part of total needs not covered by social security and pensions. He therefore concluded that the Bernheim index did not indicate a household's adequacy of retirement preparations. For example, if a household needed 100 units of wealth to retire, and it was on course to generate 61 units in social security, 30 in pensions, and three in other assets, it would have 94 percent of its retirement needs covered. The Bernheim index would indicate that the household was saving only 33 percent of what it needs $(= 3/(100-61-30))$. Finally, Gale argued that several of Bernheim's other assumptions were faulty, including a likely understatement of pension benefits, the exclusion of all housing wealth and inheritances, a common retirement age of 65, and no allowance for retirees' lower work-related and other expenses.

In his own research which used a variant of Bernheim's model, Gale drew on the 1992 Survey of Consumer Finances to explore what proportion of households save adequately for retirement, the traits of households who don't save, and how big their shortfall will be. He estimated that, in married couples where the husband worked full-time, 30–53 percent of households were saving inadequately. He also concluded that adequacy was higher among the more educated, those with a pension plan, and those with higher income, while it was lower among the older population. His wealth shortfall or adequacy gap measure was defined as the difference between target and actual wealth among households saving inadequately (he too ignored all housing wealth). He found that the median inadequate saver had a relatively small shortfall of $22,000 or about six months of earnings. The shortfall, however, increased significantly with age; among 60–64-year-olds, the median inadequate saver was short $75,000, or about 26 months of earnings.

As will be described in more detail below, the approach we adopt in this chapter is more direct and conservative than those of the studies just described. Where possible, we draw on existing data from the 1992 Survey of Consumer Finances rather than inferring them as Bernheim did. If there is a doubt, we attempt to skew our assumptions in favor of finding saving adequacy, particularly by allowing the saving rate of households to increase with age. Moreover, our approach is immune to some of Gale's critiques, since we measure saving adequacy in terms of the standards of current workers (rather than retirees); we include housing wealth in measured assets; we use workers' self-reported retirement ages; and we allow for a drop in living expenses on retirement. Our approach is also superior to Gale's since we incorporate households with nontraditional as well as traditional family structures in the empirical analysis.

Retirement and Financial Planning Software

There is an expanding universe of retirement and financial planning software and Internet sites available to the public offering advice on saving for retirement and other financial goals, as well as on asset allocation. These programs are often proprietary packages marketed by mutual fund and insurance companies with investment products to sell, and also include independent packages marketed by financial experts and consumer software companies. When these were first introduced, most packages focused on retirement planning, with advice on asset allocation a secondary consideration. More recently, software and Internet sites focus on asset allocation advice, with retirement planning taking a secondary role.

These software packages fill an important need. Middle-income and middle-aged Americans are increasingly holding defined contribution pension plans (and especially 401(k) and 403(b) plans), rather than traditional defined benefit plans as in the past. Most defined contribution pensions are voluntary (within legal and plan limits) and allow the plan participant to contribute at any level elected, often with encouragement from plan sponsors through employer matches. Increasingly participants feel they need education, guidance, and financial advice on the appropriate contribution to make. Moreover, most 401(k) and 403(b) plans allow for self-direction in the investment of contributions, necessitating education, guidance, and advice on asset allocation. Adding to the sense of urgency is public debate over the solvency of the social security program and the explosion of mutual fund investment alternatives.

Software packages and Internet sites are practical and economical media to provide this information to masses of people. Much can be conveyed in an engaging way through planning software; although complete customization is impossible, an intelligently designed program can allow for a myriad of situations and offer possible solutions to problems. The major cost of building such programs is in the design and testing stages; expenses for marketing and support are likely to be modest. Face-to-face meetings with a professional personal financial consultant (supported by professional-grade planning software) may produce more specific advice and may be more appropriate for especially complicated situations, though the more personal approach is generally more expensive than using a computer software package. Moreover, software offers privacy and a "do-it-yourself" approach, which make it attractive even to some who do use a personal financial consultant.

Although these programs differ in focus, sophistication, and level of detail, most share certain conceptual features. Typically they take an actuarial rather than an economic approach to saving for retirement. That is, a goal is set by the user for the desired income flow in retirement, and the appropriate savings rate — assumed to be level over the worklife — is calculated by the program to enable the user to reach his or her goal. This approach is consistent with the standard design of defined contribution plans. That is, employer contributions are usually constant as a share of salary over the worklife of the participant, and continuous participation is highly encouraged. Moreover, the actuarial approach is consistent with many tax rules governing pensions, particularly nondiscrimination requirements, which make it difficult for plan sponsors to tailor contribution rates to age, income level, or job tenure.[2] The software programs do not attempt to optimize saving and borrowing rates over the life cycle in response to a desire for a smooth consumption path or to adjust to particular age-specific expenditure patterns.[3]

Another feature common to planning packages is the use of risk tolerance questionnaires to assess the appropriateness of various asset classes for investor portfolios. Some of the packages, especially those appearing more recently, also use optimization techniques and modern portfolio theory to advise on the selection of efficient portfolios that maximize expected returns for a given level of risk. Finally, nearly all the packages provide a basic education on important financial planning principles including the time value of money, the benefit of tax deferral, the importance of diversification among asset classes, the trade-off between risk and return, and so on.

The Quicken Financial Planner

The universe of personal financial planning software is vast and changing, so we selected a widely used package for our analysis known as the Quicken Financial Planner from Intuit. The main purpose of the QFP is to evaluate and give advice on the steps necessary to assure full financial preparedness for retirement. To do this, the Planner poses a series of questions about the current demographic and economic characteristics of all members of a household, their personal plans and preferences, their expectations of future personal and general economic conditions, their pension coverage, and complete details of their personal balance sheet, both assets and liabilities. The QFP also asks about household asset allocation choices and risk preferences. The planning exercise is a search for answers to the following questions: can the household achieve a specified replacement rate of income in retirement under the current plan, and, if not, what changes, especially in saving, need to be made?

The Planner is a fairly sophisticated and comprehensive planning package, one that incorporates most of the essential elements of financial planning, albeit with some significant weaknesses. Like older-generation packages, its strength is in retirement planning; nevertheless, the QFP also covers asset allocation. It appears useful for households at most income and wealth levels, except perhaps those at the very bottom and the very top of the income and wealth distributions (or those with unusual financial situations). Moreover, it is more widely utilized than its competitors among independent packages and therefore may directly influence saving and asset allocation behavior for reasonably large numbers of the population. Finally, despite its sophistication, QFP is relatively easy to use and avoids the use of confusing economic and financial jargon.[4]

Analyzing Americans' Retirement Plans

In an ongoing project of the Federal Reserve Board, the Survey of Consumer Finances (SCF) collects information from a representative sample of American households about many of the demographic, economic, and financial factors required by the Planner. It is perhaps the most complete publicly available and nationally representative survey of Americans of all ages. The SCF provides a variety of financial data that we use as the basis of our empirical analysis of the prescriptions of the Quicken Financial Planner and the Planner's assessment of the adequacy of Americans' retirement savings. Hence we can use the SCF as a source of data to feed the QFP model to generate insights about households' retirement prospects. If and when data are missing, we employ information from the empirical economics literature, other surveys, and common sense.

Outline of the Procedure

Our approach had three steps. First, we created an extract containing household data from the 1992 SCF and any additional assumptions; this was formatted for input to the QFP. Second, we submitted this input file to two helpful staff members at Intuit who read our generated input file, entered the data into the QFP, and saved machine readable versions of the QFP output. Finally, the output was returned to us and entered into our statistical analysis package.

In designing the input file several assumptions and modifications were required to fit the input data into the QFP format.

Sample Selection

Using the QFP to generate a financial plan for retirement made sense for only a subset of the SCF respondents. For example, in order for "retirement" to be meaningful, we felt it reasonable to ensure that at least one member of each household was employed in a job from which he or she could "retire." Hence a first criterion for selecting SCF households for our sample was that either the respondent or the spouse/partner had to be employed full-time. Survey observations representing roughly 61 million of the 96 million households in the United States met this criterion in the 1992 SCF.[5]

We also wanted to ensure that the households we ran through the Planner represented middle America to the greatest degree possible. To this end, we excluded SCF respondents with unusually large non-financial wealth (over $1 million); these people are probably concerned with different estate planning issues than the average user of a financial software program. Additionally, we excluded people with relatively high annual earnings (over $125,000) since they too may be different from the "typical" household.[6] We also imposed an age limit on the sample, including only households with a respondent or spouse at least age 25 but younger than 71. Of those households in which there was at least one full-time worker, roughly 96 percent met this criterion.

Additional sample selection decisions pertain to the difficulty of translating SCF information into inputs for the QFP. Table 1 describes the procedure generating the sample used for the Planner exercise, and shows that lack of a retirement age (due to no full-time job or nonresponse) was a major reason for sample omission. After the age, employment, and retirement screens were applied, the remaining sample represented 42.7 million households. The table also shows some of the other reasons households were excluded from the exercise.[7]

Variable Construction

The SCF affords ample data to create most inputs required by the QFP, but there are a few instances where information is lacking.[8]

Retirement date. One of the central issues in retirement planning is the timing of the decision to retire. Unfortunately, the SCF does not ask respondents "At what age do you plan to retire?" (Indeed, because "retirement" can mean different things to different people, it would not necessarily be productive to get a response to this particular question.) The survey questionnaire does ask currently employed individuals several questions regarding expectations about future labor supply.[9] We use those responses to estimate retirement dates for the respondent and/or spouse/partner. This information is likely to be least accurate for determining retirement intentions for younger households, but it was the best available information in the survey regarding the timing of retirement.[10]

Other demographic data. The SCF contains information on age, sex, and a self-assessment of health status. We use all of this information to generate a life expectancy for the sample members that is based on the default values reported by the QFP plus 10 years. We add the 10 years to reported life expectancies for several reasons. First, it does not appear that the QFP builds in any anticipated increase in life expectancy over time. Since life

TABLE 1: Sample Characteristics

Reasons for Selection of Sample Members	Observations Removed		Observations Remaining After Sequential Removal	
	Count (n)	Weight (mil.)*	Count (n)	Weight (mil.)*
Total 1992 SCF sample size, first implicate	–	0.0	3,906	95.9
Data included from an absent spouse	9	0.2	3,897	95.7
Respondent birth year indicates age under 25 or over 70	686	18.3	3,212	77.4
Respondent does not have valid information to generate a retirement age	1,902	48.5	1,863	44.1
Respondent has spouse under 25 or over 70	276	6.8	1,832	43.2
Neither spouse nor respondent has a full-time job	1,040	29.7	1,796	42.7
First mortgage has unusual features	14	0.3	1,788	42.5
Second mortgage has unusual features	8	0.2	1,783	42.4
Special assets owned by household of over $1 million	626	1.4	1,491	41.7
Household income from employment cannot cover taxes, loan payments, etc.	1,013	22.0	1,408	40.1
Respondent or spouse has future job or spouse no main job	265	7.4	1,268	36.1
Other rejections/problems	5	0.2	1,263	35.9
Income or earnings of $125,000 or more**	197	2.0	1,066	33.9

Source: Authors' calculations based on 1992 SCF data.
*This column contains the total SCF sample weight of the observations, in millions of households.
**These observations flagged after the removal of all other observations for all other reasons; they are maintained on datafile for robustness checks.

expectancy has trended upward over time and is likely to continue to do so in the future, we felt it prudent to build this expectation into the analysis. Second, the Planner does not offer a way to set aside financial resources for unforeseen medical or health expenses in retirement. Lacking a direct way to protect against such risk, we felt that extending life expectancy seemed appropriate. Finally, the QFP does not take into account household uncertainty with regard to the length of life, so a risk averse person might legitimately use a longer life expectancy.

College expenses. Using SCF data in 1992, we include information for the oldest five children in each household under the age of 22. This is helps determine when the household is likely to experience outlays for college expenses. We assume that children rely on household resources to fund undergraduate expenses only, and we assume that all children will attend college from the age of 18 to 22. To estimate college costs, we assume that all households reside in the state of Ohio and pay college expenses at one of three Ohio institutions determined by the (1992) level of household income salary. In households with salary incomes of under $40,000, children are assumed to attend a community college. For those with income in the range $40,000–$100,000, children are assumed to attend a public, four-year, state university. In households in which salary income is over $100,000, the children are assumed to attend a private college. It is further assumed that each child will contribute $2,000 per year toward college expenses. In addition, the cost of college is offset according to income. For household incomes under $35,000, financial aid is assumed to cover all college expenses not covered by the student's contribution. For incomes between $35,000 and $70,000, financial aid is assumed to cover half of the remaining college cost. There is assumed to be no financial aid for households with over $70,000 in annual income. These assumptions are roughly consistent with Department of Education information regarding college financial planning.

Salary growth. The SCF provides detailed information on respondents' and spouses' current salaries and earnings. We also determine whether each respondent is self-employed, which enables use of the Planner's ability to calculate social security taxes differently for wage/salary earners and the self-employed. In contrast, the SCF provides no indication of the respondents' long-term expectations with regard to salary growth, though it is reasonable to expect that people anticipate pay increases over time, and also that pay growth rates are likely to be higher for younger than for older individuals. Therefore we assumed that there are three "stages" of earnings growth anticipated: people age 25–35 are assumed to have real pay grow at 5 percent per year; people age 36–50 are assumed to have pay grow at 1 percent; and no real growth rate in pay is allocated to people over the age of 50.[11]

In addition, for tax purposes, all households are assumed to reside in the state of Ohio; the QFP uses 1992 earnings to evaluate the average income tax rate for the household before and after retirement.

Taxable financial assets. From the SCF we obtain information on household checking and savings accounts, money market accounts, CDs, stocks, bonds, mutual funds, brokerage call accounts, and the value of other managed accounts. Each of these items is entered into the QFP as part of the taxable portfolio of assets. The SCF does not ask any specific questions about any amounts that households plan to save in taxable forms. As a result, we cannot use the Planner's ability to account for a household's taxable saving plan. (However, we do use the Planner's "sweep" feature to "simulate" saving — we return to this below.)

Tax deferred retirement saving vehicles. With regard to IRA and Keogh accounts, the SCF asks respondents only about how much money the households have accumulated currently in these accounts. There is enough information to construct a crude estimate of how the accumulations are allocated among asset classes; however, there is no information on typical contributions to these accounts, so we cannot use the QFP to predict future contributions. With regard to employer-provided pension and savings plans on the "main job" of the respondent and spouse, the SCF asks for information for up to three pension plans for the respondent and three for the spouse / partner. These plans can be either defined benefit or defined contribution, and for the purposes of generating information regarding tax deferred savings plans, we are only interested in the defined contribution accounts. (We enter the information about DB plans in the QFP section on anticipated pension benefits.) There are SCF data on the level of current employee contributions to these plans, as well as the level of contributions provided by an employer. But we lack information about contributions that an employer may "match" in the context of a 401 (k) or other plan. We use available data on current contribution amounts to enter each DC pension into the Planner as a separate savings plan. We also use SCF data on current accumulations and allocations of accumulations in account-type plans.

Home equity/mortgages. There is extensive SCF information that can be used to evaluate home equity levels. This includes the purchase date of the home, home mortgages, expenses associated with the home (association or property management fees), and (in a few cases) rental income associated with the home. In a few cases, mortgage loans associated with homes could not be translated into the simple structure that the QFP requires. In particular, individuals whose mortgage loans as reported in the SCF "had no set number of years" or "no set number of payments" were dropped from the sample.

It is widely known that residential housing constitutes a very large share of the net worth of American households. It is also a well-established empirical fact that people do not always consume their entire home equity to finance retirement. On the other hand, some retirees relocate and at the same time, "trade down" their homes, effectively liquidating at least a portion of their housing wealth. We felt it was therefore reasonable to assume that upon the retirement of the last individual in the household, homeowners would purchase a new residence worth 75 percent of the value of the original home. All remaining mortgage payments, if any, would be translated at the point of trade-down into a new loan, and if the individual was over 55 at retirement, the one-time capital gain exemption is used, according to the tax law in effect in 1997. All remaining after-tax proceeds from the transaction, if any, were deposited in the taxable savings portfolio.

Debt. In addition to collecting information about home mortgages, the SCF gathers information on other consumer loans. We included in the analysis lines of credit, educational loans, loans/mortgages on other real estate holdings, and other consumer loans; only loans with a standard payment schedule are used (in the case of lines of credit, we assume a 10-year repayment period and monthly payments on these borrowings).[12]

Special assets and businesses. The SCF includes a great deal of information about special assets that might be owned by a household. These include the value of loans or land contracts held by the household, shares of non-residential real estate, and other property, as well as information on the value of business interests owned. All of this information was used in generating asset level data, but none of these assets is assumed to generate current or future income. This is because there is no detailed information as to the household's plans for the assets, or whether any current income flow from the asset is stable over time. We do assume that these special assets increase in value with inflation. We note that these assumptions imply that "special assets" simply serve to raise the net worth of households and do not otherwise affect the retirement plans. Our primary motivation for tracking these assets was to assure that none of our sample households owned more than $1 million in these types of special assets.

Expenses. The SCF did not ask respondents about current or future living expenses, which means that we had no direct measure of net saving. We dealt with this in the planning exercise using several strategies. First, we assumed that living expenses in 1992 made up the balance of current income after taxes on earnings, planned saving, housing expenses, and debt payments.[13] Second, we assumed that living expenses increase with inflation and real income increased at a slightly higher rate (related to age, described above). Third, we assumed that individuals "sweep" all excess cash into taxable savings. Finally, we assumed that living expenses fell 20 percent at the point of retirement, and by a further 20 percent when one member of a couple died.

These assumptions amount to presuming that discretionary saving in 1992 equaled the (after-tax) earnings on accumulated savings. This satisfies a number of "reasonability" requirements. First, individuals with a "taste for saving" (evidenced by higher accumulation of assets by 1992) save more than others. Second, the assumption is consistent with a "mental accounts" approach toward saving, in which only current cash flow generated by labor earnings is spent to cover consumption. Third, it presumes that individuals save more as they approach retirement due to increases in labor income relative to living expenses, as well as the compounding of interest. Fourth, it seems reasonable to assume that living expenses will decline slightly at the point of retirement (perhaps due to the disappearance of "work related" expenses). These assumptions, on net, are quite conservative for the purpose of our analysis; while current taxable savings is small according to our assumptions, future savings is probably overestimated, particularly in young families. More specifically, the "expenses equal to current disposable earnings" assumption implies that the principal repayment of debt is net saving. Once loans are repaid (including mortgages), the entire payment amount is credited to taxable saving, whereas in actuality some of these payments will be diverted to other forms of consumption.

Risk and return. The SCF asks a single question regarding the willingness of the respondent to take financial risks, characterizing the respondent's attitude as (a) willing to take substantial financial risks expecting to earn substantial returns, (b) willing to take above average financial risks expecting to earn above average returns, (c) willing to take average financial risk expecting to earn average returns, or (d) not willing to take any financial risk. We map these responses into return categories in the QFP. Thus for households saying (a) we assume they invest consistent with a 10 percent annual rate of return on financial investments; those saying (b) are given a 9 percent rate; those responding (c) are given a 7.5 percent rate; and the remainder are assigned a 6 percent rate.

Social security and other pensions. The 1992 SCF did not ask respondents about anticipated social security benefits.[14] In order to generate the needed input for the social security section of the QFP, we placed each individual into one of the four "rough estimate" bands offered in the Planner using the highest salary (in 1992 dollars) that each individual was forecast to attain according to projected earnings path. Turning to pensions, a great deal of information was available on anticipated pension benefits, all of which we used in the Planner, along with the assumption that benefit amounts were fixed in nominal terms after retirement.[15] In addition the approach assumed that company pensions used a joint and survivor formula with 50 percent to the surviving spouse.

Special features. Two of the Planner's special features proved useful in our exercise. First, we allowed the QFP to sweep all excess[16] cash flow generated by the household into taxable savings. Initially, swept amounts were zero for almost every household, since, by definition, living expenses are a residual of earnings minus all outflows except college expenses. However, because younger households were assumed to have earnings that rose faster than living expenses, loans were eventually paid off, and a few households had some special income (e.g., lump sum pensions, trust accounts, rental income from housing), these amounts were often positive and sizeable in later years. Second, we allowed the Planner to sell financial assets to cover cash shortfalls in years prior to retirement. Thus we permitted household to "raid" tax-deferred retirement accounts for the purposes of meeting unexpected expenses. Note that given our assumptions, the only possible "unexpected" expense would be college.

Empirical Findings

To understand the results we generate using the QFP and SCF respondent data, we must call attention to some of the implications of assumptions made thus far. For example, we assumed that living expenses increased with inflation but labor income rose at least as fast if not faster. This implies that the analysis boils down to an actuarial calculation of whether household retirement plans are consistent with (1) the level of accumulated assets in 1992; (2) college expenditures; (3) planned saving in employer-sponsored tax-deferred saving plans; (4) future social security and pension benefits; and (5) life expectancy. Given that we defined living expenses as a residual, the only reasons for plan failure prior to retirement are that college expenses proved too large to be affordable, or that the household had no financial assets to start with. As we shall show, the latter reason turns out to be by far the more frequent explanation for early failure in retirement financial plans. After retirement, a household's plan could fail as a result of inconsistencies in any or all of the plan's dimensions.

Household Characteristics

Summary statistics for the households used in the analysis appear in Table 2. All summary statistics presented here (and elsewhere unless otherwise noted) use SCF sample weights. Deletion of some observations from the file means that the resulting sample is no longer representative of the entire U.S. population; nevertheless, sample weights are still necessary to reduce the relative impact of SCF over-sampling of wealthy individuals. The un-weighted final number of observations included 1,066 households.

As expected, the households examined have characteristics reflective of "middle America." The median age of respondents in the sample was 42 years, and the median number of persons in each household was 3. Median life expectancy assigned to the respondents was 93. Households in the sample, on average, appeared to be intending to retire somewhat early, as the median retirement age was 61, while the median number of years remaining in the plan after the first retirement in the household was 40. The estimated

TABLE 2: Characteristics of Included Sample

Characteristic	Mean	Median	Std. Dev.
Age of respondent at end of 1992	43.3	42	10.7
Respondent age at death	94.5	93	2.5
Persons in household	2.8	3	1.4
Age of respondent at time of 1st retirement	59.0	61	8.8
Number of years in plan before 1st retirement	15.8	14	10.5
Number of years in plan after 1st retirement	41.5	40	9.3
Number of years in plan	57.3	58	10.5
Number of children	0.98	1	1.11
Total 1991 income (from SCF)	$ 42,000	$ 37,000	$ 25,000
Total salary income as recorded by QFP	$ 41,000	$ 39,000	$ 24,000
Total living expenses entered into QFP	$ 24,000	$ 22,000	$ 14,000
QFP net worth in 1992	$ 105,000	$ 53,000	$ 211,000
QFP net worth at retirement	$ 397,000	$241,000	$ 501,000
QFP net worth at end of plan	$1,080,000	$221,000	$2,246,000
Total sample observations	1,066		
Total weighted observations	33,934,884		

Source: Authors' calculations based on 1992 SCF data.
Notes: All dollar amounts in 1992 real dollars. Sample includes individuals with less than $125,000 in income and salary.

1992 salary entered into QFP had a median of $39,000.[17] Median net worth of the sample members in 1992 was $53,000 (average net worth was nearly twice that, indicating a very skewed distribution of wealth.)[18]

Measures of Success and Failure

Table 3 summarizes output from the QFP, showing information regarding the "success" or "failure" of household retirement plans for the overall sample and also for selected subgroups. The bottom line is that slightly over one-half (52 percent) of the SCF households are predicted to fail to finance their retirement.

It is informative to differentiate between two separate stages at which retirement plan failures can occur. First, we track the number of failures that occur before the date at which the spouse or respondent retires (here we use the earlier of the retirement dates if there is a working spouse or partner in the household). Second, we track the number of failures that occur after the retirement date. We also measure the degree of failure or success of the retirement plan. Table 3 indicates the average number of years in the retirement period where the household lacks sufficient financial resources; this is a measure of the degree of the shortfall in retirement plans. We note that the mean reported is tabulated only across those households whose plans are at least take them into the retirement period — that

TABLE 3: Retirement Financial Failure Patterns

	Sample Count		Failed at Any Time		Failed Before Retirement		Failed After Retirement		Years Left Unfunded After Retirement**	Years Funded After Retirement***
	Mil.	%*	Mil.	%*	Mil.	%*	Mil.	%*	Average Yrs	Average Yrs
Entire sample	33.93	100.0	17.64	52.0	5.15	15.2	12.49	36.8	31.4	23.5
Respondent over age 50	9.90	29.2	6.03	60.9	1.22	12.3	4.82	48.6	28.5	19.7
Has children	16.01	47.2	7.91	49.4	3.08	19.2	4.83	30.2	33.3	25.0
Has personal loans	5.77	17.0	2.63	45.6	1.18	20.5	1.45	25.1	32.0	25.4
Has home mortgage	16.32	48.1	6.67	40.9	1.56	9.5	5.11	31.3	31.3	28.9
Has home	21.35	62.9	10.16	47.6	2.21	10.4	7.95	37.2	30.8	26.1
Has pension	21.61	63.7	9.83	45.5	2.33	10.8	7.50	34.7	30.0	26.7
Total financial investments										
None	3.78	11.1	3.78	100.0	3.78	100.0	0.00	0.0	N/A	0.0
Under $4,999	8.47	25.0	4.55	53.7	0.97	11.5	3.57	42.2	33.6	21.1
$5,000–$24,999	9.36	27.6	4.76	50.9	0.38	4.1	4.38	46.8	33.8	25.3
$25,000–$99,999	8.32	24.5	3.08	37.0	0.02	0.2	3.06	36.8	28.8	30.7
Over $100,000	4.00	11.8	1.48	36.9	0.00	0.0	1.48	36.9	24.5	31.5
Education of head										
Less than High School	3.30	9.7	2.26	68.4	0.87	26.2	1.39	42.2	33.6	14.1
High School Diploma	10.20	30.1	6.34	62.2	1.99	19.5	4.35	42.7	31.3	20.5
Some College	6.22	18.3	2.90	46.6	0.80	12.9	2.09	33.7	32.0	24.8
College Degree	10.42	30.7	4.91	47.1	1.29	12.3	3.62	34.7	31.7	26.2
Prof. Degree	3.79	11.2	1.24	32.6	0.20	5.3	1.04	27.3	26.6	30.1
1992 earnings										
Less than $20,000	6.54	19.3	3.84	58.8	2.35	35.9	1.50	22.9	29.9	17.0
$20,000–$39,999	10.95	32.3	5.44	49.6	1.08	9.8	4.36	39.8	32.0	23.3
$40,000–$79,999	13.52	39.8	6.97	51.6	1.59	11.8	5.38	39.8	31.7	25.3
Over $80,000	2.93	8.6	1.39	47.4	0.13	4.6	1.25	42.8	29.9	30.3

Source: Authors' calculations based on 1992 SCF data.
*Percent of total observations in row.
**Includes only those observations that fail during retirement; i.e. does not include failures before retirement.
***Includes all observations with plan failures (both before and after retirement) as well as those with successful plans.

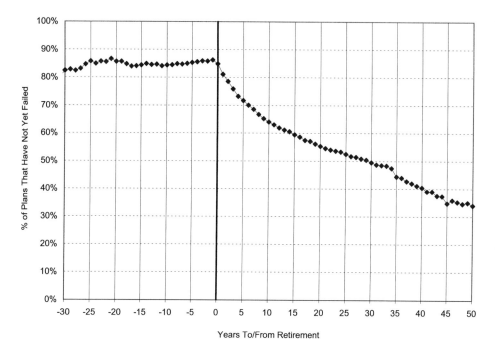

Figure 1. Retirement plan success rates. Source: Authors' calculations based on 1992 SCF data.

is, households whose plans fail before the retirement year are excluded. Table 3 also shows the average number of years for which the plan indicates there will be sufficient financial resources. Here, all observations in the sample are included in these averages.

Figures 1–3 also summarize the Planner's calculations graphically. Each of these figures plots "success rates" for the plans over time, where time is measured relative to the household retirement date. In the figures, the "success rate" is defined as the (weighted) number of plans that have not failed as of each year, divided by the total (weighted) number of plans observed in each year. All plans are (as a result of our sample selection criteria) observed at the point of retirement; however, the sample size shrinks in both directions away from this point. The figures plot the success rates for periods of up to 30 years before retirement to up to 40 years after retirement.

Turning to the specific results, the first row of Table 3 shows that success rates are constant in the years prior to retirement but then decline steadily following retirement. The first row of Table 3 indicates that 15 percent of the households in the sample run out of financial assets before retirement.

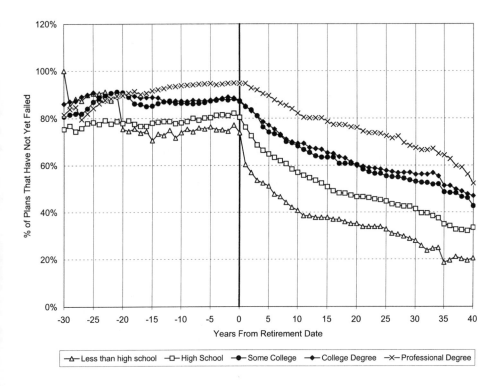

Figure 2. Retirement plan success rates by education of respondent. Source: Authors' calculations based on 1992 SCF data.

This seems like a large number, given that our assumptions imply that college expenses are the only unexpected outflows that occur prior to retirement. The reason why so many households fail before retirement is that roughly 11 percent of the sample starts the plan with no financial assets at all.[19] In other words, they were failing before they ever began. In addition, a closer examination showed that only 3 percent of the sample failed before retirement as the result of inability to pay for college expenses. In the remaining 1 percent of cases, the household failed to fund the initial retirement year.

By the tenth year of the retirement period, household success rates dropped from roughly 85 percent to around 65 percent. That is, 20 years into retirement, roughly 45 percent of the households failed in retirement planning; after 30 years, over 50 percent failed. In other words, at some point following retirement, 37 percent of the households in the sample ran out of assets.

Of course this statistic is influenced by the assumptions and underlying

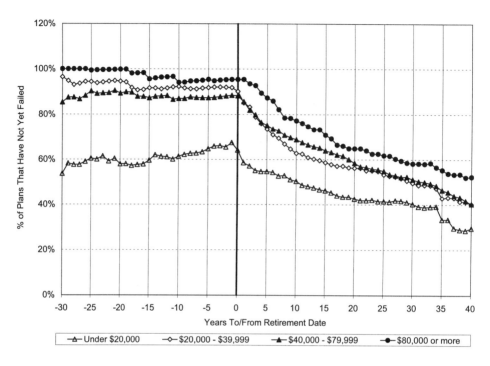

Figure 3. Retirement plan success rates by 1992 earnings level of household. Source: Authors' calculations based on 1992 SCF data.

data used in the study, whereas for any individual household, success or failure will be determined by its specific levels of initial wealth, salary, life expectancy, and timing of retirement. In order to attempt to further evaluate the relative importance of some of these factors, we divide the sample into several subgroups on the basis of key characteristics of interest.[20]

This analysis reveals that older households (where the respondent was at least 50 in 1992) are more likely to fail than the sample as a whole. This is due, in part, to the assumption that real earnings will rise at least for a while among the young, whereas wage growth is flat for older households. This finding is particularly important because one might have expected the opposite; that is, older households have more assets and are closer to retirement, so they might be expected to be better prepared for retirement. Households with personal loans, and especially mortgages, are less likely to fail than the population as a whole — this is perhaps due to the assumption that once loans are repaid, loan payments are in effect treated as net saving. Households with homes and mortgages are not very different from others in the population in terms of success rates before retirement; however, these households have generally higher success rates after retirement. Those with mortgages have the highest success rates: at a point 30 years after retirement, 60 percent of these households' plans had not yet failed, compared to the 50 percent failure rate on average. Probably not surprisingly, households with children have lower success rates than the rest of the population before retirement, probably attributable to the college expenses. After retirement, these households appear to have greater success rates than other households in the population.

The lower portion of Table 3 tabulates failure rates by three additional household characteristics: the total amount of financial assets owned by the households as of 1992, the education of the respondent, and the 1992 household earnings level. With regard to financial wealth, there is nothing unexpected here, as there is nearly a monotonic decrease in the failure rates as asset totals rise. Failures before retirement are concentrated among those who begin their plans with few assets. Failure is more common among the less educated than among the more educated, both before and after retirement. Figure 2 shows that the success rate for those with less than a high school education falls precipitously following retirement: as of retirement, there is a 20 percent difference between the success rate of the most highly educated (96 percent) and the least educated (76 percent). Only five years after retirement, this gap doubles to nearly 40 percent. Plan success rates also vary by income level (see Figure 3). Success rates among the lowest income households are remarkably low before retirement, but rise until the point of retirement. This indicates that a significant number of individuals in this category come under observation with zero financial assets.[21] Another interesting aspect of the income chart is that the relative decline in the success rate over the first 20 years in retirement is much lower for the low than for the higher income groups. For example, the highest income group hits retirement with a success rate of roughly 95 percent. After 20 years in retirement, the success rate among this group is only 65 percent—a drop of 30 percent. For the lowest income group, individuals reach retirement with a success rate of about 65 percent. After 20 years, this falls to around 45 percent, a drop of 20 percent. An important factor accounting for this difference is social security benefits.

Table 3 also indicates how years of life remaining in the plan affect performance. Failure rates are larger for those who must pay for college expenses and those with personal loans (but note there is a very small base for those with personal loans), and the data offer one way of thinking about the degree of success of the financial plans. Some good news can be found in the analysis: on average, households are able to fund almost 24 years of retirement. The number of retirement years that can be financed increases almost monotonically with starting wealth and reflects the same patterns across sub-groups as the failure rate data.

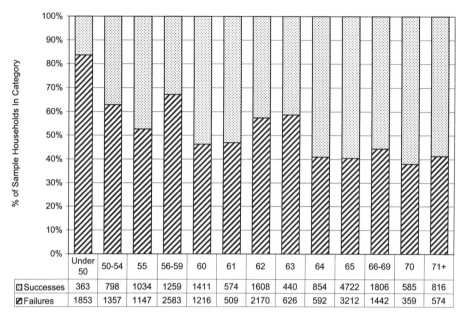

	Under 50	50-54	55	56-59	60	61	62	63	64	65	66-69	70	71+
Successes	363	798	1034	1259	1411	574	1608	440	854	4722	1806	585	816
Failures	1853	1357	1147	2583	1216	509	2170	626	592	3212	1442	359	574

Retirement Age of Head

Note: Number of success and failures in thousands of households.

Figure 4. Retirement plan successes and failures by retirement age of head (thousands of households). Source: Authors' calculations based on 1992 SCF data.

The incidence of plan success and failure is categorized by the respondent's anticipated retirement age in Figure 4. There are clearly higher failure rates among those intending to retire "early" (before age 60); in fact, failure rates for those planning to retire prior to age 50 top 80 percent. By contrast, those with retirement ages of 64 or later have failure rates of around 40 percent. Later retirement dates allow for more saving in the context of the planner's calculations, which accounts for some of these differences. It may also be true that some individuals were simply overly optimistic when reporting an "early" retirement date.

Another way of looking at the patterns of shortfalls pertains to the number of years of living expenses that household plans fail to finance. Perhaps the most interesting thing revealed in Table 4 is that the degree to which household retirement plans fail is relatively less severe for those in the lowest income group.[22]

We also compute the total real flow of dollars left uncovered by household assets after the failure of a plan, to estimate the seriousness of plan failures.

TABLE 4: Summary of Retirement Plan Shortfalls: Years of Living Expenses Left Unfunded After Plan Failure

Characteristic	Average	Median	Std. Dev.
Entire sample	18.9	17.9	10.2
Over age 50	16.0	15.0	8.0
Has children	18.8	17.9	10.0
Has home mortgage	17.8	17.1	9.2
Has home	18.3	17.9	9.5
Has pension	16.9	15.7	8.8
1992 financial wealth			
Under $4,999	19.3	18.5	10.0
$5,000–$24,999	20.4	19.5	11.1
$25,000–$99,999	17.4	16.3	8.7
Over $100,000	16.6	15.0	10.1
Education of head			
Less than high school	19.2	17.0	8.8
High school diploma	18.4	17.9	10.3
Some college	19.2	17.9	9.1
College degree	19.5	18.2	11.8
Prof. degree	17.6	17.5	8.2
1992 earnings			
Less than $20,000	14.0	10.7	8.9
$20,000–$39,999	19.8	18.4	10.6
$40,000–$79,999	19.2	18.7	9.6
Over $80,000	19.9	19.5	11.1

Source: Authors' calculations based on 1992 SCF data.
Note: Includes only those households whose plans fail after retirement and have shortfalls.

We find in Figure 5 that average unfinanced expenses for households whose plans fail is roughly $300,000 ($1992). There is also a reasonably wide distribution of shortfall amounts. Roughly 20 percent of the failures face financial shortfalls of under $50,000, about six percent fail by over $1 million, and the rest are in between.

Comparison with Previous Studies

Despite the fact that we use an entirely different modeling approach with distinct assumptions and data from those of the prior studies cited above, our results are remarkably similar to those reported by Bernheim and Gale. For example, Gale reports that 53 percent of the population is not saving adequately when he excludes housing wealth — almost the same fraction as in our study. As here, both Bernheim and Gale conclude that savings inade-

TABLE 5: Shortfalls Identified by Financial Planner (real 1992 dollars)

Cash Flow Direction	Average	Median	Std. Dev.
Total amount of shortfall[a]	$(297,000)	$(273,000)	$455,000
Total amount of excess[b]	$ 389,000	$ 227,000	$569,000

Source: Authors' calculations based on 1992 SCF data.
[a] includes only plan failures.
[b] includes only plan successes.

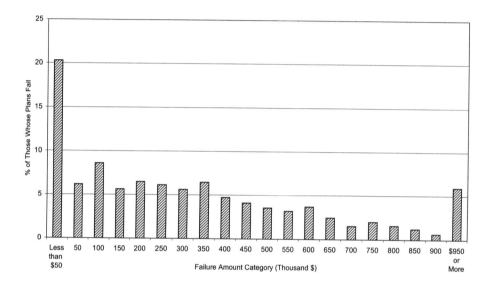

Note: Categories are equally spaced $50,000 bins from $0

Figure 5. Distribution of retirement plan failure amounts. Source: Authors' calculations based on 1992 SCF data.

quacy is particularly acute among people with low educational levels, older groups, and those without pensions.

Conclusion

A majority of American households are predicted to fall short in funding retirement, based on our research using a standard financial planning package and a dataset containing high-quality information on consumer assets and saving. We find that those most likely to fail in their retirement saving plans are households headed by the less educated, those with less financial wealth, and those lacking a pension. At the same time however, the lower-income and less-educated face a smaller shortfall than do the higher-paid and better educated. Finally, we find that the rise in failure rates over the retirement period is slower among low-income households than among the more highly paid.

We come to these conclusions after combining the Quicken Financial Planner model with data from the 1992 Survey of Consumer Finances. Like many financial planning software tools, QFP provides a useful framework for assessing retirement income needs and for tailoring individual plans for financing retirement. We also note that financial planning software programs in general suffer from limitations. In general, most do not recognize many uncertainties facing households, including uncertainty regarding life expectancy and returns on financial and human capital assets.

Our research suggests several areas where improvements might be made in future data collection efforts for retirement researchers. Because the timing of the retirement decision is such an important aspect of the financial situation of households, it would be useful to obtain more detail regarding household retirement expectations. Additional information would also be invaluable on features of workers' defined contribution pension plans, including employer match rates. Finally, a better assessment of household retirement assets requires additional information on after-tax structured savings plans (through direct deposits or any other mechanism), along with data on planned contributions to or withdrawals from IRAs.

Our analysis could be expanded in several directions. One interesting question is how sensitive the results are to assumptions, particularly regarding the sample construction, anticipated retirement ages, net costs of college, and future levels of social security benefits. It would also be interesting to compare results obtained here with those that that would be produced by other datasets including the Health and Retirement Study (Moore and Mitchell, this volume). Finally, it would be instructive to compare our findings using the Quicken Financial Planner with those produced using other software packages.

Though our analysis indicates that many Americans are far from financially prepared for retirement, we take as encouraging the development of sophisticated software planning programs such as the QFP. Indeed, as financial planning software becomes more accessible and more sophisticated, households will surely become better informed, and ideally better protected, against the strains of retirement and other financial challenges.

Appendix: A Detailed Description of the Quicken Financial Planner

The Quicken Financial Planner appears on the computer screen as a tabbed notebook, with major categories of data inputs or outputs listed on the right-side tabs, such as "Income," "Personal," or "Results." Upon opening each right-side tab, several upper tabs appear, each containing one or several notebook pages. One can open the notebook at any right-side tab or can proceed sequentially by hitting "Next" at the bottom of every page. As we will see, the Planner is explicitly designed to aid in financial planning for retirement, children's college education, and life insurance needs; one can, in addition, create other goals. In this section, we will proceed sequentially, using the version of the Planner available at the beginning of 1997.

Personal

In this category, there are three upper tabs labeled "You," "Spouse," and "Children." Thus, it is possible to create a financial plan for an individual, a couple, or an entire household. For the respondent and spouse, the name and birth dates are requested, as is the desired retirement age for each. The retirement age is described as when retirement benefits start, for example, social security, and it is also the default age for when labor income ends. The Planner next asks questions about self-reported health, gender, and smoking status to determine the respondent's and spouse's life expectancies. A life expectancy is returned by the program, which the Planner encourages the respondent to increase manually by 10 years to allow for the possibility of living beyond the average life expectancy. Whatever age is entered determines the length of the retirement period for later use in the plan. Finally, the names and birth dates of dependent children are requested.

Income

This right-hand tab has two upper tabs, "Salaries" and "Special Income." In "Salaries," current and expected future labor incomes are requested for the respondent and spouse. In particular, for each current and expected future job, salary (in today's dollars), expected dates of tenure, expected rate of increase in salary, employment status (regular or self-employed), and payroll tax status are requested. If a significant promotion is expected, it would be entered separately as a future job. Similarly, temporary non-participation in the labor force can be recognized. As mentioned above, the default ending date for a job is the desired retirement age, but this may be overridden. In "Special Income," gifts, inheritances, royalties, and distributions from trust funds may be entered. Either a one-time transfer or a flow of income may be recorded in today's dollars, at any expected future date(s).

Taxes and Inflation

This category has three upper tabs, "Income Taxes," "Other Taxes," and "Inflation." In the "Income Taxes" tab, the respondent inputs combined federal and state average income tax rates, before and after retirement, for the household. The respondent is given a choice of two methods to do the estimation. One is a "demographic average," the average tax rate paid by the average person in the respondent's state of residence with the same level of household income; the other is the "tax return" method, where an average tax rate is calculated based on the household's adjusted gross income and the actual taxes paid last year, as reported on federal and state tax returns. The respondent is then asked to input the average tax rate he or she expects to face in retirement; the program advises that the pre-retirement tax rate be used unless it is expected that income will drop significantly in retirement. Whether before or after retirement, the respondent is told by the Planner to avoid inputting a marginal tax rate.

In the "Other Taxes" tab, the Planner explains how social security and Medicare taxes are automatically reflected in the program's calculations. Finally, the "Inflation" tab shows a chart with historical inflation rates since 1927, and counsels that a 3 percent inflation rate is a reasonable estimate of future trends, given past experience; the respondent can, however, select any desired inflation rate from 0 to 20 percent.

Saving

This major tab has three upper tabs, labeled "Tax-deferred," "Taxable," and "Investments." In the "Tax-deferred" tab, the respondent inputs both spouses' planned contributions to all types of tax-advantaged accounts, including 401(k) and 403(b) plans, IRAs, and Keogh plans. In addition, employer contributions to such plans are captured here. In particular, for each active tax-advantaged plan, the respondent is asked over what period contributions will be made, the level of employee contribution (in percentage or dollar terms), and the level of employer contribution (as a match, up to what limit, and/or any profit sharing). The direct limitations of the Internal Revenue Code on contributions are automatically imposed; limitations arising from the operation of non-discrimination requirements at the plan level, however, are not imposed. Similar questions are posed in the "Taxable" tab for taxable regular saving plans, such as Christmas clubs, EEE government savings bond plans, and so on.

In the "Investments" tab, details are entered about the holdings of financial assets separately for tax-deferred and taxable accounts, by major asset classes, such as stocks, bonds, money market funds, guaranteed investment contracts, and so on. One can enter these holdings either as a rough estimate, where the asset class designations are ignored, or as an itemized list, where the asset class designations are requested; if a mutual fund is entered, Morningstar performance and star-rating information is available.[23]

Assets

In this category, information about nonfinancial assets of the household is entered in three separate tabs, "Homes," "Life Insurance," and "Special Assets." In the "Homes" section, information about each primary residence currently owned or planned to be owned is requested. In particular, the Planner asks for the expected length of stay in the home, the purchase price and date, the current market value, the expected rate of increase in value, annual expenses and property taxes incurred, rental income, and any mortgages secured by the property, including original loan balance, interest rate, and term. In the "Life Insurance" section, information about any term or cash-value insurance policies is requested, including the policy's start and end dates, death benefit, annual premium, and, if relevant, cash value (currently and at retirement). In the "Special Assets" section, information about assets which produce income or can be sold to fund retirement, such as businesses, vacation homes, other real estate, and so on, is requested; the specific questions here are similar to those asked in the "Homes" section of the Planner. Unless specified by the respondent, however, the Planner will not sell either homes or special assets to fund retirement. There are no questions in the Planner concerning personal property because such property is not expected to be sold at any time or in any circumstance.

Loans

This category has one upper tab, labeled "Loans." The Planner asks the respondent to enter information about current loans and any major loans anticipated in the future. Relevant loans include auto loans, business loans, and loans to pay for college expenses for the respondent, spouse, or children. Credit card payments should be included in expenses (see next major tab), and mortgages have already been entered. The Planner asks for each loan, its start date, original and current balance, interest rate, term, frequency of payments, and whether any balloon payments are expected. It can calculate the current principal and interest payments and the current balance if sufficient information is input.

Expenses

This major tab has three upper tabs, "Living Expenses," "College Expenses," and "Special Expenses." In the "Living Expenses" tab, the respondent has a choice between two methodologies for estimating household's expenses for food, clothing, uninsured medical bills, credit card payments, and so on: the "Rough Estimate" and the "Itemized List." In the Rough Estimate approach, the Planner simply asks for the respondent's estimated living expenses before and after retirement. As guidance, the Planner provides an abbreviated statement of cash flow subtracting payments for taxes, loans, housing, insurance premiums, and savings from current income to arrive at a remainder available for living expenses. In the "Itemized List" approach, the respondent is invited to enter self-defined categories of expenses with start and end dates and annual amounts. The Planner then totals pre- and post-retirement living expenses from this list.

In the "College Expenses" tab, the Planner asks for parents' plans for each child's college education. It requests information about the expected age of college entrance, the duration of college, the name of the institution to be attended, the expected rate of tuition inflation, anticipated annual financial aid, and expected annual student and gift contributions to the cost of college. For each institution of higher education drawn from a fairly comprehensive list (ordered by state, separately for public and private), the Planner provides current tuition and fees, additional out-of-state tuition, room and board, books and supplies, and other expenses. In the "Special Expenses" tab, the respondent enters expenses for weddings, vacations, and other large purchases, whether current or anticipated, one-time or continuous.

Retirement Benefits

This category has two upper tabs, "Social Security" and "Pensions," where periodic post-retirement payments from social security and employer-sponsored defined benefit pension plans are estimated. The age at which benefits begin defaults to the retirement age entered in the "Personal" tab, described above. Under the "Social Security" tab, respondent and spouse estimate their anticipated social security income using one of two methods: the "Rough Estimate" or the "Social Security Administration Estimate." The rough estimate method asks in which of four earnings bands the respondent and spouse expect to find themselves; an estimate of social security income is then produced based on those answers. Income is adjusted for the expected retirement age according to the social security benefit formula. Under the Social Security Administration estimate method, the respondent inputs social security income from the official response to the Request for Personal Earnings and Benefits Estimate Statement form mailed to the Social Security Administration. Finally, the respondent is allowed to reduce the estimate of future social security income to reflect views of likely future policy changes in the program. The "Pensions" tab asks the respondent and spouse to enter anticipated yearly benefits from employer-sponsored defined benefit plans, if any (in today's dollars). The Planner also asks whether benefits will be adjusted to reflect the cost of living and whether the spouse will receive benefits upon the death of the respondent.

Return

In the "Return" section, there are three tabs: "Risk & Return," "Before Retirement," and "After Retirement." In the "Risk & Return" tab, basic investment information is provided, highlighting the historical annual returns experienced on various asset classes and the variability of those returns. The respondent is asked to select the portfolio returns he or she believes are achievable given general risk preferences and investment time horizon. The returns selected may differ before retirement and after retirement. One of 10 model portfolios is shown for each return selected (at 50 basis point intervals) between 5.5 and 10 percent. The Planner relies on Callan Associates, an independent investment consulting firm, to estimate an efficient investment frontier to develop these portfolios. It is also important to note that the Planner uses the selected return in its calculations, *not* the expected return which would result from the actual portfolio held by the respondent and spouse, as entered above in the Saving / Investments tab.

Advanced Planning Options

In the Planner menu there is a general function called "Advanced Planning Options" with five tabs: "Cash Shortfalls," "Investment Mixes," "Realized Gains," "International," and "Sweep." These functions allow for quite sophisticated modeling by the respondent. In "Cash Shortfalls," the respondent is asked about plans to sell investments (tax-deferred or taxable) to cover pre-retirement shortages; the default answer is No. In "Investment Mixes," the respondent is asked whether the same selected return should apply to the three portfolios: "Self Tax-deferred," "Spouse Tax-deferred," and "Taxable"; the default answer is Yes. In "Realized Gains," the respondent is asked what percentage of the gains in the taxable portfolio will be subject to income and capital gains taxes every year; the default answer is 100 percent. In "International," the respondent is asked whether international stock and global bonds should be included in the investment mix; the default answer is Yes. Finally, in "Sweep," the respondent is asked what percent of surplus cash flows are swept into taxable savings; the default answer is 0 percent.

Results

This major tab contains four upper tabs, "First Glance," "Assumptions," "Forecasts," and "What If." In "First Glance," the respondent is told the good or the bad news: whether he or she can anticipate having the money needed to retire. If the news is bad, a brief statement of the nature of the problem is given, including the year when assets are depleted. Regardless of the nature of the news, a graph of the life cycle of the household portfolio value is shown on the screen.

In the next tab, "Assumptions," the respondent can review all inputs and assumptions; the program also provides more information about problems that the household might encounter in the plan and offers hints for solving some of those problems. The Planner automatically makes appropriately sized withdrawals from tax-deferred accounts in accordance with the minimum distribution requirements of the Internal Revenue Code and IRS regulations, if that is indicated after the respondent and spouse turn age 70½.

In the "Forecasts" tab, graphs, tables, and narrative descriptions of the household's situation are available in the following areas: Portfolio Value, Net Worth, Cash Flow, Income, Expense, Savings, and Withdrawals. It should be noted that the Planner defines net cash flow in a unique way: it is the surplus or deficit produced by the planned sources and uses of annual money flows. If the advanced planning option of not selling assets is chosen, a deficit is not financed, and if the sweep option is not activated, a surplus is not invested; rather, the respondent is simply alerted by the Planner to deficit problems.

In the "What If" tab, a bar is shown indicating the percent of years of retirement funded; green shows the years funded, red shows the years with a shortfall. Below the bar is a listing of assumptions that can be changed ("what ifs") to improve the performance of the plan. There is a "Solve It" function key on the notebook page, which produces the exact change necessary in a particular assumption to result in a successful plan, that is, a fully financed retirement. The "Solve It" functions key operates one assumption at a time; there is no way to automatically make changes in several assumptions simultaneously, although this can be done manually. By trial and error one can then arrive at a fully funded retirement. The variable assumptions include the retirement ages, portfolio returns, saving contributions, percent of post-retirement living expenses covered, and life expectancies.

Action Plan

The final major tab, "Action Plan," contains the following upper tabs: "Summary," "Action Steps," "Insurance Needs," and "Print Plan." "Summary" shows a screen with the Plan Summary of the plan incorporating whatever changes were made in the prior section of the program. "Action Steps" highlights the saving and investment schedules needed to implement the chosen financial plan and to follow the Planner's asset allocation advice; it also offers some generic advice on estate tax matters. "Insurance Needs" is an independent calculator that uses data already inputted and asks for preferences on the size of a desired estate and other post-mortem expenses; it then gives advice on the optimal amount of term life insurance to have. Finally, "Print Plan" encourages the respondent to print out the complete plan, which contains the graphs and narrative of the type already exhibited as well as a year-by-year schedule of saving and investment needed to make the plan work.

Critiques

The Quicken Financial Planner is quite comprehensive and one of the best we have seen among planning packages available to the general public. However, it is not without faults, logical inconsistencies, and scope for improvement. Some of these improvements would be easy to accomplish; others, however, would require more work.

We believe that the Planner should regard both life expectancy and risk tolerance as facts rather than changeable assumptions. We can construct an example of the program's somewhat odd results when the life expectancy of the spouse is allowed to change to enable the respondent to achieve a fully financed retirement. More specifically, through the "Solve It" key, the Planner allows a radical reduction in life expectancy; this change works because it reduces the length of the retirement period, and the default assumption is that an individual can live on 80 percent of what a couple needs to live. The Planner, however, is not really advocating divorce or murder because it still assumes that the spouse's salary, pension contributions, and investments are included in the plan. Similarly, it is much too easy to achieve success in the program simply by increasing portfolio return. The consequences of such a change in terms of risk are not presented clearly enough to caution against such a "quick fix."

Regarding life expectancy, the Planner does not really consider the uncertainty of the length of life, and therefore, the need for annuitization of retirement assets. It is true that the use of life expectancy plus 10 years to estimate the expected period of retirement is fairly conservative. This assumption, however, can lead people to have an unnecessarily low standard of living before and during retirement because of the need to husband resources to finance a longer than expected period of retirement. Furthermore, it can lead to insufficient assets if the respondent and spouse live to extreme old age or to unused assets on death if their lives are of average length.[24]

Also, the Planner does not consider explicitly the significant financial risks facing an aging household from uninsured health and long-term care expenditures. Although an estimate of average expenditures for such needs could be inputted, it is currently impossible for the Planner to evaluate reasonable ranges for such expenditures. Therefore respondent and spouse may remain unaware of the need for long-term care and Medigap insurance. Taking this thought further, the Planner should ask whether either spouse has or expects to have retiree health insurance from an employer, and it should then make the appropriate adjustments to projected expenses.

Because of its actuarial nature, the Planner's "What If" function does not optimize by changing borrowing and saving behavior over the life cycle to achieve the appropriate level of assets to have on hand when retirement begins. The program does allow a respondent to input different saving rates at different ages, and similarly to experiment with taking out loans of varying amounts at varying times, but the program does not suggest or encourage such an approach to planning. Varying borrowing and saving rates at different stages in the life cycle is especially appropriate if income and/or expenses vary significantly over the life cycle. It makes little sense to maintain the same rate of contributions to a 401(k) plan during an early financially stressful period as during later working years when household income may be higher and one-time expenses are lower.

If the household faces a cash flow problem even after selling taxable investments and taking out loans, say to finance its children's college education, the Planner can have the family dip into tax-deferred investments, thereby incurring a 10 percent penalty tax, as well as the payment of state and federal income taxes on the withdrawal. Yet if the household owned and occupied real estate, it would clearly be preferable to borrow against home equity; the interest on such a loan is deductible from income taxes.

The Planner provides a wealth of information about the cost (including tuition, room and board, books, and so on) of attending hundreds of different colleges and universities. Yet for most people using the Planner their horizons presumably are sufficiently long that they do not know which type of college (public or private, two-year or four-year) their children will attend, let alone the specific identity of the school. Furthermore, many households do not pay full tuition, being assisted by grants, loans, scholarships, and so on. Therefore, despite the detailed information it provides, the Planner is not sufficiently realistic about financing higher education. A better approach might be for the Planner to offer the respondent a choice of precise or ballpark estimates, similar to that offered for the social security benefit calculations.

The Planner is not truly dynamically consistent in expected rates of return. Although it allows for one rate of return during the working years and another during the retirement period, the Planner does not consider changes in expected rates of return arising from likely changes in portfolio holdings caused by aging, expected growth in wealth or income, maturing of children, lack of consistent rebalancing of assets, and so on.

The Planner uses the respondent's planned or desired rate of return on investments in its calculations. This rate of return is not necessarily related to the actual current portfolio composition of the responding household, and thus may lead to an underestimate or, more likely, to an overestimate of the household's ability to finance retirement. Probably a better approach would be to ascertain, either through information obtained about current portfolio composition or by direct question, the household's expected return on its current investment portfolio. Then a few questions could elicit the household's risk preferences and an efficient portfolio could be suggested (see Barsky et al. 1997).

Finally, the Planner does not employ the technology of stochastic intertemporal financial economics, as appears, for example, in Merton (1971), Breeden (1979), Cox and Huang (1989), and Bodie, Merton, and Samuelson (1992). Such a technology would combine the stochastic natures of asset returns, labor income, and consumption expenditures with the risk preferences of the respondent to produce an optimal financial plan. Clearly, the absence of uncertainty in financial planning programs now on the market is a major defect, because the appearance of certainty makes things look better than they are likely to be. Furthermore, significant uncertainty pertains to important public policies, such as taxes and government-sponsored retirement income and health programs, as well as to market and individual household risks factors. It must be admitted, of course, that stochastic technology needed to handle uncertainty has yet to be implemented for practical use.

Nevertheless, we do what we can with what is available—and we believe that results obtained with the Quicken Financial Planner offer results better than many other models. In particular, the Planner considers many more "real life" factors, such as financing for children's education, than do other models.

The authors thank Dennis Kwong, John Adams, and Jim Safka at Intuit for their assistance in processing the Survey of Consumer Finances data files through the Quicken Financial Planner testing program. They also thank Eric Engen, William Gale, Ron Gebhardtsbauer, Larry Kotlikoff, Joyce Manchester, Jim Poterba, Anna Rappaport, Martin Feldstein, and seminar participants at the Federal Reserve Board, the Pension Research Council, and the NBER Summer Institute for helpful comments, discussions, and suggestions. Opinions expressed are those of the authors and do not necessarily represent the views of TIAA-CREF.

Notes

1. See Radner (1998) and Moore and Mitchell (this volume) for additional economics studies on retirement preparedness.
2. An economic model that can be reconciled with the actuarial approach is the theory of self-control advanced by Thaler and Shefrin (1981), which posits that people are simultaneously farsighted planners and myopic doers. Hence they resolve their inner conflict by self-imposed rules that restrict the "doer's" opportunities and reactions. Empirical evidence suggests that this self-control theory does reflect the ethos of many financial planning packages (Warshawsky 1987).
3. Kotlikoff and Bernheim have a software package called "Economic Security Planner" that employs an economic approach to retirement planning. Here life

insurance and savings recommendations are based on what the household needs to maintain its living standard under different mortality contingencies, through different stages of the life cycle, and in light of particular planned expenditures, such as financing a child's college education. Other unique features include the conceptual integration of life insurance and saving decisions, and the display of the consequences of alternative insurance and saving decisions; these features demand a sophisticated optimization algorithm.

4. For more detail on the QFP see the Appendix.

5. These tabulations use the entire 1992 SCF sample. As described below, our QFP work uses only data from the first implicate of the SCF sample, so the numbers in Table 1 may vary slightly from these statistics.

6. The results of the exercise are similar when these individuals are included.

7. One reason for exclusion — because "respondent or spouse has future job" — is attributed to an error in the input file discovered after the study was completed. We hope to correct this in ongoing research but do not anticipate that adding such cases will change our results. Because non-response is an important problem in the context of wealth surveys, the SCF designers have used a "multiple imputation" process to deal with missing data since 1989. This procedure requires that the dataset contain multiple copies of the responses of each interviewed household, called implicates, which differ from one another in terms of imputed data. This methodology multiplies the number of observations in the final public use dataset by a factor of five for example, 3,906 households responded to the 1992 survey, but there are 19,530 implicates. Processing more than about 1,500 observations through the procedure we have outlined would have been impractical. As a result, in this chapter we use only the first implicate for each household in the dataset. The statistical validity of the analysis is served better by taking the average of the values of each SCF data item across all implicates, but where the Planner required a discrete answer regarding ownership of certain assets or types of assets, we cannot use the average of the implicates.

8. The Health and Retirement Study (see Chapter 1) contains much useful data relating to retirement finance; we did not use that dataset here because we sought data on households of all ages, rather than only those nearing retirement.

9. For example, Question 45(11) of the SCF asks individuals with full-time jobs: "Thinking now of the future, what year do you expect to stop working full-time?" A similar question is asked of individuals working part time who are planning to return to full-time work.

10. An alternate formulation of the question posed to full-time workers might result in a higher response rate to the retirement question. For example, it would be helpful to follow up individuals who claim that they will never stop working full-time by asking if or when whether they ever anticipate significantly reducing the total number of hours spent at their job per year in the future. For those who provide a valid answer, it would be worth learning why they will stop working full-time (retirement, childcare, or other).

11. These age-earnings profiles are drawn from Murphy and Welch (1990).

12. While core questions are asked about each type of loan, slightly different information is collected for each different type of loan, and there are many areas where responses can invalidate the answers.

13. In a small number of cases, this balance was negative; i.e., individuals could not fund all these payments out of current earnings, and these cases were dropped from the sample. This is generally due to the existence of large loan payments for people with substantial income from sources other than earnings.

14. The SCF does contain information about social security benefits currently received. However, since the QFP provides its own estimates of social security benefits, we use that information here.

15. We include lump-sum pension benefits as one-time "special income" rather than as pension income. One unresolved issue with the SCF data was whether the respondent factored inflation into estimates of future pension benefits. The SCF asks the individual to report the benefit amounts as "as a percentage of pay at retirement or as an amount when you start receiving them." We assume that the amount responses were in real 1992 dollars and that the benefit amount increased with inflation until benefits began to be receivedfrom that point onward, we assumed no nominal benefit increase. We did not consider inheritances in the analysis because the SCF data were imprecise on this point.

16. Excess cash flow is generated when income is greater than all expenses plus planned saving.

17. With regard to the financial data, the households had median total income of $37,000. This is based on household responses to the SCF query regarding income received in 1991. In the 1992 SCF sample (representing 96 million households), median household income was $26,000.

18. Median net worth (including defined contribution pension assets) for the entire 1992 SCF sample was $50,000.

19. We were somewhat surprised by the result that 11 percent of the sample had no financial assets in 1992. As a check, we tabulated financial asset values for the entire 1992 SCF population (96 million households) where we found that approximately 9.2 million households (9.6 percent) had no financial assets, a result that is not too different from that reported in the text.

20. The sensitivity of this measure was checked by adding 10 years to the QFP's suggested life expectancy assumptions; it is interesting that only three percent of the sample had plan failures in the final decade of their plan. While changing the life expectancy assumption would not necessarily result in exactly a 3 percent reduction in the failure rate (this change alters several parameters in the model), we are confident that the impact of the life expectancy extension on the overall rate of failure is relatively minor.

21. Recall that in this category, college expenses are assumed to be covered by the student's own contributions and financial aid; therefore the plans cannot fail before retirement as a result of college expenses. Since the success rate is generally rising until the time of retirement, it is also the case that among individuals in this category, those whose plans begin closer to retirement are more likely to have at least some financial assets.

22. It is important to note that we use no real discount rate in these calculations (a year of living expenses 10 years after retirement is given the same dollar value as the first year of living expenses after retirement.)

23. In the Planner menu a "Mutual Funds" function is also available, which provides a tool for selecting mutual funds meeting respondent-determined criteria, such as star rating, manager tenure, minimum investment, and so on, in the asset classes (basic or extended) chosen. In addition, some general guidance about selecting mutual funds is given.

24. In recent research, Mitchell, Poterba, Warshawsky, and Brown (forthcoming, 1999) offer an economic model of the "consumer surplus" created by life annuities, and they compare this surplus with the load factor experienced by the average consumer if he or she were to purchase commercially available single-premium immediate life annuities.

References

Barsky, Robert B., F. Thomas Juster, Miles S. Kimball, and Matthew D. Shapiro. 1997. "Preference Parameters and Behavioral Heterogeneity: An Experimental Approach in the Health and Retirement Study." *Quarterly Journal of Economics* (May): 537–79.

Bernheim, B. Douglas. 1992. "Is the Baby Boom Generation Preparing Adequately for Retirement?" Technical Report. Princeton, N.J.: Merrill Lynch, September.

Bernheim, B. Douglas and John Karl Scholz. 1993. "Private Saving and Public Policy." In James Poterba, ed., *Tax Policy and the Economy* 7: 73–110.

Bodie, Zvi, Robert Merton, and William Samuelson. 1992. "Labor Supply Flexibility and Portfolio Choice in a Life Cycle Model." *Journal of Economic Dynamics and Control* 16: 427–49.

Breeden, Douglas. 1979. "An Intertemporal Asset Pricing Model with Stochastic Consumption and Investment Opportunities." *Journal of Financial Economics* 7: 265–96.

Congressional Budget Office. 1993. "Baby Boomers in Retirement: An Early Perspective." CBO Report. Washington, D.C: U.S. Government Printing Office, September.

Cox, John and Chi-Fu Huang. 1989. "Optimal Consumption and Portfolio Policies when Asset Prices Follow a Diffusion Process." *Journal of Economic Theory* 49: 33–83.

Gale, William. 1997. "Will the Baby Boom Be Ready for Retirement?" *Brookings Review* (Summer): 5–9.

Merton, Robert. 1971. "Optimum Consumption and Portfolio Rules in a Continuous-Time Model." *Journal of Economic Theory* 3: 373–413.

Mitchell, Olivia S., James M. Poterba, Mark J. Warshawsky, and Jeff Brown. 1999. "New Evidence on the Money's Worth of Individual Annuities." *American Economic Review.*

Moore, James and Olivia S. Mitchell, "Projected Retirement Wealth and Savings Adequacy." This volume.

Murphy, Kevin and Finis Welch. 1990. "Empirical Age-Earnings Profiles." *Journal of Labor Economics.* 8: 202–29.

Radner, Daniel. 1998. "The Retirement Prospects of the Baby Boom Generation." *Social Security Bulletin* 61: 3–19.

Thaler, Richard and Hersh Shefrin. 1981. "An Economic Theory of Self-Control." *Journal of Political Economy* 89: 392–406.

Warshawsky, Mark. 1987. "Sensitivity to Market Incentives: The Case of Policy Loans." *Review of Economics and Statistics* 69: 286–95.

Chapter 3
Projected Retirement Wealth and Saving Adequacy

James F. Moore and Olivia S. Mitchell

Future retirees will bear a larger responsibility for ensuring their own well-being in retirement, judging from projected social security system insolvency and the national shift from defined benefit to defined contribution private pension plans. Yet household saving rates in the United States have dropped from over 10 percent in the 1950s to around 3 percent in the first half of the 1990s (Gokhale et al. 1996). This discouraging pattern raises serious concerns about Americans' ability to maintain consumption levels in old age. They are underscored by a recent research controversy over whether workers are adequately prepared for retirement. A comparison of baby boomers' assets to those of their parents recently argued that saving for retirement is on track (CBO 1993). But, using a different benchmark, a recent study concluded that U.S. households were saving at only one-third the rate needed to fund a comfortable retirement (Bernheim 1992, 1994). The present work contributes to this debate by using the Health and Retirement Study to explore patterns of asset accumulation and saving shortfall among a cohort of older Americans. Our goals are to determine (1) how much retirement wealth older people on the verge of retirement actually have, and (2) how much more they would need to save if they wished to preserve consumption levels after retirement. Our research shows that the median older household is projected to have retirement wealth of approximately $400,000, yet will still need to save 16 percent of annual income to preserve pre-retirement consumption. This summary statistic conceals extraordinary heterogeneity in both assets and saving needs in the older population.

In what follows we first discuss the rationale for the replacement rate model and prior studies examining saving behavior. Next we describe wealth levels and composition for HRS households in 1992, and show how those wealth patterns would be expected to change at retirement ages of 62 and 65. These wealth measures are then converted to saving rates, which are then compared to optimal saving rates required to smooth lifetime consumption. A final section spells out implications.

Saving Patterns and Replacement Rates in a Life Cycle Model

Economic models of saving behavior rely on a life cycle model in which individuals are posited to maximize utility by smoothing consumption through time. In this framework, people are predicted to save when they have periods of relatively high income, and dip into accumulated savings or borrow when income is relatively low, including in retirement.[1] One recent study implementing an augmented life cycle model derived optimal saving rate paths using dynamic programming, in which the optimal saving path proves to increase with age up to retirement (Bernheim 1992).[2] Predicted saving rates are then compared with actual rates derived in empirical analysis of respondents. Bernheim concluded that workers in his sample saved at only one-third (35 percent) the prescribed rate that they should have been saving, if they sought to meet target consumption goals. However, this estimated shortfall omitted from people's wealth levels the value of their net housing wealth, on the argument that relatively few people liquidate their housing on retirement.[3] His calculations of saving shortfalls if housing assets are included in retirement wealth is somewhat lower — on the order of about 16 percent per year. The extent to which Bernheim's results are generalizable is unclear, however, because his sample is relatively small and better off than the average population. In addition he focuses on the typical saving pattern rather than examining the dispersion in saving shortfall, a topic of central interest below.

A different approach to the retirement saving question relies on a "replacement rate" approach. As we describe below, this methodology evaluates the ratio of household income needed to finance desired retirement consumption relative to annual pre-retirement income. The object here is to equate pre-retirement and post-retirement consumption on an expected value basis.[4] Recent work by Palmer (1988, 1991, 1993) uses several cross-section Consumer Expenditure Surveys to examine this issue, and concludes that gross replacement rates have varied over time depending on tax changes and household saving rates.

An invaluable dataset with which to explore older Americans' wealth positions as they near retirement is the Health and Retirement Study (HRS: see Chapter 1). This extensive questionnaire on wealth and income was addressed to a nationally representative sample of 7607 households in 1992, where at least one respondent was age 51 to 61.[5] Under certain restricted conditions, researchers may also access special files needed for measuring pension and social security wealth (described in more detail below). One other study using these data, Mitchell, Olson, and Steinmeier (this volume, hereafter MOS), explores expected present values of social security benefits for HRS respondents. A second analysis, by Gustman, Mitchell, Samwick, and Steinmeier (this volume, hereafter GMSS) examines both pension and social security wealth for these same households, using actual pension information and imputed or estimated social security data.

These two studies reveal that estimated median total household wealth for HRS respondents on the verge of retirement totaled approximately $340,000 in 1992 (with mean values of approximately half a million dollars). Total wealth depends on four components: net financial wealth, net housing equity, and the present value of expected pension and social security benefits. At face value, these wealth amounts would seem to indicate that the "average" HRS household is in relatively good shape for retirement. But Mitchell and Moore (this volume, hereafter MM) assess the adequacy of these asset accumulations, and suggest that the median older American family faces a substantial saving shortfall. Specifically, MM project anticipated wealth as of age 65 for a hypothetical median couple, and then compared this with the level of wealth needed to sustain the family's pre-retirement consumption derived from targets offered by Palmer (1994). The required saving rate needed to build assets to desired levels for this representative HRS household is quite high — 13–23 percent of gross income per year in the decade leading up to retirement. In the next section we will explore whether that conclusion — derived for a representative couple — is informative for the older population as a whole.

Initial and Projected Wealth in the Health and Retirement Study

The present study improves on previous analyses in three ways. First, we evaluate retirement wealth and saving needs for the entire nationally representative sample of HRS households. This is important since focusing on a median family conceals wide differences across the population, and asset levels are quite diverse across older households. Second, our approach determines replacement and saving rates jointly, given the household's earnings level and projected assets to age 62 and 65. Third, we assess saving needs in the older population as a whole, and describe these patterns by income and wealth level.

The starting point for our analysis is an examination of HRS households' net wealth levels. The primary components of this wealth can be broadly categorized into four groups[6]:

1. net financial wealth, including saving, investments, business assets, and nonresidential real estate less outstanding debt not related to housing;
2. net housing wealth, or the current market value of residential housing less outstanding mortgage debt;

3. pension wealth, or the present value of employer-sponsored retirement benefits; and
4. the present value of social security benefits.

"Current" values for net financial wealth and net housing wealth are those reported by respondents in the HRS 1992 survey. Values for pension and social security wealth reflect actuarial present values of these contingent income sources based on service and salary through 1992 (see the Appendix). Pension wealth for respondents with employer-provided pensions is calculated using software developed at the Institute for Social Research at the University of Michigan. This software uses information collected from employers of HRS participants to calculate benefit streams based on workers' salary and service. Social security wealth is calculated using administrative records on covered earnings and benefit formulas available from the Social Security Administration, as described in MOS.

Values of current wealth by deciles are reported in Table 1. One result that will not be surprising to many is the wide disparity of wealth across the population, even though the group is on the verge of retirement. The mean value in the tenth, or wealthiest decile, is $1.8 million, or 45 times that of the mean value for the poorest decile. The composition of this wealth also differs dramatically across wealth deciles. For the poorest decile, the value of anticipated social security benefits is greater than total wealth (107 percent), as a result of negative net housing wealth. At the other end of the wealth distribution, expected social security benefits comprise less than one-tenth of household wealth.

Graphical representations of the data are also useful. Dollar estimates of total wealth appear in Figure 1, and fractions of wealth are given in Figure 2. Mean values for almost all sources monotonically increase in total wealth, but the relative importance of the individual components varies across the group. For example, to focus first on social security payments, the present value of these benefits falls as a fraction of total wealth as wealth levels rise, because of the plan's redistributive benefit formulas. Net housing wealth is negative for the lowest decile, indicating that these households have over-levered their housing stock. Beyond the poorest group, housing assets rise as a fraction of wealth, attaining almost one-fifth of wealth for households in the middle of the total wealth distribution, and then fall in relative importance for the wealthiest households. Net financial wealth is rare among the poorer half of the wealth distribution: households in the bottom two-fifths have less than $50,000 in assets of this sort. Only the top two-fifths of the population have more than $100,000 in net financial assets.

Looking across the entire HRS sample, we see that the median household group holds slightly over $325,000 in total wealth, while the mean household has almost $480,000. Not only do levels differ; composition also varies across the mean and median household. At the median, the split can be

TABLE 1: Mean Value and Composition of HRS Wealth (1992) by Wealth Decile

Wealth Decile	Total Wealth	Net Housing Wealth	Net Financial Wealth	Social Security Wealth	Pension Wealth
1	$ 39,470	$(5,719) -14%	$ 1,520 4%	$42,312 107%	$ 1,356 3%
2	97,452	11,052 11%	10,579 11%	69,239 71%	6,583 7%
3	156,288	24,951 16%	18,235 12%	93,920 60%	19,181 12%
4	219,797	37,095 17%	32,632 15%	115,224 52%	34,845 16%
5	287,692	53,787 19%	55,020 19%	128,377 45%	50,809 18%
6	364,802	68,637 19%	75,793 21%	136,116 37%	84,255 23%
7	459,858	81,432 18%	109,811 24%	142,981 31%	125,635 27%
8	590,079	95,414 16%	159,054 27%	149,310 25%	186,301 32%
9	804,934	112,039 14%	265,967 33%	158,976 20%	267,953 33%
10	1,764,414	180,894 10%	1,032,049 58%	161,605 9%	389,865 22%
Total sample					
Mean	478,313	65,940 14%	175,974 37%	119,793 25%	116,606 24%
Median 10%	325,157	59,746 18%	66,530 20%	133,606 41%	65,275 20%

Source: Authors' calculations. All values in 1992 dollars and calculated using HRS sampling weights.

characterized as a "rule of fifths." Social security constitutes two-fifths of total wealth, and the other three asset categories each comprise a fifth. This balance is shifted for the mean, since net financial wealth plays a much more prominent role for wealthier households (it comprises as much as two-thirds of wealth for the wealthiest group represented).

It is interesting to compare our results to those reported by GMSS who obtained a mean value of almost $500,000 in total net wealth, and $340,000 for the median 10 percent of households.[7] These are very close to our estimated values of $478,000 and $325,000 respectively. Our figures differ because,

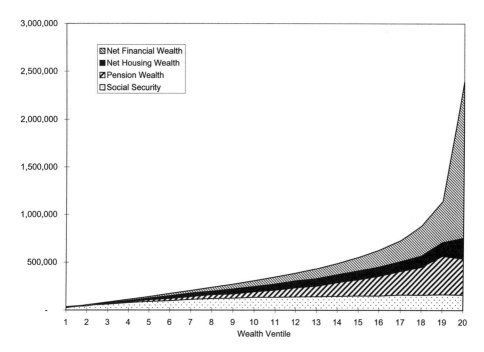

Figure 1. Composition of HRS (1992) wealth by type. Source: Authors' calculations.

first, GMSS calculate a value for retirement health insurance ($7,600 at the mean) which we do not include; and second, our analysis uses social security wealth from actual administrative earnings records. By contrast, GMSS do not use the restricted administrative records data, but instead estimated it from self-reported earnings data. Their estimated figures of $134,000 and $145,000 for the mean and median values are slightly higher—around 10 percent—than our mean and median of $120,000 and $134,000 calculated using actual Social Security Administration records.[8] Our estimates for pension wealth are very close to theirs, differing by less than 1 percent ($1,000) at the mean ($117,000 versus $116,000).

Having established current wealth levels and distributions for the HRS, the next step is to project existing assets to an assumed retirement age. We do this because two households holding the same initial wealth in different forms could prove to be in quite different circumstances a decade later, even assuming no additional saving out of earnings. To examine this possibility we project assets to two assumed retirement dates, the early and normal retirement ages for social security. Age 62 is the age of earliest entitlement for early social security retirement benefits and also corresponds to the modal retirement age in the United States. The social security normal re-

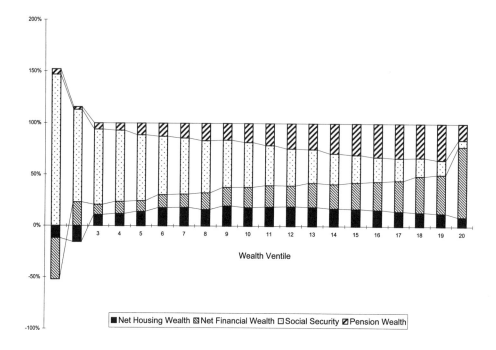

Figure 2. Composition of HRS wealth (1992) as percent of total wealth. Source: Authors' calculations.

tirement age, historically 65, is the age at which an individual is eligible for full, unreduced social security benefits and is a traditional benchmark age.[9]

While it is easy to specify an assumed retirement age for an individual, it is more problematic for a married couple. Spouses do not necessarily retire at the same time, and even when they do it is not clear which partner's age keys the decision. In the present study we follow HRS practice, where the survey interviewer designated as the primary respondent the household member with the greatest knowledge of the household's financial matters. Usually this respondent was age-eligible for the HRS survey; in this case we assume the retirement assumption is triggered on this person's attainment of age 62 or 65. If the primary respondent was not HRS age eligible, this guarantees that the secondary respondent is age eligible. In this instance, we assume that the retirement age is keyed off the attainment of 62 or 65 by this household member.

Asset values for each of these classes are projected to these retirement dates using a range of projection technologies and assumptions.[10] *Net financial wealth* is projected forward using averages of market returns based on historical rates. Historical return rates are drawn from Ibbotson (1996). *Housing wealth* is projected forward using survey data on the purchase price of the respondent's house, year of purchase, outstanding debt owed on homes, and mortgage payment amount and frequency. The process consists of increasing the market value of the house into the future, and also reducing the debt outstanding on the house. We assume that the market value of the house grows in line with the general inflation rate so there is no real appreciation in housing values; rather what does change is the amount owed on the house for those with outstanding mortgage values. Each mortgage payment decreases the remaining principal on the mortgage. Respondents' *pension and social security wealth* values are projected assuming workers remain employed to their respective retirement ages. Pension benefits are derived based on the plan provisions of employer-provided pensions and respondents' answers to salary and years of service (where appropriate). Social security projected amounts are computed as described in MOS. Present values of benefits are calculated using mortality, interest rate, inflation, and wage growth assumptions as described in the Appendix; all values are in 1992 dollars.

Initial and projected wealth values for HRS respondents are reported in Table 2. Median household wealth is anticipated to grow by almost 20 percent in real terms by age 62, to slightly over $383,000. If retirement were postponed until 65, the median household wealth value would rise by approximately 30 percent, or $421,000. Mean increases are similar in percentage terms and translate to wealth figures of approximately $566,000 and $625,000 at ages 62 and 65 respectively.

While percentage changes are similar by decile, those in the top two wealth deciles are projected to have amassed considerable additional net worth. The second wealthiest decile has more than $1 million dollars on average, and the wealthiest has more than $2.3 million. For the wealthiest decile, this is largely due to financial and business assets which make up some 60 percent of assets ($1.4 million). Pension assets make up 23 percent ($535,000 on average), leaving social security and, surprisingly, net housing wealth as relatively unimportant, 8 percent each. Yet this is still almost $200,000 for each. Pension wealth plays a larger role for the ninth decile, comprising some 38 percent of total wealth.

The most dramatic change in projected benefits is attributable to increases in pension wealth, which is found to rise by one-third by age 62, and by one-half by age 65 for the mean household. For the median respondent family, pension present value figures rise by nearly one-half and three-quarters for the same ages. By contrast, social security wealth increases only 7–8 percent by age 62, and by about 20 percent by age 65. Much of this difference is attributable to the well-known nonlinear accrual pattern common to employer pensions, rewarding additional service at older ages. A smoother pattern characterizes social security benefits, since most HRS households have already reached entitlement and additional service changes their benefits by relatively little.[11] About the mean and median, the different rate of

TABLE 2: Mean Value of HRS Wealth (1992 and Projected) by Wealth Decile

Wealth Decile	Current Wealth	Projected Wealth at Age 62	Projected Wealth at Age 65
1	$ 39,470	$ 43,804	$ 49,031
2	97,452	109,578	121,123
3	156,288	182,494	202,946
4	219,797	256,636	283,184
5	287,692	338,153	372,701
6	364,802	429,253	471,308
7	459,858	543,397	595,408
8	590,079	699,681	763,756
9	804,934	944,894	1,030,054
10	1,764,414	2,117,052	2,362,963
Total sample			
Mean	**478,313**	**566,431**	**625,066**
Housing	65,940	76,410	80,507
Financial	175,974	205,653	228,133
Social Security	119,793	128,712	142,018
Pension	116,606	155,656	174,408
Median 10%	**325,157**	**382,678**	**420,537**
Housing	59,746	71,097	75,047
Financial	66,530	71,004	71,175
Social Security	133,606	143,864	160,824
Pension	65,275	96,713	113,491

Source: Authors' calculations. All values in 1992 dollars and calculated using HRS sampling weights.

growth of these asset classes has relative little impact in changing the composition of projected wealth. Pension wealth does play a slightly larger role at the assumed retirement ages, mostly gaining a few percentage points from net housing wealth and social security.

As social security plays a much greater role for the poorest decile, their wealth gains to age 62 and 65 are relatively modest. The value of their social security wealth rises by about $6,000 to age 65, matched by gains in housing wealth. Unfortunately, about half this gain is offset by declines in the average value of their financial and other assets, mainly due to decreases in vehicle value.[12] At 65 this poorest decile still has total wealth of under $50,000, the vast majority of which (98 percent) is comprised of future social security benefits.

It is important to note that averaging may mask significant differences at the household level. For example, a household with $100,000 in pension wealth and no housing assets at 55 looks very different at 62 from an equivalent household with a $100,000 house that is completely paid for. Both households will look different from a household with the same $100,000 in net housing wealth but with a substantial mortgage outstanding. Nonetheless, as we shall show below, prospects are slim for projected movement across wealth deciles with age. Most of those households that are projected to change deciles move up or down a only single decile. In other words, initial wealth is the best predictor of projected retirement wealth: our estimated correlation between initial and projected wealth to age 62 is 0.97. There is a much weaker correlation between initial earnings and initial wealth, of 0.44, and a nearly identical correlation between earnings and projected wealth.

Saving Needs, Replacement Rates, Wealth, and Income

Having established that asset holdings are quite diverse in the HRS, the question remains as to what this implies about saving needs and replacement rates for retirement. In this section we assess target replacement and saving rates jointly, given initial earnings levels and the households' projected assets at age 62 and 65.

To solve for saving and replacement rate targets simultaneously, we begin with the basic replacement rate concept. This equates net income pre-retirement to net income post-retirement[13]:

$$Y_P - T_P - S = Y_F - T_F , \qquad (1)$$

where Y_P is pre-retirement income, T_P is pre-retirement taxes, S is saving, Y_F is post-retirement income, and T_F is post-retirement taxes. Rearranging (1), dividing through by Y_P, and expressing saving as a percent of income, $S = s Y_P$, gives the formula for replacement rate, RR.

$$RR = \frac{Y_P(1-s) - T_P + T_F}{Y_P} = \frac{Y_F}{Y_P} . \qquad (2)$$

The replacement rate gives a target income level such that a household may smooth consumption before and after retirement.

The future income stream, Y_F, may then be converted to a level of wealth needed to sustain that income level in retirement by multiplying by an appropriate annuity factor, AF.[14] Thus the wealth level required to maintain a smooth consumption profile in retirement is:

$$AF * Y_F = AF * RR * Y_P = AF[Y_P(1-s) - T_P + T_F] . \qquad (3)$$

The difference between this need level and the projected value of assets already held by any given household, *PROJ*, is the amount that must be saved between now and retirement, or the shortfall in projected retirement assets. This wealth shortfall may be defined as:

$$AF * Y_F - PROJ = AF[Y_P(1-s) - T_P + T_F] - PROJ . \qquad (4)$$

The wealth shortfall may finally be used to determine a prescribed saving rate. This rate represents what the households would need to save as a percent of income each year until retirement to achieve the projected consumption standard. Assuming that a wealth shortfall is met by saving some level percent of earnings per year, the amount saved at retirement would be:

$$\sum_{t=1}^{T} Y_C \, (1+wg)^t \, (1+rtn)^{T-t} \, s = s \, Y_C \sum_{t=1}^{T} (1+wg)^t \, (1+rtn)^{T-t} = s \, Y_C \, Z \, , \qquad (5)$$

where Y_C is the household's current income and wg and rtn are assumed rates of wage growth and return on savings, respectively. Using (4) and (5) we can then solve for a rate of saving s. Equating the two expressions and solving for s gives

$$s = \frac{AF[Y_C \, (1+wg)^T - T_P + T_F] - PROJ}{Y_C[Z + AF \, (1+wg)^T]} \, . \qquad (6)$$

We note that it is not appropriate simply to pick a desired replacement rate and solve for the resulting saving rate, or vice versa. This is because a given replacement rate might imply an infeasible saving rate given a household's earnings and projected assets. In addition, taxes depend on how much the household has saved.[15] Thus replacement rates and saving rates are determined jointly through an iterative process. We first select an arbitrary replacement rate as a starting point and use this replacement rate to determine an initial level of post-retirement income and taxes. Then resulting taxes are substituted into equation (6) to obtain an implied saving rate. This saving rate is then substituted into equation (2) to determine a new replacement rate. The process is then iterated until saving and replacement rates converge such that both equations (2) and (6) hold. For our calculations, reported earnings are used to determine taxes using the IRS regulations in place for the 1991 tax year. Taxes are calculated using the standard deductions and married couples are assumed to file jointly.[16]

Saving and Replacement Rate Results

Saving and replacement rates are reported for the 6,306 HRS households who reported positive earned income in 1991. For this group, the median prescribed saving rate for retirement at age 62 in this sample is 16.1 percent, which corresponds to a replacement rate of 69 percent. The saving rate drops to a more modest 7.3 percent if retirement is delayed to age 65, with a replacement rate of 78.1 percent. In other words, the later the retirement date, the lower is the prescribed saving rate needed to achieve consumption smoothing.

Figure 3 illustrates the distribution of prescribed saving rates across HRS

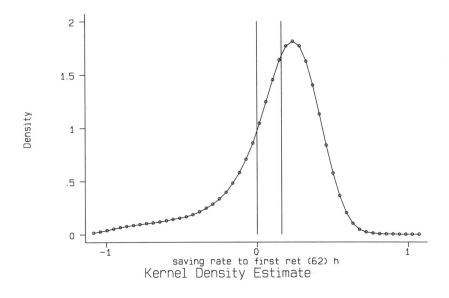

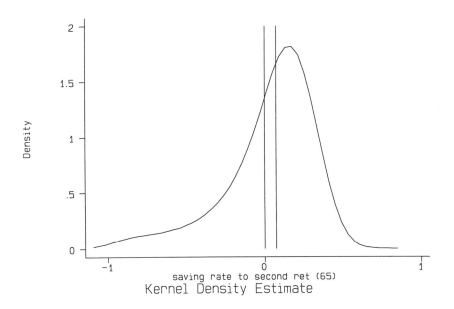

Figure 3. Distribution of prescribed saving rates: ages 62 (top) and 65 (bottom).
Source: Authors' calculations.

households, who are alternatively assumed to retire at either age 62 or 65. Vertical lines represent, respectively, a zero prescribed saving level, and the median of the distribution. Both distributions have large tails below zero, indicating that there is a substantial segment of the population for whom additional saving is not prescribed. For retirement at 62, almost a third (31 percent) of the population is in this zero or negative saving category; for retirement at age 65, some 40 percent of the population is estimated to not need any further saving out of earnings beyond accumulation occurring "automatically" through asset appreciation. The peak of the density functions lies to the right of the medians, indicating that the modal, or most commonly prescribed, saving rate is in excess of the mean and median rates.

To further describe the heterogeneity of saving and replacement rate patterns across the HRS sample, we report median values in Table 3 sorted by 1992 wealth and earnings deciles.[17] One conclusion is that saving rates fall monotonically, and replacement rates rise, with wealth. Another conclusion is that many people are unlikely to be able to save significantly for retirement without making drastic changes in their current consumption levels. For the poorest decile, retirement at age 62 would require saving nearly 40 percent of pretax earnings. Waiting to retire until 65 would require a more modest, yet still substantial, 27 percent of gross earnings. The pattern of saving shortfall extends quite far up the wealth distribution: for each of the first four wealth deciles, prescribed saving rates to age 62 are greater than 20 percent of earnings and rates to age 65 are 13% or higher. By contrast, prescribed saving rates are quite small at the top of the wealth distribution. Those in the wealthiest decile have more than sufficient assets to fund a comfortable retirement, and for some, negative rates indicate that they could dip into their stock of assets to enhance current consumption.[18]

Another interesting result is that saving patterns switch sign for households in the eighth and ninth wealth deciles, inasmuch as they have positive prescribed saving rates to age 62, but negative ones to 65. This indicates that their "optimal" retirement age assuming no further saving might lie somewhere between these two ages. Households towards the middle of the wealth distribution have what are substantial but perhaps not impossible savings targets if they want to retire at age 62, needing to save 11–18 percent of income. This would yield replacement rates of about two-thirds of current earnings. If they continued to work to age 65, annual saving needs would be cut in half, and replacement rates rise to approximately three-quarters of current earnings.

A more traditional way of examining replacement and saving rates is to tally these by household income rather than by wealth. The data in Panel B of Table 3 indicate that saving rates are quite negative for the lowest earnings decile: these households would desire to consume out of wealth prior to retirement if they could. In practice, however, such households probably

Table 3: Median Prescribed Saving and Replacement Rates

A. By 1992 wealth decile

| | Median | Saving to Age 62 (%) | | Saving to Age 65 (%) | |
Wealth Decile	Household Net Wealth	Saving Rate	Replacement Rate	Saving Rate	Replacement Rate
1	43,900	38.3	48.7	26.9	58.8
2	97,600	32.7	52.5	21.3	61.7
3	156,600	26.8	58.3	15.5	67.7
4	220,500	24.0	60.3	13.6	69.1
5	286,500	18.1	67.5	8.9	76.1
6	364,000	17.0	67.0	8.5	75.6
7	458,900	11.4	73.3	3.0	81.4
8	587,800	7.0	78.9	−0.9	87.1
9	792,600	1.0	88.3	−6.1	96.6
10	1,363,000	−25.4	126.8	−35.0	137.1
Total sample	325,000	16.1%	69.0%	7.3%	78.1%

B. By 1992 earnings decile

Earnings Decile	Household Earnings	Saving Rate	Replacement Rate	Saving Rate	Replacement Rate
1	4,500	−122.5	218.8	−132.8	227.8
2	11,930	5.9	84.8	−4.6	93.4
3	17,500	13.5	75.1	2.2	84.6
4	24,000	15.1	73.3	4.3	82.2
5	30,000	18.0	68.6	7.3	77.8
6	37,000	16.7	67.1	8.1	75.6
7	45,000	17.0	64.3	9.8	73.6
8	54,050	18.4	62.3	10.6	72.0
9	70,000	20.3	60.2	12.6	69.8
10	102,000	23.7	57.8	16.5	67.6
Total sample	33,000	16.1	69.0	7.3	78.1

Source: Authors' calculations. All values in 1992 dollars and calculated using HRS sampling weights.

face substantial liquidity constraints in that their wealth is not immediately available for consumption. This would be the case for workers anticipating social security or pension benefits at some future age.[19]

The results in Table 3B also show that prescribed saving rates rise with earnings. Those in the second pay decile need to save a little less than 6 percent of income to achieve a replacement rate of 85 percent by age 62. Without additional savings, they could achieve current living standards by retiring sometime before reaching 65. For higher earner deciles, double-digit saving is required to retire at 62 with the same relative standard of

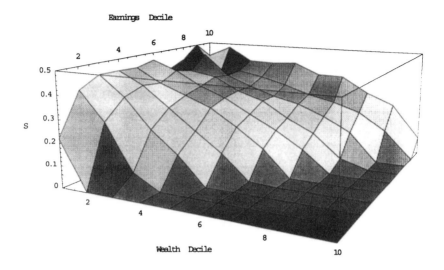

Figure 4. Prescribed saving rates by 1992 earnings and wealth for retirement at age 62. Shading represents median prescribed saving rate for each earnings-wealth decile pair. Source: Authors' calculations.

living. Delaying retirement to age 65 cuts required saving by 7–11 percent, depending on the family's earnings decile. Similarly, replacement rates fall with earnings but rise with retirement age.

A conclusion that our data on assets and pay highlights is that saving and replacement rates obscure the intertwined relationship between income and wealth. Of course, people with higher earnings also tend to have greater wealth, but this relationship is far from perfect, given that the correlation between earnings and initial wealth is only 0.44. Figure 4 plots prescribed saving rates as a function of both earnings and wealth. Median prescribed saving rate values by earnings-wealth decile pairs are presented for an assumed retirement age of 62.[20] Figure 5 presents the same information in a contour plot with contour lines at 5 percent intervals. These figures illustrate substantial heterogeneity in prescribed saving rates within the same income decile: most households fall along the "diagonal" with wealth increasing with earnings, but there are some households with substantial wealth given their earnings, as well as others whose net wealth seems low in comparison to earnings. The "diagonal" corresponds to the sloped region in Figure 4, running from the bottom left corner to the top right corner of the figure. The closeness of the contour lines in Figure 5 point out that the topology of the surface in Figure 4 is rather steep. In other words, saving rates for households falling along the diagonal are very sensitive to small changes in income or assets.

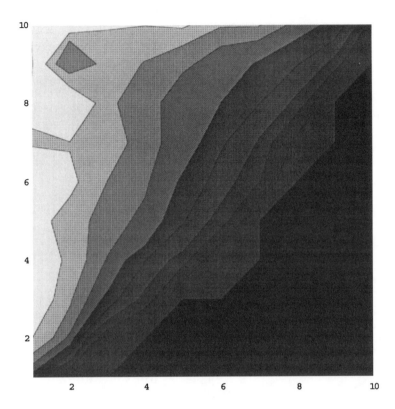

Figure 5. Contour plot of prescribed saving rates to age 62 for retirement at age 62. X-axis is wealth decile; Y-axis is earnings decile. Shading represents different prescribed levels of saving: darkest regions represent zero or negative prescribed saving, lighter regions need for greater saving. Contour lines are at intervals of 5.0 percent, corresponding to Figure 4. Authors' calculations.

Descriptive regressions of prescribed saving rates in Table 4 summarize some of the complex multivariate relationships. Coefficients are calculated using median regressions to minimize the effects of extreme observations. For each retirement age, we first relate saving rates as quadratic functions of income and earnings alone, and then add age and other indicator variables indicating whether the household is comprised of a single male or female (versus a married couple), whether individuals in that household have pension wealth, and whether the household owns its own home.

All estimated parameters are statistically significant at conventional levels. The estimates suggest that, about the median earnings level of $33,000, the effect of an extra $100 per year in earnings is to raise the prescribed saving rate by 0.095 percent (for retirement by 62) or by 0.097 percent (at age 65). That is, given the median saving rate of 16.1 percent, raising the

TABLE 4: Descriptive Regression of Prescribed Saving Rates

	Prescribed Saving Rate to Age 62		Prescribed Saving Rate to Age 65	
Household earnings	1.01	1.03	1.09	1.05
(*10^{-5})	89.46	125.94	89.14	101.37
Earnings squared	−1.18	−1.22	−1.35	−1.24
(*10^{-7})	−66.24	−95.43	−69.76	−76.85
Total household wealth	−9.93	−9.73	−1.01	−9.60
(*10^{-7})	−93.44	−119.81	−87.07	−93.79
Wealth squared	9.71	9.18	9.12	7.27
(*10^{-9})	45.75	57.93	39.34	36.29
Single male		−0.07		−0.13
		−9.06		−12.77
Single female		0.02		−0.05
		3.02		−6.04
Primary respondent age		0.004		0.002
		9.11		2.72
Have pension		−0.03		−0.04
		−7.18		−6.49
Own home		−0.08		−0.08
		−13.08		−10.31
Constant	0.13	−0.01	0.01	0.04
	24.87	−0.442	2.217	1.3
Pseudo R^2	0.09	0.09	0.09	0.09
N	6306	6306	6306	6306
Wtd. sum of absolute deviations	7808.74	7782.49	7782.49	7978.5

Source: Authors' calculations.
Notes: Coefficients estimated using median regressions to minimize effects of extreme outliers. Coefficients calculated using HRS household sampling weights. T-statistics appear below estimated coefficient values.

rate to 16.195 percent implies that $47.5 of the additional $100 in income would be saved.[21] The effect of $1000 more total wealth on prescribed saving is about the same for the median household, but in the opposite direction, causing the saving rate to 62 to fall 0.097 percent. This translates to approximately $32 less in saving in the first year. The coefficients for single men and women reflect the impact of different mortality rates by sex; since women live longer than men, they need to save at a greater rate, and this difference is rather substantial. For example, if age 62 retirement is the target, a woman's prescribed saving rate would exceed the otherwise equivalent man's by 9.1 percent. The results also show that owning a home and having an employer-sponsored pension affect prescribed saving substantially. Since "current" pension wealth and net home values are captured in the initial household wealth variable, these estimated coefficients reflect additions to future wealth — in pensions due to additional service, contributions, and portfolio returns where applicable, and in housing stock due to the paying down of outstanding mortgage debt and home appreciation. The regressions indicate that the presence of a pension reduces prescribed saving by 3–4 percent per year, while saving done through the home is equivalent to saving an additional 7.6 percent out of annual earnings at the median.

Discussion

We have explored the adequacy of asset holdings in the Health and Retirement Study, a nationally representative survey of older Americans on the verge of retirement. We conclude that, despite seemingly large accumulations of total retirement wealth, the majority of older households will not be able to maintain current levels of consumption into retirement without additional saving. In particular, the median HRS household has more than $380,000 dollars in projected wealth by age 62, but it would still have to save an additional 16 percent of earnings to smooth consumption for age 62 retirement.

Another lesson from our analysis is the importance of retirement decisions in generating adequate retirement consumption. Delaying retirement by only three years reduces the saving burden substantially, and allows for a sizable increase in consumption both before and after retirement. In our sample, if retirement were delayed to age 65, the asset base would total $421,000 and prescribed additional saving would be a relatively manageable 7 percent of earnings at the median.

We also show that initial and projected assets are distributed quite unevenly across the older population. Therefore, conclusions about the median household conceal extraordinary heterogeneity in saving needs among these households. Small changes in earnings or assets may lead to sizable differences in prescribed saving rates near the median. Average current holdings of the wealthiest HRS decile are 45 times those of the poorest decile, and 48 times that of the poorest by age 62. This difference arises mainly because of pension and financial wealth, since social security wealth is relatively evenly distributed and housing wealth does not comprise a large fraction of assets for the wealthiest. Assets are more evenly distributed across the other deciles, with the second highest group having 8 times more total wealth than households in the second lowest.

How do our conclusions square with other research on saving patterns? One way to compare them is to see how well prescribed saving rates from our methodology align with actual rates, as in Table 5. Here we tabulate our saving rates for HRS married couples and actual saving rates derived from

TABLE 5: Comparison of HRS Prescribed Saving Rates and CES Actual Rates

Household Earnings	HRS Prescribed Saving Rates (%)			Actual CES Saving Rates (%)
	Age 62	Age 65		
20,000	6.0	−1.9	?	2.3
30,000	16.8	8.5	>	2.8
40,000	17.7	10.0	>	3.3
50,000	17.9	11.1	>	3.7
60,000	20.2	13.1	>	4.1
70,000	20.3	13.5	>	4.5
80,000	21.1	14.2	>	5.0
90,000	20.5	13.3	>	5.4

Source: Authors' calculations.
Notes: Prescribed saving rates calculated using HRS (1992); Median values given for married couples with earnings within ±$5000 of reported earnings using HRS household sampling weights. CES saving rates taken from Palmer's (1994) calculations using the 1990 Consumer Expenditure Survey for respondents age 50–64. Rates are adjusted to reflect saving as a percent of total earnings.

the 1990 Consumer Expenditure Survey (CES) for the worker group age 50–64 (Palmer 1994). The evidence indicates that actual saving rates are only about a third of the levels prescribed by our calculations.[22]

Another approach is to compare our results to those of Bernheim (1994), who presents after-tax "target" saving rates about twice as large as ours for similarly aged households. For example, his target saving rates for a married couple age 55–64 with (without) a pension and earnings of $30,000 are 12.1 percent (18.1 percent); at $50,000 19.2 percent (24.3 percent); and at $75,000 22.9 percent (28.1 percent). Adjusting these rates to reflect saving as a percent of gross income reduces them by approximately 20–30 percent. However, as noted earlier, Bernheim's target rate calculations omit housing wealth, which if included would substantially narrow the difference between our prescribed saving rates.[23]

A third way to assess the comparability of our results with those in the literature is to compare projected replacement rates. Figure 6 shows our HRS target replacement rates with those generated using the 1990 CES (Palmer 1994), and some differences emerge. The HRS profiles both fall with earnings, in contrast to those derived from the CES data which are flatter and rise for higher incomes. Part of the difference between our results and Palmer's is that his method implicitly assumes that observed saving rates are optimal. To the extent that retirement income is not provided by social security, pensions, or existing assets and needs to be provided by additional saving, this will lead to Palmer's replacement rates overstating actual replacement rates.[24] Palmer's research also assumes an age 65 retire-

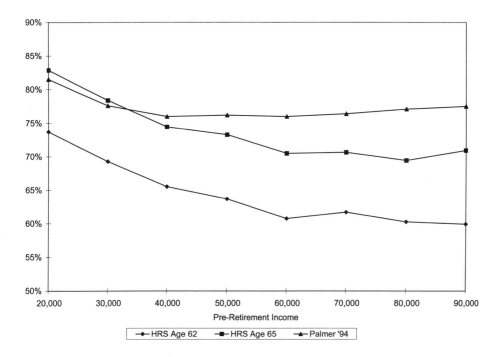

Figure 6. Comparison of replacement rates. Source: Authors' calculations.

ment age. We also note that the age-65 replacement rate for the HRS sample is substantially above the age 62 rate, illustrating the importance of retirement ages in the methodology. If retirement occurs earlier, and empirical evidence suggests it does, this is further cause to believe that average actual replacement rates fall below those estimated by Palmer.

One question we have not yet explored in any depth is why observed saving patterns appear to fall short of target saving benchmarks, both ours and others such as Bernheim's. One possible answer is that some households are simply too poor to defer consumption, but this appears unlikely for those other than the poorest in our sample. Other possible explanations center around informational issues, for example, households may simply underestimate their likely life expectancy in retirement, though recent research by Hurd and McGarry (1995) suggests that HRS respondents have quite reasonable forecasts of survival probabilities into old age. An additional hypothesized explanation is that people discount the future to varying degrees and some may do so very heavily. The rich set of standard and experimental questions in the HRS and future information provided by these households may provide clues to discovering the answers.

Appendix: Wealth Projections Using the Health and Retirement Study

In this Appendix we describe briefly the methods used to project elements of retirement wealth forward to age 62 and 65 for the HRS sample described in the text.

Social Security Wealth

Social security wealth measures are contained in the Earning and Benefits File (EBF), a restricted dataset available under controlled access conditions and described in MOS (1996). This file reports covered earnings under the social security law and estimated old-age and disability benefit amounts for HRS respondents who gave permission for administrative data to be linked to their survey responses. Retirement benefits are calculated based on earnings through 1991 and projected earnings to age 62 (the eligibility age for early retirement benefits), and also to the social security normal retirement age (65 for most HRS participants). In addition the EBF file indicates household wealth figures, which for married couples include spouse and survivor benefits.

Assumptions used to compute these benefit amounts are consistent with those used by the Social Security Administration (SSA) under its "intermediate assumptions" scenario outlined by the Social Security Trustees to forecast the system's fiscal status. Details of the calculations of social security benefit amounts, present values, and other available variables are described in MOS. Of the 7,607 HRS households, 4,334 had useable social security wealth from the EBF file.

For those households where earnings records were not available, values were imputed using the HRS dataset. Separate regression models were constructed for married couples and households with single individuals. The coefficients of the prediction model were estimated using the sample for which EBF social security wealth was available. Regressor variables used were those common to all households in the HRS dataset and include male earnings, female earnings, financial net wealth, net housing wealth, respondent's age, spouse's age, a dummy for white primary respondents, and a dummy for single female, with the log of social security wealth as the dependent variable. Estimated coefficients were used out of sample to estimate social security wealth for those households not appearing in the EBF.

Pension Wealth

The Institute for Survey Research (ISR) at the University of Michigan asked HRS respondents covered by employer-provided pensions for permission to contact their employers for information about these pension plans. Having obtained the names and addresses of the employers, ISR requested a pension plan Summary Plan Description (SPD) for each worker's current and past plans, and followed up with requests for the SPD at the U.S. Department of Labor where employer-supplied documents were not obtained. The SPDs were then coded using a format developed at ISR, and combined with a special software program developed by Curtin and others (1997). The software uses information collected from the SPDs to calculate benefit streams based on respondents' salary profiles and service, at alternative retirement ages. Vested terminated benefits as well as benefits available from current pension plans are included in the analysis in this paper. The employer-sponsored pension information and pension provider software are in the developmental phase and can currently be accessed only under restricted conditions.

Mortality, interest rate, inflation, and wage growth valuation assumptions are consistent with those used by the Social Security Administration in its annual reporting to Congress. For defined benefit plans, present values are calculated assuming a 2.3 percent real interest rate and a 4.0 percent inflation assumption (implying a 6.3 percent nominal discount rate). For defined contribution plans, real returns on contribution balances are assumed to be 4.0 percent annually (8.0 percent nominal). The same assumption is used for calculating present values. The pension provider software does not permit different assumptions for contribution growth and discounting, but we feel it is appropriate to use the higher discount rate in the defined contribution pensions plans due to the greater uncertainty of future benefit levels. Defined benefit plans sponsored by HRS participants' current employers are assumed to pay cost-of-living adjustments of half the inflation rate, mirroring historical practice. Benefits from previous employers and defined contribution plans are assumed to have no cost-of-living adjustment. The percentage of plans for which we were able to use the ISR software to estimate the present value of plan benefits varied by plan type, but was generally 60–70%.

For those households where pension plan data were not generated by the ISR software, values were imputed using the HRS dataset. Separate regression models were constructed for each pension type. Regressor variables used were those common to all households in the HRS dataset and include earnings, age, service in the plan, industry dummies, job description, race, sex, and union status. The log of pension wealth is the dependent variable. Estimated coefficients were used out of sample to estimate pension wealth for those households with missing pension data.

Housing Wealth

Net housing wealth reported in the HRS is the value of owner-occupied primary housing less debt owed on the property. The projected net value we use in this study is derived as the projected market value of the housing less projected debt. We assume that the market value of housing assets is constant in real dollars, or in other words, the increase in home value is equal to the assumed rate of inflation. Projecting debt is more complicated, as will be explained.

The HRS provides information on first mortgages, second mortgages, home equity loans, and lines of credit against housing equity. To roll forward debt we need a) the outstanding balance on the mortgage or other debt, b) the payments and frequency of payments on that debt, and c) the interest rate on the debt. The HRS provides the first two of these three, necessitating the use of alternative sources for the mortgage rate.

Given the purchase date of the house, a datum reported by HRS respondents, we use historical interest rates as proxies for current rates. However, this ignores the possibility that the homeowner refinanced the mortgage. We know that interest rates fluctuate over time, and a common "rule of thumb" has the mortgage holder refinance when rates drop by more than 200 basis points (2 percent). Therefore, for example, using the May 1980 average 30-year mortgage rate for a house purchased in May 1980 would be likely to overstate the actual interest costs for many if not most households. A different approach would be to take the purchase price of the house reported in the HRS, the payment amount, and some assumption regarding the term of the mortgage (e.g., assume a 30-year fixed-rate mortgage). This has the problem that many households' mortgage payments include their property taxes, homeowners' insurance premiums, or both. Imputing mortgage interest rates from the raw payments would bias upward the derived mortgage interest rates.

Data from another survey mitigate some of these problems. The American Housing Survey (AHS 1993) provides interest rate data for houses in its sample. From this source, we calculate a series of actual mortgage rates paid by averaging conditional on year of home purchase and use these to roll forward first-mortgage debt. Analysis of these rates as opposed to issue rates indicates that they embed substantial refinancing for periods such as the early 1980s. For years prior to 1953 where data are thin, or where HRS households do not indicate a year of purchase, we use the average mortgage interest rate for the sample, approximately 8.5 percent.

The AHS also has data on tax and insurance payments. These, in addition to tax payment information contained in the HRS, are used to calculate an effective mortgage payment, or the amount of the mortgage that actually services the debt. HRS households indicate whether given payments include taxes, insurance, both, or neither. When taxes are given, these are used to reduce mortgage payments. When they are not, the average rate of tax as a percent of payment as calculated from the AHS is used instead. A similar procedure is used for insurance payments when they are included in mortgage payments. The AHS derived values for taxes and insurance are 18.11 percent and 5.90 percent of mortgage payments, respectively.

For second mortgages and home equity loans the HRS does not contain information on year of issue. These amounts are therefore projected forward using the average rate on such debt from the AHS, approximately 9.5 percent.

Missing observations on mortgage payment amounts are imputed assuming a 30-year fixed mortgage at the rate associated with the purchase year when purchase year and price are available. When this information is unavailable, it is assumed that the payments are such that the mortgage is paid off at age 70. For missing secondary debt, a 10-year term is assumed to pay off the remaining balance. There are respectively 123, 47, and 36 missing payments imputed in this manner.

Other Financial Wealth

"Other financial wealth" includes such assets as savings, investments, business assets, and nonresidential real estate less outstanding debt not related to housing. Asset values in 1992 are provided by HRS respondents. To obtain projected net financial assets, as noted in the text, we project individual components of this asset category separately. That is, equity components of assets are projected in line with historical equity returns, bond returns are used to project fixed income holdings, and personal business assets are projected using the equity rate of return. Assumed growth rates are geometric averages of real returns over the period 1926–95 as calculated using the Stocks, Bonds, Bills, and Inflation series from Ibbotson Associates.

The components of net financial wealth as tabulated in the HRS and the rates used to project them:

- Vehicle and RV wealth — depreciated over ten years using straight line depreciation.
- Checking, savings, money market accounts — Real T-bill rate (0.5 percent)
- CDs, savings bonds, T-bills — Real T-bill rate (0.5 percent)
- IRA and Keough accts. — 50/50 corporate bonds/stocks (2.3 percent/ 7.2 percent)
- Stocks, mutual funds — stocks (7.2 percent)
- Business equity — stocks (7.2 percent)
- Other assets, real estate, second home — held constant in real terms
- Other debt, second home debt — held constant since we lack other information to estimate changes in value

Research support for this study was provided by the Wharton School, the Penn Aging Research Center, and the Boettner Center of Financial Gerontology. The authors remain solely responsible for opinions contained herein.

Notes

1. Franco Modigliani was a believer in this model, which garnered him the Nobel prize. When asked what he would do with his prize money, he is alleged to have responded that he would spend $1/T$ of it, where T represented the remaining (and assumed known) years of life remaining.

2. Bernheim solves backward from the household's last possible period, T, in which all wealth and income is assumed to be exhausted. Then the household is posited to maximize utility in period $T-1$ given uncertainty of living to period T. Actual consumption (and hence saving) is determined by solving for C_{T-1} given $U(C_T)$, the utility of consumption; β, the rate of pure time preference (discount); p_{T-1}, the probability of surviving from time $T-1$ to time T; and the objective function max $U(C_{T-1})+p_{T-1}\beta U(C*T)$. The process is then resolved for periods back to the starting point, and under a range of assumptions regarding other variables.

3. Whether housing wealth should be included in a tally of retirement assets is a hotly debated issue. Retirees are often reluctant to move from the houses they lived in while working, in which case they see their housing wealth as an emergency contingency fund (and possibly as a bequest). In addition, moving costs can make accessing housing equity expensive. However, we note that housing wealth may be used to increase consumption through mechanisms such as second mortgages, home equity loans, and reverse mortgages, so in this paper we include housing wealth in the set of assets that could finance retirement.

4. From a theoretical economic perspective, this is less appealing than a true life cycle dynamic programming approach, as it ignores utility theory and behavioral responses to uncertainty. However, it is a popular model among retirement planning practitioners and can be seen as a relatively tractable approximation or rule of thumb to the life cycle model.

5. The HRS is structured as a longitudinal or panel dataset with households re-sampled every two years, and should prove a fertile source for researchers in the future. Currently only the first wave is available in public release, and only public release data can be merged with the pension and social security data to be described below.

6. All wealth values reported in this paper are weighted by HRS sample weights.

7. The value for the median 10 percent is the mean value for those households falling between the 45th and 55th percentile of the wealth distribution. This value is presented instead of the true median to allow for representative disaggregation.

8. GMSS recognize the upward bias of their numbers but were not permitted at that time (February 1997) to combine pension with social security administrative data.

9. Legislation is increasing the normal retirement age to 67 over a period of several years, and for a few HRS respondents the normal retirement age will be age 66.

10. More discussion of projection methodology and rates of growth is given in the Appendix.

11. In other words, the payroll tax at older ages is more of a true tax than at younger ages, where additional benefits may be accrued by extra years of contribution to social security.

12. We assume vehicles depreciate over a 10-year period.

13. One could extend the analysis by allowing for changes in specific consumption prior to and after retirement, and Palmer (1994) does this. In this paper we do not model this possibility and note that consumption choices are a decision variable rather than an exogenous variable, dependent on assets and income.

14. Annuity factors are calculated with the same assumptions as those used for valuing pension and social security wealth, a real interest rate of 2.3 percent, and the moderate assumptions used in the long range projections of the Social Security Administration. Annuity factors employ the SSA mortality tables (see MOS). For

married couples the annuity factor used was a Joint and Survivor annuity paying 75 percent to the surviving spouse.

15. Depending on how the saving is done, the rate of saving may affect either pre-retirement taxes, post-retirement taxes, or both. For our current calculations we assume saving out of earnings is done on an after-tax basis so it only affects post-retirement taxes; all pension saving is assumed to be pre-tax.

16. We do not account for state and local taxes in this chapter's analysis. To the extent that these differ pre- and post-retirement, this may bias calculated replacement rates. If pre-retirement state and local taxes were higher than post-retirement taxes, our replacement rates would be too high.

17. Medians are presented instead of means as they give a more accurate representation of typical values within deciles. Means give curious results because of the presence of outliers; for example, a saving rate value for a household where earnings are at the lower extreme for earnings within a wealth decile might indicate significant dissaving as optimal behavior, possibly to the tune of large multiples of earnings. Averaging that value with others more representative of the subsample would drastically understate the prescribed saving rate for the "typical" household.

18. Of course, it is possible that these households may have a strong bequest motive, in which case the pure replacement model may understate their need and taste for saving. To the extent that there is heterogeneity in the desire to provide bequests, those with a stronger motive are likely to have accumulated greater assets to date and appear here as "over-savers."

19. In addition, their "desire" to consume out of future income may be overstated, inasmuch as earnings exclude noncash transfers such as food stamps and housing subsidies to the very poor.

20. Plots for age 65 retirement look qualitatively very similar.

21. Additional savings equals savings on the additional dollars of income plus increase in saving on previous income, i.e., $0.16195 * 100 + 0.00095 * 33,000$.

22. Palmer (1994) shows that the 1984 and 1988 CES saving rates are higher for certain earnings groups, yet they still fall short of our median prescribed rates.

23. Another way to think about housing wealth is that mortgage payments have both an investment component and a consumption component. The investment component recognizes the purchase of the house as an investment in a tangible asset. The consumption component represents what the homeowner would pay for housing services, or for the non-homeowner, rent. Since shelter is a large consumption expense, paying off the mortgage represents a substantial decrease in income required to cover consumption needs or a prefunding of later housing consumption.

24. Schieber (1996) offers additional criticism of Palmer's methodology arguing that his figures are upwardly biased.

References

Bernheim, B. Douglas. 1992. "Is the Baby Boom Generation Preparing Adequately for Retirement?" Technical Report. Princeton, N.J.: Merrill Lynch.

——. 1994. "The Merrill Lynch Baby Boom Retirement Index." Summary Report. Princeton, N.J.: Merrill Lynch.

Case, Karl E. 1994. "Land Prices and House Prices in the United States." In Yukio Noguchi and James M. Poterba, eds., *Housing Markets in the United States and Japan*, Chicago: University of Chicago Press.

Curtin, Richard T. 1997. "Employer Sponsored Pension Plan Documentation: Pension Estimation Program Software Documentation." University of Michigan, Ann Arbor.

Congressional Budget Office. 1993. "Baby Boomers in Retirement: An Early Perspective." CBO Report. Washington, D.C.: U.S. Government Printing Office, September.

Gokhale, Jagadeesh, Laurence J. Kotlikoff, and John Sabelhaus. 1996. "Understanding the Postwar Decline in U.S. Saving: A Cohort Analysis." *Brookings Papers on Economic Activity* 1: 315–407.

Gustman, Alan L., Olivia S. Mitchell, Andrew A. Samwick, and Thomas L. Steinmeier. "Evaluating Pension Entitlements." This volume.

Hurd, Michael D. and Kathleen McGarry. 1995. "Evaluation of the Subjective Probabilities of Survival in the Health and Retirement Study." *Journal of Human Resources* 30 (Supplement): S268–92.

Ibbotson Associates. 1996. *Stocks, Bonds, Bills, and Inflation: 1996 Yearbook*. Chicago: Ibbotson Associates.

McGill, Dan M., Kyle N. Brown, John J. Haley, and Sylvester J. Schieber. 1996. *Fundamentals of Private Pensions*. 7th edition. Pension Research Council. Philadelphia: University of Pennsylvania Press.

Mitchell, Olivia S. and James F. Moore. 1998. "Can Americans Afford to Retire? New Evidence on Retirement Saving Adequacy." *Journal of Risk Insurance*, 65, 3:371–400.

Mitchell, Olivia S., Jan Olson, and Thomas L. Steinmeier. "Social Security Earnings and Projected Benefits." This volume.

Palmer, Bruce A. 1988. *The Impact of Tax Reform on Wage Replacement Ratios*. Atlanta: Georgia State University, Center for Risk Management and Insurance Research.

——. 1991. *1991 Georgia State University/Alexander & Alexander Consulting Group RETIRE Project Report*. Atlanta: Georgia State University, Center for Risk Management and Insurance Research.

——. 1993. *1993 Georgia State University/Alexander & Alexander Consulting Group RETIRE Project Report*. Atlanta: Georgia State University, Center for Risk Management and Insurance Research.

——. 1994. "Retirement Income Replacement Ratios: An Update." *Benefits Quarterly* (Second Quarter): 59–69.

Schieber, Sylvester J. 1996. "Conceptual and Measurement Problems in Contemporary Measures of Income Needs in Retirement." *Benefits Quarterly* (Second Quarter): 56–68.

Social Security Advisory Council (SSAC). 1996. *Report of the 1994–1996 Advisory Council on Social Security*, Volumes 1 and 2. Washington, D.C.: Social Security Administration.

U.S. Department of Commerce, Bureau of the Census. 1994. *American Housing Survey, 1991: National File*. Washington, D.C.: U.S. Government Printing Office.

Chapter 4
Making the Most of 401 (k) Plans: Who's Choosing What and Why?

Robert L. Clark, Gordon P. Goodfellow,
Sylvester J. Schieber, and Drew Warwick

Pension assets grew faster than total wealth in the United States during the 1980s, leading one researcher to conclude that "pensions are how America saves" (Shoven 1995). At the same time that pension wealth has grown in importance, there has been a revolution in the pension industry as defined contribution plans in general, and 401(k) plans in particular, have become the pensions of choice. During the late 1970s, there were approximately twice as many active participants in private defined benefit plans as in private defined contribution plans. Today, the situation is almost exactly reversed. This shift from defined benefit to defined contribution pension plans has been accompanied by a shift in the responsibility for financing and managing retirement accruals from firms to individuals. By the end of the 1980s, three-fourths of the contributions going into private pension plans went into defined contribution plans, and nearly half of these contributions went into plans partly dependent on voluntary contributions by workers. Projecting trends on pension contributions, the U.S. Department of Labor (1997) concluded that it will not be long before more money is going into private 401(k) plans than all other private pension plans combined, if we are not there already. Most of the contributions to these plans will be directly from workers.

During the same period, there was a similar shift in the responsibility for managing assets in employer-sponsored retirement plans. Defined benefit plan sponsors assume the responsibility of managing the pension assets in their retirement trusts, since they bear the risks associated with investment performance of pension funds. Today, the overwhelming majority of workers participating in 401(k) plans (and their public and nonprofit sector counterparts) are required to manage the investment of their retirement savings directly. In this new world, not only do workers have to determine when to start saving for their retirement and how much to contribute to their retirement accounts, they also have to decide the allocation of pension funds across various types of assets.

Because of these fundamental changes in retirement plans and the importance of individual decision-making, we developed a new data file of the participants in 87 401(k) plans. This unique data file enabled us to examine individual savings and investment choices associated with these plans. Specifically, we examined who participated in these plans, how much they contributed when they did, and how they managed their assets as they accrued them.

We first describe the data file used in this analysis and present the characteristics of the participants in the plans. Next, we assess the factors related to participation and contribution rates in these plans, and then evaluate the general level of assets being accumulated. The next step is to examine the portfolio allocations and the associated characteristics of workers related to variations in asset allocations. Finally, we look at how participation, contribution rates, and asset allocations vary by the sex of the participants in these plans.

Description of the Data

Our analysis of individual contribution and investment decisions in 401(k) plans was based on administrative records of 87 plans in operation during 1995. All information reported covered the 1995 calendar year. Of these plans, 41 were administrative recordkeeping clients of Watson Wyatt Worldwide; 46 were not. The smallest plan in the group had just under 25 participants, and the largest plan had approximately 15,000 participants. The plans analyzed here were not chosen on a random probability basis, but there is no reason to believe that the variation in characteristics of these plans was dissimilar to that of 401(k) plans generally.

A total of 234,573 workers were employed at some time during 1995 by the sponsors of these plans. Information for each worker included age, annual pay, 1995 contributions to the 401(k) plan, 1995 account balances, amount of funds in each investment option provided by the plan sponsor, years of service with the company, and employee's name.[1] Not all the employees were included in the sample used in the analysis for a variety of reasons. Workers under age 20 or over age 64 were omitted, as were part-year employees. Also eliminated were workers who did not have at least one year of service, because some plans had a one-year-of-service participation standard. In addition, employees with annual earnings of less than $10,000 per year were deleted from the sample, because we were interested in examining the behavior of full-time workers and the administrative records did not include an hours measure that could be used for such screening. After these deletions, the base file used in the analysis contained 156,376 workers eligible to participate in the 401(k) plans in 1995.

Utilization of 401 (k) Plans

Since employee contributions to 401(k) plans are voluntary, workers must decide whether or not to designate a portion of pre-tax earnings as contributions to the plan. In general, individuals are free to select any contribution amount from zero up to the maximum annual level specified by the firm or the legal limit ($9,240 in 1995). In evaluating the effectiveness of voluntary contributory retirement plans, analysts have been concerned about variations in the participation and contribution rates in these plans by workers at different levels of annual earnings. Part of the policy concern is to avoid providing higher-income workers a disproportionate share of the advantages of the preferential tax treatment afforded these plans.[2] Of course, there is also some interest in the potential of these plans to provide adequate retirement security to a broad cross-section of workers. Earlier research using similar data has concluded that the decision to participate in these plans and the amounts contributed vary with plan characteristics and with worker's age and earnings (Clark and Schieber 1998). That is where we begin the current analysis.

Policymakers concerned about the growth of voluntary retirement plans have also focused on the willingness of other specific groups of individuals to participate in 401(k) plans and on how the management of retirement assets varies across socioeconomic groups. For example, some argue that young people may not begin to save early enough or may save too little to accumulate sufficient assets by the time they retire. Others believe that low-wage workers and women might be overly risk averse and thus tend to invest too conservatively. For these reasons, it is important to examine carefully the investment choices of workers of different ages, sexes, and levels of earnings. The age and earnings distribution of persons employed by the sponsors of these 87 plans is shown in Table 1. These data indicate that half of the entire sample had annual earnings of $15,000 to $34,999 in 1995 and an additional third of the employees had earnings of between $35,000 and $74,999. Younger workers were more likely to have had lower earnings — 82 percent earned less than $35,000 per year, while persons 40 to 59 years of age were more likely to have had higher earnings.

Participation in 401 (k) Plans

Young, low-income workers were much less likely to participate in a 401(k) plan than older, high-income individuals. For example, fewer than half of all workers age 20–29 earning less than $15,000 per year contributed to their 401(k) plan. In contrast, over 92 percent of workers aged 50 and older with earnings in excess of $60,000 participated in their company plan. It is important to recognize that pension participation varies with both age and income. Furthermore, it should be recognized that older workers were more

TABLE 1: Age and Earnings Distribution of Employees (%)

Age group	Annual Earnings ($000)							
	10.0–14.9	15.0–24.9	25.0–34.9	35.0–44.9	45.0–59.9	60.0–74.9	75.0–99.9	100+
20–29	12.4	37.8	31.4	12.1	5.0	0.8	0.4	0.2
30–39	6.1	21.8	27.0	18.8	14.1	5.9	3.5	2.7
40–49	6.5	20.5	22.8	16.2	14.7	7.7	5.8	5.9
50–59	8.2	23.0	22.4	13.9	13.5	6.8	5.7	6.5
60–65	10.4	28.1	21.6	12.9	11.0	6.0	4.4	5.6
All ages	7.7	24.4	25.5	15.9	12.6	5.8	4.1	4.0

Source: Authors' calculations from a file containing data on 87 401(k) plans and 156,376 persons employed by plan sponsors and eligible to participate in the plans in 1995.

likely to be participating in the pension plan than the average of all workers. This indicated that the number of people who will accumulate pension accounts sometime during their life is greater than that shown by a single cross-section of the proportion of workers who are participating in a plan during that year.[3]

Table 2 reports the proportion of eligible workers who contributed to their 401(k) plans during 1995 by various ages and levels of annual earnings. These data reveal important earnings and age patterns in the proportion of earnings contributed to the 401(k) plan. The effect of increases in annual earnings on the likelihood that a worker will participate in the plan was also clearly shown in these data. Only 60 percent of all workers with annual earnings between $10,000 and $14,999 participated in the 401(k) plans, while approximately three quarters of those earning between $15,000 and $34,999 made contributions during 1995. Over 80 percent of workers with annual earnings between $35,000 and $59,999 participated, and over 90 percent of those earning in excess of $60,000 made contributions. Holding age constant, the proportion of workers who participated in the plan increased rapidly with income up to the earnings level of $60,000 to $74,999. Further increases in income did not seem to affect participation.

Participation rates also rose with age, from 66 percent for those aged 20–29 to 79 percent for 30–39-year-olds, and over 80 percent of workers aged 40 and over. This age-related increase in participation was much larger among low-income workers. For most workers, their earnings increases as they age. Therefore, a lifecycle pattern of participation is best viewed as a movement along the diagonals of the table.

Multivariate statistical analysis of participation in a 401(k) plan produced estimates of the partial effects of earnings, age, and tenure on the probability of workers making contributions to their 401(k) accounts in 1995. Since the information in Table 2 suggested that these variables had a nonlinear effect, the estimated equation included age and age squared, tenure and tenure squared, and earnings and earnings squared. In addition, the equation included dichotomous variables indicating the worker's sex and a series of dichotomous variables identifying the 401(k) plan in which the person was enrolled.[4]

The estimated marginal effects indicated that the probability of participation in the plan increases with age, tenure, and earnings, but at a decreasing rate. Given the nonlinearity of the relationships between participation and age, tenure, and earnings level, the best method of assessing their effects was to plot the implied participation probabilities as age, tenure, and earnings vary. Figure 1 shows the increase in the probability of 401(k) participation with increases in earnings for a hypothetical male worker age 40 and having 10 years of tenure employed by the largest plan sponsor in our sample.[5] The probability of 401(k) participation for such a worker earning less than $25,000 was approximately 55 percent, while a similar worker earning

TABLE 2: 401(k) Participation Rates by Age and Earnings (%)

	Annual Earnings ($000)								
Age group	10.0–14.9	15.0–24.9	25.0–34.9	35.0–44.9	45.0–59.9	60.0–74.9	75.0–99.9	100+	All Earnings
20–29	43.5	61.7	71.4	79.5	86.3	91.3	91.0	91.1	66.2
30–39	59.3	71.5	76.6	81.2	87.7	91.3	93.6	89.0	78.6
40–49	63.7	76.0	78.8	81.8	86.1	90.3	92.0	89.2	81.1
50–59	73.8	81.5	82.4	85.0	87.8	92.9	95.1	92.3	84.7
60–65	75.9	82.0	80.9	84.9	90.5	96.6	93.1	92.4	84.4
All ages	59.6	72.1	77.1	81.8	87.2	91.4	93.2	90.2	78.6

Source: See Table 1.

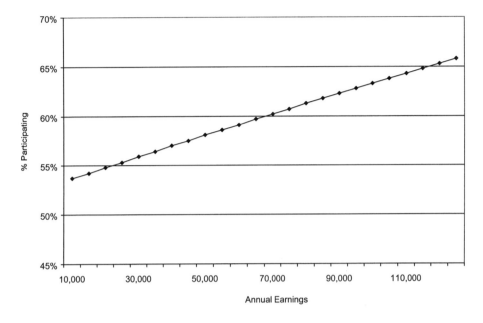

Figure 1. 401 (k) participation rates for men by earnings (%). Values are based on the logit regression in column 2, Appendix Table 1. Values are for employees of the largest plan sponsor, age 40, with 10 years tenure.

$75,000 had a participation probability of about 60 percent. Participation rates for men with annual earnings of $125,000 exceeded 65 percent. The estimation procedure constrained the participation probabilities for women to have the same relationship with increases in annual earnings as that shown for men in Figure 1; however, the probability of participation was predicted to be about 2 percentage points higher at each level of income.

The effects of advancing age and tenure on 401 (k) participation probabilities are shown in Figure 2 for two different earnings levels, $25,000 and $75,000. In this case, the profiles are for a man hired by the firm at age 30; thus as age increases by one year, so does tenure. The profiles show that the probability of participation in the plan at age 30 was just under 50 percent for men earning $25,000, and about 53 percent for those with $75,000. These probabilities rose slightly with age until the mid-40s and then declined. The predicted participation rates for women had the same age pattern as that shown in Figure 2, they were slightly higher at each age.

An alternative specification used to examine the participation decision introduced two company-specific pension variables that were expected to influence whether a worker would participate in the 401 (k) plan. Specifically, we hypothesized that a worker will be more likely to make a contribu-

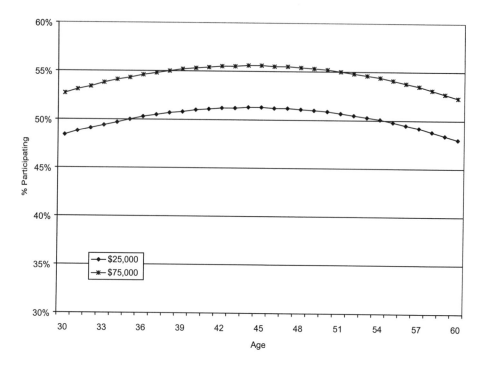

Figure 2. 401(k) participation rates for men by age and earnings (%). Values are based on the logit regression in column 2, Appendix Table 1. Values are for employees hired at age 30 by the largest plan sponsor, with either $25,000 or $75,000 annual earnings.

tion to the plan when the company provides a matching contribution, and the higher the match rate, the more likely a worker will be to participate in the plan. We also argue that the existence of a company defined benefit plan will influence 401(k) participation. Hence, we asked whether the projected age-65 replacement rate from the defined benefit plan affects the likelihood that a worker will make a contribution to the 401(k) plan.[6] The individual 401(k) plan indicators were not included in this specification of the participation equation.

The estimates indicate that workers were, in fact, more likely to participate in the 401(k) plan the higher the company match rate. The estimated effects indicated that each 10 percentage point increase in the match rate increased the probability of 401(k) participation by 3 percentage points. This finding is consistent with workers responding to the economic incentive of a higher return on their own investment when the match is included (Clark and Schieber 1998). The estimated effects of a higher defined benefit replacement rate indicated that a 10 percentage point higher projected rate at age 65 reduced the probability of participating in the 401 (k) plan by 0.4 percentage points. This finding suggested that workers had a target level of retirement savings in mind when they decided whether to participate in these plans, so that employees covered by more generous defined benefit plans desired to save less in their 401 (k) plans.

Contribution Rates by 401 (k) Participants

Annual employee contributions as a percent of salary are shown in Table 3 by various age and earnings groups. The entries indicate the average percentage of earnings contributed to the plan by those workers who made a contribution during 1995. The table also reports combined employee and employer annual contributions. For all participants with annual earnings under $45,000, employee contributions were between 6 and 7 percent of earnings, while combined contributions represented about 10 percent of compensation. For workers earning $45,000–$99,999, employee contributions totaled 7–8 percent of earnings, and combined contributions amounted to 11–12 percent. Finally, contributions as a percent of earnings were lower for persons earning in excess of $100,000. The decline in the contribution rate for highly compensated workers was presumably driven by the maximum contribution rates imposed by the company and/or the tax code.

Among those workers contributing to a plan, age effects were greater than the earnings effects described above. The contribution rates increased with age for all workers and within each income category. Participants age 20–29 contributed 5 percent of their earnings, while those age 30–39 contributed almost 7 percent. The contribution rate continued to increase with age, as persons age 50–59 contributed 8 percent of earnings and those age 60–65 contributed 9 percent.

A multivariate analysis of contribution rates enables us to determine how these rates vary with age, tenure, earnings, sex, and dichotomous variables indicating the plan in which the person was enrolled (see the first two columns of Appendix Table 2).[7] The analysis of contribution rates included only persons who made a contribution in 1995 to their 401 (k) plan. The results show that contributions as a percent of pay were flat up to the $65,000 earnings level. Above $65,000, discrimination limits and dollar cap limits imposed by the tax code reduced contribution rates relative to workers' pay.

Figure 3 plots the interacting effects of age and tenure on the probability of men participating in a 401 (k) plan, derived from the same multivariate analysis. The values were calculated for a 401 (k) participant earning $40,000 per year, who was hired at age 30. The combined effects of increasing age and tenure on the contribution rate to the plan were strongly posi-

TABLE 3: 401(k) Contribution Rates by Age and Earnings (% of Annual Earnings)

Age group	Annual Earnings ($000)								
	10.0–14.9	15.0–24.9	25.0–34.9	35.0–44.9	45.0–59.9	60.0–74.9	75.0–99.9	100+	All Earnings
Employee contributions as a percentage of earnings									
20–29	4.4	4.4	4.9	6.1	6.8	7.5	5.6	4.2	5.0
30–39	6.4	6.4	6.1	6.5	7.2	7.5	7.2	5.5	6.6
40–49	7.5	7.3	6.6	6.8	7.3	7.6	7.4	5.9	7.0
50–59	8.2	9.1	8.1	8.1	8.3	8.4	7.6	6.0	8.2
60–65	9.3	10.4	8.9	9.2	9.4	8.8	7.9	5.6	9.2
All ages	6.9	6.9	6.4	6.9	7.5	7.8	7.4	5.8	6.9
Employee contributions plus employer match as a percentage of earnings									
20–29	6.8	7.6	8.5	9.6	10.5	10.9	8.1	5.7	8.4
30–39	9.6	9.9	9.7	10.1	11.1	11.5	11.1	8.2	10.2
40–49	10.7	10.9	10.2	10.2	11.1	11.5	11.5	9.2	10.6
50–59	11.4	13.0	12.0	11.8	12.2	12.2	11.7	9.3	12.0
60–65	12.1	14.5	13.3	12.7	13.5	13.0	11.7	8.5	13.1
All ages	9.9	10.4	10.1	10.4	11.3	11.7	11.4	8.9	10.5

Source: See Table 1.

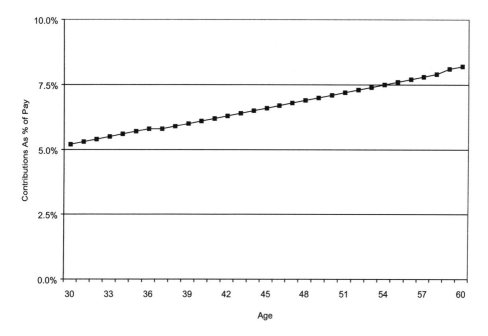

Figure 3. 401(k) contribution rates for men by age (as % of annual pay). Values are based on the OLS regression shown in column 2, Appendix Table 2. Values are for employees hired at age 30 by the largest plan sponsor, with annual earnings of $40,000.

tive, with contributions rising from 5 percent to 8 percent between age 30 and age 60.

We also developed an alternative specification of the contribution rate equation that included the 401(k) match rate and the level of generosity of the defined benefit plan where there was one. The results are shown in the third and fourth columns of Appendix Table 2. The negative coefficient on the match rate provided further support for the target saving hypothesis. The estimated coefficient indicates that each 10 percentage point increase in the match rate was associated with a reduction in the contribution rate of 0.4 percentage points. In this equation, the replacement rate from the defined benefit plan had a positive effect on the 401(k) contribution rate, was at odds with the target savings model. This finding is, however, consistent with Ippolito's (1997) hypothesis of saving preferences. This model predicts that workers with high saving preferences will want both defined benefit and defined contribution retirement savings plans. The coefficient indicated that each 10 percentage point increase in the projected replacement rate from the defined benefit plan increased the contribution rate by 2 percentage points.

TABLE 4: Average Account Balance by Age and Earnings

	Annual Earnings ($000)								
Age group	10.0–14.9	15.0–24.9	25.0–34.9	35.0–44.9	45.0–59.9	60.0–74.9	75.0–99.9	100+	All Earnings
Balances from employee contributions									
20–29	1,258	2,128	3,646	6,811	10,862	15,000	13,444	14,799	4,026
30–39	2,802	4,238	7,003	11,423	17,813	26,875	34,106	43,745	12,411
40–49	4,661	6,234	9,804	16,726	25,755	39,919	52,644	73,109	21,884
50–59	6,811	9,759	15,677	26,221	38,689	55,534	71,594	117,054	32,145
60–65	8,290	14,442	20,908	30,732	46,830	64,523	80,600	145,358	36,082
All ages	4,184	5,711	8,920	15,276	24,673	38,700	51,945	81,367	18,562
Total balances									
20–29	2,200	3,907	6,781	11,881	18,783	23,834	19,810	21,928	7,169
30–39	5,328	7,539	12,762	20,454	30,905	44,944	55,993	68,937	21,409
40–49	8,226	10,974	17,461	29,131	44,731	65,955	89,316	121,279	37,359
50–59	11,304	16,506	26,430	42,934	63,941	88,733	119,121	202,854	53,770
60–65	13,081	23,318	34,391	50,655	78,417	103,810	123,932	239,431	58,797
All ages	7,250	9,908	15,731	26,342	42,168	63,413	86,537	136,447	31,511

Source: See Table 1.

Investment Patterns of 401(k) Assets

Participating in a 401(k) plan and contributing reasonable amounts to the plan play an extremely important role in determining the amount of money that these plans will produce for retirement income purposes. Thus, it is important to examine retirement fund balances attributable to employee contributions as well as total 401(k) accumulations. Table 4 reports the 401(k) account balances of all workers who had contributed to one of the sample plans in the past (even though they might not have done so during 1995).[8] Not surprisingly, Table 4 reveals a strong relationship between earnings, age, and 401(k) plan balances. In the bottom three earnings classes, which include workers with earnings up to $35,000 per year, the average cumulative total balances in the plans were roughly equal to one-half a year's earnings. Average account balances rose steadily with increases in earnings until they approached annual earnings for workers earning between $75,000 and $100,000. Fund balances across different age groups varied significantly with earnings. For example, accumulated balances of workers in their mid-60s with earnings up to $25,000 were roughly 6 times those of workers in their 20s with similar earnings. For those earning $35,000 to $75,000, the differential for these age groups dropped to only 4 times. At earnings levels above $75,000, the differential ranged from 8 to 10 times.

To examine the investment choices of plan participants, the 87 firms were divided into two groups, depending on whether the 401(k) plan offered company stock as an investment option in the plan. In our sample of plans, 58 did not offer company stock as an investment option for plan participants, and 29 companies did. Plans with company stock options employed one of three types of investment options: 16 plans simply offered company stock as an investment option that participants could invest in if they so chose without any incentives or requirements that they do so; 9 plans contributed matching contributions only to the company stock account and allowed plan participants free choice as to whether they wanted to invest their own contributions in company stock; and 4 plans required that employee contributions be made to the company stock account in order to qualify for matching employer contributions that also went to the company stock account.

Focusing first on the 58 plans without any company stock investment option, Table 5 reports the proportion of total 1995 contributions allocated to the purchase of equities and fixed-income assets. Two consistent patterns emerge from these data. First, the proportion of contributions allocated to fixed-income assets increased with age. The proportion of new contributions devoted to fixed-income assets increased from approximately 43 percent for workers under age 40 to about 55 percent for participants age 50 and older. The increase in fixed assets with age was observed within each of the earnings categories. Second, as annual earnings increased, the propor-

TABLE 5: Allocation of 401(k) Contributions by Age and Earnings; 401(k) Plans without Company Stock as an Investment Option (%)

Age group	Annual Earnings ($000)								
	10.0–14.9	15.0–24.9	25.0–34.9	35.0–44.9	45.0–59.9	60.0–74.9	75.0–99.9	100+	All Earnings
Percent of contributions in equities									
20–29	53	53	59	63	68	68	69	74	58
30–39	46	49	54	61	63	67	70	75	57
40–49	46	48	47	56	58	60	64	70	54
50–59	38	42	43	49	53	57	58	66	47
60–65	37	35	37	43	45	58	51	61	41
All ages	45	48	50	57	60	62	64	70	54
Percent of contributions in fixed-income assets									
20–29	47	47	41	37	32	32	31	26	42
30–39	54	51	46	39	37	33	30	25	43
40–49	54	52	53	44	42	40	36	30	46
50–59	62	58	57	51	47	43	42	34	53
60–65	63	65	63	57	55	42	49	39	59
All ages	55	52	50	43	40	38	36	30	46

Source: Authors' calculations. Allocations are calculated only for employees making a contribution in 1995. Plan information is from a file containing data on 58 401(k) plans that did not provide the option of investing in company stock.

tion of new contributions designated for the purchase of fixed-income assets declined. Workers with annual earnings under $35,000 allocated slightly more than half their contributions to fixed-income assets, while individuals with earnings in excess of $60,000 put only 30 to 40 percent of their contributions in fixed-income accounts.

Among participants in the 29 plans that offered or required some purchase of company stock, we found that these workers designated much less of their 401(k) contributions to fixed-income assets (33 percent in Table 6 compared to 46 percent in Table 5). This was true for each of the age/earnings entries shown in the two tables. The first panel of Table 6 shows that low earners (those with earnings between $10,000 and $15,000) allocated 38 percent of their contributions to company stock; at earnings of $15,000 to $25,000 the share contributed to company stock dropped to 28 percent; and it peaked at 41 percent for those earning $45,000 to $60,000. The proportion of contributions devoted to company stock declined slightly at earnings levels over $75,000. In general, the proportion of contributions allocated to company stock rose with age until 50 to 59, and then declined.

We also examined summary investment information for 401(k) aggregate account balances reported in Table 7. The data show that the individual portfolio composition of account balances was remarkably close to the allocation of 1995 contributions. Workers with earnings in excess of $15,000 held less of their 401(k) balances in fixed-income assets as annual earnings increased. Also, workers without a company stock investment option consistently put 10 to 15 percentage more of their 401(k) contributions and total account balances in fixed-income asset accounts, as compared to those with a company stock option.

To clarify how the availability of company stock as an investment option affected 401(k) asset allocations between equities and fixed-income assets, we estimated Tobit equations (reported in Appendix Tables 3 and 4). The investment in fixed-income assets was clearly different between plans that offer company stock as an investment option and those that did not. For both sets of plans, there was a negative relationship between earnings level and investment in fixed-income assets, although it was much stronger in the case of plans with company stock than in those without it (see Figure 4). The combined effects of age and tenure reflected in Figure 5 was positive for both sets of plans, although it was somewhat more so for plans with company stock.

In plans that provided an employer match in company stock (but the employee was not constrained to put his or her own contributions in the company stock fund), the percent of participant contributions to fixed-income assets increased by 12 percent relative to plans where company stock investment was totally voluntary. Among the plans that required the employee to contribute to the company stock fund in order to qualify for a

TABLE 6: Allocation of Contributions by Age and Earnings: Plans with Company Stock as an Investment Option (%)

Age group	Annual Earnings ($000)								
	10.0–14.9	15.0–24.9	25.0–34.9	35.0–44.9	45.0–59.9	60.0–74.9	75.0–99.9	100+	All Earnings
Percentage of contributions in company stock									
20–29	26	23	28	37	36	34	17	12	28
30–39	40	30	32	37	38	37	37	30	35
40–49	44	31	33	39	41	41	39	39	37
50–59	41	30	32	39	46	48	44	42	39
60–65	39	28	30	37	39	35	31	28	33
All ages	38	28	31	38	41	41	39	38	35
Percentage of contributions in other equities									
20–29	39	32	34	36	43	48	71	72	35
30–39	35	32	31	33	38	41	45	55	35
40–49	31	29	29	30	33	36	41	45	32
50–59	29	25	24	25	27	28	36	39	27
60–65	29	24	22	22	22	34	40	46	27
All ages	33	30	30	31	34	36	41	45	32
Percentage of contributions in fixed-income assets									
20–29	35	45	38	27	21	18	12	16	37
30–39	25	38	37	30	24	22	18	15	31
40–49	25	40	38	31	26	22	21	16	31
50–59	30	45	44	36	27	24	20	19	34
60–65	32	48	48	41	39	31	29	26	41
All ages	29	42	39	31	25	23	20	17	33

Source: Authors' calculations. Allocations are calculated only for employees making a contribution in 1995. Plan information is from a file containing data on 29 401(k) plans that did provide the option of investing in company stock.

TABLE 7: Allocation of 401(k) Contributions and Balances by Earnings (%)

	Annual Earnings ($000)								
	10.0–14.9	15.0–24.9	25.0–34.9	35.0–44.9	45.0–59.9	60.0–74.9	75.0–99.9	100+	All Earnings
Employer plans without company stock as an investment option									
Contributions in equities									
	45	48	50	57	60	62	64	70	54
Balances in equities									
	47	48	50	57	60	63	65	71	53
Contributions in fixed-income assets									
	55	52	50	43	40	38	36	30	46
Balances in fixed-income assets									
	53	52	50	43	40	37	35	29	46
Employer plans with company stock as an investment option									
Contributions in company stock									
	38	28	31	38	41	41	39	38	35
Balances in company stock									
	41	30	35	43	45	44	42	38	38
Contributions in other equities									
	33	30	30	31	34	36	41	45	32
Balances in other equities									
	33	30	30	30	32	34	38	43	32
Contributions in fixed-income assets									
	29	42	39	31	25	23	20	17	33
Balances in fixed-income assets									
	27	40	35	27	24	22	20	19	30

Source: See Table 1.

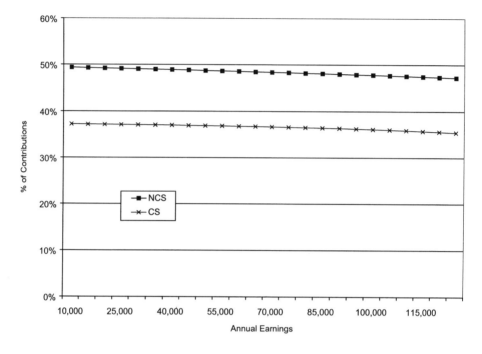

Figure 4. Allocation of 401(k) contributions to fixed-income assets by men by earnings, for plans with and without company stock investment options (%). Values are based on the Tobit estimates in columns 2 and 3, Appendix Table 3. Values are for employees age 40 with 10 years of tenure. Intercepts should not be interpreted as representing an average difference between plans with and without company stock. CS/NCS refer to plans that respectively do or do not offer company stock as an investment option.

match, participant contributions to fixed-income assets were reduced by 25 percent. In this latter case, it was clear that forcing employees to take company stock to qualify for a match caused participants to substitute out of fixed-income assets.

Examining only plans that include company stock as an investment option, we estimated the allocation of participant contributions to company stock and other equities. The relationship between earnings level and investment in both company stock and other equities was positive, although somewhat less so in the case of company stock. Estimates indicated that plan requirements that a portion of 401(k) contributions be invested in company stock were successful in getting participants to invest funds in that fashion. Our analysis indicated that the more restrictive the constraint, the more effective it was in increasing the allocation to company stock. In the case of

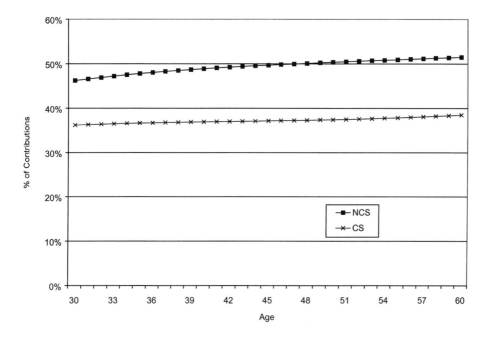

Figure 5. Allocation of 401(k) contributions to fixed-income assets by men by age, for plans with and without company stock investment (%). Values are based on the Tobit estimates in columns 2 and 3, Appendix Table 3. Values are for employees hired at age 30 with annual earnings of $40,000. Intercepts should not be interpreted as representing an average difference between plans with and without company stock. CS/NCS refer to plans that respectively do or do not offer company stock as an investment option.

the other equities equation, it was clear that company stock constraints pushed people out of other equity holdings.

Sex Differences in 401 (k) Decisions

One area that is of particular interest to analysts of defined contribution plans is the relative behavior of men and women. For example, several studies based on a small number of pension plans have reported that women demonstrate greater risk aversion in allocating assets within their self-directed defined contribution plans than men (Bajtelsmit and VanDerhei 1997; Hinz, McCarthy, and Turner 1997), and that women are even less likely than men to allocate wealth into defined contribution plans (Jianakopolos, Bernasek, and Bajtelsmit 1998). To shed some light on the relative participation and investment behavior of men and women, we created a subfile of workers that includes the sex of each employee.[9] Out of the original 156,376 workers used in the analysis, the sex was determined for 142,543. Of these, 46 percent were classified as female. The women were disproportionately represented in the earnings categories below $35,000 per year, as were women in their 20s.

Our earlier analysis as well as research by others indicated that women behave differently from men in deciding to participate in 401(k) plans, in the amount they contribute, and in the allocation of their pension funds. Using our newly developed data file, we were able to examine the 401(k) choices of men and women in much more detail than previous studies had done. Our findings indicated that women were not more reluctant 401(k) participants, and they did not seem to be more risk averse in investing their self-directed defined contribution assets.

Sex Differences in 401(k) Participation

A summary of participation rates by sex, age, and earnings categories is presented in Table 8. In general, women were slightly more likely to participate (80 percent) in their companies' 401(k) plans than men (78 percent). A greater proportion of women participated in the plan in every age and income category for workers with less than $60,000 per year. Of the 40 age/earnings categories shown in Table 8, the male participation rate exceeded the female rate in only eight categories, with four of these being for workers with annual earnings in excess of $100,000 (shown in boldface).

One reason that women generally participated in 401(k) plans more frequently than men may relate to differences in household income. Our administrative data did not include information on marital status of workers, total household income, or the working status of spouses. But in an analysis not reported in detail here we examined the March 1996 Current Population Survey and found that working women were likely to be in families with higher overall family income levels than working men with equivalent annual earnings.[10]

The difference in family income level between men and women at comparable earnings levels means that some of the differential in how women behave in 401(k) plans compared to men may be a factor of variables we cannot measure here. If the decisions about participating, contributing, or investing in a 401(k) plan were made on the basis of total resources available to workers, viewing these factors on the basis of earnings alone might be misleading. For example, comparing working men and women at earnings levels between $25,000 and $35,000, the women's mean family income tended to be about $15,000 higher than for men. If 401(k) usage is based on family income instead of individual worker's earnings level, it suggests that we should be comparing a woman with annual earnings of $25,000 in 1995 with a man earning closer to $40,000 rather than one earning $25,000. Since we do not know other family resources for workers in this analysis, we decided

TABLE 8: Participation Rates by Sex, Age, and Earnings (%)

Age group	Annual Earnings ($000)								
	10.0–14.9	15.0–24.9	25.0–34.9	35.0–44.9	45.0–59.9	60.0–74.9	75.0–99.9	100+	All Earnings
Women									
20–29	47.8	65.2	77.9	87.5	90.9	90.0	86.7	100.0	68.7
30–39	63.8	74.7	82.0	88.4	91.7	94.3	93.3	78.9	80.1
40–49	68.0	79.5	83.5	88.1	91.9	94.9	94.0	82.0	82.4
50–59	78.0	84.6	87.8	92.8	93.8	97.6	97.7	87.8	86.5
60–65	79.8	87.7	88.9	93.3	92.2	91.7	100.0	78.6	87.6
All ages	64.3	76.0	82.7	89.0	92.0	94.8	94.1	81.8	79.9
Men									
20–29	34.1	56.1	64.6	76.4	85.3	**92.4**	**93.6**	84.6	63.8
30–39	49.3	65.9	72.1	77.8	86.2	90.7	**93.8**	**91.4**	77.7
40–49	53.4	67.1	73.4	78.2	84.5	89.3	91.5	**90.1**	80.2
50–59	62.1	73.8	75.8	81.1	86.0	92.2	94.6	**92.5**	83.4
60–65	69.2	70.2	71.3	82.0	89.9	**97.0**	92.2	**93.3**	82.3
All ages	48.8	64.6	71.4	78.3	85.6	90.7	92.9	91.2	77.7

Source: See Table 1.
Note: Entries for men in boldface show age and earnings cells where men's participation rate is greater than women's.

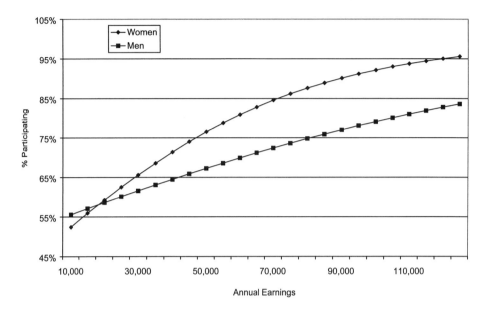

Figure 6. 401(k) participation rates by sex and earnings (%). Values are based on the logit estimates in column 2, Appendix Table 5. Values are for employees of the largest plan sponsor, age 40, with 10 years tenure.

that it would be most appropriate to estimate probability models of participation, contributions, and account management separately for men and women.

Sex differences in the decision to participate in a 401(k) plan were examined by estimating separately the participation equation for men and women (results are shown in Appendix Table 5). The estimates indicate that age, tenure, and annual earnings were all important determinants of participation for both men and women and that each of these effects was nonlinear. Figure 6 shows the estimated effect of earnings by sex on 401(k) participation for hypothetical male and female workers age 40 with 10 years of earnings. A somewhat surprising finding is that the probability of participating in a 401(k) plan was higher for women than for men, for annual earnings in excess of $15,000. Furthermore, this difference widened at higher levels of annual earnings. Women with earnings over $75,000 had a probability of participating in the plan over 12 percentage points higher than for men.

Patterns of participation also differed by sex and age (Figure 7). For workers with earnings of $40,000 per year, the predicted probability of making a 1995 contribution to the 401(k) plan increased with age and tenure for both men and women until the early 50s and then declined slightly.

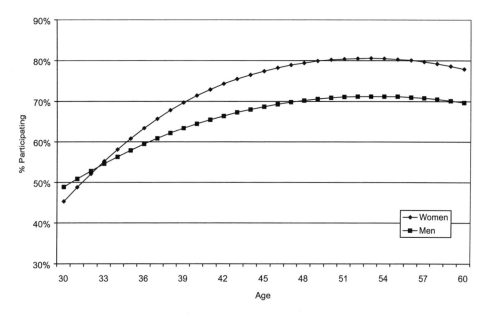

Figure 7. 401 (k) participation rates by sex and age (%). Values are based on the logit estimates in column 2, Appendix Table 5. Values are for employees of the largest plan sponsor, hired at age 30, with annual earnings of $40,000.

Among young workers, men were more likely to participate in their plans; however, for persons over age 33, women had a higher probability of participation. The sex gap in participation reached 10 percentage points by age 50.

Sex Differences in 401 (k) Contribution Rates

Another surprising result is that women contributed a higher proportion of earnings to 401 (k) plans than did men with similar earnings. Average contribution rates by age, sex, and earnings are shown in Table 9. These data reveal an interesting pattern of age/earnings differences in contribution rates by sex. The bold entries in the second half of the table indicate that the contribution rate for that age/earnings level was greater for men than for women. Men at low earnings levels contributed a higher proportion of their earnings than did women at similar earnings levels at all ages. Some of these age/earnings differences in contribution rates were in excess of two percentage points of earnings. For workers with earnings in excess of $25,000, men age 20 to 29 continued to contribute at higher levels than women; however, for older workers, women contributed a greater proportion of their annual pay.

Multivariate model of contribution rates was estimated separately for men

TABLE 9: 401(k) Contribution Rates by Sex, Age, and Earnings (% of Annual Earnings)

Age group	Annual Earnings ($000)								All Earnings
	10.0–14.9	15.0–24.9	25.0–34.9	35.0–44.9	45.0–59.9	60.0–74.9	75.0–99.9	100+	
Women									
20–29	4.2	4.2	4.5	5.6	6.8	6.0	5.3	2.9	4.5
30–39	6.0	6.1	6.1	6.6	7.6	7.5	6.9	5.3	6.4
40–49	6.8	7.0	6.8	7.4	8.1	8.2	8.1	5.9	7.1
50–59	7.7	8.9	8.3	9.2	9.0	9.5	7.8	6.8	8.6
60–65	8.9	10.6	9.0	10.4	8.8	10.1	10.7	4.8	9.8
All ages	6.5	6.7	6.4	7.3	8.0	8.0	7.5	5.7	6.8
Men									
20–29	**4.7**	**5.1**	**5.4**	**6.3**	**7.0**	**7.3**	**5.4**	**4.8**	**5.7**
30–39	**7.7**	**6.9**	6.1	6.4	7.1	7.4	**7.2**	**5.4**	**6.7**
40–49	**10.3**	**8.3**	6.4	6.5	7.0	7.4	7.2	5.8	6.9
50–59	**10.8**	**9.8**	7.7	7.5	8.1	8.3	7.6	6.0	7.9
60–65	**11.6**	10.2	9.0	8.4	9.1	8.7	7.6	**5.7**	8.7
All ages	**8.6**	**7.3**	6.3	6.6	7.3	7.6	7.3	**5.8**	6.9

Source: See Table 1.
Note: Entries for men in boldface show age and earnings cells where men's average contribution rate is greater than women's.

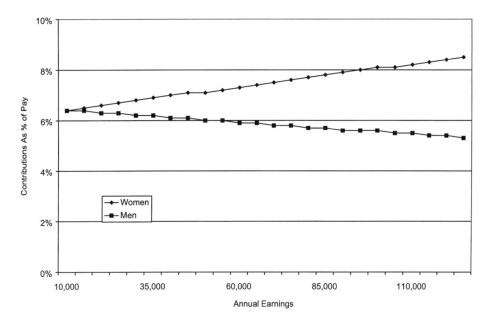

Figure 8. 401 (k) contribution rates by sex and earnings (%). Values are based on the OLS estimates in columns 2 and 4, Appendix Table 6. Values are for employees of the largest plan sponsor, age 40, with 10 years tenure.

and women (Appendix Table 6), and the results are used to examine how age and earnings affect differences in sex-specific contribution rates. Figure 8 shows that for workers age 40 with 10 years of tenure, the contribution rate for women was greater than that for men for all but the lowest income workers, and the difference widened as earnings increased. The estimated effects indicated that with the exception of workers under age 33, working women of all ages contributed a higher proportion of annual earnings to their 401 (k) plan. Together with the findings concerning participation, these effects indicated that women workers offered 401 (k) plans were at least as active participants as men, controlling for differences in age, tenure, earnings, and plan features. We next examined whether men and women behaved differently in the investment of their 401 (k) contributions and account balances.

Sex Differences in 401 (k) Accumulations

An analysis of account balances by sex showed that men had larger account balances than women. In our sample, men had balances of $24,880, or over twice the size of the average female balance of $11,360. However, this obser-

TABLE 10: Average Account Balances by Sex, Age, and Earnings

	Annual Earnings ($000)							
Age group	10.0–14.9	15.0–24.9	25.0–34.9	35.0–44.9	45.0–59.9	60.0–74.9	75.0–99.9	100+	All Earnings
Women									
20–29	1,246	2,025	3,259	6,377	9,012	13,893	10,087	8,153	3,074
30–39	2,608	4,122	7,038	11,832	18,002	25,736	30,527	36,294	9,146
40–49	3,893	5,890	10,041	17,910	27,521	40,444	48,644	58,644	13,786
50–59	4,937	9,219	16,336	28,287	39,795	53,001	62,161	99,353	17,377
60–65	6,374	12,564	21,289	34,374	53,487	64,274	78,379	72,657	19,853
All ages	3,430	5,493	9,173	16,301	24,672	35,422	42,473	53,983	11,360
Men									
20–29	**1,351**	**2,334**	**4,150**	**6,996**	**11,420**	**14,286**	**13,966**	19,787	**5,201**
30–39	**3,426**	**4,511**	6,981	11,249	17,787	**27,158**	**34,797**	45,575	**15,100**
40–49	**7,345**	**7,317**	9,628	15,989	25,038	39,495	52,574	74,426	**28,426**
50–59	**13,164**	**11,306**	15,060	25,193	38,261	**56,531**	71,672	117,724	**44,637**
60–65	**14,604**	**19,641**	20,883	30,227	46,250	63,429	**82,559**	152,961	**52,520**
All ages	**6,622**	**6,224**	8,640	14,689	24,639	**39,491**	53,326	84,638	24,880

Source: See Table 1.
Note: Entries for men in boldface show age and earnings cells where men's average account balance is greater than women's.

vation did not hold for all ages and earnings levels (see Table 10). Men's balances were consistently larger than women's for workers in their 20s and at the bottom and top of the earnings distributions. In the middle of the earnings distribution, however, women had larger accumulated account balances, and in some cases these differences were fairly large. One explanation for men having larger account balances despite being less likely to participate in the plan and having lower contribution rates may be that older men had longer job tenure than similar aged women. The general observation that men tended to have higher earnings than women will also tend to produce higher 401(k) account balances.

Sex Differences in 401(k) Investments

Each of the 401(k) plans in our sample required participants to make investment decisions. These choices were classified into fixed-income assets and equities, and, as noted above, some plans also required that workers to devote a portion of their holdings to the purchase of company stock. Table 11 illustrates several key findings. First, women devoted less of their contributions to the purchase of company stock than did men, and they held a lower percentage of their total account balances in company stock than did men (29 percent compared to 45 percent). Women were also more likely to hold fixed-income assets than men (40 percent compared to just over 25 percent). This pattern of investment of 401(k) accounts persisted for all age groups.

Examining the account balances for men and women in the 58 plans that did not have a company stock investment choice reveals a dramatically different picture (see Table 12). With the exception of young men at the low and high tails of the earnings distribution, women generally held a higher proportion of their 401(k) assets in equities in plans not offering company stock. These results suggested that previous findings that women tended to devote a higher percentage of their retirement savings to low-risk/low-return assets were wrong.

To further examine this issue, we estimated sex-specific equations for the allocation of 1995 contributions and account balances separately for plans with and without company stock investment options. In the first set of estimates we looked at differences in the investment in fixed-income assets (Appendix Tables 7 and 8). The results showed that, controlling for age and tenure, there was a slightly negative relationship between earnings level and share of 401(k) assets held in fixed-income assets in plans that did not have a company stock option (Figure 9). This relationship was slightly more pronounced for women than men, but still relatively moderate. The relationship between earnings level and fixed-income asset holding was much more pronounced in cases where the plan includes company stock as an investment option. In these plans, women were estimated to hold considerably

TABLE 11: Allocation of 401(k) Contributions and Balances By Sex and Earnings: Plans with Company Stock as an Investment Option (%)

	Annual Earnings ($000)								
Sex	10.0–14.9	15.0–24.9	25.0–34.9	35.0–44.9	45.0–59.9	60.0–74.9	75.0–99.9	100+	All Earnings
Employee contributions in company stock									
Women	25	25	26	30	32	29	28	27	27
Men	60	35	37	42	43	43	41	39	41
Employee contributions in other equities									
Women	38	30	32	37	40	45	47	51	34
Men	25	31	28	28	33	35	40	45	32
Employee contributions in fixed-income assets									
Women	36	45	42	32	27	26	25	22	39
Men	15	33	35	30	25	22	19	16	27
Employee-financed 401(k) balances in company stock									
Women	26	26	28	34	36	30	31	27	29
Men	65	37	42	48	47	47	44	40	45
Employee-financed 401(k) balances in other equities									
Women	39	30	31	35	37	44	44	49	33
Men	24	33	29	28	30	33	37	42	31
Employee-financed 401(k) balances in fixed-income assets									
Women	36	44	41	31	27	26	25	24	38
Men	12	30	29	25	22	21	19	18	24

Source: See Table 6.

TABLE 12: 401(k) Account Balances Held in Equities by Sex, Age, and Earnings: Plans without Company Stock as an Investment Option (%)

Age group	Annual Earnings ($000)								
	10.0–14.9	15.0–24.9	25.0–34.9	35.0–44.9	45.0–59.9	60.0–74.9	75.0–99.9	100+	All Earnings
Women									
20–29	55	57	60	67	67	75	72	30	58
30–39	48	52	56	63	66	67	74	77	55
40–49	49	51	51	60	59	60	68	70	52
50–59	42	46	48	56	58	61	60	69	46
60–65	40	37	43	48	61	49	50	87	39
All ages	47	51	53	61	62	63	69	72	52
Men									
20–29	**58**	46	57	64	**70**	72	**83**	**84**	57
30–39	**50**	45	51	59	63	**68**	72	**78**	59
40–49	47	39	39	53	57	60	63	**71**	54
50–59	39	31	32	44	49	54	57	64	46
60–65	32	23	28	41	40	**56**	50	61	40
All ages	**48**	40	46	55	59	62	64	71	54

Source: See Table 5.
Note: Entries for men in boldface type show age and earnings cells where men's average allocation of account balances to equities is greater than women's.

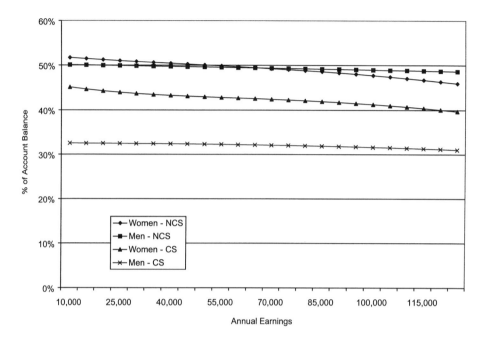

Figure 9. Allocation of 401(k) contributions to fixed-income assets by sex and whether the plan offers company stock as an investment option (% of total account balances). Values are based on the Tobit estimates in columns 2 and 4, Appendix Tables 7 and 8. Values are for employees age 40, with 10 years tenure. Intercepts should not be interpreted as representing an average difference between plans with and without company stock. CS/NCS refers to plans that respectively do or do not offer company stock as an investment option.

more fixed-income assets than men and their holding of these assets was more sensitive to earnings level than men's.

The estimated effects suggested that a requirement that the employee's contributions be to company stock in order to qualify for a company match had a roughly equivalent effect on men and women in reducing their overall holding of fixed-income assets. When the employer match was in the form of company stock, but was not conditioned on the employee investing in this form, both men and women were predicted to hold more fixed-income assets at the mean. The estimated effect on men, however, was nearly 4.5 times as strong as for women.

Examining the effect of age on investment choices, we found that where there was no company stock investment in the plan men and women tended to invest in fixed-income assets in a very similar pattern at each age-tenure combination, with there being an overall positive relationship between investing in this form and age. When company stock was part of the invest-

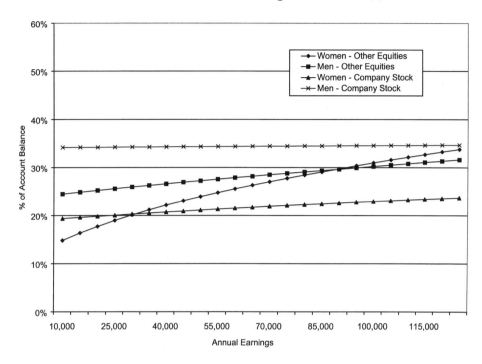

Figure 10. Allocation 401(k) contributions to company stock and other equity investments by sex and earnings, plans with company stock as an investment option (% of total account balances). Values are based on the Tobit estimates in columns 2 and 4, Appendix Tables 9 and 10. Values are for employees age 40, with 10 years tenure. Intercepts should not be interpreted as representing an average difference between plans with and without company stock.

ment portfolio, however, there was clearly some substitution of other assets for fixed-income holdings and the substitution was clearly much stronger for men than for women.

Estimates for equity and company stock holdings are reported in Appendix Tables 9 and 10. For plans with company stock investment, the relationship between earnings and investment behavior of men and women is interesting (Figure 10). The earnings effect on company stock investment for men was negligible — they were estimated to hold a relatively constant percentage of total assets in this form no matter what their earnings. Among women, however, higher earners were willing to take on the greater risk of company stock as compared to their counterparts further down the earnings spectrum. The relationship between earnings and holding of other equities was positive for both men and women, although it was slightly more so for women than men. The combination of these findings suggested that overall, women were somewhat more sensitive to investment risk across the earnings spectrum than men, and that the inclusion of company stock in the 401(k) portfolio increased that sensitivity.

Conclusion

This research confirms and extends previous research regarding American workers' use of 401(k) pension plans as retirement savings vehicles. We find that 401(k) plan participation is more age sensitive at lower earnings levels than higher. Participation among workers earning $10,000–$15,000 per year rises from 44 percent for those 20–29 to over 70 percent for those age 50 and older. In comparison, over 90 percent of all workers earning in excess of $60,000 participate in 401(k) plans regardless of age. We have shown that given participation, age is more important in determining contribution rates than earnings. Among those making a 401(k) contribution in 1995, the contribution rates of persons age 50 and older was over fifty percent higher than that of workers 20–29 (over 8 percent of earnings compared to 5 percent).

These patterns are consistent with earlier studies, as are our results that older people tend to invest more conservatively than younger ones, and that people with lower earnings invest more conservatively than more highly paid workers. One finding that has not received prior study is that the allocation of workers' current contributions to 401(k) plans is remarkably similar to the allocation of total assets in plans when controlling their age, earnings levels, and sex. Our analysis also showed that the inclusion of company stock as an investment option in the plans did influence how people invested their 401(k) assets and that it had a differential effect on the patterns of investment of men and women. Women with relatively low earnings who participated in plans with company stock requirements tended to allocate about 10 percent less of their account balances to fixed-income assets, while higher-earning women in plans with company stock requirements devoted over 20 percent less to fixed-income assets. In contrast, men with low earnings held over 25 percent less in fixed-income assets while men with higher earnings devoted almost 25 percent less to fixed-income assets.

One area we explored in detail pertains to differences between men and women in their utilization of 401(k) plans. We find that women behaved differently from men in these plans and the differences were not just a matter of degree. Specifically, women's participation rates increased more steeply with increases in annual earnings, and with age and tenure, than did men's. Women's contribution rates rose significantly with earnings, while men's declined slightly. Furthermore, women's contributions rose more steeply with age than did men's. Overall, we found that men had more money in their plans than did women, but these sex differences may be attributable to differences in their earnings, contribution rates, and job tenure. We also found that women generally are not more conservative in their investment behavior than men after controlling for earnings, age, and other important determinants of investment behavior. In general, we believe our results suggest that women are as effective in their use of 401(k) plans as their male counterparts. Beyond the youngest ages and lowest earnings levels they participate and contribute at rates equal to or exceeding those of men.

These findings have important implications for understanding national retirement policy in the twenty-first century, and they provide new insights into how workers make voluntary retirement savings decisions. Key insights include:

1. When offered the option of participating in a voluntary 401(k) plan, most workers choose to make annual contributions.
2. The probability that workers make an annual contribution and the amount of the contribution increase with age and earnings.
3. Women are equally (or more) likely than men to contribute to 401(k) plans.
4. Participants tend to have balanced portfolios, with about half of contributions and account balances being devoted to equities and half to fixed-income assets.
5. The proportion of balances and contributions allocated to equities increases with annual earnings and declines with age.
6. In plans without company stock requirements, women hold as much or more of their 401(k) balances in equities than men. When company stock requirements are imposed, men tend to hold a larger portion of their assets in company stock.

These findings suggest that most workers will be able to adjust to the ongoing changes in private pensions—the continuing shift toward voluntary defined contribution plans—by regularly contributing to their new pension plans. Our analysis also indicates that further education of young workers and those with low earnings is needed to insure that they begin saving early enough and contribute sufficient funds to provide for an adequate retirement income. Finally, these findings may provide some indication of how workers would behave under a revised social security system that included individual accounts. Our analysis indicates that most workers maintain diversified accounts and tend to move toward portfolios with less risk at older ages. This should dispel some of the concerns associated with individual accounts as a primary component of future national retirement policy.

Notes

1. To predict individual employee sex, we used a name recognition algorithm described below.

2. There has been some debate over the incidence of federal pension tax expenditures. For different views of the incidence of the tax expenditures for employer pensions, see Munnell (1991), Goodfellow and Schieber (1993), and Clark and Wolper (1997).

3. This observation has important implications for understanding the role of pensions in providing retirement income. Specifically, it is probable that more people will accumulate retirement benefits than is indicated by cross-sectional participation rates. This higher career coverage rate by pensions implies that more workers receive the advantage of pension tax expenditures than that implied by the cross-sectional data. In particular, young, low-wage workers are likely to obtain pension coverage later in their careers.

4. The probability of workers making a contribution to the their 401(k) plan in 1995 is estimated using a logit procedure. Results from the logit estimation of the probability of participation appear in the first two columns of Appendix Table 1.

5. The statistical model estimates individual intercepts for the probability of participation for each plan; however, the response to the other explanatory variables is not a function of the plan which covers the worker. The largest plan sponsor in our sample had a relatively low percentage of its employees participating in the 401(k) plan. As a result, the participation probabilities shown in Figures 1 and 2 are lower than are estimated for most of the plans in the sample.

6. This variable was derived based on the benefit formula of the defined benefit pension plan, projected growth in annual earnings, and the assumption that the worker remains with the company until age 65. The company dummy variables were not included in this equation, since these two variables were expected to capture much of the variation in participation across the individual companies. These results are shown in the last two columns of Appendix Table 1.

7. Contribution rates were estimated using ordinary least squares.

8. While 1995 participation in the plan was not a criterion for being included in Table 4, the other screening criteria were still applied. That is, we still only included workers earning $10,000 per year or more, those with one year of service or more, and so forth.

9. Determination of the sex of employees was not straightforward because the administrative records do not include a specific designation of the sex of the worker. We had access to administrative employment records of another firm with similar data on approximately 16,000 employees that included the individual plan participants' first names and an indicator of their sex. We sorted this file by first names and tabulated the sex distributions with each name. We used the results of this exercise to assign a sex classification to each individual in our sample. Any name where more than 80 percent of the individuals with that name were of one sex was classified as being a sex-specific name. All individuals with that name were assigned that sex. For example, people with the name Ann were virtually always identified as females in our source file. Thus, anyone in our sample with the name Ann was classified as a female. In cases where a name did not include at least 80 percent persons of one sex, we characterized that name as having an indeterminate sexual classification. For example, names like Brett or Chris that are often associated with either men or women did not meet our identification criterion. All individuals classified as being of indeterminate sex on the analysis file were then visually reviewed for possible reclassification. Where it was relatively clear to us that the name was associated with a man or woman, it was reclassified accordingly.

10. Other than at the lowest earnings level, working men were consistently more likely to be married than working women, but they were far more likely to be married to a spouse who did not work outside the home for pay. Indeed, for working men

earning more than $25,000 per year, the probability of having a wife who did not work for pay increased with the husband's earnings. Almost 80 percent of married women who work earn less than their husbands (Winkler 1998). This means that if you compare a man and a woman at the same earnings level, each of whom has a working spouse, it is likely that the woman will be in a household with higher total earnings than the man. The man is likely to have a wife earning less than he is and the woman is likely to have a husband earning more than she is. The lower probability of having a man having working spouse accentuates the likelihood that men at a given earnings level will end up in households with lower total income than women with similar earnings levels. Controlling for earnings level, working women consistently have higher average family incomes than their male counterparts at any given earnings level.

References

Bajtelsmit, Vickie A. and Jack A. VanDerhei. 1997. "Risk Aversion and Pension Investment Choices." In Michael S. Gordon, Olivia S. Mitchell, and Marc M. Twinney, eds., *Positioning Pensions for the Twenty-First Century*. Pension Research Council. Philadelphia: University of Pennsylvania Press: 45–66.

Clark, Robert L. and Sylvester J. Schieber. 1998. "Factors Affecting Participation Rates and Contribution Levels in 401(k) Plans." In Olivia S. Mitchell and Sylvester J. Schieber, eds., *Living with Defined Contribution Pensions: Remaking Responsibility for Retirement*. Pension Research Council. Philadelphia: University of Pennsylvania Press: 69–97.

Clark, Robert L. and Elisa Wolper. 1997. "Pension Tax Expenditures: Magnitude, Distribution, and Economic Effects." In Sylvester J. Schieber and John B. Shoven, eds., *Public Policy Toward Pensions*. Cambridge, Mass.: MIT Press: 41–84.

Goodfellow, Gordon and Sylvester J. Schieber. 1993. "The Role of Tax Expenditures in the Provision of Retirement Income Security." In Richard V. Burkhauser and Dallas L. Salisbury, eds., *Pensions in a Changing Economy*. Washington, D.C.: EBRI: 79–94.

Hinz, Richard P., David D. McCarthy, and John A. Turner. 1997. "Are Women Conservative Investors? Gender Differences in Participant-Directed Pension Investments." In Michael S. Gordon, Olivia S. Mitchell, and Marc M. Twinney, eds., *Positioning Pensions for the Twenty-First Century*. Pension Research Council. Philadelphia: University of Pennsylvania Press: 91–106.

Ippolito, Richard A. 1997. *Pension Plans and Employee Performance*. Chicago: University of Chicago Press.

Jianakopolos, Nancy A., Alexandra Bernasek, and Vickie L. Bajtelsmit. 1998. "Women, Risk Taking, and Pension Decisions." Paper presented at the Annual Meetings of the American Economic Association, January 3. Chicago.

Munnell, Alicia. 1991. "Are Pensions Worth the Cost?" *National Tax Journal* 44: 393–403.

Shoven, John B. 1995. *Return on Investment: Pensions Are How America Saves*, Washington, D.C.: Association of Private Pension and Welfare Plans, September.

U.S. Department of Labor, Pension and Welfare Benefits Administration. Winter 1997. *Private Pension Bulletin, Abstract of 1993 Form 5500 Annual Reports*. Washington, D.C. U.S. Government Printing Office.

Winkler, Anne. 1998. "Earnings of Husbands and Wives in Dual-Earner Families." *Monthly Labor Review* 12, 4 (April): 42–48.

APPENDIX TABLE 1: Logit Estimates of Participation Rates in 401(k) Plans

Variable	Marginal Effect	Standard Error	Marginal Effect	Standard Error
INTERCEPT	−0.47	0.11	−0.234	0.10
AGE	0.51	0.01	0.01	0.01
AGE SQUARED	−0.19	0.01	−0.01	0.01
TENURE	0.20	0.003	0.01	0.003
TENURE SQUARED	−0.07	0.00	−0.00	0.00
EARNINGS	0.15	0.004	0.03	0.004
EARNINGS SQUARED	−0.004	0.001	−0.01	0.001
FEMALE[a]	0.02	0.02	0.07	0.01
SEX UNKNOWN[a]	−0.001	0.02	0.02	0.02
COMPANY DUMMIES[b]	Yes		No	
MATCH RATE			0.03	0.02
REPLACEMENT RATE AT AGE 65			−0.04	0.04
Likelihood ratio chi-square	19,1976.32		8,346.79	
N	156,009		152,914	
Percent correctly predicted	74.5		67.3	
McFadden's pseudo R-square	0.123		0.052	

Source: Authors' estimates of the probability of employees' participation in the 401(k) plan using a Logit procedure.

[a] Equations include dichotomous variables indicating sex, if known, or whether this information is missing.

[b] Estimates shown in column 2 include the effect of dichotomous variables indicating the specific 401(k) plan covering each employee. These variables are not included in the estimates of marginal effects shown in column 4.

APPENDIX TABLE 2: OLS Estimates of Percentage of Earnings Contributed to Plan by Participants

Variable	Marginal Effect	Standard Error	Marginal Effect	Standard Error
INTERCEPT	0.06	.003	0.05	.003
AGE	−0.001	.00	0.00	.00
AGE SQUARED	0.002	.00	0.001	.00
TENURE	0.001	.00	0.001	.00
TENURE SQUARED	−0.003	.00	−0.01	.00
EARNINGS	−0.001	.00	−0.001	.00
EARNINGS SQUARED	0.00	.00	0.00	.00
FEMALE[a]	−0.003	.00	−0.003	.00
SEX UNKNOWN[a]	0.001	.001	−0.00	.001
COMPANY DUMMIES[b]	Yes		No	
MATCH RATE			−0.03	.001
REPLACEMENT RATE AT AGE 65			0.02	.001
N	122,511		120,010	
R-squared	0.37		0.05	
Rbar-squared	0.37		0.05	
F	758.41		598.80	
Std. error of estimate	0.06		0.07	

Source: Authors' estimates of contribution rates for employees making a contribution to their 401(k) plan using ordinary least squares.

[a] Equations include dichotomous variables indicating sex, if known, or whether this information is missing.

[b] Estimates shown in column 2 include effect of dichotomous variables indicating the specific 401(k) plan covering each employee. These variables are not included in the estimates shown in column 4.

APPENDIX TABLE 3: Tobit Estimates of Percentage of Participants' Contributions Directed to Investments in Fixed Assets

Variable	Plans with no company stock		Plans with company stock	
	Marginal Effect	Standard Error	Marginal Effect	Standard Error
INTERCEPT[a]	0.60	0.04	0.80	0.04
EMPLOYER MATCH IN COMPANY STOCK			−0.24	0.01
CO STOCK INVESTMENT REQUIRED FOR MATCH			−1.09	0.002
AGE	−0.17	0.02	−0.02	0.002
AGE SQUARED	0.02	0.002	0.03	0.002
TENURE	0.02	0.001	0.02	0.001
TENURE SQUARED	−0.04	0.003	−0.03	0.003
EARNINGS	−0.01	0.001	−0.03	0.001
EARNINGS SQUARED	0.003	0.00	0.01	0.00
FEMALE[b]	0.09	0.01	0.08	0.01
SEX UNKNOWN[b]	0.06	0.01	0.06	0.01
COMPANY DUMMIES[c]	Yes		Yes	
Uncensored	33,959		33,883	
Right censored	11,491		7,418	
Left censored	11,313		24,447	
N	56,763		65,748	

Source: Authors' estimates of the allocation of contributions to fixed-income assets using a Tobit procedure.

[a] The intercept in column 4 is an average of three 401(k) plans with omitted dummy variables.
[b] Equations include dichotomous variables indicating sex, if known, or whether this information is missing.
[c] Estimates shown in columns 2 and 4 include the effect of dichotomous variables indicating the specific 401(k) plan covering each employee.

APPENDIX TABLE 4: Tobit Estimates of Percentage of Participants' Contributions Directed to Investment in Company Stock and Other Equities by Participants in Plans with Company Stock

Variable	Company stock		Other equities	
	Marginal Effect	Standard Error	Marginal Effect	Standard Error
INTERCEPT[a]	−0.29	0.03	0.20	0.04
EMPLOYER MATCH IN COMPANY STOCK	.58	0.01	−0.39	0.01
CO STOCK INVESTMENT REQUIRED FOR MATCH	1.22	0.01	−0.58	0.01
AGE	0.02	0.002	0.01	0.002
AGE SQUARED	−0.02	0.002	−0.01	0.002
TENURE	−0.05	0.001	−0.02	0.001
TENURE SQUARED	0.01	0.002	0.03	0.003
EARNINGS	0.002	0.001	0.03	0.001
EARNINGS SQUARED	−0.00	0.00	−0.03	0.001
FEMALE[b]	−0.03	0.004	−0.02	0.005
SEX UNKNOWN[b]	−0.02	0.007	−0.04	0.008
COMPANY DUMMIES[c]	Yes		Yes	
Uncensored	33,681		39,176	
Right censored	9,810		349	
Left censored	22,257		26,223	
N	65,748		65,748	

Source: Authors' estimates of the allocation of contributions to company stock and other equities using a Tobit procedure.
[a] The intercepts are an average of three 401(k) plans with omitted dummy variables.
[b] Equation include dichotomous variables indicating sex, if known, or whether this information is missing.
[c] Estimates shown in columns 2 and 4 include the effect of dichotomous variables indicating the specific 401(k) plan covering each employee.

APPENDIX TABLE 5: Logit Estimates of 401(k) Plan Participation Rates for Men and Women

	Men		Women	
Variable	Marginal Effect	Standard Error	Marginal Effect	Standard Error
INTERCEPT	−0.39	0.16	−0.57	0.17
AGE	0.01	0.01	0.01	0.01
AGE SQUARED	−0.01	0.01	−0.01	0.01
TENURE	0.01	0.004	0.03	0.01
TENURE SQUARED	−0.00	0.00	−0.001	0.00
EARNINGS	0.03	0.01	0.07	0.01
EARNINGS SQUARED	−0.01	0.002	−0.04	0.01
COMPANY DUMMIES[a]	Yes		Yes	
Likelihood ratio chi-square		10,458.58		8,119.95
N		77,010		65,208
Percent correctly predicted		74.8		74.9
McFadden's pseudo R-square		0.13		0.12

Source: Authors' estimates of the probability by sex of employees' participation in the 401(k) plan using a Logit procedure.
[a] Estimates shown in columns 2 and 4 include the effect of dichotomous variables indicating the specific 401(k) plan covering each employee.

APPENDIX TABLE 6: OLS Estimates of Percentage of Earnings Contributed to Plan by Participants for Men and Women Separately

	Men		Women	
Variable	Marginal Effect	Standard Error	Marginal Effect	Standard Error
INTERCEPT	0.06	0.004	0.06	0.01
AGE	−0.001	0.00	−0.001	0.00
AGE SQUARED	0.002	0.00	0.003	0.00
TENURE	0.001	0.00	0.002	0.00
TENURE SQUARED	−0.002	0.00	−0.01	0.00
EARNINGS	−0.001	0.00	0.002	0.00
EARNINGS SQUARED	0.00	0.00	−0.001	0.00
COMPANY DUMMIES[a]	Yes		Yes	
N	59,804		52,088	
R-squared	0.32		0.41	
Rbar-squared	0.32		0.41	
F	308.30		395.37	
Std. error of estimate	0.05		0.06	

Source: Authors' estimates of contribution rates by sex for employees making a contribution to their 401(k) plan using ordinary least squares.
[a] Estimates shown in columns 2 and 4 include the effect of dichotomous variables indicating the specific 401(k) plan covering each employee.

APPENDIX TABLE 7: Tobit Estimates of Percentage of Men's and Women's 401(k) Contributions Directed to Investments in Fixed-Income Assests: Plans with Company Stock

Variable	Men		Women	
	Marginal Effect	Standard Error	Marginal Effect	Standard Error
INTERCEPT[a]	0.64	0.06	0.98	0.07
EMPLOYER MATCH IN COMPANY STOCK	−0.15	0.02	−0.40	0.03
CO STOCK INVESTMENT REQUIRED FOR MATCH	−0.96	0.02	−1.26	0.02
AGE	−0.02	0.003	−0.02	0.003
AGE SQUARED	0.03	0.003	0.02	0.004
TENURE	0.02	0.001	0.02	0.002
TENURE SQUARED	−0.03	0.004	−0.03	0.01
EARNINGS	−0.02	0.001	−0.06	0.003
EARNINGS SQUARED	0.01	0.001	0.10	0.01
COMPANY DUMMIES[b]	Yes		Yes	
Uncensored	17,555		13,749	
Right censored	2,610		4,177	
Left censored	14,801		7,929	
N	34,966		25,855	

Source: Authors' estimates of the allocation by sex of account balances to fixed-income assets using a Tobit procedure.
[a] The intercepts are an average of three 401(k) plans with omitted dummy variables.
[b] Estimates shown in columns 2 and 4 include the effect of dichotomous variables indicating the specific 401(k) plan covering each employee.

APPENDIX TABLE 8: Tobit Estimates of Percentage of Men's and Women's 401(k) Contributions Directed to Investments in Fixed-Income Assets: Plans with No Company Stock

Variable	Men		Women	
	Marginal Effect	Standard Error	Marginal Effect	Standard Error
INTERCEPT	0.62	0.06	0.66	0.06
AGE	−0.02	0.003	−0.01	0.003
AGE SQUARED	0.02	0.003	0.02	0.003
TENURE	0.02	0.001	0.02	0.002
TENURE SQUARED	−0.03	0.004	−0.05	0.006
EARNINGS	−0.01	0.001	−0.04	0.002
EARNINGS SQUARED	0.002	0.00	0.02	0.001
COMPANY DUMMIES[a]	Yes		Yes	
Uncensored	15,161		15,434	
Right censored	4,888		5,467	
Left censored	4,789		5,332	
N	24,838		26,233	

Source: Authors' estimates of the allocation by sex of account balances to fixed-income assets using a Tobit procedure.

[a] Estimates shown in columns 2 and 4 include the effect of dichotomous variables indicating the specific 401(k) plan covering each employee.

APPENDIX TABLE 9: Tobit Estimates of Percentage of Men's and Women's 401(k) Balances Directed to Investments in Other Equities: Plans with Company Stock

Variable	Men		Women	
	Marginal Effect	*Standard Error*	*Marginal Effect*	*Standard Error*
INTERCEPT[a]	0.34	0.05	0.08	0.06
EMPLOYER MATCH IN COMPANY STOCK	−0.45	0.02	−0.27	0.02
CO STOCK INVESTMENT REQUIRED FOR MATCH	−0.60	0.01	−0.55	0.02
AGE	0.004	0.002	0.01	0.003
AGE SQUARED	−0.009	0.003	−0.01	0.003
TENURE	−0.01	0.001	−0.03	0.002
TENURE SQUARED	0.02	0.003	0.05	0.005
EARNINGS	0.03	0.001	0.06	0.003
EARNINGS SQUARED	−0.02	0.001	−0.11	0.01
COMPANY DUMMIES[b]	Yes		Yes	
Uncensored	20,522		15,917	
Right censored	291		35	
Left censored	14,153		9,903	
N	34,966		25,855	

Source: Authors' estimates of the allocation by sex of account balances to fixed-income assets using a Tobit procedure.

[a] The intercepts are an average of three 401(k) plans with omitted dummy variables.

[b] Estimates shown in columns 2 and 4 include the effect of dichotomous variables indicating the specific 401(k) plan covering each employee.

APPENDIX TABLE 10: Tobit Estimates of Percentage of Men's and Women's 401(k)
Balances Directed to Investments in Company Stock

	Men		Women	
Variable	*Marginal Effect*	*Standard Error*	*Marginal Effect*	*Standard Error*
INTERCEPT[a]	−0.18	0.05	−0.42	0.04
EMPLOYER MATCH IN COMPANY STOCK	0.56	0.02	0.62	0.02
CO STOCK INVESTMENT REQUIRED FOR MATCH	1.19	0.01	1.25	0.05
AGE	0.01	0.002	0.02	0.002
AGE SQUARED	−0.02	0.003	−0.02	0.003
TENURE	−0.01	0.001	−0.004	0.001
TENURE SQUARED	0.02	0.003	−0.025	0.004
EARNINGS	0.001	0.001	0.01	0.002
EARNINGS SQUARED	−0.00	0.001	−0.01	0.01
COMPANY DUMMIES[b]	Yes		Yes	
Uncensored	18,421		12,613	
Right censored	6,649		2,403	
Left censored	9,896		10,839	
N	34,966		25,855	

Source: Authors' estimates of the allocation by sex of account balances to company stock using a Tobit procedure.

[a] The intercepts are an average of three 401(k) plans with omitted dummy variables.

[b] Estimates shown in columns 2 and 4 include the effect of dichotomous variables indicating the specific 401(k) plan covering each employee.

Chapter 5
Explaining Retirement Saving Shortfalls

Olivia S. Mitchell, James F. Moore,
and John W. Phillips

Much has been made in the popular press and among researchers of the failure of Americans to save adequately for their own retirement. U.S. households saved around 10–12 percent of income between the 1950s and the
1970s, but the national saving rate dropped sharply over the 1990s. This
pattern raises serious concerns regarding Americans' ability to fund adequate and sustainable post-retirement consumption levels. This concern is
sharpened in view of projected social security shortfalls and the national
pension shift from defined benefit to defined contribution plans (Mitchell
et al. 1999). Clearly, future retirees will bear a larger responsibility for ensuring their own wellbeing in retirement, yet there is reason to believe that they
are seriously underestimating their retirement saving needs.

   Our objective in this chapter is to use the Health and Retirement Study to
explore the factors that appear to drive retirement saving shortfalls, and for
whom the shortfalls appear most serious. The HRS offers a unique opportunity to analyze the household wealth of families on the verge of retirement, inasmuch as it contains detailed questions on housing, pensions,
social security, and other financial wealth (Juster and Suzman 1995). In
what follows we first briefly review what is known about saving profiles for
older Americans and outline the nature and scope of saving shortfalls. We
then go on to describe several factors that might be anticipated to affect
people's ability to meet these saving targets, and explore the impact of
socioeconomic factors, health status factors, and preference proxies on the
shortfall pattern with a multivariate statistical analysis.

Modeling Saving Shortfalls

There is some controversy regarding projections of the future retirees' likely
wellbeing at older ages. A Congressional Budget Office study (1993) com-

pared the income and accumulated assets of the baby boom generation to those of their parents, and it concluded that boomers seem to be on track for retirement. By contrast, Bernheim (1992, 1994) used an augmented life cycle model as a benchmark and produced dramatically contradictory results. Specifically, he argued that U.S. households were saving at about one-third of the level that was adequate to fund retirement.

Our goal in the present analysis is to use estimated measures of pension and social security wealth, and derived saving shortfall measures, to determine what factors influence observed shortfall patterns. Related research by Moore and Mitchell (this volume, hereafter MM) used the Health and Retirement Study to show that saving shortfalls are considerable for many older Americans, with the typical older household needing to save 16 percent more of annual income to reach target retirement saving levels. There we did not, however, establish the kinds of factors that appear to explain the shortfalls.[1]

For the empirical evaluation, we begin with measures of current retirement wealth for respondents in the HRS datafile surveyed in 1992. These represent expected present values of contingent future income (pensions, social security) combined with current values of financial assets and housing wealth. In that year, mean total household wealth—which included net financial wealth + net housing equity + pension wealth + social security wealth—stood at around half a million dollars, with the median household having approximately $325,000 in total retirement wealth.[2]

It might seem that such a sum would be sufficient to leave the median older household in good shape for retirement, but further analysis indicates the inadequacy of asset accumulation for many HRS households. In order to establish this, we first forecast financial wealth to respondents' retirement ages by projecting four types of household assets, with future growth rates depending on their past trajectories: 1) net financial wealth, which includes such assets as savings, investments, business assets, and nonresidential real estate less outstanding debt not related to housing; 2) net housing wealth—the current market value of residential housing less outstanding mortgage debt; 3) pension wealth, or the present value of retirement benefits; and 4) present value of social security. The forecasting methodology for financial wealth uses the techniques developed in MM. For instance, housing wealth is projected using HRS responses on the purchase price of each participant's house, year of purchase, and mortgage payment amount and frequency. Interest rates are drawn from the average interest rate for households in the American Housing Survey with the same year of purchase. Given these interest rates, we then determine amortization schedules for mortgages and project reduction in housing debt over time. This in turn implies an increase in net housing wealth. Pension wealth is projected to retirement based on the plan provisions of employer provided Summary Plan Descriptions and HRS data on salary and tenure of service where appropriate. Individuals are assumed to remain with their current employer until the retirement age. Assumed asset allocation for pension saving is in accordance with that observed by Schieber and Goodfellow (1998), and returns assumed on defined contribution pensions are consistent with historical averages derived from Ibbotson (1996). Mortality is assumed to be as per actuarial tables obtained from the Social Security Administration. Social security wealth is derived from the earning and benefits file (EPBF) as described in Mitchell, Olson, and Steinmeyer (this volume, hereafter MOS).[3]

Deriving saving shortfalls requires that we then project retirement wealth forward to age 62 for each HRS household, and then compute how much additional saving beyond existing assets and pension plans would actually be needed to smooth that family's consumption patterns as of that retirement date.[4] The benchmark used to determine adequacy of saving is the replacement rate, an income level in retirement that is sufficient to smooth consumption before and after retirement (allowing for changes in tax status and the change from saving to spending in retirement).[5] Each household's replacement rate is solved for in conjunction with the determination of its saving rate, so as to determine how much income it would need in retirement to attain pre-retirement consumption levels.[6] For example, if the determined rate was 0.80 for a household with an income of $50,000 per year pre-retirement, the suggested annual income level in retirement is $40,000 for that household given differences in taxes and saving. More generally, assets needed at retirement are the result of taking into account 1) household income at retirement, 2) the appropriate replacement rate for that income level, and 3) a joint and survivor annuity factor allowing for the age composition of the household (either individual or married couples).

The rate of saving necessary to meet these levels is solved for simultaneously with the household's replacement rate. Given a replacement rate, the shortfall between a household's projected value of assets and its projected need determines its prescribed saving rate. This rate represents a prescription of what the older household would need to save as a percent of income each year until retirement to achieve that projected need. If the resultant projected saving rate were too small (large) to meet the projected need, the replacement rate is lowered (raised) until replacement and saving rates come into balance.

Saving Shortfalls on the Verge of Retirement

Retirement wealth levels are unevenly distributed across the older U.S. population, a point depicted in Table 1. Here overall wealth levels are given as of 1992, and also as of the respondent's retirement age.[7] The results show that a household in the median decile of the sample could anticipate retirement assets of about $380,000 for retirement at 62, with social security benefits representing more than a third of this sum, private pensions close to $100,000,

TABLE 1: Household Wealth by Marital Status in the HRS, 1992 and Projected to Retirement

Wealth Quintile	Wealth in 1992	Projected Wealth at Age 62	Projected Wealth at Age 65
Married			
1	$ 139,814	$ 169,416	$ 195,352
2	227,529	331,893	369,843
3	421,118	502,080	553,291
4	631,667	734,102	801,873
5	1,458,433	1,724,998	1,909,038
Nonmarried			
1	$ 33,094	$ 38,004	$ 41,905
2	73,986	83,549	91,408
3	134,602	163,658	179,562
4	253,469	306,548	335,424
5	689,344	810,585	882,090
Overall mean	$ 478,313	$ 566,431	$ 625,066
Housing	65,940	76,410	80,507
Financial	175,974	205,653	228,133
Social security	119,793	128,712	142,018
Pension	116,606	155,656	174,408
Median 10%	$ 325,157	$ 382,678	$ 420,537
Housing	59,746	71,097	75,047
Financial	66,530	71,004	71,175
Social security	133,606	143,864	160,824
Pension	65,275	96,713	113,491

Source: Authors' calculations using 1992 HRS data. All values in 1992 dollars and calculated using HRS sampling weights.

and housing and other financial wealth amounting to about $70,000 each. Examination of wealth patterns by marital status indicates that households headed by unmarried persons are substantially worse off than are their married counterparts. Married couples in the poorest quintile have four times more total wealth than do unmarried households ($140,000 versus $33,000 in present value). Indeed, wealth held by the *poorest* married quintile is equivalent to wealth held by unmarried people in the *middle* of their wealth distribution.

One reason that unmarried households might be anticipated to command less wealth *at retirement* is that they had lower "initial" levels when first queried in 1992. Another reason is that their asset composition is such that they can experience a lower growth trajectory for wealth until retirement age. As an example, we find that the poorest nonmarried groups are projected to only gain another $5,000–10,000 by retirement, while the poorest married households anticipate wealth gains of some $30,000. At the top of the wealth distribution, wealth gains are expected to be proportionately larger for both the unmarried and married households.

Given the diversity in wealth levels across the HRS population, it should not be surprising that prescribed saving rates also vary across households on the verge of retirement. Saving needs, summarized by earnings and wealth, appear in Table 2 for both married and nonmarried households. Here we see that the poorest households have prescribed saving rates of over 30 percent per year, double the median saving shortfall of 16 percent. Conversely, the very richest segment of the population has more than sufficient assets to smooth consumption.[8]

A somewhat surprising finding evident from Table 2 is that households with the highest earnings levels are also those facing some of the largest saving shortfalls because many high-earner households have insufficient retirement assets. To illustrate, high-earner married couples would need to save close to one-quarter of their total annual incomes if they are to achieve consumption smoothing. We also see that replacement rates fall with earnings for married couples, because taxes and required savings rise. By contrast, this pattern does not hold for unmarried households: instead, prescribed saving rates fall across the top four earnings groups. This may be the result of greater pension wealth for this group, or it could reflect nonmarried persons' greater sensitivity to future retirement needs.

Why is it that, for married households, saving shortfalls become more serious as earnings rise but fall with wealth? One reason is that earnings and wealth are not particularly highly correlated — the correlation coefficient is only 0.4, indicating that many households with high incomes have relatively little wealth and vice versa. This produces the uneven topology of prescribed saving needs depicted in Figure 1.[9] In addition, we see that many households are not in need of undertaking additional saving — these are the households with large amounts of wealth relative to their earnings (the right front section of Figure 1). It should be noted that as wealth falls and earnings rise, prescribed saving rates rise. The increase is fairly sharp initially, and then levels off as earnings rise (wealth falls); the slope of the surface is the result of the countervailing forces of replacement rates falling as saving rates rise, yielding a natural cap for required saving rates.[10]

Next we explore how households who do face saving needs compare to those who do not. To do this, we first define a qualitative variable set to 1 if the household has unmet saving needs and 0 otherwise. Using a vector of control variables to be described shortly, we use a statistical technique (multinomial Probit) to explore the factors associated with the probability of having a shortfall. Subsequently we examine the extent of shortfalls for the subset of the population needing to save more. This second analysis uses a multivariate regression model, controlling for selectivity possibly associated with this two-step procedure.[11]

TABLE 2: Saving Rate Shortfalls in the HRS by 1992 Wealth and Earnings

	By Wealth Decile		
Wealth Decile	Median Household Net Worth	Saving Rate to Age 62 (%)	Replacement Rate (%)
Married			
1	$ 144,600	31	53
2	276,600	22	62
3	418,400	17	66
4	622,500	06	80
5	1,117,800	−14	109
Nonmarried			
1	$ 36,800	36	52
2	61,900	34	52
3	132,500	24	62
4	247,200	12	75
5	510,000	−5	96
All	$ 325,000	*16*	*69*

	By Earnings Decile		
Earnings Decile	Household Earnings	Saving Rate to Age 62 (%)	Replacement Rate (%)
Married			
1	$ 10,400	−40	135
2	26,000	15	73
3	40,000	19	64
4	56,000	20	60
5	88,000	23	58
Nonmarried			
1	$ 5,000	−11	103
2	13,000	27	59
3	20,000	26	60
4	29,400	20	64
5	47,000	15	69
All	$ 33,000	*16*	*69*

Notes: See Table 1.

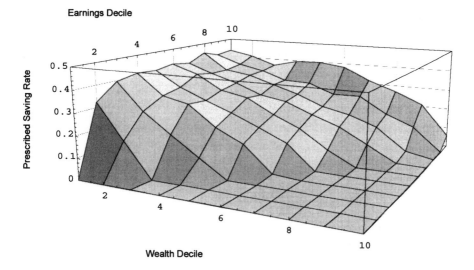

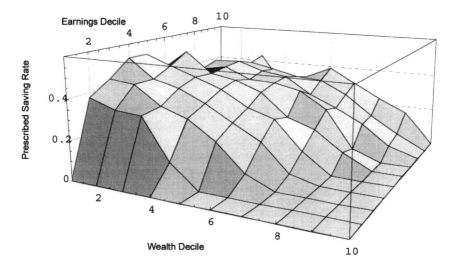

Figure 1. Prescribed saving rates for retirement at age 62 by marital status: married couples (top), single households (bottom). Source: Authors' calculations.

The saving shortfall outcomes are related to a set of control variables, which for ease of discussion, we cluster into three groups: a vector representing *conventional socioeconomic* factors (SES); a vector of *health status* controls (H); and a vector of factors we think of as *preference proxies* (P) indicating attitudes toward risk and the future. Since the saving and consumption patterns of married and nonmarried households may differ, we evaluate separate estimates for these two groups. In the case of married couples, both respondent and spouse variables are included in the analysis.

The SES variables are controls that most economists would agree would be likely to influence saving, namely a measure of lifetime earnings, education, census region, race, age, and family status (e.g., number of children and whether ever divorced, widowed, or married).[12] The specific lifetime earnings measure we employ is the respondent's average indexed monthly earnings (AIME), obtained from Social Security Administration records linked to the HRS file. In general, one might expect that more educated, older respondents with higher lifetime earnings would be less likely to face saving shortfalls; holding other things constant, households with children might have been able to save less. People who have experienced divorce and/or widowhood might also be anticipated to face greater shortfalls to the extent that these events often dissipate assets.

To capture respondents' health status, we include self-reports of respondents' difficulty performing any activities of daily living (ADL), smoking and drinking habits, depressive symptom scores, memory recall test scores, and self-assessments of their probability of living to age 75.[13] Many economic studies have used self-reported ADL and drinking/smoking variables, though here their anticipated effect on shortfall is not a priori clear. For example, ADL difficulty could suggest a level of disability that could affect a respondent's ability both to work and to save; smoking clearly lowers life expectancies; and moderate drinking may be beneficial to longevity. (Heavy drinkers would be expected to live less long.) Poor health can shorten both worklife and life expectancy, so we include control variables for people's self-assessed probability of living to age 75. This variable is anticipated to increase the chance of having a reported shortfall: thus someone who feels more likely to live to age 75 than the general population would find it reasonable to save more than average. Controlling on this, it is still possible that health problems could have ambiguous effects. That is, people in poorer health could have fewer assets because health problems are expensive to treat, but they may also have a smaller shortfall since poor health reduces earnings — and earnings are used to compute shortfalls. Once earnings are controlled, one might anticipate that poor health would increase the need for additional retirement saving. The depression and memory scores are included to determine whether shortfalls arise due to people's inability to cope with complex and long-term retirement planning computations.[14]

Finally, we include three variables intended to reflect differences across people in terms of their preferences and attitudes toward risk and the future. A first attitudinal factor evaluates people's planning horizon, elicited by a question in the survey asking them over what horizon period they make "family savings and spending" decisions. A second attitudinal factor pertains to respondents' risk aversion: this measure is derived from a series of hypothetical questions posed during the interview regarding the respondent's willingness to accept a job that would pay more, on average, than his or her current job, but with a higher variance.[15] The responses form an ordered mutually exclusive set of four groups, where higher values indicate greater risk aversion. We control for the "most risk averse" group in our analysis.[16] The final variable we assess asks HRS participants if they had ever contacted the Social Security Administration to have their retirement benefits estimated. It is anticipated that those people who made such inquiries regarding future benefits would be most likely to be cognizant of retirement needs and to make more concerted efforts to meet retirement saving targets.

Relative Importance of Explanatory Factors

Results from the first-stage examination of the multiple factors associated with having a saving shortfall appear in Tables 3 and 4; these provide estimated Probit coefficients and standard errors for married versus unmarried households, separately.[17] Turning first to the married households, our results indicate that some but not all socioeconomic variables are strong predictors of the likelihood of a shortfall. That is, older people are less likely to have a shortfall; nonwhites are at substantially more risk. Having experienced widowhood decreases the likelihood of a shortfall for the primary respondent. The number of children associated with the household increases the likelihood of a shortfall. Earlier we saw that retirement saving needs rise with earnings; here we note that the likelihood of a shortfall is also positively related to lifetime earnings.[18] For spouses, the only significant socioeconomic variable is age, and the effect on the likelihood of a shortfall matches that of the respondent.

Turning now to the role of poor health, we find that it is not a significant determinant of the probability of having a saving shortfall among married households.[19] Smokers appear to undersave relative to the target, but those who consume alcohol are better prepared for retirement. This may be because moderate alcohol consumption has come to be seen as having a positive health effect, though we note that empirically only those taking 3 or more drinks per day have the smaller shortfall. Smokers may know they are less likely to survive than average and hence undersave, though this effect should be controlled for because we include respondents' subjective probabilities of survival to age 75. Interestingly, many of the included health status

TABLE 3: Any Shortfall (0,1) at Age 62 for Married Households (N=4,646)

	Primary Respondent	Spouse
Conventional socioeconomic variables[a]		
AIME/1,000	0.04**	0.03
	(0.01)	(0.02)
Less than high school degree	0.00	0.01
	(0.02)	(0.02)
College graduate	0.01	0.04
	(0.02)	(0.03)
Graduate school	0.03	−0.01
	(0.03)	(0.03)
Ever divorced	0.02	0.00
	(0.02)	(0.02)
Ever widowed	−0.10*	−0.02
	(0.04)	(0.04)
Total children	0.01*	—
	(0.00)	
Respondent is female	−0.02	—
	(0.03)	
Age	−0.02**	−0.02**
	(0.00)	(0.00)
Respondent is Black	0.07**	—
	(0.03)	
Respondent is Hispanic	0.12**	—
	(0.03)	
Health indicators[b]		
Difficulty with any ADL	−0.01	−0.01
	(0.03)	(0.03)
Subjective probability of living to 75	0.00	0.00
	(0.00)	(0.00)

variables are not statistically significant, including the ADL measure and respondents' depression and memory scores.

Still focusing on married persons, it is of interest to ask whether undersaving appears related to either spouse's self-reported attitude about risk aversion. The evidence suggests no statistically significant impact, and likewise respondents having a long financial planning horizon have the same likelihood of experiencing a shortfall as do others. Respondents who had contacted the Social Security Administration for benefit estimates did not appear to be any more or less likely to have a saving shortfall.[20]

Turning now to results for unmarried households, we note several similarities and a few important differences. Lifetime earnings and age have similar influences on the probability of a shortfall for both groups. By con-

Table 3: *Continued*

	Primary Respondent	*Spouse*
Depression score	0.00	0.00
	(0.00)	(0.00)
Depression score squared	−0.00	0.00
	(0.00)	(0.00)
Initial recall	−0.03	0.00
	(0.00)	(0.00)
Ever smoked cigarettes	0.03*	0.03*
	(0.02)	(0.02)
Alcohol consumed: 1–2 drinks/day	−0.01	−0.02
	(0.02)	(0.02)
Alcohol consumed: 3+ drinks/day	−0.07*	−0.01
	(0.04)	(0.04)
Preference proxies[c]		
Relative risk aversion: most risk averse	−0.02	0.03
	(0.02)	(0.02)
Long planning horizon	−0.02	−0.01
	(0.02)	(0.02)
Contacted SSA regarding SS benefits	0.01	0.02
	(0.02)	(0.02)

Source: Authors' calculations using 1992 HRS data.
Notes:
* Significant at the 5 percent level.
** Significant at the 1 percent level.
— Not applicable.
[a] Probit regressions include census region dummy variables and a missing spouse indicator not reported. Categorical variables respondent white and high school degree omitted.
[b] Probit regressions include flag for missing cognitive score not reported. Categorical variable alcohol group 1 omitted.
[c] Probit regressions include a flag variable for missing risk aversion not reported. Categorical variables less risk averse and shorter financial planning horizon omitted.

trast, singles' education plays a much bigger role — higher education has a strong beneficial effect in reducing nonmarried persons' chance of having a retirement shortfall. Also nonmarried respondents who experienced a divorce are more likely to experience a shortfall. Nonmarried women are at greater shortfall risk than their male counterparts, even after controlling for other factors including lifetime earnings; this is primarily because women live longer in retirement and their assets must be spread over additional years. After controlling for all these human capital and family structure characteristics, race and ethnicity have no influence on the likelihood of a shortfall for the nonmarried population.

As with the married households, we also find that health and preference variables contain little explanatory power in explaining shortfalls among

TABLE 4: Any Shortfall (0,1) at Age 62 for Nonmarried Households (N=1,655)

	Primary Respondent
Conventional socioeconomic variables[a]	
AIME/1,000	0.05**
	(0.02)
Less than high school degree	0.09**
	(0.03)
College graduate	−0.08*
	(0.04)
Graduate school	−0.09*
	(0.04)
Ever divorced	0.11**
	(0.03)
Ever widowed	−0.04
	(0.03)
Total children	0.00
	(0.01)
Respondent is female	0.09**
	(0.03)
Age	−0.01**
	(0.00)
Respondent is Black	0.06
	(0.03)
Respondent is Hispanic	0.05
	(0.05)
Health indicators[b]	
Difficulty with any ADL	−0.12**
	(0.05)
Subjective probability of living to 75	0.00
	(0.00)
Depression score	0.00
	(0.01)
Depression score squared	0.00
	(0.00)
Initial recall	0.01
	(0.01)
Ever smoked cigarettes	−0.03
	(0.02)
Alcohol consumed: 1–2 drinks/day	0.00
	(0.03)
Alcohol consumed: 3+ drinks/day	−0.07
	(0.06)
Preference proxies[c]	
Relative risk aversion: most risk averse	0.01
	(0.02)
Long planning horizon	−0.02
	(0.02)
Contacted SSA regarding SS benefits	−0.04
	(0.03)

Notes: See Table 3.

nonmarried households. The single factor that is statistically significant has a rather surprising effect—namely, ADL difficulty—where people reporting an ADL difficulty were less likely to experience a shortfall. Other factors, including risk aversion and reported financial planning horizon, were not statistically significant.

Next we turn to the subset of people confronting a saving shortfall—or alternatively, those for whom we have identified a positive prescribed saving rate. Here the goal is to understand what affects the magnitude of prescribed saving rates conditional on having a shortfall, an analysis that appears in Tables 5 and 6.[21]

Focusing first on the married group, we find once again that the SES variables are highly correlated with married households' saving needs. Conditional on having a shortfall, each additional $1,000 of lifetime earnings dictates roughly a 2 percent reduction in the prescribed saving rate. In other words, for married households, having higher lifetime earnings increases the likelihood of having a shortfall, but those with higher lifetime earnings do not need to save as much to reach their retirement target. Education also matters: having a graduate degree cuts prescribed saving rates by one percent for the respondent and two percent for the spouse. Divorce raises prescribed saving rates by 2 percent. Interestingly, the ages of spouses work in opposite directions: older primary respondents need more saving (approximately 0.1 percent per year) but older spouses require less (−0.2 percent per year). This is probably due to the fact that an older primary respondent has less time remaining until retirement, while having an older spouse indicates fewer future years of expected consumption in retirement. Nonwhite married households with a shortfall have larger prescribed saving rates than their white counterparts.

Among the married group, having poor health is not particularly useful as a predictor of saving rate shortfalls: none of the included health variables (for respondent or spouse) have a statistically significant impact on prescribed saving rates. Only one of the preference variables proves important: respondents indicating they have a longer planning horizon (relative to the omitted category of under five years) are in better shape financially with smaller saving rate shortfalls.

Turning now to the nonmarried having prescribed saving needs, many fewer factors are important in explaining observed shortfalls. In fact, only two of the socioeconomic variables are significant (AIME and age), though their magnitudes are quite large relative to married respondents. An additional $1,000 in AIME decreases the prescribed saving rate by 5 percent, and age increases it by 1 percent per year.

Health measures, which did not explain married household behavior, are more important for nonmarried households. Specifically, respondents with a higher measured level of cognition have lower prescribed saving rates, while smokers have higher prescribed rates than do nonsmokers. As with

TABLE 5: Extent of Saving Shortfall at Age 62 for Married Households

	Primary Respondent	Spouse
Conventional socioeconomic variables[a]		
AIME/1,000	−0.02**	−0.01
	(0.00)	(0.01)
Less than high school degree	0.01	0.01
	(0.01)	(0.01)
College graduate	0.01	0.01
	(0.01)	(0.01)
Graduate school	−0.02*	−0.02*
	(0.01)	(0.01)
Ever divorced	0.01	0.02**
	(0.01)	(0.01)
Ever widowed	−0.02	0.00
	(0.01)	(0.01)
Total children	0.00	—
	(0.00)	
Respondent is female	−0.01	—
	(0.01)	
Age	0.001*	−0.002**
	(0.00)	(0.00)
Respondent is Black	0.02*	—
	(0.01)	
Respondent is Hispanic	0.03**	—
	(0.01)	
Health indicators[b]		
Difficulty with any ADL	0.01	0.00
	(0.01)	(0.01)
Subjective probability of living to 75	0.00	0.00
	(0.00)	(0.00)
Depression score	0.00	0.00
	(0.00)	(0.00)
Depression score squared	0.00	0.00
	(0.00)	(0.00)
Initial recall	0.00	0.00
	(0.00)	(0.00)
Ever smoked cigarettes	0.00	0.00
	(0.00)	(0.01)
Alcohol consumed: 1–2 drinks/day	−0.01	0.01
	(0.01)	(0.01)
Alcohol consumed: 3+ drinks/day	0.00	0.02
	(0.01)	(0.01)
Preference proxies[c]		
Relative risk aversion: most risk averse	0.00	−0.01
	(0.01)	(0.01)
Long planning horizon	−0.01*	0.00
	(0.00)	(0.01)
Contacted SSA regarding SS benefits	0.00	0.00
	(0.01)	(0.01)
Inverse Mills ratio	−0.02	—
	(0.02)	

Notes: See Table 3.

TABLE 6: Extent of Saving Shortfall at Age 62 for Nonmarried Households

	Primary Respondent
Conventional socioeconomic variables[a]	
AIME/1,000	−0.05**
	(0.01)
Less than high school degree	0.00
	(0.01)
College graduate	0.01
	(0.01)
Graduate school	0.00
	(0.01)
Ever divorced	0.00
	(0.01)
Ever widowed	−0.02
	(0.01)
Total children	0.00
	(0.00)
Respondent is female	−0.02
	(0.01)
Age	0.01**
	(0.00)
Respondent is Black	−0.01
	(0.01)
Respondent is Hispanic	−0.01
	(0.02)
Health indicators[b]	
Difficulty with any ADL	0.01
	(0.02)
Subjective probability of living to 75	0.00
	(0.00)
Depression score	0.00
	(0.00)
Depression score squared	0.00
	(0.00)
Initial recall	−0.03*
	(0.00)
Ever smoked cigarettes	0.04**
	(0.01)
Alcohol consumed: 1–2 drinks/day	−0.01
	(0.01)
Alcohol consumed: 3+ drinks/day	0.01
	(0.02)
Preference proxies[c]	
Relative risk aversion: most risk averse	−0.01
	(0.01)
Long planning horizon	−0.02**
	(0.01)
Contacted SSA regarding SS benefits	−0.01
	(0.01)
Inverse Mills ratio	−0.07**
	(0.02)

Notes: See Table 3.

154   Olivia S. Mitchell, James F. Moore, and John W. Phillips

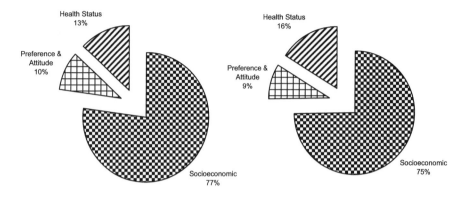

Figure 2. Explained variance in prescribed saving rates by current marital status: married (left), nonmarried (right). Source: Authors' calculations.

the married group, the only significant preference variable is long financial planning horizon: those with a longer planning horizon appeared to do a better job saving for retirement.[22]

An alternative way to describe empirical patterns uses an analysis of variance (ANOVA) to summarize the relative contribution of each of the clusters of variables in explaining observed patterns. Our results appear in Figure 2 disaggregated by marital status. Among married households, we find that SES factors account for 77 percent, health 13 percent, and preference proxies only 10 percent of explained variance. For nonmarried households, SES factors again play the largest role (75 percent), followed by health (16 percent) and preference proxies (9 percent). In short, the socioeconomic factors explain most of what can be explained in the data. This suggests that people's saving shortfalls are primarily driven by socioeconomic factors; of these, the most important quantitatively are education and AIME, with marital history and ethnicity also being significant. Nevertheless, poor health and preferences have a stronger effect among the unmarried, which is of interest inasmuch as this group is likely to be most vulnerable to poverty in old age.[23]

A further ANOVA breakdown appears in Figure 3, illustrating how respondent and spouse characteristics contribute to explaining saving shortfall patterns. Our estimates indicate that spousal factors account for about half of the total variance attributable to SES factors. In particular, saving shortfalls are less prevalent when spouses are more educated. Spouse effects are also important among the health and preference variables, though respondent preference variables explain almost twice the variance in prescribed rates compared to spousal preference variables.

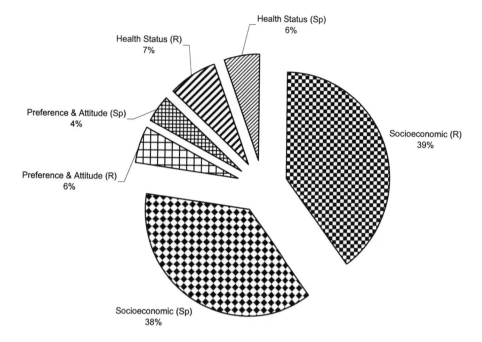

Figure 3. Explained variance in prescribed saving rates for married couples by respondent ans spouse attributes. Source: Authors' calculations.

Conclusions

Our research represents a step toward understanding why so many older Americans face retirement saving shortfalls. Using retirement wealth shortfalls in the HRS, we have shown that the probability of having a saving shortfall, as well as the size of the saving rate needed to make up the deficit, is related to factors that economists conventionally employ when explaining saving patterns. These include respondents' and spouses' educational attainment, lifetime earnings, marital and children status, and ethnicity. Overall, socioeconomic variables are key in explaining variation in saving rates needed for retirement; health and preference proxies are also crucial, together accounting for 20–25 percent of explained variance.

We find it interesting that several other factors—including depression, memory problems, and earlier-than-predicted mortality—appear not to explain saving shortfalls. Some health-related factors do have explanatory power, including alcohol consumption (associated with improved proximity to the saving target) and smoking (taking respondents farther from their goals). We also find modest effects from ADL difficulty and cognition scores, though these effects are limited to the unmarried sample. Only one of the preference proxies used helps us understand which people undersave and why: that is, households with longer financial planning horizons have lower prescribed savings rates.

Finally, the analysis indicates that in understanding married couples' wealth situation, it is useful to take into account economic, health, and preference proxies for *both* respondents and spouses. Spousal effects account for about half of the explained variance in saving shortfall patterns for married households.

Appendix

In this Appendix we describe data construction methods used to derive the key wealth and saving shortfall variables used in this chapter. The retirement wealth measures we use for 1992 as well as retirement at age 62 and 65 follow Moore and Mitchell (this volume). Prescribed saving and replacement rates are also calculated as on Moore and Mitchell; the process is an iterative one that uses 1) projected assets at an assumed retirement date, 2) projected earnings just prior to retirement, and 3) an annuity factor that makes allowance for the age and sex characteristics of the household.

In addition to the wealth and saving measures described elsewhere, we also obtain several additional variables from the HRS survey for use in this analysis. For example, respondents are asked to indicate their likelihood of living to age 75 using a scale of 0 to 10. Individuals who report higher values believe that the probability they will survive to age 75 is high, while low values suggest pessimism regarding survival to 75. Participants are also asked a number of directed questions about their willingness to exchange their current wage income for a wage that has a gamble associated with it. For example, the first question gives the option of an alternative with a 50 percent chance of doubling income, but a 50 percent chance that it will reduce income by one-third. Participants answering that they would take the risk are offered a choice where the lesser of the two outcomes is worse (a reduction of one-half) and those answering that they would not take the risk are given a gamble where the lesser outcome is a loss of one-fifth. The four categories can be used to rank risk aversion from most risk averse (category 4) to least risk averse (category 1). We then identify those in the most risk averse group with a dichotomous variable.

In order to ascertain respondents' mental condition, ISR interviewers recite a list of twenty nouns to the respondent, asking him or her to recall as many words from that list as possible. This sum represents the "initial memory" variable we use in the analysis (Wallace and Herzog 1995). Respondents are also asked a set of questions measuring depressive symptoms, taken from the Center for Epidemiology Studies Depression Scale (CES-D). For questions that relate to depressive symptoms (e.g., "I felt everything I did was an effort"), respondents rate how often they had these symptoms over the past week using a four-category scale to measure "intensity." The sum of the responses to these 11 questions is the depression score used in the analysis, where higher depression scores imply a higher level of depressive symptoms.

The authors acknowledge financial support for this study provided by the Pension Research Council of the Wharton School, the Penn Aging Research Center, the Boettner Center at the University of Pennsylvania, and the National Institute on Aging. Opinions are solely those of the authors and not those of institutions with which they are affiliated.

Notes

1. We build on Moore and Mitchell (this volume, MM), Mitchell, Olson, and Steinmeier (this volume, MOS), and Gustman et al. (this volume) in these calculations.

2. These estimates use the Social Security Administration's intermediate economic and demographic assumptions. See the Appendix for further discussion.

3. See the Appendix for more discussion of data creation issues.

4. Age 62.5 is the modal retirement age currently, where retirement is defined as the age at which people apply for social security benefits.

5. Palmer (1991, 1993) analyzes replacement rates using the Consumer Expenditure Survey; this research is reviewed and alternative approaches offered by McGill et al. (1996).

6. This iterative approach to solving for the household's saving shortfall is described in MM.

7. Descriptive statistics on the HRS sample under study in this chapter are given in Appendix Tables 1, 2 along with variable definitions. Appendix Table 3 summarizes the 1992 wealth distribution derived for the HRS sample with a simple multivariate regression model similar to that of Smith (1995). We find that our empirical results for factors associated with wealth levels in the HRS are quite consistent with the prior study.

8. In fact this group could begin consuming assets by an amount worth 5–14 percent of annual income if all that was of interest was consumption-smoothing. Clearly other goals, including the passing on of assets via bequests, are also viable for this segment of the population.

9. The figures present the median prescribed saving rates in wealth-earnings deciles by marital status. Sample medians mask the fact that variation remains in each decile pair grouping but they do provide a representation of average conditional behavior.

10. The surface is smoother for married than for unmarried households, due to a larger sample size for the former group.

11. The method is a standard Heckit procedure with the selection correction term (inverse Mills ratio) included among second stage regressors; standard errors are corrected using the appropriate joint estimation technique (Greene 1997).

12. Variable definitions appear in the Appendix.

13. A detailed description of HRS health measures can be found in Wallace and Herzog (1995).

14. Etner et al. (1997) find that depression reduces employment among the broader population; it has not been established whether this effect is important in the saving and retirement decision.

15. Barsky et al. (1997) use the risk aversion measure to analyze risk-taking behavior (stock ownership, cigarette smoking, drinking, etc.) in the HRS. They find that the risk aversion measure is correlated with these "risky" behaviors.

16. We use a dichotomous variable "most risk averse" where the omitted category is the remaining three "less risk averse" groups.

17. In addition to the controls mentioned above, flags are incorporated for missing values of variables and the mean of all nonmissing responses was used as a replacement. Most values of these flags are not statistically significant and hence are not individually reported in Tables 3–6.

18. We recognize that current household earnings affect prescribed saving needs in a complex way. For one thing, families with higher earnings will have a higher need for wealth in retirement to sustain their higher consumption patterns when young. This generates a mechanical (positive) link between earnings and saving needs. However having higher earnings levels at any given date probably also indicates that a household has a higher "ability to save" over its remaining years in the labor force, a result that may produce an inverse link between earnings and saving needs on the verge of retirement. Having higher earnings also is likely to be associated with (unmeasured) high tastes for work, such that these respondents are less likely to retire early. Such workers might have measured saving shortfalls, which in fact they could make up by retiring later. Since it is not clear whether current earnings determines shortfalls or vice versa, we use a "lifetime" earnings measure (AIME) in our estimates rather than current earnings. Though AIME and current earnings are positively correlated, the degree of correlation is rather small, only 0.35.

19. Using the HRS, Smith (1997) shows that poor health is associated with lower wealth *levels*, a finding we confirm in Appendix 2 using our own set of explanatory factors in the HRS sample. By contrast, our goal in Table 3 is to show how saving *shortfall* measures are related to respondent and spouse variables. Our results thus show that health conditions as measured here play only a minor role in predicting which households should increase their saving rates in order to meet retirement consumption needs.

20. One explanation for the statistical insignificance of the health and preference measures is that they may be correlated, confounding our estimates. To determine how important this might be to our results, we also explored how results changed on SES variables if we deleted all health and preference controls from the canonical specifications in Tables 3 and 4. We then added a single health or preference variable at a time and reestimated the new specification, comparing the coefficient value of the lone health/preference variable in the new specification with the same coefficient in the canonical set. The results indicate that coefficients on included variables in both sets of models are similar, so that correlation among health variables probably does not alter our results.

21. The statistically significant coefficient on the inverse Mills ratio indicates that failing to correct for selectivity would produce biased estimates of covariate effects.

22. In sensitivity analysis not reported in the tables in detail, we sequentially varied the assumed retirement age and also the truncation point for determining which households have a saving shortfall to see what impact this had on results reported in the text. Qualitative conclusions are unchanged.

23. For a discussion of nonmarried people's particular vulnerability to old-age poverty, see Levine, Mitchell, and Moore (this volume).

References

Barksy, Robert B., F. Thomas Juster, Miles S. Kimball, and Matthew D. Shapiro. 1997. "Preference Parameters and Behavioral Heterogeneity: An Experimental Approach in the HRS." *Quarterly Journal of Economics* (May).
Bernheim, B. Douglas. 1992. "Is the Baby Boom Generation Preparing Adequately for Retirement?" Technical Report. Princeton, N.J.: Merrill Lynch.
Bernheim, B. Douglas. 1994. "The Merrill Lynch Baby Boom Retirement Index." Technical Report. Princeton, N.J.: Merrill Lynch.
Case, Karl E. 1994. "Land Prices and House Prices in the United States." In Yukio Noguchi and James M. Poterba, eds., *Housing Markets in the United States and Japan.* Chicago: University of Chicago Press.
Congressional Budget Office. 1993. "Baby Boomers in Retirement: An Early Perspective." Washington, D.C.: U.S. Government Printing Office, September.
Etner, Susan L., Richard G. Frank, and Ronald C. Kessler. October 1997. "The Impact of Psychiatric Disorders on Labor Market Outcomes." *Industrial & Labor Relations Review* 51, 1: 64–81.
Gokhale, Jagadeesh, Laurence J. Kotlikoff, and John Sabelhaus. 1996. "Understanding the Postwar Decline in U.S. Saving: A Cohort Analysis." *Brookings Papers on Economic Activity* 1: 315–407.
Greene, William. 1997. *Econometric Analysis.* 3rd edition. Englewood Cliffs, N.J.: Prentice Hall.
Gustman, Alan L., Olivia S. Mitchell, Andrew A. Samwick, and Thomas L. Steinmeier. "Evaluating Pension Entitlements." This volume.
Ibbotson Associates. 1997. *Stocks, Bonds, Bills, and Inflation: 1996 Yearbook.* Chicago: Ibbotson Associates.
Juster, F. Thomas, and Richard Suzman. "Overview of the Health and Retirement Study." *Journal of Human Resources* 30 (Supplement): S7–56.
Levine, Phillip B., Olivia S. Mitchell, and James F. Moore. "Women on the Verge of Retirement: Predictors of Retiree Wellbeing." This volume.
McGill, Dan M., Kyle N. Brown, John J. Haley, and Sylvester J. Schieber. 1996. *Fundamentals of Private Pensions.* 7th edition. Pension Research Council. Philadelphia: University of Pennsylvania Press.
Mitchell, Olivia S. and James F. Moore. 1998. "Can Americans Afford to Retire? New Evidence on Retirement Saving Adequacy." *Journal of Risk and Insurance* 65, 3: 371–400.
Mitchell, Olivia S., Robert J. Myers, and Howard Young, eds. *Prospects for Social Security Reform.* Pension Research Council. Philadelphia: University of Pennsylvania Press, 1999.
Mitchell, Olivia S., Jan Olson, and Thomas Steinmeier. (MOS). "Earnings and Projected Benefits File in the Health and Retirement Study." This volume.
Moore, James F. and Olivia S. Mitchell. (MM). "Projected Retirement Wealth and Savings Adequacy." This volume.
Palmer, Bruce A. 1991, 1993. "Georgia State University/Alexander & Alexander Consulting Group RETIRE Report." Center for Risk Management and Insurance Research, Georgia State University.
Schieber, Sylvester J. and Gordon Goodfellow. 1998. "Self-Directed Pension Accounts." In Olivia S. Mitchell and Sylvester J. Schieber, eds. *Living with Defined*

Contribution Pensions. Pension Research Council. Philadelphia: University of Pennsylvania Press.

Smith, James P. 1995. "Racial and Ethnic Differences in Wealth." *Journal of Human Resources* 30 (Supplement): S158–83.

Social Security Advisory Council (SSAC). 1996. *Report of the 1994–1996 Advisory Council on Social Security,* Volumes I and II. Washington, D.C.: Social Security Administration.

Wallace, Robert B. and A. Regula Herzog. 1995. "Overview of Health Measures in the Health and Retirement Study." *Journal of Human Resources* 30 (Supplement): S84–107.

U.S. Department of Commerce. 1994. *American Housing Survey, 1991: National File.* Bureau of the Census, Washington, D.C.: Bureau of the Census.

APPENDIX TABLE 1: Means and Standard Deviations — Married Respondents (N=5,234)

	Respondent		Spouse	
Conventional socioeconomic variables[a]				
Earnings ($)	27,650	45,747	15,777	20,201
Less than high school degree (%)	0.22	0.41	0.25	0.43
College graduate (%)	0.12	0.33	0.09	0.29
Graduate school (%)	0.10	0.30	0.06	0.23
Ever divorced (%)	0.26	0.44	0.22	0.42
Ever widowed (%)	0.04	0.19	0.04	0.19
Total children (#)	3.35	2.06	—	—
Respondent is female	0.37	0.48	—	—
Age	56.19	5.49	54.81	6.28
Respondent is Black (%)	0.07	0.26	0.07	0.25
Respondent is Hispanic (%)	0.07	0.25	0.07	0.25
Health indicators[b]				
Difficulty with any ADL	0.09	0.29	0.09	0.27
Subjective probability of living to 75	0.65	0.28	0.66	0.26
Depression score	4.29	4.05	4.51	4.21
Initial recall score	7.61	2.50	7.84	2.51
Ever smoked cigarettes (%)	0.66	0.48	0.60	0.48
Alcohol consumed: none	0.35	0.48	0.38	0.49
Alcohol consumed: 1–2 drinks/day	0.60	0.49	0.55	0.50
Alcohol consumed: 3+ drinks/day	0.06	0.23	0.05	0.21
Preference proxies[c]				
Relative risk aversion: less risk averse	0.38	0.50	0.46	0.49
Relative risk aversion: most risk averse	0.62	0.49	0.54	0.50
Planning horizon: < 5 years	0.61	0.48	0.67	0.48
Planning horizon: 5+ years	0.39	0.49	0.33	0.47
Contacted SSA regarding SS benefits (%)	0.25	0.43	0.16	0.36
Wealth variables				
Saving rate shortfall at age 62 (%) (n=3,155)	0.24	0.12	—	—
Saving rate shortfall at age 65 (%) (n=2,824)	0.18	0.11	—	—
Current period total wealth ($)	589,760	649,982	—	—

Notes: See Table 3.

APPENDIX TABLE 2: Means and Standard Deviations — Unmarried Respondents
(N=2,373)

	Mean	Standard Deviation
Conventional socioeconomic variables[a]		
Earnings	18,215	26,877
Less than high school degree	0.31	0.46
College graduate	0.09	0.28
Graduate school	0.08	0.27
Ever divorced	0.64	0.48
Ever widowed	0.28	0.45
Total children	2.60	2.10
Respondent is female	0.68	0.47
Age	55.95	3.27
Respondent is Black	0.18	0.39
Respondent is Hispanic	0.09	0.28
Health indicators[b]		
Difficulty with any ADL	0.14	0.35
Subjective probability of living to 75	0.14	0.31
Depression score	6.49	5.63
Initial recall score	7.27	2.70
Ever smoked cigarettes	0.67	0.47
Alcohol consumed: none	0.40	0.49
Alcohol consumed: 1–2 drinks/day	0.54	0.50
Alcohol consumed: 3+ drinks/day	0.06	0.23
Preference proxies[c]		
Relative risk aversion: less risk averse	0.38	0.50
Relative risk aversion: most risk averse	0.62	0.49
Planning horizon: < 5 years	0.68	0.45
Planning horizon: 5+ years	0.32	0.47
Contacted SSA regarding SS benefits (%)	0.17	0.37
Wealth variables		
Saving rate shortfall at age 62 (%) (N=1,198)	0.26	0.14
Saving rate shortfall at age 65 (%) (N=936)	0.20	0.11
Current period total wealth	238,793	374,629

Notes: See Table 3.

APPENDIX TABLE 3: Wealth Level Regression: Full Sample

	Coefficient	Standard Error
Conventional socioeconomic variables[a]		
Household income category 2	38904.85**	14055.21
Household income category 3	89890.63**	16954.62
Household income category 4	176310.7**	19863.14
Household income category 5	522416.5**	33803.07
Less than high school degree	−43300.39**	14810.53
College graduate	103631.7**	28732.31
Graduate school	207372.8**	36357.02
Married couple/partnered	145671.6**	17165.84
Ever divorced	−80121.58**	14860.13
Ever widowed	−17636.31	14054.36
Respondent is Black	−95180.33**	11137.88
Respondent is Hispanic	−132231.6**	23911.22
Health indicators[b]		
Categorical health: excellent	102057.3**	21363.15
Categorical health: very good	84463.51**	19755.65
Categorical health: good	65989.85**	16546.74
Categorical health: fair	62191.03**	16045.98
Relative mortality optimism	2612.305**	2088.487
Preference proxies[c]s		
Planning horizon: 1 year	−31245.51	20895.16
Planning horizon: a few years	15297.14	17217.03
Planning horizon: 5–10 years	16311.26	19307.04
Planning horizon: 10+ years	118679.2**	35307.86

Notes: See Table 3.

Part II
Facing the Challenges
of Retirement

Chapter 6
Women on the Verge of Retirement: Predictors of Retiree Wellbeing

Phillip B. Levine, Olivia S. Mitchell
and James F. Moore

The economic status of Americans age 65 and over has risen for several decades. On average, members of this age group—which used to be the nation's poorest—are now at least as well off economically as younger people (U.S. Senate 1991). However, pockets of poverty remain. In particular, older women have benefited from rising prosperity, but not to the same degree as older men: currently, women age 65 and over are about twice as likely to live in poverty as compared to men of the same age.[1] Against this backdrop, some surmise that older women's risk of poverty may worsen in the future. Women comprise a disproportionate share of the elderly and are more likely to experience hardship resulting from chronic health problems, widowhood, and lower labor market activity (Ory and Warner 1990). Therefore, as the older population grows and becomes more heavily female, problems associated with aging may intensify for women.

Past researchers seeking to understand why older women fare worse in old age have focused primarily on marital status changes as a cause of poverty. Many studies suggest that widowhood is strongly related to poor economic outcomes; for example, women face a significant probability of falling into poverty following their husband's death.[2] In addition, women's wealth has been found to decline at widowhood due to the loss of their husbands' pension benefits (Hurd and Wise 1989). Some analysts have examined the effect of divorce, concluding that divorce too is associated with loss of income for older women (Crown et al. 1993).

Our study takes a different tack, exploring the influence of socioeconomic factors on older women's wellbeing. Specifically, we examine how people's work histories, health, and time transfers to family members affect retired women's standing, relative to men's. We separately analyze the wellbeing of older whites from blacks and Hispanics because these factors may

have differential impacts on wellbeing by ethnic group.[3] Understanding
how these factors contribute to differences in wellbeing between older men
and women may have important implications for pension, social security,
and labor market policy. If women who work more during their lifetime are
less likely to face economic hardship in later life, then the trend toward
greater female labor force participation would be anticipated to reduce
disparities in later life. If poor health leads to a significant decrease in
economic wellbeing, then policies designed to alleviate income loss may be
desirable, including larger disability payments and/or job retraining. If
women face hardship because they spend time caring for very old parents in
poor health, then policies aimed at the long-term health needs of the very
old may be crucial. To the extent that these factors are more likely to affect
wellbeing for women of a particular ethnicity, potential policy responses
might effectively target that group.

Little previous research has explored these determinants of older wom-
en's wellbeing, and the few existing studies produce mixed results. For example, Burkhauser et al. (1985) provides weak evidence that poor health
reduces wellbeing, but Boskin and Shoven (1988) report no effect. Differences in methodologies make it difficult to compare those studies directly. A
handful of older papers indicated that more consistent labor force attachment was positively related to greater income security among older people
in decades past,[4] but little recent work has been done on this subject. Analysis of newer cohorts of women is required, particularly given the massive
changes in women's labor supply over the last several decades. Intrafamily
transfers have been identified by some researchers as potentially burden-
some to people in late middle age,[5] but the published literature has no
recent empirical work on this relationship.

Our goal therefore is to examine women's economic wellbeing at the end
of their work lives, and to show which factors appear to be associated with
women's relatively poor economic status in old age. We use the Health and
Retirement Study (HRS), reporting a rich variety of data on people in late
middle age, to evaluate the relative contributions of three factors believed to
influence women's wellbeing in retirement. These three factors are wom-
en's lifetime labor market attachment, women's health status and history,
and women's family responsibilities including transfers of time to family
members.

Methodology

An examination of the determinants of economic wellbeing requires us to
define economic status and then specify models appropriate for estimating
its determinants. In this section, we describe the variables employed to
measure wellbeing and its determinants, along with the strengths and weaknesses of each of these measures.

Measuring Wellbeing

Existing studies have focused on two approaches to measure wellbeing: using income-based measures, and using wealth-based measures. *Income* is comprised of labor earnings, income from interest and dividends, and transfer payments. *Wealth* consists of financial assets, housing value, and the present discounted value of future annuity payments, like social security and private pensions.

Income- and wealth-based measures of wellbeing each have distinct strengths and weaknesses.[6] Analysts often prefer to use income, inasmuch it is relatively easy to measure and interpret and is readily gathered in household surveys. But if one thinks of wellbeing as reflecting consumption, income is an imperfect measure. For example, income overstates wellbeing if taxes and work-related expenses that reduce consumption are not subtracted; conversely, income understates wellbeing to the extent that owner-occupied housing provides consumption flows not reflected in income measures. A different criticism of income-based measures of wellbeing is that they exclude payments made in kind, such as food stamps and housing subsidies. A final issue is that income-based measures of wellbeing must take into account family size, so many experts develop "equivalence scales," in order to make income comparisons across different-sized families scaled by family size. This approach is implicit in the widely used federal government poverty line, used by most empirical researchers on economic wellbeing in the United States.[7]

These limitations imply to some that wealth-based measures would more closely reflect a family's available consumption, favoring these over income-based measures. This is most sensible when a measured wealth figure acknowledges the value of a respondent's future social security and pension payments, as well as the value of net housing and financial assets. For instance, an older person with little cash income might hold a sizable investment portfolio that she continually reinvested instead of converting the returns to income. In this case, her cash income would be low, but her command over consumable resources would be high. Nevertheless, most national surveys do not collect good data on wealth from respondents. Fortunately, the Health and Retirement Survey contains the necessary elements for this analysis, as will be detailed below. There are some remaining issues to be settled, however, even if wealth measures are available. One is that wealth-based measures of wellbeing require the analyst to make judgments regarding the value of different types of assets. For instance, housing could be included in a measure of wealth or, alternatively, might be excluded if it is assumed that the owner faces substantial costs in accessing the net equity. Differences in family size also may present problems when examining wealth, raising questions about an appropriate equivalence scale similar to those raised above.

Our approach in this study is to construct and examine several measures of wellbeing, so that our results may be compared to earlier work and examined for sensitivity to measurement concepts. First, we use three different income-based measures to establish a household's level of wellbeing: its level of income, its poverty status, and its income-to-needs ratio. These measures have been widely used in prior studies,[8] though these do not examine older respondents in the HRS. Levels of income are directly observable in our data. Poverty status is a dichotomous variable indicating whether income is above or below the official poverty line set by the government. The poverty line is meant to measure the minimum level of income needed to purchase a subsistence level of goods and services and is adjusted for family composition. The income-to-needs ratio represents the ratio of the level of income to the poverty line, for a family of a particular composition. Although the equivalence scale built into the official definition of poverty is controversial, we use it because it is the most common method of adjusting for family composition. Finally, we examine pretax income, since the public release version of the HRS does not include state-level IDs with which to impute state taxes.

We also use wellbeing measures that rely on projected retirement income. That is, we compute respondents' expected future social security and pension benefits, and value anticipated assets at retirement age (taken here to be age 62). Then we value annual household income as of that point, measured as the annuitized value of wealth obtained by converting the stock of an individual's wealth into a flow of funds.[9] This projected retirement income measure represents the annual payments that a given level of wealth would yield if it was drawn down to zero over an individual's (or family's) remaining life expectancy.[10] We examine projected retirement income directly, along with the ratio between projected retirement income and the poverty line (analogous to the income-to-needs ratio) and projected poverty status in retirement.

One important question pertains to the distinction between an individual's resources and his or her family's resources. Income and wealth in the HRS are considered to be household-based measures, making it is impossible to attribute resources to each individual member within a household. This issue is important in the present analysis because resources separately available to husbands and wives from pooled income or wealth cannot be separately allocated. As a result, our analysis assumes that they are consumed jointly. Therefore differences in measured wellbeing by sex can only result from measured differences in the wellbeing of nonmarried men and women. We explore the empirical effects of this implication of the data below.

Statistical Specifications

To examine the relationship between wellbeing and its potential determinants holding other factors constant, multivariate techniques are required. We devise and estimate models of the following form for older men and women in the HRS, following Blau and Graham (1990), who examine wealth accumulation among young persons.

$$WB_{ige} = WH_{ige}b_{1ge} + H_{ige}b_{2ge} + T_{ige}b_{3ge} + X_{ige}b_{4ge} + S_{ige}b_{5ge} + u_{ige} \qquad (1)$$

where

$$i = 1, \ldots, N, \quad g = f, m, \quad e = w, nw.$$

In this equation, WB represents a continuous measure of economic well-being; WH captures work history; H represents measures of health status; T represents time transfers to family members; X represents demographic characteristics of the individual (including marital status); S represents characteristics of the respondent's spouse for those respondents who are married;[11] u represents an error term; the subscript i indexes individuals (N indicates the sample size); the subscript g indexes sex (m for male, f for female); and the subscript indexes ethnic group (w for white, nw for non-white, either black or Hispanic).[12] Details on all variables appear below. As indicated by the subscripts, these models are estimated separately by ethnic/sex groups so that results can be compared across groups.[13]

For dichotomous measures of wellbeing like poverty status, we estimate Probit models:

$$\text{Prob } (WB_{ige} = 1) = f(WH_{ige}b_{1ge} + H_{ige}b_{2ge} + T_{ige}b_{3ge} + X_{ige}b_{4ge} + S_{ige}b_{5ge}) \qquad (2)$$

where

$$i = 1, \ldots, N, \quad g = f, m, \quad e = w, nw.$$

All variables are defined as above except that WB equals 1 if income or projected retirement income falls below the poverty line and 0 otherwise. These models are estimated separately for white and nonwhite men and women, so that results may be compared across demographic groups.

In both sets of equations, the coefficients b_1, b_2, and b_3 represent, respectively, the effects of work history, health status, and transfers on economic wellbeing within a given ethnic/sex group. If b_1 is statistically significantly greater than zero, then we would conclude that there is a positive association between work history and wellbeing. If b_2 is significantly less than zero, then we would conclude that poor health is negatively associated with wellbeing. If b_3 is significantly less than zero, then those who spend time taking care of parents or children are more likely to experience economic hardship.

A potential statistical problem might bias the coefficient estimates if there are variables omitted from the X vector that are correlated with both wellbeing and work history, health status and/or intrafamily transfers. A possible solution for this problem is to control on the respondent's earnings: that is, people who earn more on their jobs during their work lives may be less likely to experience economic hardship and, for example, may be in better health due to greater resources available to obtain good medical care. However, including earnings as an explanatory variable is itself problematic since earnings are a component of many wellbeing measures. In other words, including earnings would be analogous to regressing one variable on itself and would introduce endogeneity. We suggest, however, that our approach to modeling wellbeing obviates this statistical concern. This is because we include the most important determinants of earnings, namely human capital variables such as education and labor market experience (Willis 1986). Since the specifications represented in equations (1) and (2) include these characteristics, our models may be interpreted as a reduced form of a system of equations where the structural equation includes earnings. Earnings are therefore implicitly controlled for, so potential omitted variable bias is avoided.

An additional statistical problem may result from the specification of work history characteristics, since respondent wellbeing (particularly current wellbeing) is likely to be influenced by one's current employment status. Thus, those people who withdraw from the labor force later may be better off because their earnings are greater, other things equal. Current employment status, for this reason, should not be used in a model of older people's economic wellbeing since those with few resources may be more likely to work.[14] One possible solution to this problem would be to specify a model of the labor force participation decision along with the model of economic wellbeing, and to estimate the system of equations jointly. Instead, acknowledging the difficulty of estimating simultaneous structural models of retirement behavior, we instead exclude measures of current employment status. Therefore we interpret results as a reduced form specification of a general structural retirement model.[15]

A related problem would arise if the number of total years worked in the labor market were included as an explanatory variable in the wellbeing equation. Clearly a worker who retires earlier will have worked fewer years, all else held constant. To the extent that economic status affects the decision to retire, the number of years spent in the labor market will be endogenous as well. We therefore create measures of early work history, prior to the age of 50. Because relatively few workers have retired by this age for economic reasons, this variable should be exogenous to current wellbeing.

Another issue encountered here involves the distinction raised earlier between the economic wellbeing of married versus nonmarried men and women. Because the wellbeing of married men and women is identical by construction, differences in wellbeing and its correlates by sex may be detected only by comparing nonmarried individuals. Our equations (1) and (2) include all men and women, controlling for differences in spouse's characteristics so as to take advantage of the larger sample sizes and thus obtain precise estimates of the coefficients. But at the same time these equations impose a restriction that the nonmarried and married persons' parameters are identical. To test the effect of this assumption, we also estimate equations (1) and (2) for the subsample of nonmarried men and women. Because of the considerably smaller size of this subsample, whites and nonwhites are pooled when estimating these models.

Before turning to the results, we note that interpretation of findings requires some care. The form of the model suggests that parameter estimates indicate a causal relationship between the relevant righthand variable and economic wellbeing. Such an interpretation would be incorrect if any of the right hand side variables are endogenous. For example, wealthier respondents who have access to better quality medical care might be in better health. In this case, a positive relationship would be observed between health and wellbeing that would not be causal; improving women's health relative to men through active federal policies, for example, might not reduce the gap in wellbeing under these circumstances. To the extent that such endogeneity exists, the results presented here can only be interpreted as descriptive, expressing relationships between variables without indicating causality. Statistical techniques that can examine the scope of this problem are left to future work.

Predicting Wellbeing

Parameter estimates from these models are used to derive predictions regarding women's wellbeing at the end of their worklives, associated with differences in work history, health status, and intrafamily transfers. For instance, we know that female labor force participation rates for women have risen continuously over the past several decades. As a result older women will have work histories that converge, over time, to the patterns exhibited by older men. We use our regression results to simulate how older women's wellbeing would change if their work histories were to become identical to those of older men. Similar analyses are conducted for health status and intrafamily transfers.

Methodologically, the difference in wellbeing between older men and women is decomposed into the portion due to differences in characteristics and the portion due to differences in returns to those characteristics between the two groups.[16] More specifically, we compute:

$$\overline{WB^m} - \overline{WB^f} = \sum_{i=1}^{k} \beta_i^m * (\overline{X_i^m} - \overline{X_i^f}) + \sum_{i=1}^{k} \overline{X_i^f} * (\beta_i^m - \beta_i^f),$$

where WB represents a particular measure of economic wellbeing; b represents the vector of regression coefficients estimated from equation (1) above; represents a vector of mean characteristics, f and m represent men and women respectively; and k indexes characteristics. The first expression on the right-hand side of this equation is said to represent the "explained" part of the differential in wellbeing because it is attributed to the different characteristics of men and women.[17] The second expression is said to represent the "unexplained" part of the differential because it produces differences in wellbeing even if men and women had the same characteristics.[18]

Our simulation strategy determines the percentage reduction in the gap in wellbeing between men and women that would occur if both had identical characteristics. Formally, this involves estimating

$$\frac{\sum_{i=1}^{k} \beta_i^m * (\overline{X}_i^m - \overline{X}_i^f)}{\overline{WB}^m - \overline{WB}^f} * 100 \ .$$

This expression represents the gap in wellbeing that can be "explained" by differences in characteristics as a percentage of the size of the gap. Analogous statistics are estimated for each measure of wellbeing and by ethnic group as well as for nonmarried men and women.

Empirical Context

The dataset employed in this research is wave 1 of the Health and Retirement Study (HRS) (see Chapter 1). Respondents answered 90-minute interviews on four main subject areas: work and pensions, health and functioning status, family structure and transfers, and economic status. This data source is ideally suited to the present research because it contains a wide array of information regarding respondents' income, wealth, work history, health status, and intrafamily transfers of time as well as their demographic characteristics. Full information in all of these areas is available for women, in contrast to many previous data collection efforts such as the Retirement History Survey. By explicit design, the HRS oversamples blacks and Hispanics at twice their proportional rate in the population. This was done to permit extensive examination of groups previously understudied, so that findings can be of benefit to diverse racial and ethnic groups. Throughout our analyses of older women's wellbeing, we devote careful attention to key differences between whites and nonwhites (both black and Hispanic).[19]

Measures of Wellbeing

We begin by examining wellbeing measures that rely on current income and projected retirement income. In the HRS, respondent income included earnings, unemployment compensation, social security, private pensions, and interest and dividends; thus was provided a complete picture of total household current income. These current income data are used to create a household's current poverty status and income-to-needs ratio, by merging federal definitions of the poverty line for families of different sizes and composition in 1992, the year the Wave 1 HRS survey was conducted. Projected wellbeing measures required projecting expected retirement income to age 62. A unique aspect of the HRS is that administrative records on earnings histories and employer-supplied pensions were obtained from respondents furnishing appropriate signed consent forms.[20] Thus projected social security payments are devised based on the workers' earnings histories from the Social Security Administration regarding their future benefit levels, and expected pension benefits are derived from the Pension Provider Survey.[21] Therefore retirement benefits are measured with an unusually high degree of precision for this nationally representative sample. For married couples, expected benefits of both respondents are summed to obtain a measure of projected social security benefits for the family. The final source of projected retirement income is income from assets.[22] Here we convert asset values to an annuitized flow of funds, separately examining the influence of including or excluding the value of owner-occupied housing. Although families may not actually translate their assets into cash in this manner, this approach is useful in representing the flow of resources over which the family could have command if it so chose. This approach is therefore consistent with wealth-based measures of wellbeing, as described earlier.

Determinants of Wellbeing

Three sets of determinants of wellbeing are considered in the analysis to follow: work history, health history and status, and intrafamily transfers of time. The HRS contains detailed information on each of these factors. Survey responses regarding each respondent's work history include the length of time spent on a current or most recent job, and the number of years spent in the next most recent job that lasted five or more years. From this information, we construct three alternative measures of a respondent's work history. We create two different dummy variables, indicating whether or not a respondent worked at all before age 50, and the second indicating whether any jobs were held for longer than five years. We then create a measure of the length of time spent on the worker's longest job before age 50 that represents the maximum value of the available job duration measures. These measures are all based on the respondent's work history before age 50 to avoid potential endogeneity biases, as described above.

Each respondent is asked his or her health status and history as well. Several different objective measures are available, including reported physical limitations and incidence of specific illnesses. A respondent's physical limitations are measured using the reported level of difficulty of completing given tasks, ranging from running a mile, to picking up a dime from a table, to getting dressed without help. Many of these limitations are correlated, so including the entire set of them is superfluous. Instead, we select a subset that is intended to cover a range of limitations from relatively mild to more severe. These measures include the ability to run one mile, walk several blocks, or carry a 10-pound bag with little or no difficulty. We also examine the effects on wellbeing of specific health problems experienced by HRS respondents either currently or in the past. These illnesses include cancer, heart problems, high blood pressure, arthritis, lung disease, and diabetes.

The HRS also collects data on transfers of time to parents and grand-children. A discrete measure is used indicating whether any time is spent with a parent or grandchild over the past twelve months. In addition, we use a continuous measure of the amount of time spent, for those with a positive time transfer, and zero otherwise.

Empirical Results of Wellbeing Analysis

Evidence on the determinants of measures of wellbeing is taken up next. In each case, the unit of analysis is age-eligible respondents to the HRS (those respondents and spouses between the age of 51 and 61), weighted to repre-sent the national population from which the probability sample was drawn.

Measures of current and projected future economic wellbeing by demo-graphic group are reported in Table 1. The results reinforce the view that older women are substantially worse off financially relative to older men. For example, older white men have a median household current income about 20 percent greater than white women. This difference is not entirely driven by differences in household composition since the median income-to-needs ratio is 15 percent greater for men relative to women. The female poverty rate among whites is 1.5 times that of men in this sample as well. For non-whites, the median family income gap is similar at 16 percent, but the lower absolute income levels of nonwhites imply that both poverty rates based on current income are much higher than for whites.

Table 1 also reports statistics regarding projected retirement income, and here the results show a substantial drop in family income for men and women of all ethnic groups.[23] Projected income declines are on the order of about one-quarter to one-third across all demographic groups, but the like-lihood of being poor is much larger for nonwhites than for whites. This may suggest that the bottom part of the white income distribution is somewhat protected from income loss, though women less well than men; by contrast, projected poverty rates for nonwhite men rise to 32 percent and for women to 44 percent.

A striking result in Table 1 is that the sex difference in retiree wellbeing is anticipated to be considerably smaller than the white/nonwhite difference. For instance, although white women are projected to be almost twice as likely than white men to live in poverty, nonwhite women are seven times more likely. Below we examine the factors associated with these differences in detail.

Current and future measures of wellbeing by marital status are given in

TABLE 1: Measures of Wellbeing by Race and Sex[1]

	White		Nonwhite	
	Men	Women	Men	Women
Based on current income				
Median family income	49,000	40,580	30,855	24,652
Median income-to-needs ratio (%)	4.63	4.04	2.67	2.14
% in poverty	4.3	6.9	16.9	22.7
Number of observations	3,373	3,600	1,216	1,564
Based on projected retirement income[2]				
Projected median retirement income	31,682	27,685	16,485	12,484
Projected median retirement income, excl. annualized value of housing wealth	27,104	23,471	14,193	10,270
Projected median income-to-needs ratio (%)	3.21	2.97	1.43	1.13
Projected median income-to-needs ratio excl. annualized value of housing wealth	2.77	2.49	1.24	0.95
Projected % in poverty	6.7	11.3	32.2	43.8
Projected % in poverty, excluding annuitized value of housing wealth	8.8	14.9	37.4	50.2
Number of observations[3]	3,216	3,451	1,091	1,416

Source: Authors' calculations.
Notes: [1] All dollar figures in 1992 dollars. Estimates are weighted to provide nationally representative statistics.
[2] For retirement at age 62.
[3] Means for some variables are estimated from fewer observations due to missing data.

Table 2. Though we would anticipate that married men's and women's wellbeing would be equivalent on average, our results here indicate that average household income for married women is somewhat below the average household income for married men. The discrepancy is due to the sampling structure of the HRS. In particular, age-eligible respondents are between 51 and 61 years old, and in the United States, men tend to marry women who are younger they are. Therefore HRS respondent males will tend to be married to women at least four years younger than they are — who are more likely to be working — while age-eligible HRS respondent women will tend to have older retired husbands. This finding reinforces the notion that we need to control for spouse's characteristics when married men and women are included the analysis, as represented by equations (1) and (2).

This consideration is not relevant, of course, for single men and women, where we note that unmarried women have one quarter less current income than unmarried men, and the gap rises to over one-third after they reach retirement age. The table also makes clear that unmarried men and women are considerably less well off than those who are married, even after control-

TABLE 2: Measures of Wellbeing by Marital Status and Sex[1]

	Married		Nonmarried	
	Men	*Women*	*Men*	*Women*
Based on current income				
Median family income	49,500	45,000	25,300	20,000
Median income-to-needs ratio (%)	4.42	4.22	2.74	2.13
% in poverty	4.1	5.0	17.8	22.5
Number of observations	3,668	3,442	921	1,722
Based on projected retirement income[2]				
Projected median retirement income	30,775	30,564	12,580	8,819
Projected median retirement income, excl. annualized value of housing wealth	26,536	26,118	10,864	6,864
Projected median income-to-needs ratio (%)	2.94	3.12	1.53	1.00
Projected median income-to-needs ratio excl. annualized value of housing wealth	2.54	2.67	1.33	0.79
Projected % in poverty	6.9	5.9	30.3	44.8
Projected % in poverty, excluding annuitized value of housing wealth	9.4	8.4	33.5	52.3
Number of observations[3]	3,437	3,242	870	1,625

Source: Authors' calculations.
Notes: See Table 1.

ling for household size in measures like the income-to-needs ratio. Current poverty rates for this cohort on the verge of retirement are 18–23 percent for the nonmarried group, four to five times higher than among their married counterparts. Projected poverty differences after retirement rise, with unmarried persons facing poverty rates of 30–45 percent, or up to nine times higher than the married members of the cohort.

Components of household income are displayed by race in Table 3, and by marital status in Table 4. Evaluated at the mean or the median, earnings represent the largest component of household income at the time the respondents are first observed. Values of the other components of income are virtually uniformly equal to zero, even though means are occasionally substantial. This indicates that distributions of non-earned income are highly skewed, for all marital groups and both ethnic groups explored. Thus the mean of income from capital (like interest and dividends), from pensions and annuities, and from other family members is nontrivial, though medians are tiny indeed. In the two largest income categories, earnings and capital income, men receive more than women, on average. Among the nonmarried, women receive larger flows of income from other family members and from pensions and annuities. This latter finding is consistent with survivor benefits paid to widows through social security.

TABLE 3: Current Income Components by Race and Sex: Mean/Median[1]

	White		Nonwhite	
	Men	*Women*	*Men*	*Women*
Family earnings	45,456/38,200	34,196/26,250	29,600/25,000	19,862/24,000
Capital income (interest, dividends, etc.)	7,628/200	6,622/180	2,414/100	1,580/0
Disability benefits	666/0	648/0	674/0	501/0
Income from pensions and annuities	2,546/0	4090/0	1,548/0	2,426/0
SSI or other welfare program	156/0	149/0	418/0	588/0
Unemployment/worker's compensation	399/0	308/0	488/0	353/0
Other sources of income	163/0	250/0	90/0	182/0
Income from other family members (besides spouse)	3,559/0	4,153/0	4,062/0	6,358/0
Total family income	61,875/49,000	51,114/40,580	42,368/39,918	33,617/30,855

Source: Authors' calculations.
Notes:
[1] All dollar figures in 1992 dollars.
[2] Estimates obtained from reported income and income imputed by the Institute for Survey Research at the University of Michigan. Estimates are weighted to provide nationally representative statistics.

TABLE 4: Current Income Components by Marital Status and Sex: Mean / Median[1]

	Married		Nonmarried	
	Men	*Women*	*Men*	*Women*
Family earnings	45,271 / 39,000	37,281 / 30,500	25,259 / 16,744	15,010 / 11,013
Capital income (interest, dividends, etc.)	6,807 / 50	6,775 / 100	4,012 / 0	1,736 / 0
Disability benefits	642 / 0	725 / 0	774 / 0	359 / 0
Income from pensions and annuities	2,458 / 0	4,708 / 0	1,581 / 0	1,649 / 0
SSI or other welfare program	146 / 0	138 / 0	539 / 0	570 / 0
Unemployment/worker's compensation	455 / 0	387 / 0	296 / 0	192 / 0
Other sources of income	139 / 0	129 / 0	164 / 0	428 / 0
Income from other family members (besides spouse)	3,918 / 0	4,203 / 0	2,796 / 0	6,056 / 0
Total family income	62,529 / 49,500	56,482 / 45,000	39,337 / 25,300	26,902 / 20,000

Source: Authors' calculations.
Notes: See Table 3.

Descriptive statistics regarding the components of projected retirement income appear by race in Table 5, and by marital status in Table 6. When households are differentiated by race (Table 5), projected social security benefits are roughly equivalent by sex. The differences that emerge in projected wellbeing of men and women occur because men are more likely to live in households with greater projected pension benefits and asset holdings (and, hence, larger projected annuity flows from assets). As expected, these differences are compounded when nonmarried men and women are compared (Table 6). Older women's households are projected to receive lower amounts of income in virtually every category across demographic groups. In most cases, mean as well as median values reported in Tables 5 and 6 are either very small or zero for all components besides housing. Even evaluated at the mean, the value of owner-occupied housing represents around a quarter to a third of total net worth for this cohort on the verge of retirement.[24] With the exception of owner-occupied housing, asset values in each category are uniformly higher for nonmarried men than for nonmarried women.

Using conventional tests of significance, there appears to be no difference in overall net worth between men and women regardless of race, evaluated at either means or medians. When we focus on nonmarried men and women only, however, we see that median values of net worth are roughly similar, but the mean value is almost twice as high for men as for women. These findings indicate that the distribution of net worth for nonmarried men is more heavily skewed than it is for women; that is, there are more very wealthy nonmarried men than nonmarried women. Strikingly, differences in net worth are far greater between whites and nonwhites than they are between men and women. Evaluated at the median, for example, white men have more than three times the assets of nonwhite men.

In Tables 7 and 8 we report values of the three sets of factors of most interest to our study, namely health, work history, and family transfers. When we compare averages of each variable by race, marital status, and sex, it is clear that these three factors differ dramatically across groups. The first block of each table reports the percentage of respondents who report they are able to perform certain activities. Men report many fewer physical limitations than women, as measured by indicators of the ability to run one mile, walk several blocks, or carry a 10-pound bag with little or no difficulty. Although 95 percent of white men can carry a 10-pound bag (such as a bag of groceries, as worded in the survey), only 83 percent of white women can do so. Among nonmarried respondents, 94 percent of men but only 76 percent of the women can perform this task with little or no difficulty. Across measures and holding sex constant, whites and married respondents appear to have fewer limitations than nonwhites and those who are not married.

These physical limitation patterns are also correlated with health differences by sex, as is evident from the second panel of Tables 7 and 8. Here we see that women and nonwhites report a higher prevalence of many serious

TABLE 5: Projected Retirement Income and Wealth Components by Race and Sex: Mean / Median[1]

	White		Nonwhite	
	Men	*Women*	*Men*	*Women*
Projected retirement income				
Annual social security benefit	12,562/13,340	11,126/12,319	9,283/9,199	7,345/6,432
Annual pension benefit	10,607/4,483	8,774/3,362	6,554/1,714	5,334/0
Annuity value of asset holdings (incl. housing)	19,826/8,030	17,609/7,703	6,111/2,447	6,234/2,159
Annuity value of asset holdings (excl. housing)	15,209/3,600	13,094/3,224	3,647/242	3,971/128
Current asset holdings				
Home	106,485/53,000	71,324/53,000	36,501/22,000	33,519/19,000
Other real estate	64,583/0	53,878/0	22,951/0	30,174/0
Vehicle	17,842/10,000	15,335/9,000	9,473/5,000	7,047/2,500
Liquid assets (checking/savings account, etc.)	26,585/7,000	26,214/7,000	8,131/800	6,731/200
Stocks	25,339/0	25,574/0	3,346/0	4,940/0
Bonds	3,740/0	3,225/0	139/0	582/0
IRA	23,872/0	24,544/0	5,484/0	5,855/0
Business	63,595/0	46,374/0	12,994/0	10,308/0
Other assets	11,547/0	11,552	2,117/0	2,148/0
Amount of debt	3,808/0	3,166	3,120/0	2,136/0
Mean current net worth	304,741	274,856	98,015	99,169
Median current net worth	132,750	129,250	39,075	34,000

Source: Authors' calculations.
Notes: See Table 3.

TABLE 6: Projected Retirement Income and Wealth Components by Marital Status and Sex: Mean/Median[1]

	Married		Nonmarried	
	Men	Women	Men	Women
Projected retirement income				
Annual social security benefit	13,133/13,678	12,777/13,199	6,244/6,240	4,603/4,704
Annual pension benefit	10,398/4,912	9,928/4,603	6,088/0	3,388/0
Annuity value of asset holdings (incl. housing)	17,266/7,082	18,123/7,720	11,910/2,323	6,252/1,954
Annuity value of asset holdings (excl. housing)	12,875/2,785	13,457/3,150	9,459/611	3,902/175
Current asset holdings				
Home	69,501/51,000	72,530/55,000	33,056/0	34,578/8,000
Other real estate	58,319/0	60,636/0	34,561/0	18,840/0
Vehicles	16,876/10,000	16,726/10,000	10,639/3,500	5,028/2,000
Liquid assets (checking/savings account)	22,572/5,500	25,477/6,900	18,202/0	9,993/500
Stocks	21,026/0	24,298/0	13,473/0	9,383/0
Bonds	2,745/0	2,779/0	2,944/0	1,717/0
IRA	21,324/0	24,822/0	9,742/0	7,015/0
Business	55,053/0	50,180/0	30,804/0	6,011/0
Other assets	8,748/0	10,474	10,243/0	5,164/0
Amount of debt	3,951/0	2,946/0	2,327/0	2,669/0
Mean current net worth	272,215	284,977	161,338	95,059
Median current net worth	120,000	129,900	34,000	29,800

Source: Authors' calculations.
Notes: See Table 3.

TABLE 7: Characteristics of HRS Sample by Race and Sex[1]

	White		Nonwhite	
	Men	*Women*	*Men*	*Women*
Physical limitations (%)				
Able to run 1 mile with little or no difficulty	38.4	23.7	44.7	28.6
Able to walk several blocks with little or no difficulty	88.8	85.5	83.0	78.9
Able to carry a 10-pound bag with little or no difficulty	95.4	83.4	88.3	74.6
Illnesses (%)				
Have had cancer	3.2	8.3	3.0	5.5
Have heart problems	15.5	10.5	13.0	11.7
Have high blood pressure	12.3	12.9	17.5	25.0
Have arthritis	31.0	43.8	30.0	45.7
Have lung disease	8.5	8.7	4.9	7.8
Have diabetes	6.5	5.6	11.4	14.6
Work history				
Ever worked before age 50 (%)	96.0	84.4	89.9	78.2
Ever held job lasting longer than 5 years before age 50 (%)	90.2	65.0	80.4	62.6
Length of longest job held before age 50 (yrs.)	17.0	8.7	12.9	8.8
Family transfers				
Spent time caring for grandchildren in past year (%)	22.8	33.1	20.6	30.1
Hours spent caring for grand-children in past year[2]	388	725	601	1,199
Spent time caring for parents/in-laws in past year (%)	4.5	6.0	3.8	5.9
Hours spent caring for parents/in-laws in past year[2]	479	920	394	980
Number of observations[3]	*3,382*	*3,632*	*1,221*	*1,590*

Source: Authors' calculations.
Notes:
[1] Estimates are weighted averages to provide nationally representative statistics.
[2] Conditional on spending some time caring for grandchildren/parents.
[3] Means for some variables are estimated from fewer observations due to missing data.

TABLE 8: Characteristics of HRS Sample by Marital Status and Sex[1]

	Married		Nonmarried	
	Men	*Women*	*Men*	*Women*
Physical limitations (%)				
Able to run 1 mile with little or no difficulty	40.2	25.9	36.9	22.1
Able to walk several blocks with little or no difficulty	88.8	86.0	83.4	79.6
Able to carry a 10-pound bag with little or no difficulty	95.3	95.3	93.5	76.4
Illnesses (%)				
Have had cancer	3.2	7.4	2.7	8.4
Have heart problems	14.8	10.0	16.0	12.5
Have high blood pressure	12.8	13.2	15.3	20.6
Have arthritis	30.3	42.1	33.2	48.8
Have lung disease	7.5	7.3	9.3	11.2
Have diabetes	7.2	6.6	8.6	9.6
Work history				
Ever worked before age 50 (%)	95.8	83.5	90.9	82.0
Ever held job lasting longer than 5 years before age 50 (%)	90.1	63.2	80.7	67.4
Length of longest job held before age 50 (yrs.)	16.7	8.4	14.0	9.4
Family transfers				
Spent time caring for grandchildren in past year (%)	25.7	35.7	8.2	25.1
Hours spent caring for grand-children in past year[2]	420	782	465	938
Spent time caring for parents/ in-laws in past year (%)	4.9	6.2	2.2	5.4
Hours spent caring for parents/ in-laws in past year[2]	428	855	835	1,139
Number of observations[3]	*3,681*	*3,498*	*922*	*1,724*

Source: Authors' calculations.
Notes: See Table 7.

diseases and health problems: for instance, older women are half again as likely as men to report they have arthritis. Women are considerably more likely to have had cancer as well. Among nonmarried respondents, for example, 8 percent of women compared to 3 percent of men reported having had cancer. In contrast, however, men are more likely to report heart problems than women. Differences by race and marital status can be observed as well: in particular, nonwhite and nonmarried respondents are considerably more likely to report high blood pressure and diabetes than white and married respondents.

A third dimension along which we expect older men and women to differ is with respect to work histories. This is confirmed in the third panel of Tables 7 and 8, where we see that almost all (90 percent) of the white men worked on a job lasting at least 5 years before the age of 50, but only two-thirds of white women worked on a job lasting that long. Corresponding figures were somewhat lower for nonwhite men — 80 percent, but similar for nonwhite women — 63 percent. More striking are the results about the longest job people held prior to age 50. Men averaged 13–17 years, while women of both ethnic groups averaged only 9 years. On average, married women had longest job tenures of one year less than their nonmarried counterparts (8 versus 9 years), but similar percentages had ever worked prior to age 50 (82 and 84 percent).

The final panel in Tables 7 and 8 describes respondents' time transfers to parents and/or grandchildren. As expected, older HRS women are considerably more likely to make such transfers; also, those women who do so spend considerably more time in this activity than men. Transfers to grandchildren are also considerably more likely than transfers to parents. Among the women, for example, one third provide cared for their grandchildren, but only 6 percent provide care for their parents. By contrast, about one-fifth of the men cared for their grandchildren, but 4–5 percent cared for their parents. A substantial difference is evident by marital status: only 8 percent of nonmarried men spent time caring for grandchildren, whereas a full 25 percent of nonmarried women took care of their grandchildren (among both sexes, nonmarried persons afforded relatively little care for their parents). Of course many currently nonmarried persons have previously been married.

Multivariate Statistical Findings

Taken as a whole, the statistics presented thus far suggest that (1) older women on the verge of retirement are in worse health than men in several but not all dimensions; (2) these women have had weaker labor force attachment over their lifetimes than men; and (3) these women spend more time than men caring for other family members. These observed differences between men and women may help explain sex-based differences in wellbeing, and in this section we use multivariate techniques presented above to explore these links.

Before presenting the results, however, we first split the sample by poverty status and sex, and compute summary statistics of health status, work history, and intrafamily transfers for each subgroup. The purpose of this exercise is to determine whether there are any simple correlations between each of these characteristics and economic wellbeing. The results, appearing in Table 9, indicate the anticipated patterns. Men and women who are in poverty are uniformly in poorer health, have weaker labor market histories, and, among those that care for parents and/or grandchildren, contribute more time to this activity.

In order to make our presentation more accessible, parameter estimates of multivariate models of wellbeing are relegated to the Appendix. Here we simply note that the parameter estimates obtained from these models are used to decompose the gap in economic wellbeing into the fraction explained by health, work history, and intrafamily transfers. Following equation (3), we determine the fraction of the difference in wellbeing by sex/ ethnic group and report the results in Tables 10A–C. For simplicity, results are derived using male coefficients but we note that results obtained using female coefficients are qualitatively similar.

The results of this exercise lead us to conclude that work history patterns are strongly related to observed differences in wellbeing experienced by older men and women in the HRS sample. Focusing first on whites (Table 10A), we see that the gap in current family income would be diminished by 25 percent, if women had the same labor market history as men. Similarly, observed differences in current poverty rates and the income-to-needs ratio would have been cut by 34–44 percent. Differences in health by sex also explain a sizable portion of the sex difference in current wellbeing among whites, but intrafamily time transfers apparently play no consistent role. Thus health differences are associated with about a 20–25 percent difference in wellbeing between white men and women, irrespective of the measure of wellbeing employed. The estimated effects of time transfers are somewhat erratic, with differences by sex explaining virtually none of the difference in log family income, about 13 percent of the difference in income-to-needs, and actually indicate that more women would fall into poverty if the difference in time transfers between white men and women were eliminated. This final statistic may indicate endogeneity in these transfer measures; those respondents who spend time caring for family members are the ones who can afford to do so.

A parallel analysis for nonwhite men and women appears in Table 10B, with similar but not identical findings. Labor market history explains roughly 26–40 percent of the income gap between men and women, as for whites.

TABLE 9: Characteristics of HRS Sample by Poverty Status and Sex[1]

	Men		Women	
	In Poverty	*Not in Poverty*	*In Poverty*	*Not in Poverty*
Health measures (%)				
Able to run 1 mile with little or no difficulty	24.8	40.6	18.5	25.5
Able to walk several blocks with little or no difficulty	66.6	89.2	63.8	86.4
Able to carry a 10-pound bag with little or no difficulty	76.0	93.1	61.2	83.8
Have had cancer	5.8	3.0	6.9	7.8
Have heart problems	23.2	14.4	18.8	9.8
Have high blood pressure	20.5	12.7	24.2	14.5
Have arthritis	39.7	30.2	59.2	42.4
Have lung disease	18.3	7.1	14.7	7.8
Have diabetes	10.5	7.2	15.4	6.6
Labor market history measures				
Ever worked before age 50 (%)	84.5	95.6	68.7	84.7
Held job lasting longer than 5 years before age 50 (%)	71.6	89.5	45.1	66.7
Length of longest job held before age 50 (yrs.)	11.4	16.5	5.5	9.1
Intrafamily transfers				
Spent time caring for grandchildren in past year (%)	13.8	23.1	30.3	32.7
Hours spent caring for grand-children in past year[2]	475	422	1,255	772
Spent time caring for parents/in-laws in past year (%)	3.7	4.4	5.0	6.1
Hours spent caring for parents/in-laws in past year[2]	988	435	1,730	857
Number of observations[3]	*380*	*4,222*	*648*	*4,574*

Source: Authors' calculations.
Notes: See Table 7.

More different however is the key role of health problems, which now explain an equally large share of the gap. Finally, time devoted to caring for parents and grandchildren does not predict gaps in wellbeing, as was true for whites. In fact, the negative sign indicates that the gap would possibly increase if men and women spent the same amount of time caring for family members.

We repeat the analysis for nonmarried men and women separately in

TABLE 10: Decomposition of Differences in Current Measures of Wellbeing

Measure of Current Wellbeing	% of Differential Explained		
	Log Family Income	Income-to-Needs Ratio	Probability of Being in Poverty[1]
A. Between White Men and Women			
Health history and status	18.5	24.2	21.5
Labor market history	25.4	43.5	33.5
Transfers of time to family	1.0	12.7	−20.6
B. Between Nonwhite Men and Women			
Health history and status	32.9	36.7	43.2
Labor market history	25.6	22.7	41.0
Transfers of time to family	−6.0	−1.0	−25.3
C. Between Unmarried Men and Women			
Health history and status	34.4	20.6	57.7
Labor market history	35.4	16.4	82.2
Transfers of time to family	−3.1	20.0	−55.0

Source: Authors' calculations.
Notes: [1] Coefficients estimated from linear probability model using male coefficients.

Table 10C, of special interest because of the particular vulnerability to poverty. Of course, the sample size is reduced, which in turn cuts the precision of the estimated parameters. But here too, we find that labor market attachment and health factors play the key role in explaining differences in current economic wellbeing. These results further confirm that intrafamily transfers do not provide a particularly powerful explanation for differences in wellbeing between men and women.

Turning to anticipated future patterns of wellbeing, Table 11 reinforces and extends previous findings. First, we emphasize the fundamentally key role of differences in labor market attachment for whites and nonmarried persons. Thus, if a white woman reached retirement age having had a typical man's lifetime labor force pattern, her retirement income and income relative to needs would be at least equal to or greater than her male counterpart's.[25] A nonmarried woman with a labor market history like that of a man would do almost as well. Since nonwhite women tend to be more closely attached to the job market over their lifetimes, the role of labor market differences is relatively smaller, but it remains key: 45 percent of the gap by sex is attributable to these factors. For both ethnic groups, health problems are also a factor driving differences in wellbeing, particularly for men and women whose income is low relative to needs. We again show that time

TABLE 11: Decomposition of Differences in Projected Measures of Wellbeing

Measure of Projected Wellbeing in Retirement	% of Differential Explained		
	Log Family Income	Income-to-Needs Ratio	Probability of Being in Poverty[1]
A. Between White Men and Women			
Health history and status	23.7	39.9	25.8
Labor market history	106.8	176.3	74.8
Transfers of time to family	5.9	10.8	3.6
B. Between Nonwhite Men and Women			
Health history and status	27.0	102.6	24.6
Labor market history	44.6	194.3	55.7
Transfers of time to family	−3.2	−9.2	−18.9
C. Between Unmarried Men and Women			
Health history and status	1.1	13.0	15.3
Labor market history	85.8	38.9	100.1
Transfers of time to family	15.0	19.8	10.3

Source: Authors' calculations.
Notes: See Table 10.

transfers to family members are weak predictors of women's relative income and poverty disadvantage.

Conclusions

Researchers seeking to understand causes of poverty among older women have focused, in the main, on marital status changes as a cause of poverty. Here we explore how other factors affect older women's wellbeing, focusing specifically on labor market attachment, health, and transfers of time to family members. Because there is some debate in the literature over how best to measure wellbeing, we use three measures: family income, the ratio of family income to needs, and the poverty line. We compute these as of the date respondents answered the HRS survey, and also at age 62, the modal retirement age in the United States. To obtain projected figures we annuitize retiree wealth by converting people's asset holdings into a cash flow available for consumption needs, along with projected social security and pension benefits. These computations, displayed by sex, ethnic group, and marital status, are then related to people's work histories, health, and intra-family transfers of time. We use multivariate regression estimates to simulate how patterns of wellbeing might change if older women's characteristics were to become more like men's.

Our results show that older women on the verge of retirement have less income, and are projected to have less income when retired, than their male counterparts. Similarly, nonwhites are in worse condition than whites in terms of income, poverty status, and income-to-needs ratios. And nonmarried women have less income now, and their deficit will drop farther in retirement.

We also show that older women are more vulnerable than men because they are in worse health than men in many respects; they had weaker labor force attachment over their lifetimes; and they spend more time than men caring for other family members. These different lifetime experiences translate into wellbeing in interesting ways. First, differences in health and labor market history explain a significant share of differences in the current income of men and women on the verge of retirement. Perhaps one-quarter to one-half of the overall gap in current wellbeing can be explained by each of these factors; taken together, they explain between half to three quarters of the gap. Second, the same two factors are even more important in explaining differences in projected wellbeing in retirement, with labor market histories dominating for whites and nonmarried persons. Thus, from one-half to all of the gap in projected wellbeing can be explained by these two factors alone. Third, transfers of time to family members appear to be a weak predictor of both current and future wellbeing. On the basis of these findings, health problems play an important role for women, and medical advances may not necessarily benefit women relative to men. In that event, the wellbeing gap between older men and women may persist to the extent that men and women experience different health challenges in their later years. On the other hand, it seems reasonable to project a narrowing of differences in economic wellbeing between men and women in the future. As women's labor force attachment continues to increase, future cohorts of women approaching retirement will have accumulated more years of work experience, enhancing their wellbeing relative to men.

The authors acknowledge research support for this study provided by the AARP Andrus Foundation, Wellesley College, the Wharton School, and the National Bureau of Economic Research. Opinions are solely those of the authors and not those of institutions with which they are affiliated.

Notes

1. See, e.g., McLanahan et al. (1989); Smolensky et al. (1988); Older Women's League (1995).

2. See Burkhauser et al. (1991); Boskin and Shoven (1988); Burkhauser and Duncan (1989); Holden et al. (1988); and Holden et al. (1986).

3. Although some research has separately examined the wellbeing of women of

different racial/ethnic groups (cf. Torres-Gil, 1986; Markides et al., 1990; Wilson-Ford, 1990), this work has been hindered by small sample sizes in existing datasets, a defect remedied in the present study.

4. See, e.g., O'Rand and Landerman (1984) and Van Velsor and O'Rand (1984).

5. Among these are Stone (1990) and Wood (1991).

6. See, e.g., Palmer et al. (1988); Ruggles (1990); and Moon (1977).

7. For a discussion of equivalence scales see Ruggles (1990) and Nelson (1993). Some analysts extend income-based measures to include the value of in-kind income. A problem with this approach is that there is no agreed-on method to value it. (Some use the cost of providing the benefit, another seeks to determine what an individual would be willing to pay to receive it. Economic theory tells us that the two concepts are not the same.) No consensus exists in the literature, and most economic wellbeing studies of younger persons also focus on cash income, so we follow this approach here when measuring income of older women.

8. See Burkhauser and Duncan (1988), Holden et al. (1988), and Smolensky et al. (1988).

9. Burkhauser et al. (1985), Moon (1977), and Hurd (1989) employ similar measures.

10. Actual consumption patterns through retirement may differ from these projected annuity payments (due to time preferences or bequest motives, for instance), but this measure adequately represents the resources available for consumption over the remainder of the household's life.

11. Components of this vector take on the value zero for those respondents who are not married. These variables must be included because the measures of wellbeing relate to households, not individuals.

12. Separate analyses of Hispanic and black men and women are hampered by sample sizes that are too small to yield robust results.

13. In all cases, F-tests reject the hypothesis that coefficients are equal across groups.

14. The problem is actually worse when using income-based measures of wellbeing since income includes earnings, which are positive only for those respondents who are currently employed. Previous studies have not recognized this issue.

15. See Lumsdaine et al. (1990), Stock and Wise (1990), and Rust (1989).

16. This approach is sometimes called a "Oaxaca decomposition" in reference to the work of Oaxaca (1973) that first used this approach to explore the components of the male-female wage differential.

17. The terminology "explained" may be somewhat misleading since it may suggest a causal relationship between the control variables and economic wellbeing that may not be warranted, as discussed above. Nevertheless, it is common practice to use this expression and we do so throughout this analysis.

18. An important complication in this analysis is that characteristics can be valued at either the "male rate" or the "female rate" (using the regression coefficients obtained from the sample of men or of women). A common approach is to report both and to consider the sensitivity of findings to the different approaches.

19. In addition, the analysis takes account of the fact that the HRS also oversampled residents of the state of Florida; sample weights are used to convert survey responses into responses representative of the overall population.

20. See the HRS web page for more information on these restricted data (www.umich.edu/~hrswww) and the Appendix for a discussion of how these data were derived.

21. For more on these datasets see Moore and Mitchell (this volume), Gustman et al. (this volume), and Mitchell, Olson, and Steinmeier (this volume).

22. The value of assets is reported by over half the HRS respondents and imputed

for the remainder. The Institute for Survey Research at the University of Michigan, the organization administering the HRS survey, uses a "hot-deck" imputation procedure, assigning equal asset values to families with similar characteristics.

23. Moore and Mitchell (this volume) show that retirement wealth could grow if retirement were deferred to, say, age 65.

24. To the extent that housing represents an illiquid asset that cannot readily be converted into retirement income, this value should be subtracted from total net worth to provide a measure of the resources available for consumption.

25. The implication that women's wellbeing would surpass men's if their labor market histories were equalized should be interpreted with some caution. Based on the rather large differences in work history currently observed between men and women, the simulation exercise we are conducting here narrows the gap beyond much of the variation that is observed in our sample (called out-of-sample prediction). If the relationship between work history and wellbeing is nonlinear, so that the return to additional work is greater for those who have worked less than for those who have worked more, then our methodology will overstate the narrowing in wellbeing if men and women had the same work history. Nevertheless, one can strongly conclude based on this evidence that women's wellbeing would be much improved relative to men if they had the same work history.

References

Blau, Francine D. and J. W. Graham. May 1990. "Black-White Differences in Wealth and Asset Composition." *Quarterly Journal of Economics*: 321–39.

Boskin, Michael J. and John B. Shoven. 1988. "Poverty Among the Elderly: Where are the Holes in the Safety Net?" In Zvi Bodie, John B. Shoven, and David A. Wise, eds., *Pensions in the U.S. Economy.* Chicago: University of Chicago Press: 115–38.

Burkhauser, Richard V., J. S. Butler, and Karen C. Holden. 1991. "How the Death of a Spouse Affects Economic Wellbeing After Retirement: A Hazard Model Approach." *Social Science Quarterly* 72, 3 (September): 504–19.

Burkhauser, Richard V., J. S. Butler, and J. T. Wilkinson. 1985. "Estimating Changes in Wellbeing Across Life: A Realized vs. Comprehensive Income Approach." In Martin David and Timothy Smeeding, eds., *Horizontal Equity, Uncertainty, and Economic Wellbeing.* Chicago: University of Chicago Press: 69–90.

Burkhauser, Richard V. and Greg J. Duncan. 1989. "Economic Risks of Gender Roles: Income Loss and Life Events over the Life Course." *Social Science Quarterly* (March): 3–23.

———. 1988. "Life Events, Public Policy, and the Economic Vulnerability of Children and the Elderly." In John L. Palmer, Timothy Smeeding, and B. Boyle Torrey, eds., *The Vulnerable.* Washington, D.C.: Urban Institute Press: 55–88.

Crown, William H., Phyllis Mutschler, James Schulz, and Robert Loew. 1993. "The Economic Status of Divorced Older Women." Working Paper, Heller School, Brandeis University.

Gustman, Alan L., Olivia S. Mitchell, Andrew A. Samwick, and Thomas L. Steinmeier. "Pension and Social Security Wealth in the Health and Retirement Study." In Robert Willis, ed., *Wealth, Work, and Health: Innovations in Survey Measurement in the Social Sciences,* forthcoming.

Holden, Karen C., Richard V. Burkhauser, and Daniel A. Myers. 1986. "Income Transitions at Older Stages of Life: The Dynamics of Poverty." *Gerontologist* (June): 292–97.

Holden, Karen C., Richard V. Burkhauser, and Daniel J. Feaster. 1988. "The Timing of Falls into Poverty After Retirement and Widowhood." *Demography* 25, 3 (August): 405–13.

Hurd, Michael D. 1989. "The Poverty of Widows: Future Prospects." In David A. Wise, ed. *The Economics of Aging.* Chicago: University of Chicago Press: 201–30.

Hurd, Michael D. and David A. Wise. 1989. "The Wealth and Poverty of Widows: Assets Before and After the Husband's Death." In David A. Wise, ed., *The Economics of Aging.* Chicago: University of Chicago Press: 177–200.

Lumsdaine, Robin, James Stock, and David A. Wise. 1990. "Efficient Windows and Labor Force Reduction." *Journal of Public Economics*, 43, 2: 131–59.

Markides, Kyriakos S., Jersey Liang, and James Jackson. 1990. "Race, Ethnicity, and Aging: Conceptual and Methodological Issues." In Robert H. Binstock and Linda K. George, eds., *Handbook of Aging and the Social Sciences*, San Diego, Calif.: Academic Press: 112–29.

McLanahan, S., A. Sorensen, and D. Watson. 1989. "Sex Differences in Poverty, 1950–1980." *Signs* (Autumn): 102–22.

Mitchell, Olivia S. 1988. "Worker Knowledge of Pension Provisions." *Journal of Labor Economics* 6, 1 (January): 21–39.

Mitchell, Olivia S. and James F. Moore. "Retirement Wealth Accumulation and Decumulation: New Developments and Outstanding Opportunities." *Journal of Risk and Insurance*, forthcoming.

Mitchell, Olivia S., Jan Olson, and Thomas L. Steinmeier. "Social Security Earnings and Projected Benefits." This volume.

Moon, Marilyn. 1977. *The Measurement of Economic Welfare.* New York: Academic Press.

Moore, James F. and Olivia S. Mitchell. "Projected Retirement Wealth and Saving Adequacy." This volume.

Nelson, Julie A. 1993. "Household Equivalence Scales: Theory Versus Policy?" *Journal of Labor Economics* 11, 3 (July): 471–93.

Oaxaca, Ronald L. 1973. "Male-Female Wage Differentials in Urban Labor Markets." *International Economic Review* 14, 3 (October): 693–709.

Older Women's League. 1995. *The Path to Poverty: An Analysis of Women's Retirement Income.* Mother's Day Report, Washington, D.C.: Older Women's League.

O'Rand, Angela M. and R. Landerman. 1984. "Women's and Men's Retirement Income Status: Early Family Role Effects." *Research on Aging* (March): 25–44.

Ory, Marcia G. and Huber R. Warner, eds. 1990. *Gender, Health, and Longevity: Multidisciplinary Perspectives.* New York: Springer.

Palmer, John L., Timothy Smeeding, and Christopher Jencks. 1988. "The Uses and Limits of Income Comparisons." In John Palmer, Timothy Smeeding, and Barbara Boyle Torrey, eds., *The Vulnerable*, Washington, D.C.: Urban Institute Press: 9–28.

Ruggles, Patricia. 1990. *Drawing the Line: Alternative Poverty Measures and the Implications for Public Policy.* Washington, D.C.: Urban Institute Press.

Rust, John. 1989. "A Dynamic Programming Model of Retirement Behavior." In David A. Wise ed., *The Economics of Aging.* Chicago: University of Chicago Press: 359–404.

Smolensky, Eugene, Sheldon Danziger, and Peter Gottschalk. 1988. "The Declining Significance of Age in the United States: Trends in the Wellbeing of Children and the Elderly Since 1939." In John Palmer, Timothy Smeeding, and B. Boyle Torrey, eds., *The Vulnerable.* Washington, D.C.: Urban Institute Press: 29–54.

Stock, James H. and David A. Wise. 1990. "Pensions, The Option Value of Work, and Retirement." 58(5) *Econometrica* (September) 1151–80.

Stone, Roberta. 1990. "Spouses and Children of Disabled Elders: How Large a Constituency for Long-Term Care Reform?" Rockville, Md.: U.S. Department of

Health and Human Services Public Health Service, Agency for Health Care Policy and Research.

Torres-Gil, Fernando. 1986. "Hispanics: A Special Challenge." In A. Pifer and L. Bronte, eds., *Our Aging Society: Paradox and Promise.* New York: W.W. Norton: 219–42.

U.S. Senate Special Committee on Aging, the American Association of Retired Persons, the Federal Council on the Aging, and the U.S. Administration on Aging. 1991. *Aging America: Trends and Projections*, 1991 Edition. Washington, D.C.: Department of Health and Human Services.

Van Velsor, Ellen and Angela M. O'Rand. May 1984. "Family Life Cycle, Work Career Patterns, and Women's Wages at Midlife." *Journal of Marriage and the Family*: 46, 2: 365–73.

Wilson-Ford, V. 1990. "Poverty Among Black Elderly Women." *Journal of Women and Aging* 2, 4: 5–21.

Wood, John B. 1991. "Caregivers as Comptrollers: Women and Long-Term Care and Cost Containment." *Journal of Aging and Social Policy* 3, 4: 31–46.

Willis, Robert J. 1986. "Wage Determinants: A Survey and Reinterpretation of Human Capital Earnings Functions." In Orley Ashenfelter and Richard Layard, eds., *Handbook of Labor Economics.* Amsterdam: North Holland.

APPENDIX TABLE 1A: Effect of Health, Labor Market History, and Intrafamily Transfers on Current Income-Based Measures of Wellbeing, White Respondents[1] (standard errors in parentheses)

Measure of Current Wellbeing	Log Family Income		Income-to-Needs Ratio		Poverty Status[2]	
	Men	Women	Men	Women	Men	Women
Health measures						
Able to run 1 mile with little or no difficulty	0.079	0.047	0.680	0.629	−0.140	0.201
	(0.027)	(0.030)	(0.198)	(0.166)	(0.116)	(0.101)
Able to walk several blocks with little or no difficulty	0.104	0.123	0.105	0.368	−0.317	−0.434
	(0.047)	(0.040)	(0.346)	(0.221)	(0.142)	(0.104)
Able to carry a 10-pound bag with little or no difficulty	0.218	0.051	0.605	0.141	−0.066	−0.196
	(0.056)	(0.037)	(0.409)	(0.204)	(0.165)	(0.103)
Have had cancer	−0.093	0.029	−0.409	−0.212	0.330	−0.131
	(0.069)	(0.044)	(0.510)	(0.246)	(0.203)	(0.148)
Have heart problems	0.010	−0.090	−0.012	−0.035	0.071	0.068
	(0.035)	(0.042)	(0.257)	(0.233)	(0.123)	(0.120)
Have high blood pressure	−0.010	−0.044	−0.035	−0.216	0.156	0.002
	(0.038)	(0.037)	(0.281)	(0.207)	(0.130)	(0.109)
Have arthritis	0.004	−0.075	−0.048	−0.342	−0.034	0.236
	(0.027)	(0.026)	(0.201)	(0.145)	(0.102)	(0.084)
Have lung disease	−0.196	−0.016	−0.455	0.177	0.421	−0.018
	(0.046)	(0.045)	(0.336)	(0.253)	(0.129)	(0.124)
Have diabetes	0.016	−0.032	−0.108	−0.369	−0.165	−0.085
	(0.050)	(0.054)	(0.368)	(0.300)	(0.181)	(0.153)

Labor market history measures

	(1)	(2)	(3)	(4)	(5)	(6)
Ever worked before age 50	0.129	0.109	0.189	0.322	−0.148	−0.255
	(0.075)	(0.040)	(0.556)	(0.226)	(0.232)	(0.113)
Had job lasting longer than 5 years before age 50	−0.027	0.065	−0.050	0.004	0.117	−0.088
	(0.055)	(0.038)	(0.403)	(0.211)	(0.184)	(0.122)
Length of longest job held before age 50[3]	0.005	0.004	0.037	0.006	−0.009	−0.014
	(0.002)	(0.002)	(0.012)	(0.011)	(0.006)	(0.008)

Intrafamily transfers

	(1)	(2)	(3)	(4)	(5)	(6)
Spent time caring for grandchildren in past year	0.035	0.058	−0.162	0.046	−0.444	−0.217
	(0.059)	(0.045)	(0.434)	(0.252)	(0.215)	(0.133)
Hours spent caring for grandchildren in past year[4] (x 1,000)	−0.024	0.018	−0.318	0.205	−0.033	0.099
	(0.043)	(0.025)	(0.318)	(0.141)	(0.166)	(0.064)
Spent time caring for parents/in-laws in past year (x 1,000)	0.019	−0.002	0.308	−0.525	−0.160	−0.189
	(0.107)	(0.079)	(0.791)	(0.445)	(0.446)	(0.276)
Hours spent caring for parents/in-laws in past year[4] (x 1,000)	−0.148	0.026	−0.951	0.293	0.245	0.126
	(0.059)	(0.035)	(0.440)	(0.196)	(0.137)	(0.080)
Number of observations[5]	*3,156*	*3,388*	*3,172*	*3,409*	*3,172*	*3,409*

Source: Authors' calculations.

Notes:

[1] Estimates are weighted to provide nationally representative statistics. All models include the vector of demographic characteristics whose sample means are reported in Table 1, and the health status, labor market history, and interfamily transfers made by a respondent's spouse, along with spouse's demographic characteristics for married respondents.

[2] Coefficients estimated from Probit model.

[3] Conditional on ever working.

[4] Conditional on spending some time caring for grandchildren/parents.

[5] Sample sizes for models of log family income are slightly lower because individuals with no family income have been dropped from the sample.

APPENDIX TABLE 1B: Effect of Health, Labor Market History, and Intrafamily Transfers on Current Income-Based Measures of Wellbeing, Nonwhite Respondents[1] (standard errors in parentheses)

Measure of Current Wellbeing	Log Family Income		Income-to-Needs Ratio		Poverty Status[2]	
	Men	Women	Men	Women	Men	Women
Health measures						
Able to run 1 mile with little or no difficulty	-0.044	0.009	-0.120	0.105	-0.026	-0.088
	(0.053)	(0.054)	(0.191)	(0.147)	(0.134)	(0.115)
Able to walk several blocks with little or no difficulty	0.211	0.201	0.103	0.419	-0.289	-0.280
	(0.074)	(0.063)	(0.269)	(0.172)	(0.167)	(0.113)
Able to carry a 10-pound bag with little or no difficulty	0.445	0.081	1.091	0.060	-0.602	-0.258
	(0.083)	(0.060)	(0.302)	(0.162)	(0.175)	(0.111)
Have had cancer	-0.103	0.017	0.017	-0.011	0.604	-0.056
	(0.130)	(0.096)	(0.473)	(0.261)	(0.289)	(0.182)
Have heart problems	-0.267	-0.004	-0.767	-0.001	0.322	0.071
	(0.073)	(0.077)	(0.263)	(0.208)	(0.167)	(0.139)
Have high blood pressure	-0.057	-0.117	0.103	-0.352	0.189	0.066
	(0.063)	(0.055)	(0.228)	(0.148)	(0.151)	(0.105)
Have arthritis	-0.056	-0.039	-0.269	0.014	-0.004	-0.011
	(0.053)	(0.048)	(0.193)	(0.130)	(0.130)	(0.094)
Have lung disease	-0.171	-0.090	-0.697	-0.077	0.311	0.038
	(0.111)	(0.088)	(0.398)	(0.240)	(0.241)	(0.156)
Have diabetes	-0.038	-0.073	-0.462	-0.091	-0.147	0.203
	(0.075)	(0.068)	(0.273)	(0.184)	(0.187)	(0.124)

Labor market history measures						
Ever worked before age 50	0.210	−0.110	−0.062	−0.338	−0.151	0.176
	(0.097)	(0.073)	(0.348)	(0.199)	(0.199)	(0.130)
Had job lasting longer than 5 years before age 50	0.090	0.282	0.783	0.517	−0.302	−0.342
	(0.082)	(0.076)	(0.297)	(0.207)	(0.184)	(0.145)
Length of longest job held before age 50[3]	0.007	0.007	−0.002	0.029	−0.005	−0.020
	(0.003)	(0.004)	(0.012)	(0.011)	(0.009)	(0.009)
Intrafamily transfers						
Spent time caring for grandchildren in past year	0.197	−0.052	0.592	−0.267	−0.121	0.158
	(0.093)	(0.072)	(0.337)	(0.194)	(0.235)	(0.130)
Hours spent caring for grandchildren in past year[4] (x 1,000)	0.002	0.056	−0.145	0.064	−0.430	−0.097
	(0.065)	(0.033)	(0.238)	(0.089)	(0.285)	(0.060)
Spent time caring for parents/in-laws in past year (x 1,000)	−0.445	0.083	−0.802	0.318	1.676	−0.254
	(0.196)	(0.133)	(0.714)	(0.365)	(0.740)	(0.270)
Hours spent caring for parents/in-laws in past year[4] (x 1,000)	0.107	−0.105	0.048	−0.147	−6.116	0.301
	(0.141)	(0.062)	(0.517)	(0.169)	(4.301)	(0.133)
Number of observations[5]	1,055	1,351	1,068	1,371	1,068	1,371

Notes: See Appendix Table 1A.

APPENDIX TABLE 1C: Effect of Health, Labor Market History, and Intrafamily Transfers on Current Income-Based Measures of Wellbeing, Single Respondents[1] (standard errors in parentheses)

Measure of Current Wellbeing	Log Family Income		Income-to-Needs Ratio		Poverty Status[2]	
	Men	Women	Men	Women	Men	Women
Health measures						
Can run 1 mile with little or no difficulty	0.142	0.041	1.374	0.247	−0.149	−0.005
	(0.073)	(0.056)	(0.435)	(0.148)	(0.141)	(0.108)
Can walk several blocks with little or no difficulty	0.211	0.224	0.222	0.383	−0.318	−0.428
	(0.106)	(0.064)	(0.632)	(0.169)	(0.168)	(0.104)
Able to carry a 10-pound bag with little or no difficulty	0.346	0.059	0.401	0.129	−0.270	−0.250
	(0.120)	(0.062)	(0.715)	(0.162)	(0.189)	(0.102)
Have had cancer	0.001	0.114	0.056	0.277	0.443	−0.265
	(0.209)	(0.080)	(1.222)	(0.210)	(0.328)	(0.152)
Have heart problems	−0.210	−0.061	−0.410	−0.055	0.223	0.072
	(0.095)	(0.074)	(0.559)	(0.193)	(0.160)	(0.122)
Have high blood pressure	−0.085	−0.120	−0.051	−0.338	0.151	0.010
	(0.094)	(0.058)	(0.554)	(0.151)	(0.156)	(0.098)
Have arthritis	0.041	−0.126	−0.105	−0.297	−0.056	0.126
	(0.071)	(0.047)	(0.425)	(0.123)	(0.127)	(0.084)
Have lung disease	−0.327	−0.101	−0.763	−0.164	0.545	0.129
	(0.115)	(0.073)	(0.681)	(0.191)	(0.179)	(0.120)
Have diabetes	−0.022	−0.101	−0.466	−0.103	−0.104	0.030
	(0.116)	(0.081)	(0.694)	(0.210)	(0.204)	(0.133)

Labor market history measures

Ever worked before age 50	0.163	−0.046	0.112	−0.130	−0.161	0.122
	(0.142)	(0.075)	(0.837)	(0.196)	(0.217)	(0.121)
Had job lasting longer than 5 years before age 50	−0.057	0.189	0.166	0.533	−0.223	−0.182
	(0.118)	(0.072)	(0.698)	(0.189)	(0.195)	(0.125)
Length of longest job held before age 50[3]	0.010	0.010	0.030	0.011	−0.011	−0.024
	(0.004)	(0.004)	(0.027)	(0.010)	(0.008)	(0.007)

Intrafamily transfers

Spent time caring for grandchildren in past year	0.140	0.029	−0.486	−0.188	−0.625	−0.075
	(0.145)	(0.061)	(0.877)	(0.160)	(0.325)	(0.111)
Hours spent caring for grandchildren in past year[4] (x 1,000)	0.004	0.029	−0.332	0.019	0.045	0.002
	(0.189)	(0.036)	(1.143)	(0.095)	(0.386)	(0.059)
Spent time caring for parents/in-laws in past year	−0.413	0.001	−1.313	−0.076	0.621	−0.144
	(0.250)	(0.113)	(1.511)	(0.297)	(0.479)	(0.219)
Hours spent caring for parents/in-laws in past year[4] (x 1,000)	0.121	−0.086	−0.091	−0.179	−0.522	0.212
	(0.138)	(0.048)	(0.836)	(0.127)	(1.049)	(0.072)
Number of observations[5]	*830*	*1,555*	*848*	*1,582*	*848*	*1,582*

Notes: See Appendix Table 1.

[5] Sample sizes for models of log family income are slightly lower because individuals with no family income have been dropped from the sample.

APPENDIX TABLE 2A: Effects of Health, Labor Market History, and Interfamily
Transfers on Projected Retirement: Income-Based Measures of
Wellbeing, White Respondents (standard errors in parentheses)

| | Log Family Income | | | |
	Men Coef.	Std. Err.	Women Coef.	Std. Err.
Health measures				
Able to run 1 mile	0.078	0.024	0.062	0.027
Able to walk sev. blocks	0.137	0.043	0.141	0.036
Able to carry 10-lb bag	0.264	0.050	0.165	0.033
Have had cancer	−0.008	0.063	0.042	0.040
Have heart problems	0.025	0.032	−0.045	0.038
Have high blood pressure	0.046	0.035	−0.078	0.033
Have arthritis	−0.021	0.025	−0.043	0.023
Have lung disease	−0.100	0.041	−0.119	0.041
Have diabetes	−0.014	0.045	−0.080	0.048
Labor market history measures				
Ever worked before age 50	−0.049	0.068	0.140	0.036
Had 5+ yr job < age 50	0.087	0.050	−0.014	0.034
Length longest job < age 50	0.022	0.001	0.015	0.002
Intrafamily transfers				
Cared for grandkids last year	−0.023	0.053	0.096	0.041
Hours last year (1000)	−5.5E−05	4E−05	−3.5E−05	2E−05
Cared for parents/in-laws last year	−0.023	0.097	−0.009	0.072
Hours last year (1000)	6.2E−06	5E−05	−8.7E−06	3E−05
R-squared	0.384		0.523	

Source: Authors' calculations.
Notes:
[1] Estimates are weighted to provide nationally representative statistics. All models include the vector of demographic characteristics whose sample means are reported in Table 1, and the health status, labor market history, and intrafamily transfers made by a respondent's spouse, along with spouse's demographic characteristics for married respondents. The HRS data employed for this analysis is the Beta release tape.
[2] Coefficients estimated from Probit model.
[3] Conditional upon ever working.
[4] Conditional upon spending some time caring for grandchildren/parents.

Income-to-Needs Ratio				Poverty Status			
Men Coef.	Std. Err.	Women Coef.	Std. Err.	Men Coef.	Std. Err.	Women Coef.	Std. Err.
0.512	0.199	0.562	0.174	−0.013	0.009	−0.013	0.011
0.392	0.349	0.237	0.231	−0.059	0.015	−0.047	0.014
0.674	0.412	0.316	0.213	−0.091	0.018	−0.035	0.013
0.154	0.514	0.034	0.257	0.014	0.023	−0.010	0.016
0.108	0.259	0.037	0.244	0.016	0.011	0.019	0.015
0.270	0.283	−0.210	0.217	0.012	0.012	0.019	0.014
−0.131	0.203	−0.198	0.152	−0.004	0.009	0.002	0.010
−0.295	0.338	−0.223	0.264	0.057	0.015	0.052	0.017
−0.059	0.371	−0.429	0.314	0.012	0.016	0.025	0.020
−0.749	0.560	−0.049	0.236	−0.052	0.025	−0.071	0.015
0.173	0.406	−0.350	0.221	−0.051	0.018	−0.017	0.014
0.092	0.012	0.064	0.012	−0.002	0.001	−0.003	0.001
−0.215	0.437	0.130	0.264	−0.007	0.019	−0.069	0.017
−0.00026	0.0003	3.3E−05	0.0001	1.7E−05	1E−05	1.7E−05	9E−06
−0.252	0.796	−0.491	0.466	0.015	0.035	−0.008	0.029
0.00065	0.0004	3E−05	0.0002	−1.5E−05	2E−05	1.1E−05	1E−05
0.122		0.202		0.27		0.336	

APPENDIX TABLE 2B: Effects of Health, Labor Market History, and Interfamily Transfers on Projected Retirement: Income-Based Measures of Wellbeing, Nonwhite Respondents (standard errors in parentheses)

	Log Family Income			
	Men Coef.	Std. Err.	Women Coef.	Std. Err.
Health measures				
Able to run 1 mile	−0.021	0.049	0.050	0.055
Able to walk sev. blocks	0.181	0.069	0.201	0.066
Able to carry 10-lb bag	0.484	0.078	0.214	0.062
Have had cancer	0.074	0.123	0.152	0.101
Have heart problems	−0.172	0.068	−0.092	0.081
Have high blood pressure	−0.023	0.059	−0.158	0.056
Have arthritis	−0.056	0.050	−0.039	0.049
Have lung disease	−147	0.103	−0.030	0.092
Have diabetes	−0.130	0.070	−0.153	0.070
Labor market history measures				
Ever worked before age 50	−0.120	0.090	−0.146	0.077
Had 5+ yr job < age 50	0.249	0.076	0.279	0.078
Length longest job < age 50	0.024	0.003	0.023	0.004
Intrafamily transfers				
Cared for grandkids last year	−0.035	0.086	0.073	0.074
Hours last year (1000)	0.000	0.000	0.000	0.000
Cared for parents/in-laws last year	0.241	0.183	0.157	0.140
Hours last year (1000)	1E−05	0.0001	−0.0005	6E−05
R-squared	0.564		0.547	

Notes: See Table 2A.

Income-to-Needs Ratio				Poverty Status			
Men Coef.	Std. Err.	Women Coef.	Std. Err.	Men Coef.	Std. Err.	Women Coef.	Std. Err.
−0.019	0.123	0.395	0.175	−0.011	0.025	−0.037	0.024
−0.082	0.174	0.314	0.205	−0.027	0.036	−0.049	0.028
0.719	0.196	0.187	0.194	−0.150	0.040	−0.065	0.026
0.387	0.307	0.230	0.312	−0.002	0.063	−0.036	0.042
−0.125	0.170	0.006	0.248	0.080	0.035	0.013	0.033
−0.084	0.147	−0.308	0.177	0.034	0.030	0.037	0.024
−0.182	0.125	0.034	0.156	0.011	0.026	0.029	0.021
−0.182	0.258	−0.030	0.286	0.008	0.053	−0.037	0.038
−0.292	0.177	−0.244	0.220	0.055	0.036	0.013	0.030
−0.293	0.255	−0.132	0.238	−0.071	0.046	0.026	0.032
0.323	0.192	0.094	0.247	−0.090	0.039	−0.119	0.033
0.050	0.008	0.047	0.013	−0.008	0.002	−0.007	0.002
0.284	0.218	−0.041	0.232	0.021	0.045	−0.074	0.031
0.000	0.000	0.000	0.000	0.000	0.000	0.000	0.000
0.149	0.463	−0.240	0.435	−0.129	0.095	0.032	0.059
−8E−05	0.0003	−1E−05	0.0002	−7E−05	7E−05	3E−05	3E−05
0.375		0.287		0.436		0.492	

APPENDIX TABLE 2C: Effects of Health, Labor Market History, and Interfamily Transfers on Projected Retirement: Income-Based Measures of Wellbeing, Single Respondents (standard errors in parentheses)

	Log Family Income			
	Men Coef.	Std. Err.	Women Coef.	Std. Err.
Health measures				
Able to run 1 mile	0.150	0.068	0.022	0.055
Able to walk sev. blocks	0.290	0.099	0.241	0.065
Able to carry 10-lb bag	0.459	0.112	0.283	0.062
Have had cancer	−0.099	0.194	0.120	0.079
Have heart problems	−0.049	0.088	−0.142	0.074
Have high blood pressure	−0.006	0.087	−0.168	0.057
Have arthritis	0.018	0.067	−0.061	0.046
Have lung disease	−0.236	0.107	−0.151	0.073
Have diabetes	−0.121	0.109	−0.149	0.080
Labor market history measures				
Ever worked before age 50	−0.157	0.133	0.007	0.076
Had 5+ yr job < age 50	0.242	0.110	0.326	0.072
Length longest job < age 50	0.040	0.004	0.027	0.004
Intrafamily transfers				
Cared for grandkids last year	0.029	0.138	0.182	0.060
Hours last year (1000)	−3E−04	0.0002	−1E−04	4E−05
Cared for parents/in-laws last year	0.090	0.236	−0.062	0.111
Hours last year (1000)	−6E−05	0.0001	−2E−04	5E−05
R-squared	0.464		0.450	

Notes: See Table 2A.

	Income-to-Needs Ratio				Poverty Status		
Men Coef.	*Std. Err.*	*Women Coef.*	*Std. Err.*	*Men Coef.*	*Std. Err.*	*Women Coef.*	*Std. Err.*
0.396	0.462	0.253	0.143	−0.013	0.009	−0.013	0.011
−0.392	0.673	0.293	0.164	−0.059	0.015	−0.047	0.014
0.773	0.760	0.320	0.157	−0.091	0.018	−0.035	0.013
−0.143	1.302	0.437	0.204	0.014	0.023	−0.010	0.016
0.076	0.595	0.023	0.187	0.016	0.011	0.019	0.015
0.007	0.589	−0.236	0.146	0.012	0.012	0.019	0.014
−0.313	0.453	−0.137	0.119	−0.004	0.009	0.002	0.010
−0.806	0.723	−0.376	0.186	0.057	0.015	0.052	0.017
−0.914	0.739	−0.192	0.203	0.012	0.016	0.025	0.020
−0.589	0.891	−0.264	0.190	−0.052	0.025	−0.071	0.015
−0.094	0.744	0.116	0.184	−0.051	0.018	−0.017	0.014
0.142	0.028	0.062	0.009	−0.002	0.001	−0.003	0.001
−0.515	9.935	0.089	0.156	−0.007	0.019	−0.069	0.017
−1E−03	0.0012	−6E−05	9E−05	2E−05	1E−05	2E−05	9E−06
−0.027	1.607	−0.398	0.288	0.015	0.035	−0.008	0.029
−5E−04	0.0009	−1E−04	0.000	−2E−05	2E−05	1E−05	1E−05
0.151		0.281		0.207		0.336	

Chapter 7
Prospects for Widow Poverty
David R. Weir and Robert J. Willis

One important challenge for aging policy in the United States is the high poverty rate of older women living alone. A recent survey found that elderly single women were the poorest group among the aged, the only group with poverty rates significantly higher than the population as a whole, and a group much worse off (in relative terms) than older single women in other countries (Holtz-Eakin and Smeeding 1994). These findings come after decades of significant progress during which poverty rates declined for women in all marital status groups. Nevertheless, poverty persists, particularly among nonmarried women (see Table 1). Divorced women fare worst of all, suggesting that attention to the economic consequences of divorce should be a concern for aging policy. Nevertheless, our attention here is on widowhood: nearly half the elderly poor are widowed women and their poverty rates are substantially higher than for widowed men.

Financial arrangements made during marriage can largely determine the relative prospects of husbands and wives in the event of a spousal death, and before these women were widows, they were wives. The widespread availability of life insurance offers a contract mechanism whose purpose is to reduce the differences in economic status between marriage and widowhood, whatever the composition of other financial resources available to the couple. The fact that so many couples are not poor, but so many widows are, raises questions about how couples make financial decisions prior to one spouse's death.[1] Of course the problem is not limited to the poor: earlier research found that many wives at all levels of income faced reduced living standards in the event of their husbands' deaths (Auerbach and Kotlikoff, 1987). The impact of widowhood on economic status thus raises important questions of public policy. For example, some propose redistributing social security benefits toward widows and away from married couples (Burkhauser 1994; Sandell and Iams 1997). Such reforms would be self-defeating if couples responded to them by reducing life insurance, savings, or other private financial provision for widows.

TABLE 1: Poverty in the Population 65 and Older by Sex and Marital Status, 1994.

Marital Status	Population 65+ (thousands)		Fraction of Poor (%)		Share of Elderly Poverty (%)	
	Men	Women	Men	Women	Men	Women
Married	9735	9735	4.8	4.0	13.0	13.0
Widowed	1755	8636	12.2	20.0	5.9	48.4
Divorced	681	1091	16.5	25.3	3.1	7.7
Never-married	543	768	18.0	28.7	2.7	6.1

Source: Authors' calculations using data reported in Grad (1996).

In this chapter we examine the financial situation of married couples with special attention to the life-contingency structure of the various assets that comprise couples' wealth. The data come from the Health and Retirement Study (HRS), a survey that provides unusually detailed information on family finances (see Chapter 1). We focus here on 3,362 married women who were age 51–61 in 1992. All statistical results are weighted by the women's person-level sampling weight in the HRS to ensure that the results are nationally representative.

After describing the methods used to construct household wealth measures, we then compute how much would remain after the death of the husband or the wife, if that death occurred immediately. Next we convert wealth in each of the three possible surviving states into the sustainable annual consumption (annuity) that the couple or widow(er) could achieve. The results are then compared with earlier research on the adequacy of provision for prospective widows. We also compare survivors' sustainable consumption levels to poverty thresholds. This then indicates potential poverty rates in each survival state.

The Wealth of Married Couples

The standard problem in retirement planning is to provide for a relatively smooth lifetime consumption stream drawing on a varied mix of income sources and savings. An important source of uncertainty in this planning problem is uncertainty regarding age at death. In the case of a single decision-maker, the role of life insurance and life annuities in responding to that uncertainty has been extensively examined (Yaari 1965; Fischer 1973; Lewis 1979; Bernheim 1991). By contrast, we ask here how uncertainty over the timing of spousal deaths complicates the problem of smoothing income for a married couple, and how life insurance can assist in that contingent allocation.

Previous research by Auerbach and Kotlikoff (1987, 1991) has taken a related tack in assessing the "adequacy" of life insurance purchases. Those authors offered an intuitively appealing assessment of a couple's financial situation, by investigating the sustainable level of consumption per person while married, and comparing it with the sustainable level of consumption available to a widow following her husband's death. Our methods are similar, with some improvements made possible by the strengths of the HRS data. First, we convert a couple's claims to future income such as social security or labor earnings into assets, by computing their expected present discounted values (i.e., discounting by both an interest rate and the probability the person survives to receive the income). These assets are then combined with other net worth to arrive at the couple's total lifetime wealth. This wealth stock is then converted to a sustainable consumption level by assuming the purchase of actuarially fair life annuities, a process that translates an initial stock of wealth into a constant flow of income until death.[2]

Conventional Assets (Net Worth)

We begin by examining the most familiar component of wealth, namely, net worth. This is the value of all real and financial assets owned by a couple, less their debts; it includes net housing equity, stocks, and savings accounts. One strength of the HRS interview design is its persistence in inquiring into the value of conventional assets. Respondents who declined to give dollar figures were then asked follow-up questions in the form of "brackets" to place the amount of holdings into ranges of values. As a result, the HRS obtained a more complete and accurate accounting of wealth information than most other surveys (Smith 1995). Because these conventional assets are not contingent on survival, we assume that they are 100 percent heritable between spouses.[3] In terms of their ability to provide consumption, therefore, these assets afford a greater consumption stream to a single survivor than to an individual while married (since we assume the assets are shared).

Present Value of Future Income in the HRS

A household's wealth also includes claims to future income. We measure this wealth for HRS women as the expected present discounted value of these future income streams. From the standpoint of a married couple, there are three possible future states in which income might be received: while both are alive, when only the husband survives, and when only the wife survives. The life-contingency of a particular type of future income is defined by the state or states in which it is payable. The generic form of such a present discounted expected value calculation is:

$$PV_i = \sum_{t=0}^{T} Y_{i,t,s} * P_{t,s} * (1 + r)^{-t}$$

where $Y_{i,t,s}$ is income from source i in year t in survival state s, $P_{t,s}$ is the probability that a couple is in survival state s in year t, and r is a real interest rate (which we assume throughout this chapter to be three percent).

Given the way many income flows are structured, it will be useful to refer to three general types of life-contingent income streams. Single-life annuities are received over the life of an individual and do not depend on the partner's survival. For example, the husband's expected future earnings constitute the main component of wealth that is contingent on the husband living but not on the wife's survival. The other two types of contingent claims involve both spouses' survival probabilities in combination. Joint life annuities are those streams paid to the couple only while both partners survive. Survivor annuities are streams payable to a surviving partner only after the death of the other spouse. All other types of life-contingent future claims can be represented as some combination of these three types. For example, a "joint and survivor" annuity that pays one dollar while the couple survives, fifty cents to a surviving widow, and one dollar to a surviving widower is a combination of a one-dollar joint life annuity, a fifty-cent widow annuity, and a one-dollar widower annuity.

To estimate survival probabilities, we use the Social Security Administration's single-year-of-age life table projections for single-year birth cohorts by sex (Bell, Wade, and Goss 1992). Using this, we assign a mortality schedule based on his or her year of birth for each individual in the HRS. In this chapter we do not consider other determinants of differential mortality.[4]

Next we calculate present values for future earnings, pensions, and social security payments. Briefly, future earnings are projected using workers' current earnings and their expected future labor force participation rates. Pension wealth is similarly derived from respondent reports of their pension eligibility and expected accruals. Social security wealth is based on the Earnings and Benefits File (EBF), a restricted data supplement produced by Mitchell et al. (this volume) using Social Security Administration records linked to the HRS sample. We made imputations for respondents lacking records. To convert wealth into consumption annuities we use the same life tables as those used to convert income into wealth.

Empirical Wealth Estimates of Couples and Potential Widows

Married Couples

Summary characteristics for the various components of couples' wealth appear in Table 2 for the 3,362 married couples with age-eligible wives in wave 1 of the HRS, weighted by the wife's person-level sampling weight.

TABLE 2: Characteristics of Couple Wealth (HRS age-eligible wives)

Component of Wealth	Mean ($)	Share of total	Median ($)	Coeff of variation	Gini	Share of top 10%	Percent zero
Housing	80326	0.10	60000	1.37	0.52	0.34	0.11
Non-housing	230958	0.29	71000	2.46	0.74	0.61	0.04
H DC now	15892	0.02	0	4.44	0.92	0.88	0.75
W DC now	4596	0.01	0	5.77	0.95	0.96	0.83
H DB now	34565	0.04	0	2.40	0.86	0.71	0.75
W DB now	3408	0.00	0	6.63	0.98	1.00	0.96
SS to date	162846	0.21	173170	0.33	0.18	0.15	0.02
H DB to date	36641	0.05	0	3.23	0.88	0.78	0.72
W DB to date	18075	0.02	0	5.97	0.92	0.90	0.79
H earn future	115263	0.15	75754	1.38	0.61	0.40	0.28
W earn future	55882	0.07	28633	1.46	0.65	0.41	0.38
SS future	10234	0.01	4876	1.36	0.65	0.42	0.35
H DB future	8343	0.01	0	3.36	0.89	0.81	0.74
W DB future	5342	0.01	0	3.28	0.91	0.88	0.80
H DC future	4675	0.01	0	5.09	0.94	0.93	0.82
W DC future	1286	0.00	0	5.60	0.95	0.99	0.89
Total	788333	1.00	604864	0.94	0.38	0.30	0.00
Assets	311284	0.39	148500	1.93	0.63	0.51	0.03
Pensions	132823	0.17	61615	1.73	0.67	0.46	0.27
Social security Earnings	171145	0.22	129878	1.09	0.52	0.33	0.14
Owned	331772	0.42	165000	1.87	0.62	0.49	0.02
Promised	217561	0.28	191777	0.79	0.29	0.25	0.01
Expected	239000	0.30	190880	0.92	0.45	0.30	0.05

Source: Authors' calculations from HRS data.
Notes: H = husband; W = wife; DB = defined benefit; DC = defined contribution; SS = social security.

The top panel of Table 2 gives a detailed decomposition of the different components, while the second and third panels summarize in alternative ways. Total wealth averaged $788,000, with a median of $605,000. Although the minimum was a substantial negative amount, there were very few couples with nonpositive amounts of total wealth. Wealth is unequally distributed, with 30 percent held by the top 10 percent and a Gini coefficient of .38.

The leading components of wealth are nonhousing conventional assets (29 percent), social security wealth (21 percent), expected husband's future earnings (15 percent), housing equity (10 percent), and wife's expected future earnings (7 percent). All private pension sources combined amount to 17 percent. As might be expected, wealth components are more unequally distributed than the total. Compare housing and nonhousing

TABLE 3: Correlations Among Components of Couple Wealth

	Total	Housing	Financial	Social Security	Husband Pension	Wife Pension	Future SS	Husband Future
Total	1.00							
Housing	0.34	1.00						
Financial	0.85	0.19	1.00					
Social security	0.18	0.14	0.11	1.00				
Husband pension	0.36	0.12	0.08	0.08	1.00			
Wife pension	0.21	0.03	0.02	0.06	0.06	1.00		
Future social security	0.22	−0.04	0.02	−0.12	−0.00	0.04	1.00	
Husband future	0.57	0.10	0.21	−0.01	0.21	0.02	0.40	1.00
Wife future	0.26	0.02	0.04	−0.01	0.00	0.13	0.43	0.15

Source: Authors' calculations from HRS data.
Notes: N=3,362 married couples with age-eligible wives. Correlation coefficients weighted by wife's person-level weight (inverse of sampling probability). Pension wealth includes pensions already claimed or credited. Future wealth includes expected future earnings as well as future contributions or credits to pensions. See also Table 2.

wealth, for example: both have median values near $65,000, but ownership of nonhousing wealth is more concentrated and its mean is therefore much larger. Pensions are also unequally distributed, even when summed over the different types. By contrast, social security is distributed more equally than total wealth.

The bottom panel of Table 2 divides wealth into three categories: assets owned outright or already paying annuitized income, promised future payments based on past contributions (primarily social security and pensions), and expected future payments that depend on future work effort. In this cohort, the share of wealth dependent on future work is still quite large, at 30 percent.

Another way in which the components of wealth contribute to the inequality of total wealth is through their pattern of correlation, as shown in Table 3. Most of the correlation coefficients are positive, suggesting very little compensating variation in the components of wealth between categories, between spouses, or even between past and future. The rich are apparently consistently rich. This can be seen in Figure 1, which shows the composition of wealth by decile of wealth. Conventional assets increase with decile of total wealth, as does pension wealth and expected future earnings. Social security increases rapidly through the 70th percentile and then remains roughly constant. Thus, social security is like other components of

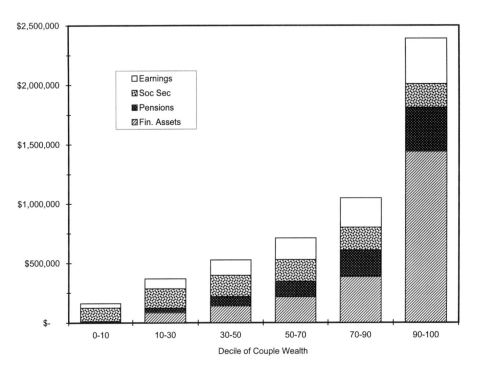

Figure 1. Sources of HRS couple wealth by decile, dollar value. Source: Authors' calculations using HRS data.

wealth in that it varies positively with the total, but it is quite different in that it is skewed "left" rather than "right." The corresponding percentage distribution appears in Figure 2. At the bottom of the wealth distribution, social security accounts for a very large share of total wealth, about 60 percent for the lowest decile, but its share declines to 7 percent among the top ten percent of the wealth distribution. Conversely, the share of conventional assets rises steadily through the middle of the wealth distribution, with social security's share declining in favor of private pensions and future earnings.

An important dimension to consider is age, shown in Figure 3. The value of future earnings declines with age as couples near retirement while the value of social security benefits rises, mainly because discounting matters less as one approaches the age of eligibility. Pensions change relatively little across age in this sample. We do not investigate this issue further here, but it appears that this is the result of two offsetting trends: a life-cycle increase in pension wealth by age and a trend toward greater use of private pensions among younger cohorts. Conventional assets also change rather little with the age of the wife.

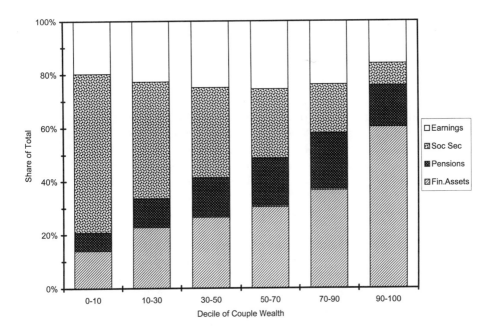

Figure 2. Sources of HRS couple wealth by decile, share of total. Source: Authors' calculations using HRS data.

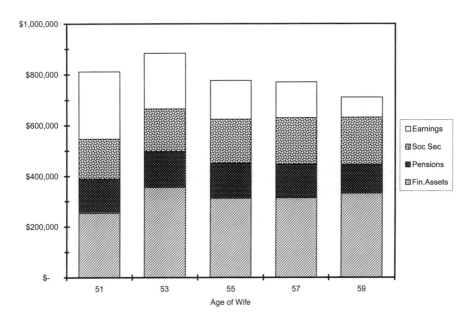

Figure 3. Sources of HRS couple wealth by age of wife. Source: Authors' calculations using HRS data.

The Wealth of Prospective Widows

We now examine what wealth would be available to these HRS women if their husbands had died suddenly around the time of the wave 1 interview. We estimate that such a prospective widow would have about $620,000 on average, with a median of $439,000. This implies that about 79 percent of couple wealth is heritable by prospective widows. On the other hand, the dispersion of widow wealth is greater than for couple wealth: the wealthiest decile of widows would have 35 percent of the wealth (compared to 30 percent for couple wealth) and the Gini coefficient of prospective widow wealth would be 0.44 (compared to 0.38 for couples).

If, instead, the wives died, the surviving husbands of these HRS women would have average wealth of $659,000, with a median of $473,000. Thus, they would be about 6 percent wealthier in widowhood than their wives on average, a meaningful but not a large difference. Widower wealth would be only slightly less unequally distributed than widow wealth: the share of the top 10 percent is 34 percent and the Gini coefficient is 0.43.

The composition of wealth for prospective widows differs from the composition of couple wealth because of the differential life-contingencies or inheritance rules governing the various assets. We assume that conventional assets are fully heritable, so these take on greater importance for widows, constituting 50 percent of total wealth on average, compared with 39 percent for couples. Social security benefits are slightly less important for widows than for couples at 16 percent, private pensions at 14 percent, and life insurance policies on the husband account for 11 percent of widows' wealth. Future earnings account for nine percent of widows' wealth (assuming widowed women do not take a job on becoming widowed).

Wealth composition also varies with the level of wealth, as shown in Figures 4 and 5. Looking at the absolute levels, conventional assets are even more concentrated among the most wealthy widows than in the couple distributions. Social security wealth is again relatively equally distributed across the wealth classes, but here too it increases with total wealth up to the middle of the distribution and never declines. Both pensions (partly inherited) and future earnings (of the widow only) increase steadily with total wealth. Even more surprisingly, so does the value of life insurance policies, which rises to an average level of over $200,000 for the richest decile of widows. This pattern, in which life insurance seems to reinforce rather than reduce the inequality of widow outcomes, is discussed at greater length elsewhere (Weir and Willis 1996).

The evidence on shares of wealth reinforces these impressions. Social security accounts for 68 percent of the wealth of the poorest prospective widows, and only 5 percent of the richest. Life insurance, future earnings, and pension income all show a gentle U-shaped pattern, rising in impor-

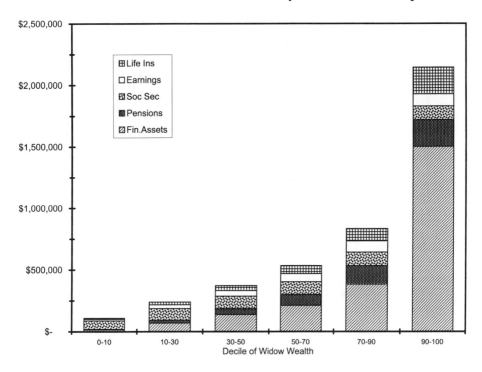

Figure 4. Sources of HRS prospective widow wealth by decile, dollar value. Source: Authors' calculations using HRS data.

tance into the middle of the distribution and falling off in the top wealth deciles. Conventional assets increase in importance.

Patterns of prospective widow wealth by age of the wife are shown in Figure 6. These patterns are similar to those for couple wealth (Figure 3). Life insurance and future earnings are more important at younger ages and decline steadily. Private pensions are relatively stable, while conventional assets and social security increase in importance with age.

The ratio of the prospective widow's to the couple's wealth, which we call the "inheritance rate," is shown in Figure 7 by source of wealth. The top panel depicts rates according to the couple's place in the distribution of couple wealth, and the rates prove to be fairly stable. By assumption, conventional assets are inherited at 100 percent so we do not show a curve for them. Nevertheless, their influence is clearly visible in the upward trend of the overall inheritance rate for total wealth (life insurance is included in the widow's wealth total, but since its share of total widow's wealth is fairly stable at around 9–12 percent it does not distort the pattern by wealth). Other

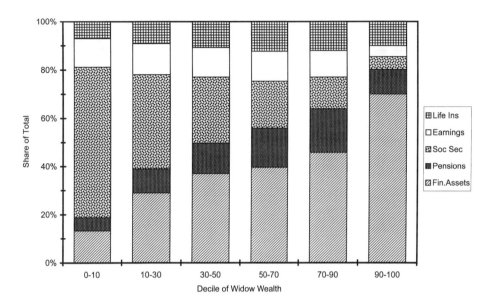

Figure 5. Sources of HRS prospective widow wealth by decile, share of total. Source: Authors' calculations using HRS data.

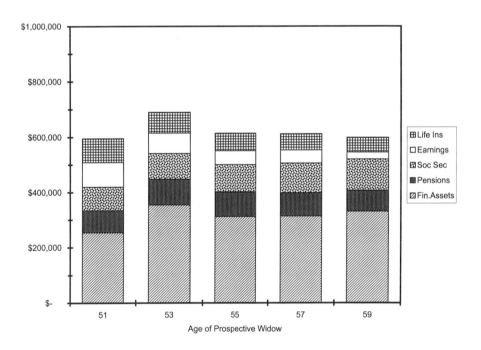

Figure 6. Sources of HRS prospective widow wealth by age of prospective widow, dollar value. Source: Authors' calculations using HRS data.

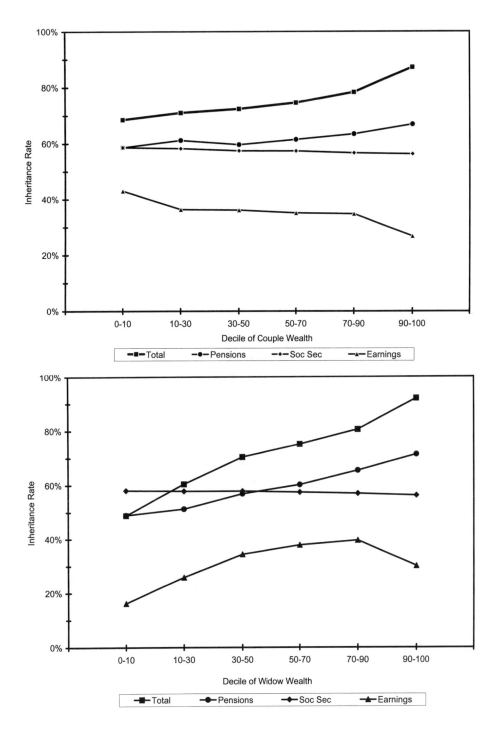

Figure 7. HRS prospective widow inheritance rates by source and decile: couple wealth (top) and widow wealth (bottom). Source: Authors' calculations using HRS data.

types of wealth are less than perfectly heritable: social security declines very slightly with total wealth; the inherited share of pensions rises with couple wealth, which means that the wife's own pensions and the husband's defined contribution pensions are an increasing share of the total; and wives contribute a slightly greater share of household earnings in the poorest households and a smaller share in the wealthiest.

The lower panel organizes the information according to the prospective widow's place in the (hypothetical) distribution of widow's wealth. Here differential inheritance rates across couples are more visible, showing that widow poverty is not simply the sequel to couple poverty. In the bottom decile of couple wealth, the average inheritance rate for all wealth was about 70 percent. In the bottom decile of widow outcomes, the average inheritance rate is only 50 percent. Social security's benefit rules ensure that inheritance rates do not vary much. Private pensions show a more sharply increasing pattern of inheritance rate by wealth. Earnings vary even more, especially at the bottom of the distribution. The poorest widows have earnings that are less than 20 percent of couple earnings.

Sustainable Consumption Paths

We next convert the wealth stock measures into estimates of sustainable individual consumption levels. Following Auerbach and Kotlikoff (1987), we do this by calculating the individual single-life annuities that could be purchased at actuarially fair rates.[5] Using the Social Security Administration's forecast life tables by age, sex, and birth cohort, we calculate for each HRS respondent an annuity rate that converts his or her stock of wealth into an annual single-life annuity payment. The inverse of the annuity rate is what used to be known as years' purchase — the multiple of the annuity payment needed to purchase it. It is simply the price (capital sum required) of a one-dollar annuity for life. For a single individual the sustainable consumption level is the present value of wealth *PVR* divided by the price of a single-life annuity *D*. Thus:

$$\text{Widow:} \quad A_f = \frac{PVR_f}{D_f},$$

$$\text{Widower:} \quad A_m = \frac{PVR_m}{D_m}.$$

Couples are slightly more complicated. To provide equal consumption annuities to both spouses, the present value of a couple's resources is divided by the sum of their individual annuity prices. But the sustainable consumption of a couple is not based on full couple wealth. As noted earlier, life insurance has no effect on full couple wealth (when it is actuarially fair term insurance). That makes it appear as if buying life insurance for surviving spouses is costless in terms of the consumption of the couple while married, when in fact it is precisely the reduction in potential married consumption that is the price paid for higher prospective widow consumption. The problem is to decide by how much to reduce the couple's available wealth for consumption (or their consumption annuities) for the purchase of life insurance. The correct amount of wealth reduction is the discounted value of all future life insurance premiums. To know this we would need to solve a dynamic program solving for optimal insurance purchases in each future year depending on the position of all other financial resources in each future year. A simpler approach uses an approximation. Optimal life insurance amounts can be expected to fall with age because the share of life-contingent assets (notably earnings) declines. If the couple maintained constant premiums at their current levels, they could buy slowly declining amounts of (term) coverage which we expect would exceed their needs as they enter retirement. We therefore deduct the annual premium reported at HRS wave 1 from the couple's combined consumption annuity.

From this point, we could follow Auerbach and Kotlikoff in comparing the potential annuities of women as wives, to the potential annuities they would be able to buy if they became widowed. The ratio of the two consumption annuities (widow/wife) is an index of adequacy of provision for widowhood. Before we do so, however, we need to consider what levels of consumption are needed in each state to produce the same standard of living. This requires a discussion of equivalence scales.

Equivalence Scales

Equivalence scales refers to the consumption needs of households of different compositions expressed relative to some "standard" household type. Developing these scales has represented a long-term challenge to economists and policy-makers alike. One debate concerns economies of scale in consumption as household size increases. That is, in comparing couples to surviving spouses, we collapse all aspects of gains to marriage into a greater efficiency of consumption. If there were no scale economies, then two people need would twice as much income as a single person. If "two can live as cheaply as one," then the income needed to support a widow at the same standard of living would be identical to the couple's income. The truth lies somewhere in between, but the range is enormous.

Equivalence scales estimated in or implied by previous work appear in Table 4, recognizing that an equivalence scale can be expressed in different ways. The first column of Table 4, following the most common format, shows how much consumption (or income or expenditure) is needed by a couple compared to a single person. The second column is simply the inverse: it shows how a single person's needs compare to those of a couple. The

TABLE 4: Consumption Ratios Implied by Different Equivalence Scales for the Elderly

Equivalence Scale	Consumption Ratios		
	Two/One	One/Two	Widow/Wife
Social Security 2-earner couple	2.00	0.50	1.00
German poverty threshold	1.81	0.55	1.10
Danziger et al. (couple/widow)	1.73	0.58	1.16
Citro-Michael	1.62	0.62	1.23
Social security 1-earner couple	1.50	0.67	1.33
Merz (US)	1.49	0.67	1.34
Danziger et al. (couple/widower)	1.36	0.73	1.47
U.S. Poverty threshold	1.26	0.79	1.59

Source: Authors' calculations from data reported in Danziger et al. (1984), Table 3; Citro and Michael (1995), pp. 165–82; and Burkhauser, Smeeding, and Merz (1996), Table 1.
Note: The indicated consumption ratios (Two/One) are ratios of the amounts of consumption expenditure needed to provide the same standard of living (or utility) for an elderly couple as compared with a single individual over 65, according to the equivalence scales estimated by the indicated author or embodied in the indicated policy rule.

third column expresses equivalence scales in terms of the ratios we will use to compare our results with Auerbach and Kotlikoff's (1987) estimates: namely, the ratio of a widow's consumption needs to that of a wife for the same standard of living. This is simply the second column times two, based on the assumption that a wife consumes one-half of the couple's total. Another equivalence is the U.S. government's poverty threshold, which assumes that a widow needs 79 percent of the income available to a married couple to achieve the same standard of living. Assuming that she had half the couple's consumption while married, her needs as a widow are 59 percent greater than they were as a wife. The German government's poverty threshold assumes much smaller scale economies, where the widow is assumed to need only 55 percent of a couple's consumption, or about a 10 percent increase over her consumption while married. Citro and Michael (1995) surveyed the literature of poverty studies to distill a "back-of-the-envelope" equivalence scale formula of n^7, where n is the number of persons in the household.

Other analysts have estimated equivalence scales allowing for differences by sex. Danziger et al. (1984) find that men's needs are much greater than women's when living alone, although both estimates detected lower scale economies than the official poverty threshold. Unfortunately, the estimated sex differences do not distinguish the elderly from younger age groups, and so are almost certainly too large.

The Social Security Administration also has an implicit equivalence scale, in that the nonworking spouse's benefit is equal to one-half of the earner's benefit, making the couple's income 1.5 times the earner's benefit. At the death of either spouse, the survivor receives the earner's benefit. This leaves a widow with two-thirds of the couple's social security income. However, working women are treated differently. At widowhood the widow receives the larger of her own or her spouse's benefit, and often this will be the husband's benefit. Thus the working widow is left in the same absolute position as if she had not worked, and in a worse position relative to her consumption in marriage. In the limit, if their individual benefits were equal, the surviving spouse receives only half the couple's social security benefits.

Widowhood and Consumption Ratios

The ratio of potential widows' to wives' consumption levels among HRS women varies substantially across respondents to the 1992 study. Table 5 shows the cumulative fraction of women whose consumption possibilities as widows would fall at or below a given threshold, as compared to their consumption as wives. The table also presents figures from 1962, derived from Auerbach and Kotlikoff (1987).

We present these for couples in three initial wealth groups. Couples with the lowest wealth are the ones we believe most relevant to the issue of widow poverty. According to the official poverty equivalence scales described in the previous section, a consumption ratio of 1.6 would be needed to keep a widow above the poverty line if the couple was just at the poverty line when the husband was alive. Relatively few women in low-income households would see even a 50 percent increase as widows (82 percent in 1969 and 79 percent in 1992).

We also see an improvement in widows' consumption levels over time. This is apparent at the more reasonable level of 1.25, corresponding to economic estimates of equivalence scales. Almost three-quarters of prospective widows in low-wealth families failed to reach this level in 1969, compared with only 55 percent in 1992. At consumption ratios of 1.0 or below, the differences are even sharper. Less than one-quarter of women in 1992 faced an absolute decline in their sustainable consumption, compared with 58 percent in 1969. These gains were even greater among the wealthier couples. The 1.25 consumption threshold was not reached by 75 percent of middle-class and 60 percent of the top group in 1969, whereas only 39 percent and 20 percent failed to reach it in 1992. Taking all wealth categories together, the potential widow's median consumption ratio rose from 1.02 to 1.36 over the two decades, while that for men rose much less, from 1.73 to 1.83. Clearly provision for widows has improved substantially more than for widowers.

One explanation for the observed changes over time arises from an examination of the composition of couple wealth. Even after adjusting for infla-

TABLE 5: Wives Whose Potential Consumption in Widowhood Would Fall Below a Given Ratio of Their Consumption in Marriage, by Wealth of Couple and Year

Cumulative Fraction with Consumption Ratio Below:	Present Value of Couple's Resources					
	Low		Middle		High	
	1969	1992	1969	1992	1969	1992
0.50	0.12	0.03	0.08	0.01	0.04	0.00
0.75	0.34	0.07	0.27	0.04	0.17	0.01
1.00	0.58	0.24	0.52	0.14	0.37	0.06
1.25	0.73	0.55	0.75	0.39	0.60	0.20
1.50	0.82	0.79	0.90	0.75	0.77	0.52
1.75	0.88	0.89	0.96	0.91	0.90	0.85

Source: Authors' calculations from HRS data for 1992 and from Auerbach and Kotlikoff (1987) Table 4, based on the Retirement History Survey for 1969.
Note: The consumption ratio is the ratio of the sustainable consumption that would be available to a woman if widowed to the sustainable consumption available to her while married. Both samples have been stratified by current couple wealth: under the 20th percentile (low), 20th to 60th (middle), and high. Each column displays the cumulative distribution of consumption ratios for a particular group.

tion (using the CPI), older couples experienced substantial real growth in all forms of wealth, with average total wealth rising from $416,000 in 1969 to $788,000 in 1992 ($1992). Of course, what matters for the relative status of widows is the life-contingent structure of that wealth, and here we find that private pensions have increased substantially. Men's pensions accounted for eight percent of couple wealth in 1969 but women's pensions were worth essentially zero. Auerbach and Kotlikoff (1987) assumed that men's pensions were strictly single-life annuities and not heritable. While spousal rights to pensions were improved over time through several regulatory changes, the increase in pensions is also key. Men's pensions were 12 percent of couple wealth in 1992 and women's pensions nearly 5 percent, which means that widows would retain nearly 11 percent of couple wealth in 1992 that they had none of in 1969. Some of the time series change is also due to growing conventional wealth, which rose from 37 percent of total couple wealth in 1969, to 39 percent in 1992.[6] Women's earnings have also increased relative to men's, so the loss of a husband's income will now have less impact on the prospective widow's wealth.

To what extent has life insurance enhanced women's protection against economic losses in widowhood? The answer appears to be "not much." Men's future earnings did become more completely insured over time (from 43 to 59 percent). Their future earnings also fell as a share of couple wealth (from 20 to 15 percent). The net result is that life insurance stayed at about nine percent of the value of couple wealth.

Prospective Poverty Rates

We are also interested in the absolute levels of resources available to wives and widows, especially at the low end of the wellbeing scale. The distribution of sustainable consumption levels of prospective widows and widowers relative to the official poverty thresholds for 1992 appears in Table 6. We find, for example, that 6 percent of the age-eligible married women in the HRS would, if widowed, have sustainable consumption levels below the official poverty threshold for single persons, and two-thirds of them (4 percent of the total) would be below 60 percent of the couple poverty line (corresponding to the Danziger or Citro-Michael equivalence scale). By contrast, only 3 percent of their husbands would be below the poverty line if widowed, and only 4 percent of the age-eligible married men in the HRS.

We must emphasize that these estimates are likely to underpredict future poverty rates for several reasons. Official poverty rates are based on a particular and restrictive definition of annual income received, whereas our estimates of sustainable consumption levels are derived from estimates of lifetime wealth whenever it was or will be earned. For example, the poverty measure does not include as income the annual rental value of home ownership. Table 6 gives some indication of this effect by reporting the distribution of sustainable consumption when the value of home equity is excluded from the definition of wealth. The inclusion of housing wealth moves many people up a category in the middle of the distribution (where housing equity is quantitatively important), but has less impact at the bottom near the official poverty threshold (where housing wealth is small). Almost nine percent of women would be below the poverty line if their housing wealth was excluded from their available consumption as widows.

We also examine how excluding other components of wealth (one at a time) affects sustainable consumption. These are calculations simply intended to give an idea of the relative importance of the different resources available to people at risk of poverty, and they do not assume behavioral responses to changes in policies or programs. Social security is the most important of the four wealth components considered here. Without social security, the simulation indicates that there would be nearly three times as many widows in poverty (17 percent). Its proportional effects on men's prospective poverty rates are about the same as for women. But since men's poverty rates are lower, social security substantially reduces the differences in poverty rates between widows and widowers.

Earlier we assumed that a spouse's defined benefit pension could be inherited at 50 percent. This proves not to be very important, and if pensions were eliminated entirely it would have little effect on poverty rates. That is because pensions only amount to about five percent of the wealth of couples at the bottom of the wealth distribution. Consequently, policies to

TABLE 6: Prospective HRS Widow(er)s Who Would Have Sustainable Consumption Levels Below the Indicated Thresholds, by Wealth Definition

Cumulative Fraction with Consumption Threshold Below:	Excluding from Widow(er) Wealth				
	Nothing	Housing	Spouse DB Pensions	Social Security	Life Insurance
Age-elegible women					
.6*PL(2)	0.041	0.052	0.046	0.125	0.049
PL(1)	0.062	0.086	0.072	0.171	0.078
1.5*PL(1)	0.131	0.204	0.157	0.284	0.167
2*PL(1)	0.229	0.323	0.265	0.386	0.285
4*PL(1)	0.585	0.672	0.631	0.684	0.657
Their husbands					
.6*PL(2)	0.020	0.030	0.021	0.073	0.022
PL(1)	0.032	0.046	0.032	0.103	0.037
1.5*PL(1)	0.070	0.104	0.074	0.170	0.076
2*PL(1)	0.118	0.183	0.124	0.246	0.137
4*PL(1)	0.415	0.526	0.427	0.554	0.445
Age-eligilble men					
.6*PL(2)	0.030	0.042	0.030	0.076	0.032
PL(1)	0.044	0.058	0.045	0.099	0.049
1.5*PL(1)	0.084	0.114	0.087	0.159	0.092
2*PL(1)	0.133	0.182	0.139	0.233	0.151
4*PL(1)	0.405	0.489	0.413	0.511	0.431

Source: Authors' calculations using HRS data.
Notes: PL(1) is the poverty line for a single person ($7,299 in 1992) PL(2) is the poverty line for a couple ($9,443 in 1992). N=3362 age-eligible married women in the HRS Wave 1, and the same number of husbands. Frequencies are weighted using the wife's person-level weight (inverse of sampling probability). N=3577 age-eligible married men, with frequencies weighted using man's person-level weight. Each column within a panel displays the cumulative distribution of consumption levels for a particular definition of wealth available to support consumption. See also Table 2.

increase the heritability of pensions might affect the well-being of the middle class, but they would not do much to alleviate poverty.

Life insurance reduces the prospective widow poverty rate from eight percent to six percent. It is therefore not entirely absent from the financial plans of even the poorest couples. As yet we cannot say how much more it might do, until we examine whether consumption could have been transferred from the married state to the prospective widow state.

The distribution of widow(er) consumption levels for different initial couple consumption levels appears in Table 7. We find that poor couples rarely produced potential widows that escaped poverty. Husbands fared little better, so it is unlikely that such persons could have purchased life insurance. Also troubling is the fate of couples within 150 percent of the poverty

TABLE 7: Prospective HRS Widow(er)s Who Would Have Sustainable Consumption Levels Below the Indicated Thresholds, by Position of Couple

Cumulative Fraction with Widow(er)'s Consumption Threshold Below:	Couple's Sustainable Consumption Relative to Poverty Threshold					
	<PL(2)	PL(2)–1.5* PL(2)	1.5*PL(2) –2*PL*(2)	2*PL(2) –4*PL(2)	>4*PL(2)	All
Age-elegible women						
.6*PL(2)	0.814	0.338	0.048	0.006	0.000	0.041
PL(1)	0.914	0.599	0.138	0.013	0.001	0.062
1.5*PL(1)	0.968	0.921	0.579	0.084	0.002	0.131
2*PL(1)	0.987	0.968	0.849	0.282	0.007	0.229
4*PL(1)	1.000	1.000	0.993	0.940	0.192	0.585
Their husbands						
.6*PL(2)	0.589	0.071	0.009	0.000	0.000	0.020
PL(1)	0.857	0.147	0.024	0.000	0.000	0.032
1.5*PL(1)	0.972	0.761	0.151	0.012	0.000	0.070
2*PL(1)	1.000	0.949	0.579	0.050	0.000	0.118
4*PL(1)	1.000	0.996	1.000	0.699	0.033	0.415
Weighted number of couples	98	122	206	1308	1628	3362

Source: Authors' calculations using HRS data.
Notes: PL(1) is the poverty line for a single person ($7,299 in 1992) PL(2) is the poverty line for a couple ($9,443 in 1992). Frequencies are weighted using the wife's person-level weight (inverse of sampling probability). The couple's sustainable annual consumption level is reduced by the (actuarially fair) premia they would need to pay per year for the current amount of life insurance in force. Each column within a panel displays the cumulative distribution of consumption levels for a particular definition of wealth available to support consumption. See also Table 2.

line. Sixty percent of the wives in that group would fall below the single-person poverty threshold if widowed, as compared with only 15 percent of their husbands. This is evidence of vulnerability to poverty differing by sex.

Characteristics of the Vulnerable

To explore in greater detail who is at risk of poverty or substantial economic loss at widowhood, we offer an overview description of how at-risk women differ from those not at risk. As we have already seen, the poorest prospective widows are much more likely to come from poor families in which the husband also faces poverty in widowhood. This effect is reinforced in Table 8 by the direct relationship between level of wealth and its life-contingent structure. The Auerbach-Kotlikoff widow/wife annuity ratios are lowest for poor widows and rise with widow's well-being. Thus, in addition to being poor, poor households transfer smaller proportions of their wealth to a widow. A

TABLE 8: Characteristics of HRS Marriages by Prospective Widow's Consumption

	Widow's Sustainable Consumption Relative to Poverty Threshold					
	<.6*PL(2)	.6*PL(2) −PL(1)	PL(1) −1.5*PL(1)	1.5*PL(1) −2*PL*(1)	2*PL(1) −4*PL(1)	>4*PL(1)
Couple poverty rate (%)	57.5	14.0	2.3	0.5	0.1	0.0
Widower poverty rate (%)	54.1	21.3	5.4	1.1	0.1	0.0
No future earnings (%)	83.8	67.8	49.5	46.2	33.4	32.3
White (%)	59.0	63.5	69.1	82.3	88.4	93.1
Health limits work (%)	49.5	39.8	34.4	21.1	18.2	10.2
Education (years)	9.6	10.1	10.5	11.3	12.0	13.6
Age (years)	54.9	55.2	55.3	56.1	56.1	56.3
Avg. past earnings ($/year)	3197	3215	4692	5502	7724	9881
Wife annuity ($/year)	4766	7132	9511	11933	16423	38614
Widow annuity ($/year)	3691	6507	9156	12786	21426	60810
Widower annuity ($/year)	7784	11367	15735	20891	29353	77411
Widow/Wife annuity (%)	77.4	91.2	96.3	107.2	130.5	157.5
Widow/Widower annuity (%)	47.4	57.2	58.2	61.2	73.0	79.6
N of couples	187	86	282	360	1187	1260
N weighted	138.6	70.4	229.9	331.1	1195.9	1386.1

Source: Authors' calculations using HRS data.

Notes: PL(1) is the poverty line for a single person ($7,299 in 1992); PL(2) is the poverty line for a couple ($9,443 in 1992). Dollar amounts are all in 1992 dollars. All calculations are weighted by the wife's person-level weight (inverse of sampling probability).

major part of this effect is the amount of financial assets, but if that were the only issue it should affect husbands and wives equally. Annuity ratios of widows/widowers suggest that gender inequality is greatest among the poorest prospective widows.

Another important determinant of the life-contingent structure of family wealth is the woman's earnings potential. The great majority of prospectively poor widows have zero projected earnings, while most of the more secure women have positive future earnings. We note that these projections are based on current earnings and respondents' stated intentions for future work; no potential changes that might result from the death of a spouse are incorporated. However, there may be little potential for increased labor supply after widowhood. Nearly half of the HRS wives who would be the poorest widows report that they already have health problems limiting their ability to do paid work, as compared with only 10 percent of wives with the best prospects for widowhood. An education deficit of almost four years separates the poorest from the most comfortable of the prospective widows, which also constrains the potential for future employment. Finally, these women's prior earnings history is consistent with a pessimistic prediction. Based only on women whose records were linked to social security records, the most vulnerable women had average lifetime earnings only about one-third as high as those with the best prospects.

The age differences in Table 8 are surprisingly large: wives projected to be poorest as widows are a full year younger than those with the highest incomes. One explanation for this is that younger women have longer to wait to receive social security benefits which, as we have seen, are the mainstay of retirement wealth for the poorest families. In our calculations, a given level of annual (expected future) social security benefits beginning at age 62 translates into less wealth (present discounted value) for a younger woman, because the benefits are discounted over more years. Younger women may think that widowhood is unlikely before they reach social security age, or that if it did occur they could make it through to social security age on some combination of increased work, family transfers, or government aid. We therefore computed how many women would be above the poverty line once they reached age 62. Table 6 shows that roughly six percent of HRS wives would have insufficient wealth to sustain a lifetime of consumption over the poverty line if they had been widowed around 1992. Of these women, 18 percent were entitled to social security benefits at age 62 that would put them above poverty. An additional nine percent would be above poverty after age 62 if they could preserve their other assets until they reached age 62. Annual social security benefits would be higher if they were claimed at the normal retirement age of 65: roughly 35 percent of the poorest widows would then be above the poverty line from social security alone, and nearly half would be if they did not consume their other assets until then. In addition to underlining once again the importance of social security in keeping the elderly out of poverty, these estimates point to the importance of choices made in the years immediately before social security eligibility in determining economic status after retirement.

Avoiding premature consumption of retirement assets is even more important for women not at risk of poverty. Among the 94 percent of wives not initially at risk for poverty in widowhood, fully 28 percent are entitled to age 62 social security benefits that are below poverty level; at 65, 16 percent are below this level. Private resources are therefore critically important in preventing poverty, and unexpected losses of future earnings or assets between now and retirement put many additional women at risk.

Conclusion

Our goal has been to direct attention to a relatively neglected but critically important aspect of married couples' financial resources: namely, the life-contingent structure of assets. Based on the rules governing transmission of different components of family wealth, we assess how much wealth would likely be available from current marriages to widows or widowers. This prospective analysis of the finances of currently married couples focuses attention on current decisions that influence what will happen after the spouse's death.

Our results using the 1992 HRS may be compared with the older analysis by Auerbach and Kotlikoff (1987). We find that wives today, if widowed, would retain a substantially greater share of their marital consumption as compared to 20 years ago. Men also do somewhat better, but the gender gap has narrowed considerably. It appears that much of the change is due to private pension wealth and its heritability, along with the rise in women's earnings and financial assets. Another explanation is that life insurance coverage of husbands' earnings increased at the same time husbands' earnings fell, resulting in less uninsured loss of husbands' income.

While a couple's overall wealth level is key in reducing the risk of widows' poverty, it is not the only factor. In particular, the composition of couples' wealth matters, too. Women with low earnings and low labor force participation are the most vulnerable. In addition, having low earnings is strongly correlated with characteristics such as poor health and low education, so poor women are also least likely to be able to respond to widowhood by increasing their future earnings.

Our results cast some doubt on the potential to solve the problem of poverty by reforming pensions or social security alone. Enhancing the heritability of assets between spouses could be justified for the middle class, on the grounds that men's potential consumption as widowers is on average substantially greater than that available to their widows. This reform would not have much effect on poverty rates, however, because of the small amounts of pension wealth available for inheritance in poor couples. Similar limitations apply to a plan to increase social security survivor benefits: its effect would be greatest on families well-removed from the risk of poverty. More re-distribution could be imposed within social security: survivor benefit re-placement rates are now the same for everyone (100 percent), but they could be made a function of income. There are good arguments against introducing means-testing into social security, however, leaving the current system of Supplemental Security Income as the most efficient means to target assistance to the needy elderly (see Manchester, forthcoming; New-mark and Powers, forthcoming).

Observed patterns of life insurance purchase by couples nearing retire-ment pose a puzzle for the life-cycle model of insurance demand and for policies built on its predictions. Life insurance in principle offers a tool to smooth consumption across the future states of the world. In practice, it appears instead to exaggerate consumption differences. This is because life insurance is purchased most heavily by the wealthy and healthy (Weir and Willis 1996). A potential explanation for this might be that life insurers price-discriminate against those who seek to purchase small quantities of insurance. Term life insurance prices per dollar of coverage decline as the quantity purchased increases, and this pattern is only partly explained by fixed administrative costs per policy (Cawley and Philipson 1996). Because low-income workers lacking employment-based access to group rates are at most risk to leave a widow in poverty, insurance access and pricing should receive more attention in future work.

Future research should also delve further into the consumption patterns of the elderly. If the official poverty index overstates economies of scale among couples, and thereby overstates the needs of unmarried individuals, then evidence on poverty among elderly widows may be seriously exagger-ated. Conversely, if elderly couples enjoy important economies of scale, a redesign of social security benefits and other policy reforms may be needed to better insure against the loss of those scale economies with the loss of a spouse. Future research should also explore whether and how couples nearing retirement think about the life-contingent structure of their asset claims, or of the tradeoffs they face among differently structured annuities.

Finally, our analysis thus far relies on analysis of the baseline HRS inter-view, which is but a single cross-section. In future research we will reexamine HRS respondents in the longitudinal file, to compare actual outcomes of loss of spouse with our predictions. This will help us say, with much greater certainty, whether the apparent improvement in married couples' financial provision for widowhood over the last 20 years will further reduce poverty among elderly widows over the next 20 years.

Olivia Mitchell and Steven Venti provided valuable guidance in the use of social security and pension records, as well as helpful comments. We are also grateful for the comments of Alan Gustman, Paul Menchik, James Smith,

Steven Sandell, David Wise, and participants in the 1997 NBER Summer Institute on Aging. Honggao Cao provided research assistance. This research was supported by the NIA (U01-AG09740; K01-AG00703).

Notes

1. Current-status poverty rates may reflect selection effects: if poorer couples are more likely to be widowed and/or if poor widows are less likely to remarry, this will increase the observed gap between widows and the still married. There is some evidence that the loss of a spouse is often a precipitating event in the transition to poverty, however. Hurd (1990: 583–84), using the Retirement History Study (RHS), reports that 37 percent of women who were widowed from a nonpoor marriage in 1975 were below the poverty line as widows in 1977, compared with only 4 percent of women whose husbands survived. Becoming widowed also reduced the chances of leaving poverty over that interval from 50 percent for couples to 15 percent for widows. Research using the Panel Study of Income Dynamics also found that the income-to-needs ratio declined after retirement at about the same rate for couples and for men who lost their wives, but it fell more quickly for widows (Burkhauser and Duncan 1991). The death of a spouse is clearly a more economically harmful event for women than for men (Burkhauser, Butler, and Holden 1991).

2. A detailed data Appendix is available from the authors on request.

3. The actual inheritance patterns of widows may vary. For instance, a couple may choose to give bequests to other heirs rather than the widow, and some debts may be avoided after the spouse dies.

4. Mortality is known to vary by income and ethnicity, and this can have important effects on the present value of similar future income streams (Panis and Lillard 1996). Individual survival probabilities may also depend on the survival of the spouse, with death rates increasing after loss of a spouse (Lillard and Panis 1996). The HRS also contains substantial amounts of health information on individuals, including questions about individuals' own survival expectations. In related work we are examining the effects of differential survival probabilities (Weir and Willis 1996), but much remains to be done. Note, however, that the effect of such mortality differentials is substantially reduced by our subsequent transformation of wealth into sustainable consumption levels.

5. This approach implicitly sets loads to zero.

6. Some of this increase may reflect improved wealth assessment in the HRS compared with the RHS data set used in the earlier analysis.

References

Auerbach, Alan J. and Laurence J. Kotlikoff. 1987. "Life Insurance of the Elderly: Its Adequacy and Determinants." In Gary Burtless, ed., *Work, Health, and Income among the Elderly*. Washington, D.C.: Brookings Institution: 229–67.

———. 1991. "The Adequacy of Life Insurance Purchases." *Journal of Financial Intermediation* 1, 3: 215–41.

Becker, Gary S. 1976. *The Economic Approach to Human Behavior*. Chicago: University of Chicago Press.

Bell, Felicitie C., Alice H. Wade, and Stephen C. Goss. 1992. *Life Tables for the United States Social Security Area: 1900–2080*. Actuarial Study No. 107, Social Security Administration. Washington, D.C.: U.S. Government Printing Office.

Bernheim, B. Douglas. 1991. "How Strong Are Bequest Motives? Evidence Based on

Estimates of the Demand for Life Insurance and Annuities." *Journal of Political Economy* 99, 5: 899–927.

Betson, David M. 1996. "Is Everything Relative? The Role of Equivalence Scales in Poverty Measurement." Unpublished paper, University of Notre Dame. March.

Burkhauser, Richard V. 1994. "Protecting the Most Vulnerable: A Proposal to Improve Social Security Insurance for Older Women." *Gerontologist.* 34, 2: 148–49.

Burkhauser, Richard V., J. S. Butler, and Karen C. Holden. 1991. "How the Death of a Spouse Affects Economic Well-Being After Retirement: A Hazard Model Approach." *Social Science Quarterly* 72, 3 (September): 504–19.

Burkhauser, Richard V. and Greg J. Duncan. 1991. "United States Public Policy and the Elderly: The Disproportionate Risk to the Well-being of Women." *Journal of Population Economics* 4, 3: 217–31.

Burkhauser, Richard V., Karen C. Holden, and Daniel A. Myers. 1986. "Marital Disruption and Poverty: The Role of Survey Procedures in Artificially Creating Poverty." *Demography* 23, 4: 621–31.

Burkhauser, Richard V. and Timothy Smeeding. 1994. "Social Security Reform: A Budget Neutral Approach to Reducing Older Women's Disproportionate Risk of Poverty." Syracuse University Center for Policy Research Policy Brief 2.

Burkhauser, Richard V., Timothy Smeeding, and Joachim Merz. 1996. "Relative Inequality and Poverty in Germany and the United States Using Alternative Equivalence Scales." *Review of Income and Wealth* 42, 4: 381–400.

Cawley, John and Tomas Philipson. 1996. "An Empirical Examination of Information Barriers to Trade in Insurance." Working Paper 132. George J. Stigler Center for the Study of the Economy and the State, University of Chicago.

Citro, Constance F. and Robert T. Michael. 1995. *Measuring Poverty: A New Approach.* Washington, D.C.: National Academy Press.

Danziger, Sheldon, J. van der Gag, Eugene Smolensky, and Michael K. Taussig. 1984. "Implications of the Relative Economic Status of the Elderly for Transfer Policy." In Henry Aaron and Gary Burtless, eds., *Retirement and Economic Behavior.* Washington, D.C.: Brookings Institution.

Fischer, Stanley. 1973. "A Life Cycle Model of Life Insurance Purchases." *International Economic Review* 14, 1: 132–51.

Friedman, Benjamin M. and Mark Warshawsky. 1988. "Annuity Prices and Savings Behavior in the United States." In Zvi Bodie, John B. Shoven, and David A. Wise, eds., *Pensions in the U.S. Economy.* NBER. Chicago: University of Chicago Press: 53–84.

Grad, Susan. 1996. *Income of the Population 55 and Older, 1994.* Washington, D.C.: Social Security Administration, Office of Research, Evaluation, and Statistics.

Grossman, Michael. 1972. "On the Concept of Health Capital and the Demand for Health." *Journal of Political Economy* 80, 2: 223–55.

Gustman, Alan L., Olivia S. Mitchell, Andrew A. Samwick, and Thomas L. Steinmeier. "Evaluating Pension Entitlements." This volume.

Holden, Karen C., Richard V. Burkhauser, and Daniel J. Feaster. 1988. "The Timing of Falls into Poverty After Retirement and Widowhood." *Demography* 25, 3 (August): 405–14.

Holtz-Eakin, Douglas and Timothy M. Smeeding. 1994. "Income, Wealth, and Intergenerational Economic Relations of the Aged." In Linda G. Martin and Samuel H. Preston, eds., *Demography of Aging.* Washington, D.C.: National Academy Press: 102–45.

Hurd, Michael D. 1989. "The Poverty of Widows: Future Prospects." In David A. Wise, ed., *The Economics of Aging.* NBER. Chicago: University of Chicago Press: 201–22.

———. 1990. "Research on the Elderly: Economic Status, Retirement, and Consumption and Saving." *Journal of Economic Literature* 28, 2: 565–637.

Hurd, Michael D. and David A. Wise. 1989. "The Wealth and Poverty of Widows: Assets Before and After the Husband's Death." In David A. Wise, ed., *The Economics of Aging*. NBER. Chicago: University of Chicago Press: 177–99.

Juster, F. Thomas and Richard M. Suzman. 1993. "The Health and Retirement Study: An Overview." HRS Working Paper Series, Core Paper 94-1001. Institute for Social Research, University of Michigan, Ann Arbor.

Kotlikoff, Laurence J. and Avia Spivak. 1981. "The Family as an Incomplete Annuities Market." *Journal of Political Economy* 89, 2: 372–91.

Lewis, Frank D. 1989. "Dependents and the Demand for Life Insurance." *American Economic Review* 79, 3: 452–67.

Lillard, Lee A. and Constantijn W. A. Panis. 1996. "Marital Status and Mortality: The Role of Health." *Demography* 33, 3 (August): 313–28.

Manchester, Joyce. 1999. "Taxing Issues for Social Security." In Olivia S. Mitchell, Robert J. Myers, and Howard Young, eds., *Prospects for Social Security Reform*. Pension Research Council. Philadelphia: University of Pennsylvania Press.

Martin, Linda G. and Samuel H. Preston, eds. 1994. *Demography of Aging*. Washington, D.C.: National Academy Press.

Mitchell, Olivia S., Jan Olson, and Thomas Steinmeier. "Social Security Earnings and Projected Benefits." This volume.

Newmark, David and Elizabeth Powers. 1999. "Means Testing Social Security." In Olivia Mitchell, Robert J. Myers, and Howard Young, eds., *Prospects for Social Security Reform*. Pension Research Council. Philadelphia: University of Pennsylvania Press: 243–68.

Panis, Constantijn W. A. and Lee A. Lillard. 1996. "Socioeconomic Differentials in the Return to Social Security." RAND Labor and Population Program Working Paper 96-05.

Quinn, Joseph F. and Richard V. Burkhauser. 1994. "Retirement and Labor Force Behavior of the Elderly." In Linda G. Martin and Samuel H. Preston, eds., *Demography of Aging*. Washington, D.C.: National Academy Press: 50–101.

Sandell, Steven H. and Howard M. Iams. 1997. "Reducing Women's Poverty by Shifting Social Security Benefits from Retired Couples to Widows." *Journal of Policy Analysis and Management*. 16, 2: 279–97.

Smith, James P. 1995. "Racial and Ethnic Differences in Wealth." *Journal of Human Resources* 30 (Supplement): S158–83.

Wallace, Robert B. and A. Regula Herzog. 1993. "Overview of the Health Measures in the Health and Retirement Survey." HRS Working Paper Series, Core Paper 94-1003. Institute for Social Research, University of Michigan, Ann Arbor.

Weir, David R. and Robert J. Willis. 1996. "Life Insurance and the Gender Bias of Poverty in Widowhood." Working Paper, University of Michigan, Ann Arbor.

Wise, David A., ed. 1989. *The Economics of Aging*. Chicago: University of Chicago Press.

Wolf, Douglas A. 1994. "The Elderly and Their Kin: Patterns of Availability and Access." In Linda G. Martin and Samuel H. Preston, eds., *Demography of Aging*. Washington, D.C.: National Academy Press: 146–94.

Yaari, Menahem. 1965. "Uncertain Lifetime, Life Insurance, and the Theory of the Consumer." *Review of Economic Studies* 32, 2: 137–50.

Chapter 8
Minorities Face Retirement: Worklife Disparities Repeated?

Marjorie Honig

Though income levels of the elderly have risen in the United States over the last three decades, the fraction of aged people in poverty is above that of many other adult age groups and is particularly high among subgroups within the elderly population. People from ethnic and racial minority groups are especially at risk: the poverty rate of elderly blacks, for example, is three times that of whites. In this chapter we ask whether this higher-than-average vulnerability to poverty in old age is the result of inadequate financial planning for retirement.

Whether households are able to forecast and then prepare adequately for retirement is a matter of considerable debate (Moore and Mitchell, this volume). Within this topic, there is additional reason for concern for the future wellbeing of minority populations. One consideration is that wealth holdings as conventionally measured are extremely low for nonwhites, both in absolute terms and as compared to those of the majority population. Thus, in 1993, the median white household held net worth (financial assets and housing equity) over 10 times larger ($47,740) than that of the median black or Hispanic household ($4,418 and $4,656 respectively).[1] Even when household incomes are held constant, large disparities in net worth remain between white and minority households in the United States.

Simple tabulations of household wealth are incomplete, however, because they omit the very important valuation of households' contingent claims on social security and employer pension benefits. In what follows, I remedy this deficiency by valuing such retirement income claims in order to include them in total wealth. The analysis uses the first wave of Health and Retirement Study data (HRS; see Chapter 1) to compare retirement wealth levels anticipated by non-Hispanic white, non-Hispanic black, and Hispanic households. My findings show that adding these previously overlooked retirement assets adds to measured wealth levels, yet wide disparities in wealth remain. On the other hand these differences are substantially narrowed as compared to those observed when retirement benefits are excluded. Specifically, median anticipated retirement wealth for white households is $391,000 ($1992), compared to $189,000 for black households, and $158,000 for Hispanic households.

The analysis proceeds in steps. I first discuss household expectations data and the rationale for their use in the present study. I then detail how we construct the key components of anticipated wealth at retirement. Both the median and mean values of wealth are given, along with data on wealth composition in the aggregate, as well as separately for the three racial and ethnic groups of special interest here. It is also informative to compare expected wealth with earnings patterns. Finally, I show how including the value of future claims on employer pension and social security payments affects measured disparities in retirement wealth between white and minority households.

Household Wealth Expectations

The focus is on households currently on the verge of retirement, and assess how well prepared they are for their future in old age. Two questions guide the analysis:

- How different will white and minority households' net worth be in retirement?
- Will these differences be larger or smaller, if we take into account workers' future claims on employer pension and social security benefits?

I rely on survey responses regarding older workers' expectations to address these questions in order to focus on the adequacy of older Americans' financial planning for retirement. In particular, I examine how wealth levels relate to respondents' expectations regarding when they will retire and how much they will receive in work-related benefits. Social security and pension wealth are computed as of people's self-reported retirement ages; we then combine these wealth forecasts with self-reported financial and housing wealth. Our measures serve to illustrate household expectations regarding the financing of their own retirement period. These responses may potentially provide a different insight into household financial planning as compared to wealth values calculated from social security and employer records, projected to a uniform retirement age such as 62 or 65 (Mitchell, Olson, and Steinmeier, this volume; Gustman et al., this volume).

We are fortunate in having a very useful dataset — the HRS — with which we may evaluate a number of direct measures of household expectations. The relevant measures for the present analysis include the expected retirement age, the expected age of receipt and anticipated amount of social security benefits, and the expected ages of receipt and anticipated benefit amounts from employer-sponsored pensions (on both current and previous jobs). Previous analyses that used earlier surveys concluded that people's responses to expectations questions regarding the timing of retirement, and the amount of benefits, corresponded quite closely to realizations (Anderson, Burkhauser, and Quinn 1986; Bernheim 1988, 1989). Our preliminary evidence on expectational measures in the HRS is equally corroborative. For instance, in waves 1 and 2 of the HRS, responses do not appear to have an unusually high random component compared to other survey information and are internally consistent (Honig 1994, 1996, 1998; Hurd and McGarry 1994, 1995).

In our view, asking people about their expected pension benefits provides useful information about how they assess their company pension plans. In the HRS, employed respondents were asked for detailed information on as many as three pension plans on their current jobs, and non-workers were asked about pensions on their last jobs. In all cases people were queried about pensions in their three most recent prior jobs. As a result, comprehensive pension expectations information is available for all those with current and past pensions. In contrast, efforts to gather employer-provided pension documents were successful for two-thirds of the pensions covering workers in the HRS, so that estimates of employer-provided information must be augmented by the researcher (Gustman et al., this volume).

Expected Retirement Wealth Levels

It is of some interest to detail how household wealth (in $1992) is measured in the HRS for the respondents' expected retirement ages.[2] For our purposes, we divide household wealth into four broad categories:

- Net financial wealth, including savings, investments, business assets, and non-residential real estate less outstanding debt unrelated to housing;
- Net housing wealth, or the market value of residential housing less outstanding mortgage debt;
- Expected pension wealth, or the present value of anticipated employer-sponsored retirement benefits;
- Expected social security wealth, or the present value of anticipated social security benefits.

Net Financial Wealth

Current (1992) values of financial assets, plus outstanding debt, are reported by the respondent designated by the household as the "financially responsible" member.[3] To obtain projected values of net financial assets as of his/her anticipated retirement date, each of the individual components are projected forward using historical averages of real market returns to each component; using geometric averages of real returns over the period 1926–95 as reported by Ibbotson Associates (1996). Growth rates used to project each component of net financial wealth appear in the Appendix.

Net Housing Wealth[4]

This component of wealth reflects the net value of owner-occupied primary housing. Estimated housing wealth at the expected retirement date of the household head is the projected real market value of the housing less projected real debt, the assumption that housing did not appreciate in real terms between 1992 and the time of retirement permits use of the current value as the best estimate of a home's projected value. Projecting debt on the property is more complicated and requires information not directly available in the HRS. The survey does, however, include respondent estimates of the value of his or her first and second mortgages, home equity loans, and lines of credit against housing equity. To project housing debt, the outstanding balance on the mortgage or other debt as well as payments on the debt and their frequency may be estimated from survey information. Debt projection also requires the current interest rate on the debt; since this is not directly available, historical interest rates are used to proxy the current rate, allowing for the possible refinancing of mortgages over time.

Pension Wealth

Employer pensions are an important component of retirement wealth, and the HRS contains a great richness of data on these plans. Respondents are queried on up to three pension plans with their current employer, the major plan with their last employer (if the respondent was not currently employed), and the major plan in the three most recent jobs prior to the current or last job. The information provided by each adult respondent in the household from all plans is used to calculate the household's expected pension wealth.

The set of questions asked of respondents differs depending on whether a pension plan is a defined contribution (DC) plan, a defined benefit (DB) plan, or a plan that combines both types. Respondents with DC plans are asked for the current balance in their account, the amount they contribute to the account, and their employer's contribution. Respondents in DB plans are asked to report the amount they expect to receive, either as a specific dollar payment or as a percent of final salary, and their expected final salary. Respondents not currently working are queried about pensions on their last job. Those with DC plans are asked for the balance in their account when they left their last employer and the date of leaving the job. Those with DB plans are asked whether they are currently receiving benefits and, if so, the amount; if not currently receiving benefits, they are asked when they expect to receive benefits. In the latter case, the amount and the expected date of receipt are requested.

Expected wealth at retirement is derived from this information. Current account balances in DC plans plus annual contributions of workers and employers are projected in real terms to each worker's anticipated retirement date. The retirement value of the expected DB pension benefit streams are derived (in $1992). For respondents with expected DB benefits from previous jobs, pension wealth at the time they expect to receive benefits is calculated and then discounted or projected to retirement. The projections include the value of benefits currently received from DB plans in previous jobs, as well as DC balances remaining with previous employers, to the retirement date.[5]

Inflation and interest rate assumptions used in these calculations (and for social security wealth, discussed below) are the "intermediate assumptions" used by the Social Security Trustees (Board of Trustees 1995) and age-specific life tables are derived from mortality data provided in Vital Statistics. I do not use race-specific mortality rates because I seek to separate the issue of differential financial planning among racial and ethnic groups from that of differential mortality. Using lower life expectancies would reduce the expected wealth of black and Hispanic households with private and public pension assets and retirement ages comparable to those of white households. Pension and social security wealth are computed as of each respondent's expected retirement date. In two-earner households, the pension and social security wealth of the member other than the head is then discounted or projected to the retirement date of the head, so that all wealth is evaluated at the anticipated retirement of the financially responsible member of the household.

Social Security Wealth

Social security wealth is calculated in a manner similar to that of DB pension wealth, with two exceptions. First, in accordance with the rules, social security benefits are assumed to be fully indexed to the cost of living, whereas among employer-pensions, only government pensions are assumed to be fully indexed. Second, since respondents are instructed to report expected social security benefits in 1992 dollars, anticipated social security benefits are assumed to be reported in real terms.[6]

Results: Expected Wealth at Retirement

The analysis sample includes 4,371 HRS households in which the "financially responsible" member worked within the last decade, reports race and ethnicity, and is neither self-employed nor reporting that he/she is retired.

TABLE 1: Expected Retirement Wealth by Wealth Decile, HRS Respondents
        (N=4,371)

Wealth Decile	Total Wealth	Net Housing Wealth	Net Financial Wealth	Soc Security Wealth	Pension Wealth
1	$ 41,850	$ 9,054	$ 4,036	$ 26,322	$ 2,438
		21%	10%	63%	6%
2	110,261	14,253	7,450	80,337	8,221
		13%	7%	73%	7%
3	160,671	30,585	16,700	92,696	20,689
		19%	10%	58%	13%
4	222,389	42,908	26,803	110,267	42,405
		19%	12%	50%	19%
5	289,430	53,797	42,375	126,543	66,715
		18%	15%	44%	23%
6	362,309	67,044	54,641	150,611	90,013
		18%	15%	42%	25%
7	455,352	88,191	75,466	164,569	127,126
		19%	17%	36%	28%
8	581,549	92,484	114,947	174,041	200,077
		16%	20%	30%	34%
9	773,362	104,067	177,011	184,338	307,945
		13%	23%	24%	40%
10	1,591,450	151,952	690,301	190,859	558,338
		10%	43%	12%	35%
Overall mean	491,539	69,264	132,686	134,641	154,948
		14%	27%	27%	32%
Median 10%	323,857	62,687	49,641	137,452	74,076
		20%	15%	42%	23%

Source: Author's calculations. All values in 1992 dollars and calculated using HRS sampling weights.

The first sample restriction is necessary because only respondents reporting employment within 10 years were queried about their expected date of retirement.[7] Household heads defining themselves as self-employed on either their current job or, if not working, their most recent job, are excluded from the sample because the concept of retirement is less well-defined for this group, and because of the focus on employer pensions in this study.[8] Because black and Hispanic populations were oversampled in the HRS, there are 853 and 397 households in the minority sample, respectively, representing these racial/ethnic groups. (Ethnicity is self-reported in the survey.)

Expected wealth at retirement is described in Table 1, which reports values by wealth decile. The mean household expects to hold close to half a million dollars in wealth at retirement.[9] The wide disparity in wealth noted earlier for the U.S. population as a whole is very much in evidence for households at retirement. The mean value of $1.6 million for the wealthiest decile is 38 times that of the mean value for the poorest decile ($42,000). Excluding claims on future social security benefits, households in the poorest two wealth deciles anticipate having under $30,000 in wealth at retirement, of which one-half is in the form of housing wealth.

Household wealth composition varies widely across the population. Thus social security comprises about two-thirds of total wealth for the poorest deciles, but its share falls steadily to just over 10 percent of the wealth for the highest decile. Pension wealth, by contrast, is under one-fifth of total wealth for households up through the fourth decile, and yet constitutes about one-third of wealth for the three wealthiest deciles. Financial wealth is also unequally distributed, remaining under 20 percent of total wealth for all but the three highest deciles. In contrast, housing wealth constitutes the second largest source of wealth for households in the bottom half of the distribution, while it comprises only 10 percent of total wealth among households in the highest decile.

The difference in the composition of wealth between mean and median households is striking. The expected wealth of the median 10 percent of the sample is about $325,000, of which one half is composed of social security wealth. Housing and pension wealth each contribute about a fifth, and financial wealth only 15 percent. Reflecting the greater importance of pension and financial wealth among households in the upper half of the distribution, the share of each of these components for the mean household is roughly equal to that of social security, with housing wealth comprising the remaining 14 percent.

As Table 1 reveals, broadening the definition of wealth by adding social security and pension assets to net worth has a dramatic effect on anticipated retirement wealth levels. For the mean household, for example, aggregate wealth increases more than two and one-half times, from just over $200,000 to $492,000. The impact is even greater for the median household: wealth nearly triples from just over $110,000 to $324,000. Before turning to a detailed examination of wealth differences between white and minority households, I first compare my findings on expected social security and pension wealth with values that could be obtained from information derived using administrative records.

It is interesting to note that mean social security and pension wealth derived from respondent reports of anticipated benefits, current account balances, and expected retirement age are surprisingly close to values estimated from social security and employer records. The comparison is made with data given in Moore and Mitchell (this volume; hereafter MM), where we first adjust that study's projected social security wealth values from $129,000 for retirement at age 62 (Table 2) to the implied wealth value at the mean expected retirement age of 63 in this sample. This adjusted value of $133,000 corresponds closely to the value of $135,000 reported here in

TABLE 2: Expected Retirement Wealth by Wealth Decile, Race, and Ethnicity, HRS
Respondents

Wealth Decile	Non-Hispanic White	Non-Hispanic Black	Hispanic
1	$ 65,017	$ 14,120	$ 3,921
1	148,206	72,126	58,878
3	217,262	104,445	92,036
4	285,277	130,668	113,492
5	353,659	164,923	137,501
6	431,330	214,066	180,749
7	530,219	274,199	236,263
8	662,343	358,891	312,875
9	864,813	511,761	423,480
10	1,774,924	996,236	792,433
Overall mean	541,719	297,163	242,462
Median 10%	390,950	189,023	157,771
Number of observations	3,128	848	395

Source: Author's calculations. All values in 1992 dollars and calculated using HRS sampling
weights.

Table 1.[10] Similarly, pension wealth adjusted to $162,000 (from $156,000,
Table 2, MM) is close to our value of $155,000.[11] This close correspondence
at the mean between household expectations of future social security and
pension wealth and values projected from employer and social security records suggests that pre-retirement households engage in some degree of
financial planning for retirement. The evidence is not completely conclu-
sive, however, since correspondence of values in the aggregate could be
consistent with large but offsetting forecast errors at the individual household level. Whether this is true will be examined in future research.

Wealth holdings by race and ethnicity are provided in Table 2, separately
for non-Hispanic white, non-Hispanic black, and Hispanic households in
the HRS. Very striking, but perhaps not surprising, is the wide disparity in
wealth between white and minority households. The mean Hispanic household expects to hold $242,000 in wealth at retirement, only 45 percent of the
wealth of white households ($542,000). The mean black household expects
to hold somewhat more wealth ($297,000), but still only 55 percent of the
wealth of the mean white household. Hispanic and black households at the
median of their respective wealth distributions fare even worse compared to
white households. Hispanics anticipate only 40 percent ($158,000), and
blacks only 48 percent ($189,000), of the wealth of the median white house-
hold ($391,000).

These disparities in anticipated wealth at retirement are pronounced and
substantially larger than those in earnings patterns across the older population. For example, Table 3 provides wealth values for households in which

TABLE 3: Wealth, Wages, and Earnings by Race and Ethnicity, HRS Wage and Salary-Earners

Wealth Measure	Non-Hispanic White $	Non-Hispanic Black $	% of White	Hispanic $	% of White
Mean					
Expected wealth	$ 556,443	$ 325,607	59%	$ 264,686	48%
Hourly wage	14.32	11.38	79%	10.07	70%
Annual earnings	32,563	24,121	74%	19,953	61%
Median 10%					
Expected wealth	403,317	214,452	53%	178,123	44%
Hourly wage	11.79	9.47	80%	7.91	67%
Annual earnings	27,181	20,626	76%	15,554	57%
Number of observations	2,820	730		311	

Source: Author's calculations. All values in 1992 dollars and calculated using HRS sampling weights.

the head is currently employed as a wage or salary earner. Focusing on the median household, we see that wealth disparities remain large even if they are somewhat attenuated when nonworkers are excluded. Hispanic households expect wealth of $178,000, only 44 percent of the wealth of white households, and black households expect wealth of $214,000, only 53 percent that of white households. Racial and ethnic differences in hourly wage rates are much smaller, by contrast. The wage rate of the median black household head ($9.47) is 80 percent of the wage rate of the white household head ($11.79); the Hispanic wage ($7.91) is 67 percent of the white wage rate. Annual earnings also are more equally distributed than wealth holdings: thus earnings of black household heads ($21,000) are 76 percent of the earnings of whites ($27,000), and earnings of Hispanics ($16,000) are 57 percent those of whites. This pattern is similar for households at the mean of their respective distributions.

Why do wealth distributions differ so much between white and minority households? A partial answer is apparent when the components of aggregate wealth are examined in Table 4. Of the four broad components of household wealth, social security wealth reflects wage income most directly, and this form of wealth is distributed most evenly among the three racial and ethnic groups. The median black or Hispanic household expects about $100,000 in social security wealth, two-thirds that of the median white household. However, social security wealth constitutes less than one-half of the wealth of white households; over 40 percent of the balance, moreover, is represented by pension wealth. The median white household expects about $100,000 in pension wealth, more than three times that of black households, and six times more than Hispanic households. In other words, the lower

TABLE 4: Composition of Expected Retirement Wealth by Race and Ethnicity, HRS
        Respondents

Component	Non-Hispanic White	Non-Hispanic Black	Hispanic
Mean	$541,719	$297,163	$242,462
Housing	76,323	38,880	40,715
	14%	13%	17%
Financial	153,111	52,255	34,112
	28%	18%	14%
Social security	140,437	110,894	108,638
	26%	37%	45%
Pension	171,849	95,133	58,997
	32%	32%	24%
Median 10%	390,950	189,023	157,771
Housing	75,891	35,994	22,339
	19%	19%	14%
Financial	60,804	18,659	14,063
	16%	10%	9%
Social security	153,239	102,567	104,555
	39%	54%	66%
Pension	101,016	31,802	16,814
	26%	17%	11%
Number of observations	3,128	848	395

Source: Author's calculations. All values in 1992 dollars and calculated using HRS sampling weights.

aggregate wealth of minority households results not only from lower wages but, to a much greater extent, from lower non-wage compensation. This consequence of being in a low-wage labor market is all the more striking when it is revealed among a population of mature workers on the verge of retirement.[12]

Differences in net worth also contribute to greater disparities in wealth. The median white household expects to hold two-and-one-half times the net worth of the median black household, and four times that of the median Hispanic household. These differences, however, are not as large as differences in pension wealth. Nonetheless, differential saving out of wage income (and inheritances), in addition to differences in nonwage compensation, contributes to the relatively greater disparities in aggregate wealth than in labor income between white and minority households. Why the racial/ethnic gap in household savings is so much larger than the gap in household income is a subject for future research.

The importance of broadening the definition of wealth to include future claims on social security and pension payments is demonstrated in Table 5.

TABLE 5: Racial and Ethnic Disparities in Retirement Wealth by Wealth Measure, HRS Respondents

Wealth Measure	Non-Hispanic White $	Non-Hispanic Black $	% of White	Hispanic $	% of White
Mean					
Net worth: housing and financial assets	$ 229,434	$ 91,135	40%	$74,827	33%
Private wealth: net worth plus pension wealth	401,283	186,268	46%	133,824	33%
Total wealth: private wealth plus SS wealth	541,719	297,163	55%	242,462	45%
Median 10%					
Net worth: housing and financial assets	136,695	54,653	40%	36,402	27%
Private wealth: net worth plus pension wealth	237,711	86,455	36%	53,216	22%
Total wealth: private wealth plus SS wealth	390,950	189,023	48%	157,771	40%
Number of observations	3,128	848		395	

Source: Author's calculations. All values in 1992 dollars and calculated using HRS sampling weights.

Here, wealth values are tabulated for alternative wealth measures. Focusing once again on the median household, whites expect to hold only $137,000 in net worth at retirement. Once pension wealth and particularly social security wealth are included, total wealth nearly triples to $390,000. Including social security and pension wealth has even more dramatic effects for minority households. Total wealth increases nearly three and one-half times for the median black household, from $55,000 to nearly $190,000, and more than fourfold for Hispanic households, from $36,000 to nearly $160,000. As a consequence of their proportionately greater holdings of pension and social security wealth, the relative disadvantage of minority households declines. The change is more pronounced for Hispanic households, whose wealth as a proportion of white household wealth increases from 27 to 40 percent. The relative position of black households improves more modestly, from 40 to 48 percent. As noted above, it is the inclusion of social security wealth, not pension wealth, that narrows the gap between white and minority households. The addition of pension wealth alone increases the relative disadvantage of both black and Hispanic median households.

The effect of adding social security and pension wealth to net worth is less

TABLE 6: Racial Disparities in Mean Wealth at Retirement by Wealth Measure Dual-
Earner Households, HRS

Wealth Measure	Non-Hispanic White	Non-Hispanic Black	
	$	$	% of White
Net worth: housing and financial assets	$266,936	$143,844	54%
Private wealth: net worth plus pension wealth	498,836	319,193	64%
Total wealth: private wealth plus SS wealth	682,754	489,246	72%
Number of observations	1,426	253	

Source: Author's calculations. All values in 1992 dollars and calculated using HRS sampling weights.

striking for the average household, though it remains important. White household wealth doubles, and the wealth of both black and Hispanic households triples. Thus the relative wealth position of black households improves from 50 percent to 55 percent of white household wealth, and that of Hispanic households from 33 percent to 45 percent. Interestingly, the relative position of the mean, in contrast to the median, black household improves with the addition of pension wealth, although by less than when social security wealth is added. Overall, broadening the definition of wealth not only increases wealth values at retirement, by threefold or more for median households, but it also narrows racial and ethnic disparities. These effects are more pronounced at the median because social security wealth, the largest component of wealth for these households, is the most equally distributed.

The improvement in the relative position of the mean black household when pension wealth is added reflects relatively larger contributions by second earners to black household wealth. Wealth differences in white and black dual-earner (head and spouse) households are reported in Table 6.[13] The impact that second earners have on wealth differences between the mean black and white households is striking. Black two-earner households expect to hold 72 percent of the wealth at retirement of white two-earner households; among all households, in contrast, blacks expect to hold only 55 percent of the wealth of white households (Table 5). Black dual-earner households hold only 54 percent of the personal net worth of white dual-earner households, but the addition of pension wealth raises their relative position by 10 percentage points. The addition of social security wealth adds another 8 percentage points. Remarkably, the expected aggregate wealth of the mean black dual-earner household ($489,246) is 90 percent of the mean wealth of all white households ($541,719; Table 5). These findings suggest that, in many black households, the role of second earners in financing post-retirement consumption may be pivotal.

Conclusion

Our analysis compares retirement wealth anticipated by households, and it reveals wide disparities between non-Hispanic white households, and non-Hispanic blacks and Hispanics. Adding pensions and social security wealth to conventionally-computed net financial wealth measures narrows the disparity, but the gaps remain large. The median Hispanic household in the HRS anticipates holding retirement assets worth only $160,000, or 40 percent of the wealth of the median white household. The median black household expects only $190,000, or just under 50 percent of the wealth of white households. These differences suggest that post-retirement consumption will prove to be substantially lower for black and Hispanic households than for their white counterparts. These differences are in part due to lower labor market earnings, and also to lower non-wage compensation — pensions.

To some extent these differences may reflect a lesser ability to save during the worklife, perhaps due to lower income, and to some extent they may be due to inadequate retirement planning. Future research will examine to what extent minority households are able to offset low net worth by working longer and by relying on pension and social security wealth of second earners in the household.

Appendix

In this appendix we outline the key data and methodological issues raised in devising the retirement wealth figures discussed in the text.

Net Financial Wealth

This wealth category includes savings, investments, business assets, and non-residential real estate less outstanding debt unrelated to housing. Components included in the HRS and the rates used to project them, drawn from historical data and Moore and Mitchell (this volume), are as follows:

- Vehicle and RV wealth — depreciated over ten years using straight line depreciation.
- Checking, savings, money market accounts — real T-bill rate (0.5 percent).
- CDs, savings bonds, T-bills — real T-bill rate (0.5 percent).
- IRAs and Keough accounts — 50/50 corporate bonds and stocks (2.3 percent, 7.2 percent).
- Stocks, mutual funds — stocks (7.2 percent).
- Bonds — bonds (2.3 percent).
- Business equity — stocks (7.2 percent).

- Other assets, real estate, second home — constant in real terms.
- Less other debt, second home debt — constant in real terms.

Net Housing Wealth

This component of wealth reflects the value of owner-occupied primary housing less outstanding debt. I estimate wealth at retirement as the projected real market value of the housing less projected real debt. The current value of the property is used as an estimate of the projected real value and projected real debt is computed using several steps. Projecting housing debt requires information on the outstanding balance on the mortgage and on debt payments and their frequency, information available in the HRS, and on the current interest rate on the debt, which is not available in the survey. I thus use historical interest rates to proxy the current rate, allowing for the possible refinancing of mortgages over time. An average of annual interest rates from the time of home purchase (available in the HRS) to 1992 is calculated from the 1993 American Housing Survey (USDC 1994; hereafter AHS). The average mortgage rate in the AHS, 8.5 percent, is used if the year of home purchase is missing or the purchase date was prior to the years covered in the survey. Information from the AHS on tax and insurance payments, in addition to related information in the HRS, is used to calculate the effective mortgage rate, that is, the rate that actually services the debt. I use the average rate from the AHS for second mortgages and home equity loans (9.5 percent), since their year of issue is not available in the HRS. Missing values on mortgage payment amounts are imputed from the average on 30-year fixed mortgages relevant to the year of home purchase, if the latter as well as purchase price are available. In the absence of this information I assume that primary mortgages are paid off by age 70 and that secondary mortgages and home equity loans are paid off over ten years.

Pension Wealth

The detailed history in the HRS on jobs and pension coverage permits the construction of expected pension wealth that covers the current job, the last job for non-workers, and up to three previous jobs for each respondent. For respondents with pension coverage on the current job, I calculate pension wealth at the expected retirement date. For those with expected DB pensions from previous jobs, I calculate pension wealth at the time of expected receipt of pension benefits and discount or project this value to the expected retirement date. I project DC balances remaining with previous employers to retirement, as well as the value of any benefits currently received from DB plans.

To convert the expected flow of benefits from a DB plan into a stock of wealth at retirement, I use age-specific survivor rates; in the absence of information about whether benefits will be paid to surviving spouses, I assume that all pensions are single-life and use the survival probabilities of the pension holder. I assume a 2.3 percent real rate of return (the historical return on corporate bonds) and use the inflation assumptions incorporated in the Social Security Trustees' intermediate assumptions. Because it is not known whether pensions on the current job are indexed for inflation, I assume that only government pensions are fully indexed and that remaining plans pay cost of living adjustments equal to one-half the inflation rate. I use similar assumptions for expected DB benefits from the most recent previous job, since respondents are asked about inflation adjustment only in the case of current benefits. I assume that benefits from prior jobs are not indexed. Resulting wealth values are then discounted to 1992 dollars since I assume that expected benefits are reported in future dollars.

Real returns on account balances in DC plans in current and previous jobs, and annual contributions to plans on the current job, are assumed to be four percent annually, approximating the historical average of a mixed-asset portfolio. Balances of account holders specifying investment in stocks or bonds exclusively are incremented annually by 7.2 percent or 2.3 percent, respectively. Wages, and thus the employer and employee contributions that are normally proportional to wages, are assumed constant in real terms, which is consistent with the observed flattening of the real-wage profile of older workers. For plans on previous jobs that are combinations of both DC and DB plans, respondents report balances in DC accounts as of the date of leaving the job. I assume these balances are outstanding only in cases in which the respondent expects future benefits from the DB component of the plan. I project these balances to 1992 assuming a four percent real rate of return and four percent inflation, then project by the real return to the expected retirement date.

Data Imputation

Calculation of pension and social security wealth in the HRS requires valid responses for queries on monetary values (such as current and expected benefits), account balances, and contributions, and on dates of expected benefit receipt and retirement. HRS respondents unable or unwilling to report a dollar value were permitted to chose a category from a series of range values. In such cases I impute an exact value using the mean of the valid responses in the interval chosen by the respondent. If categorical responses are missing, or in cases where expected retirement or pension receipt dates are missing, I use regression procedures to impute values. Imputations are based on linear regression models using age, race, sex, health, marital status, education, home ownership, earnings, income, wealth, tenure, industry, and occupation. Tenure, earnings, industry, and occupation are specific to the current or last job. Missing values of expected social security benefits or date of receipt are imputed from regressions that include the variables specified above but in which tenure is accumulated across all jobs. Account balances and employer (employee) contributions in DC plans are added to regressions of employee (employer) contributions.

In cases where the expected retirement date is missing, the expected date of social security receipt is used; if this is also missing, the expected date of pension receipt from the first plan on the current job is used. If this too is missing, the imputed value of the retirement date derived from the regression model is used.

The author thanks Olivia S. Mitchell, Joseph Piacentini, Steven S. Sandell, and Mikki Waid for helpful comments; exceptional programming assistance was provided by Anne C. Krill. The research was supported by the Brookdale Foundation through a grant to the International Longevity Center and the PSC-CUNY Research Award Program.

Notes

1. *Economic Report of the President* (1998), drawn from the Survey of Income and Program Participation.

2. Details of individual calculations, assumptions concerning interest rates, inflation, and wage growth, and methods for dealing with missing values, are discussed in greater detail in an appendix.

3. "Financially responsible member" and "household head" are terms used interchangeably in the present discussion.

4. This section follows the methodology developed in Moore and Mitchell (this volume).

5. Details of these calculations appear in the Appendix.

6. There is no similar instruction regarding the reporting of expected pension benefits; thus I assume that future pension benefits are reported in future dollars.

7. In cases where information on expected retirement date is missing, imputed values are used for these respondents only.

8. However, pension and social security wealth of spouses who have worked in the last ten years, regardless whether they are self-employed or retired, are included in estimates of household wealth.

9. Values for the median 10 percent of the sample are mean values for households between the 45th and 55th percentiles of the wealth distribution.

10. Values are adjusted by geometric interpolation of projected wealth at ages 62 and 65 in Table 2 (Moore and Mitchell, this volume).

11. Other estimates of expected social security and pension wealth using HRS data but alternative growth and inflation assumptions are Smith (1995; mean social security and pension wealth in 1992 of $121,000 and $104,000, respectively, for the full HRS sample) and McGarry and Davenport (1998; mean pension wealth of $93,000 at the expected retirement age for a sample of current or recent wage and salary earners similar to the sample used in this analysis). While social security and pension

wealth values in Table 1 are comparable to values (adjusted for retirement age) reported in Moore and Mitchell (this volume), total wealth in Table 1, $492,000, is substantially lower than the comparable adjusted value of $585,000 (from $566,000, Table 2, col. 2; Moore and Mitchell). This discrepancy in estimates of total wealth is due almost entirely to a difference of $80,000 in financial wealth ($133,000 in Table 1, compared to an adjusted value in MM of $213,000). The exclusion in this analysis of households in which the head is self-employed results in lower estimates of financial wealth because self-employed workers hold more personal assets on average than wage and salary earners and also are likely to hold business-related assets. If self-employed households are added to the sample, mean financial wealth increases more than 60 percent to $217,000 and mean total wealth increases to $568,000, close to the adjusted values derived from Moore and Mitchell.

12. I have not included imputed values of employer health insurance, which, if included, would exacerbate the disparity between white and minority households.

13. The small number of dual-earner Hispanic households prohibits their inclusion in this comparison.

References

Anderson, Kathryn H., Richard V. Burkhauser, and Joseph F. Quinn. 1986. "Do Retirement Dreams Come True? The Effects of Unanticipated Events on Retirement Plans." *Industrial and Labor Relations Review* 39: 518–26.

Bernheim, B. Douglas. 1988. "Social Security Benefits: An Empirical Study of Expectations and Realizations." In Rita Ricardo-Campbell and Edward P. Lazear, eds., *Issues in Contemporary Retirement*. Stanford, Calif.: Hoover Institution.

———. 1989. "The Timing of Retirement: A Comparison of Expectations and Realizations." In David A. Wise, ed., *The Economics of Aging*. Chicago: University of Chicago Press.

Board of Trustees of the Federal Old-Age and Survivors Insurance and Disability Insurance Trust Funds. 1995. *1995 Annual Report*. Washington, D.C.: U.S. Government Printing Office.

The Economic Report of the President. 1998. Washington, D.C.: U.S. Government Printing Office.

Honig, Marjorie. 1994. "The Subjective Probabilities of Retirement of White, Black, and Hispanic Married Women." HRS Working Paper 94-008. Institute for Social Research, University of Michigan, Ann Arbor.

———. 1996. "Retirement Expectations over Time." HRS/AHEAD Working Paper 96-038. Institute for Social Research, University of Michigan, Ann Arbor.

———. 1998. "Married Women's Retirement Expectations: Do Pensions and Social Security Matter?" *American Economic Review* 88, 2: 202–06.

Hurd, Michael D. and Kathleen McGarry. 1994. "Evaluation of Subjective Probability Distributions." HRS Working Paper 94-004. Institute for Social Research, University of Michigan, Ann Arbor.

———. 1995. "Evaluation of the Subjective Probabilities of Survival in the Health and Retirement Study." *Journal of Human Resources* 30 (Supplement): S268–92.

Ibbotson Associates. 1996. *Stocks, Bonds, Bills, and Inflation: 1996 Yearbook*. Chicago, Ibbotson Associates.

McGarry, Kathleen and Andrew Davenport. 1998. "Pensions and the Distribution of Wealth." In David A. Wise, ed., *Frontiers in the Economics of Aging*. Chicago: University of Chicago Press.

Moore, James F. and Olivia S. Mitchell. "Projected Retirement Wealth and Savings Adequacy." This volume.

Smith, James P. 1995. "Racial and Ethnic Differences in Wealth." *Journal of Human Resources* 30 (Supplement): S158–83.

U.S. Department of Commerce, Bureau of the Census. 1994. *American Housing Survey, 1993*. National File. Washington, D.C.: U.S. Government Printing Office.

Chapter 9
Early Retirement Windows

Charles Brown

Despite legal prohibitions on mandatory retirement rules in the United States, American firms still have a number of tools for influencing the retirement decisions of their workers. Pension plans, particularly those with early-retirement provisions, have received a good deal of attention from economists, as have wages (and wage-rate increases) in the pre-retirement years. Less studied are special early retirement windows, which offer for a limited time additional incentives for workers to retire. These are often called "window" offers.

Such windows are worth studying for at least three reasons. First, they are generally thought to have become more frequent, as firms attempt to downsize and the cuts are felt at management levels where firms have traditionally been reluctant to adopt permanent layoffs. Second, they represent an interesting response to age-discrimination legislation that has outlawed mandatory retirement and somewhat restricted the use of regular pension plans to achieve the same goal. Moreover, such offers are sometimes argued to themselves be discriminatory, since they tend to focus on older workers and are said to be seen by some older workers as only slightly subtler than a dead fish on the desk as a signal that it's time to move on. Third, such offers are often unanticipated by workers, certainly as of the time when they initially accepted employment with the firm and often even shortly before the window is opened. Consequently, if one worries that generous regular retirement plans have attracted workers who planned to retire early anyway (and so discount evidence that generous retirement plans *encourage* retirement), the unanticipated nature of special early-retirement windows makes them a particularly attractive quasi-experiment (Gustman, Mitchell, and Steinmeier 1994).[1]

Systematic evidence regarding the effect of such windows is limited. Most previous work has focused on responses to early retirement windows offered by a single employer.[2] In addition to worries about representatives of the employers studied, one can't observe in employer-based data whether workers subsequently work for other firms, and if so whether their earnings are substantial. The Health and Retirement Study (HRS) therefore included a series of questions about such special early retirement windows. The analysis in this chapter is based on the first two waves of the HRS, conducted in 1992 and 1994.

We begin by outlining the economic theory underlying the firm's decision to offer a window and the worker's decision whether to accept. Then the characteristics of window offers and the workers who receive them are analyzed. Next, work and retirement outcomes for workers who received window offers are compared to those who did not. Finally, multivariate analyses of receiving a window offer and the decision to accept it are summarized, and conclusions are offered.

Window Theory

Employers decide whether to offer an early-out window and, if so, the terms of the offer; workers decide whether to accept such offers. While the worker's decision has been considered in some detail in the retirement literature, modeling the employer's decision requires pulling together themes from several different literatures.

Offering a Window

An employer may be thought of as offering an early-out window when a reduction in employment is desirable, and an early-out window is an efficient way of achieving that reduction. Unlike the regular early retirement provisions of pension plans that are driven by steady-state considerations, a *special* early-retirement *window* presumably reflects a change in the firm's preferred level or skill-pattern of employment.

Reductions in a firm's overall demand for labor may be temporary or permanent. If temporary, the firm will want to reduce employment of those workers in whom it has invested the least; those with greater levels of firm-specific skills will remain employed so that they will be available (without new hiring and training costs) when demand recovers (Oi 1962; Becker 1993). Permanent reductions in demand for labor should lead to roughly proportional cuts at all skill levels, unless the production function is non-homothetic. Changes in product technology or in the composition of product demand can lead to changes in the employer's desired skill mix and lead to reductions in demand for those whose skills have become obsolete. Given a desire to reduce employment of some or all groups of workers, why would a firm *pay* workers to leave, rather than unilaterally severing their employment? One answer is that layoffs have their own cost — such workers can claim unemployment insurance, and at least part of the cost of the incremental benefits is reflected in the firm's payroll taxes for the UI program (Brechling 1977; Topel 1983; Anderson and Meyer 1993). By inducing quits and therefore reducing layoffs, early-out windows might reduce the firm's UI liability.

On closer analysis, however, early-out windows prove to be a relatively expensive way of cutting UI liabilities. Laid-off workers typically qualify for six months of unemployment benefits, at up to half their previous earnings. Each state has a maximum benefit, however, and workers with above-average earnings receive less than half their previous earnings in UI benefits. So in a worst case, where all workers file for benefits, receive benefits equal to half of their previous pay, and fully exhaust benefits before finding new work, and the benefits are fully experience rated, a layoff will cost the firm three months pay. For highly paid workers, the UI tax is much less than that.

By contrast, as we shall see, early-out windows are often worth at least three months pay, and are typically offered to well-paid workers. This suggests that some other "cost" of layoffs must account for the employer's offering early-out windows.

The key to understanding this cost is recognizing that, in normal times, both workers and employers benefit from long-term employment relationships. Workers' willingness to share the cost of acquiring employer-specific skills depends on a belief that the employment relationship will continue and promised wage premiums will be received. Both firms and workers gain from deferred-compensation contracts in which workers are motivated to work hard when they are young by the promise of above-market pay when they are older (Lazear 1979). Indeed, the typical merit grid rewards superior performance in one period with an increase in base pay; the value of that increase is clearly contingent on the worker's expectation of continued employment. Finally, long-term employment contracts can be seen as a type of insurance that risk-averse workers purchase from risk-neutral firms. Early-out windows are then offered when the firm decides that continuing the employment relationship on the implicitly agreed-on terms is no longer desirable.

This perspective suggests that early-out windows should be offered to those workers who have relatively stable, long-term employment relationships. To the extent that such arrangements are more common for those who work for large or unionized firms,[3] and among skilled rather than unskilled workers, we should expect early-out windows to be most common for these workers, too.

The hypothesis that early-out windows will be offered to stably-employed "advantaged" workers is strengthened by consideration of another alternative for the firm — waiting for workers to quit voluntarily. In markets where turnover rates are high, it is cheaper to wait than to pay.

Accepting a Window Offer

The worker's decision to accept or reject a window offer has been studied in the retirement literature, most notably by Lumsdaine, Stock, and Wise (1990). They carefully model a worker's decision to leave the firm now, relative to later retirement dates. Implicitly, the alternative to working with the current firm in their model is withdrawing from the labor force, because alternative employment is not explicitly considered. Gustman and Steinmeier (1986) suggest that "partial retirement," moving to a new job that usually pays less but allows a shorter workweek, is an empirically important alternative to retiring altogether, though its importance for workers covered by special early-out options has not been addressed.

Of course, these models predict — and Lumsdaine, Stock, and Wise confirm — that workers are more likely to accept offers that are more generous. Another important implication is that a given offer is more attractive to a worker who would have retired soon anyway. Moreover, early-out windows should be accepted by those who are pessimistic about their prospects with the firm, and value their alternatives — either withdrawing from the labor force or working elsewhere — most favorably. A subtler implication is that window offers may be accepted precisely because they are a sign that employment stability and traditional wage increases are less certain if one remains with the firm.

Working Backward

The process by which workers decide whether to accept window offers relates back to the firm's decision to offer them in two ways. First, worker decisions about whether to accept determine how generous offers must be in order to achieve a given number of departures. Second, worker decisions determine whether the employer is losing the "right" workers. Layoffs, perhaps with severance payments, can be targeted directly to those workers whose net value to the firm is smallest. Early-out windows introduce self-selection by workers. To the extent that the offers are accepted by workers who are relatively unproductive, they provide a relatively efficient way for the firm to reduce employment while maintaining the promise of stable employment. But if departures are motivated by good outside prospects, those who accept window offers may be those the firm would least want to lose.

Window Offers and Those Who Receive Them

The data analyzed in this chapter relate to those age-eligible members of the HRS sample who were interviewed in both of the first two waves (1992 and 1994). In Wave 1, all respondents who were currently employed or who had ever worked for pay for "more than a few months" and had last worked in

1972 or later—i.e., virtually all those who had worked in the last twenty years—were asked a sequence of questions on any window offers they had ever received. In Wave 2, those who worked at all between Wave 1 and Wave 2 were asked about window offers received since Wave 1. Early retirement windows are defined as special offers available only at a particular time, and so do not include the normal "early retirement" features of many pension plans. The placement of this sequence in the survey—after detailed pension questions about current and past jobs have already been asked—should have reinforced this distinction.

Among our 8,933 age-eligible respondents, 679 respondents (7.6 percent of the sample) reported that they had received one or more such window offers. Using sampling weights increases this proportion to 8.8 percent. Nearly 30 percent of those who received such an offer received more than one, almost always from the same employer.

Of those receiving special early retirement offers, 42 percent accepted the first offer they received; of those receiving more than one, a similar fraction (36 percent) accepted the most recent offer. Overall, counting offers between the first and last for those receiving more than two, about 34 percent of all offers were accepted.[4] This is not very different from the estimates based on surveys by private consulting companies—30 percent by Hewitt Associates (Shalowitz 1993) and 33 percent by Charles D. Spencer and Associates 1992)—or the 30 percent acceptance rate in Hogarth's (1988) New York State data. Of all individuals who received an offer (or more than one), just over half had accepted.

Window Offers by Age and Year

While a great deal is known about the early retirement options that are standard features of many pension plans, less is known about the ages at which individuals typically receive special early-retirement-window offers. Two related questions are whether the incidence of such windows has been increasing over time, and the extent to which windows are under-reported in the HRS. Table 1 addresses these questions, by presenting the number of windows offered by year and birth cohort.[5] Reading down the columns, we see the number of offers for HRS respondents from different birth cohorts (and hence different current ages) in any one year; reading across a row shows the history of offers for any one cohort; reading down the highlighted diagonal block shows the number of offers received in each year by those age 53–58 in that year.

One clear message from Table 1 is that early-out windows are apparently received throughout the 51–63 age range. Age 51 is not "too young" to get such an offer, and 63 is not near enough to "normal" retirement to discourage special efforts by employers. There is also a sharp increase in the number of offers in 1991–92 over earlier years. One can see the same pat-

258   Charles Brown

TABLE 1: Proportion of the Population Receiving an Early-Retirement Window
         Offer, by Birth Cohort and Year

Birth Cohort	1994	1993	1992	1991	1990	1989
1931	1.33%	1.62%	2.64%	2.99%	1.27%	**0.69%**
1932	2.02	1.50	2.15	1.05	**1.08**	**1.10**
1933	0.87	1.80	2.75	**2.10**	**0.95**	**1.08**
1934	0.91	2.81	**1.82**	**2.11**	**0.50**	**0.83**
1935	2.09	**2.00**	**2.41**	**2.04**	**1.25**	**0.15**
1936	**2.06**	**2.53**	**2.86**	**1.72**	**1.54**	**0.61**
1937	**1.66**	**1.94**	**2.14**	**0.84**	**0.58**	0.62
1938	**1.52**	**2.25**	**2.42**	**1.14**	1.36	0.36
1939	**1.89**	**1.62**	**1.75**	0.36	0.60	0.08
1940	**2.78**	**2.25**	1.99	1.21	0.37	0.36
1941	**2.26**	1.72	2.24	1.67	0.31	0.15
1931–41	1.75	2.06	2.27	1.54	0.84	0.54
Accepted offered	.25	.35	.35	.37	.37	.36

Source: Author's calculations using HRS data.
Note: 1994 data are for months prior to Wave 2 interview, which was centered on July.

tern along the highlighted diagonal block: those who were age 53–58 in
1991–92 were more likely to receive window offers than those who were 53–
58 in earlier years. The table hides a substantial increase in offers between
1993 and 1994: because the period prior to the Wave 2 interview includes all
of 1993 but on average 7 months of the following year, offers for all of 1994
were probably more than half again as numerous as reported in Table 1.[6]

The sharp increase in window offers over time is consistent with two quite
different interpretations: that such offers have increased dramatically in recent years, or that people tend to forget such offers over time. There are, unfortunately, no other consistently collected data on early-retirement windows that could serve as a benchmark for Table 1.[7] One plausible conjecture
is that, if respondents are under-reporting window offers received in earlier
years, such under-reporting is more likely for offers that were not accepted.
Accepted offers generate significant changes—a change of employer and
often a cash bonus or significant change in one's pension entitlement (more
on that below)—and so should be salient enough to be recalled and reported. In response to this conjecture, the last line of Table 1 presents the
fraction of offers *accepted* by age-eligible respondents in each year. With
the exception of 1994 (where there seem to be "too few" accepted offers),
the pattern for accepted offers is very much like that for all offers, and the
fraction of offers accepted does not diverge in any consistent way from the
36 percent rate for the entire 1989–93 period. This admittedly indirect test
suggests that much of the reported increase in window offers over time
reflects a genuine increase, and not partial recall of more distant offers.[8]

Whatever one makes of the reported increase in windows in recent years, accepted early-out windows are now a significant component of total turnover for workers in this age range. Between Waves 1 and 2, 26 percent of those who were initially wage and salary workers left their Wave-1 employers; accepted window offers account for 10 percent of these departures.

What Incentives Are Offered?

For those who receive window offers, HRS obtains relatively detailed information about the characteristics of the offers. These include whether the special retirement incentive offered took the form of a cash bonus, temporary cash payments, better pension benefits, and/or other benefits. Both the forms of the benefit and the amount were recorded. Table 2 describes these offers, separately for those who reject (all) offers and those who accept an (any) offer. For simplicity, I focus on the first offer received for the 30 percent of the sample who received more than one.[9] Dollar amounts are converted to constant 1992 dollars using the CPI.

Cash bonuses are slightly more common among rejected window offers, but the conditional mean bonus is higher for the accepted offers. The median and the unconditional means (i.e., treating those who were not offered a cash bonus as zero) are only slightly higher for accepted offers. Temporary cash payments (typically, until age 62) are much less common than simple cash bonuses, but are a bit more likely to be part of accepted offers than rejected ones.

Offers of additional pension benefits are both more common and more generous for accepted window offers than for those that were rejected. The same goes for pension plan credits for extra years of service. Accepted offers are more likely to include medical insurance, but they are less likely to include "other" incentives. Overall, while not all the differences are statistically significant, accepted offers are "better" than rejected ones.[10] Given that those who accepted offers had similar earnings to those who rejected them,[11] the generally better terms among the accepted offers is quite in line with an economic model of the decision to accept such offers.

Table 2 is constructed to highlight differences between accepted and rejected offers. But it is also important to note that amounts on offer in either column are impressive. Even for rejected offers, cash offers amounted to $23,000, while improved pensions averaged $4,000 *per year*. An extra pension credit of 3.6 years represents about a 15 percent increase (given average tenure of 23 years). Typically, an offer would be *either* cash or improved pension benefits, rather than both.[12]

Given the serious sums at stake, it is perhaps not surprising that three-fourths of those who accept the window offer describe it as important to their decision to retire at that time (rather than something they would do anyway). Those who reject the window offer are asked whether doubling the

TABLE 2: Window Offers: What Is Being Offered?

	(All) Offers Rejected (N=327)	Offer Accepted (N=352)
Cash bonus: Yes=1	.57	.51
Cash bonus:		
mean ($000)	22.99	31.65*
	(18.60)	(37.40)
median ($000)	22.40	24.00
Cash bonus/annual earnings	.54	.64*
	(.41)	(.44)
Temporary cash: Yes=1	.04	.06
Extra pension: Yes=1	.26	.33*
Extra pension:		
mean/year ($000)	3.99	6.16
	(5.43)	(8.57)
median/year ($000)	2.00	3.60
Extra pension/earnings	.10	.14
	(.13)	(.16)
Pension credit: Yes=1	.13	.17
Pension credit: years	3.58	4.47
	(2.21)	(2.28)
Perm. medical insurance: Yes=1	.02	.07*
Temp. medical insurance: Yes=1	.02	.03
Other incentive: Yes=1	.08	.05

Source: Author's calculations using HRS data.

Notes: For continuous variables, standard deviations are in parentheses below means. Means, medians and standard deviations of continuous variables are conditional—i.e., zeros are excluded. Results based on weighted data. * = significantly different (t≥1.96) from the mean for "all offers rejected."

offer would change their decision. Only a third reported that it would, which I find more surprising.

Who Receives Early Retirement Window Offers? Who Accepts Them?

Characteristics of HRS workers who received window offers are summarized in Table 3, for those who accepted their (first) offer and those who declined it. (With nearly equal numbers of workers in the "accept" and "reject" groups, the characteristics of all window recipients are a simple average of those two columns.) Also presented for comparison are characteristics of age-eligible individuals who did not receive such offers (but were employed or had worked at some time since 1972 and so could have reported receiving one).

Those receiving window offers are more advantaged economically than

TABLE 3: Characteristics of Workers by Window Status

Worker Characteristic	Never Offered Window N=7591	(All) Offer(s) Rejected (N=327)	Offer Accepted (N=352)
Male	.49*	.69	.69
Black	.10	.09	.08
Hispanic	.05*	.04	.02
Never married	.04	.04	.03
Married now	.73*	.78	.76
Married, spouse works	.48	.56	.44*
Years of schooling	12.42**	13.81	13.86
	(2.92)	(2.68)	(2.66)
Physical health ≥ good	.81**	.92	.90
Emotional health ≥ good	.83**	.90	.89
Health limits work	.20**	.08	.13
Will live to 75 (0–10)	6.46	6.70	6.53
	(2.93)	(2.83)	(2.86)
Will live to 85 (0–10)	4.28	4.38	4.34
	(3.17)	(3.14)	(3.26)
Financial horizon ≥ 5 yrs	.39	.40	.42
Accept financial risk	.23**	.16	.23*
Wealth mean ($000)	255.34	225.12	327.01*
	(546.15)	(411.34)	(546.43)
median ($000)	114	137	208
Year of birth	1936.19**	1936.33	1934.80*
	(3.17)	(3.33)	(3.09)

Source: Author's calculations using HRS data.
Notes: See Table 2. ** significantly different from the mean for all those receiving an offer (last two colums combined).

those who did not: they are more likely to be married males, they have on average a year and a half more schooling, they are healthier (though their estimates of their probabilities to living to age 75 or 85 are no higher), and they are wealthier. They are marginally more willing to accept a hypothetical job that offers a 50-50 chance of doubling or reducing family income by one third, but there is no significant difference in their financial planning horizons.

Differences between those who accept and those who reject offers are less marked, but nonetheless interesting. Those who accept offers are less likely to have a working spouse than are those who reject the offer. They are more likely to report that a health condition limits their work, though they are very similar on the other health measures. Those who accept offers are more likely to report that they would accept the hypothetical risky alternative job. It is not clear whether this finding should have been expected. On the one hand, as we will see later, a significant fraction of those who accept windows

TABLE 4: Job Characteristics of Workers by Window Status

Job Characteristic	Never Offered Window N=7509**	(All) Offer(s) Rejected N=327	Offer Accepted N=352
ln (wage/hour)	2.38	2.90	2.98*
	(.59)	(.47)	(.50)
Usual hours/week	40.61	42.10	43.25
	(13.45)	(7.66)	(8.91)
Durable Mfg.	.11	.18	.22
Trans & Pub Utilities	.06	.19	.25
Public Administration	.04	.11	.09
Manager	.15	.16	.23*
Professional	.14	.34	.27
Mech & Repair	.03	.08	.09
Tenure (years)	12.48	23.18	25.52*
	(10.90)	(8.81)	(8.93)
Union contract	.20	.56	.52*
Company size ≥ 500	.50	.82	.85*
Pension: DB	.22	.50	.67*
Pension: DC	.16	.08	.08
Pension: DB + DC	.11	.38	.23*

Source: Author's calculations using HRS data.
Notes: * = significantly different (t ≥ 1.96) from the mean for "all offers rejected." ** = signifi-cantly different from the mean for all those receiving an offer. For those who rejected or accepted window offers, job characteristics are from the employer who first offered a window; for those who never received a window offer, job characteristics are from current/last employer at wave 1. Union status and employer size are missing if window offer is from employer before current/last employer at wave 1.

later work with another employer. On the other hand, rejecting a window offered by a downsizing firm involves the risk of subsequent layoff. Those who accept window offers are wealthier than those who reject them (and it will turn out that the difference is larger than can be accounted for by the window payments themselves).

Table 4 presents differences in *job* characteristics of those who did and did not receive window offers. For those who received an offer, the job charac-teristics are those of the job that was held at the time of the offer; for those who did not receive an offer, I focused on their current/last job. Broadly, the finding from Table 3 that those who receive window offers are relatively advantaged workers is if anything stronger in Table 4: they are more likely to be employed in high-wage industries, to report their occupation is (or was) managerial or professional, they worked for their employer about twice as long, and they are more likely to be covered by union contracts and to work for large firms.[13] It therefore is no surprise that those who receive window offers earn more than those who do not, though the magnitude of the

TABLE 5: Job-related Expectations at Wave 1 and Real Wage Growth on Wave-1 Job by Window Status Between Waves 1 and 2

	No Window Offered N=4591	(All) Offers Rejected N=208	Offer Accepted N=128
How likely is layoff in next year (0–10)	1.76	1.30	1.91*
	(2.57)	(2.28)	(2.92)
Expect real earnings change (+1,0,−1)	.48	.51	.27*
	(.64)	(.61)	(.77)
Chances of finding equal job (0–10)	4.53**	3.50	3.03
	(3.73)	(3.69)	(3.40)
Chances of working past age 62 (0–10)	4.70**	3.93	2.89*
	(3.92)	(3.79)	(3.58)

Notes: See Table 4.

difference (those who received offers earned about 40 percent more per hour than those who didn't) may be.[14] Finally, those who received window offers are almost always covered by a defined benefit pension plan: windows are offered to workers who have an expectation of quasi-permanent employment, and such pensions contribute to and perhaps symbolize that stability. Among those who receive window offers, differences between those who accept and those who reject them are once again strikingly small, and conform to no simple pattern.

Workers' expectations about the future with their current employers, the difficulty of finding new jobs, and plans for future labor force participation potentially influence the decision to accept window offers. These variables were measured in Wave 1, for those who were working at that time. This means we cannot relate these variables to window outcomes prior to Wave 1, but we can compare Wave-1 values of those who accepted, rejected, or did not receive window offers between Wave 1 and Wave 2 (Table 5).

Those who receive window offers between Wave 1 and Wave 2 do not (at Wave 1) view their chances of being laid off any differently from those who did not receive a window offer. Furthermore, they have similar expectations about real wage growth on their job over the next several years. Those who receive window offers do think it would be harder to find a comparable job in the same line of work if they were to lose their current job. This is consistent with earlier evidence that windows are offered to workers with long-term attachment to their employers. Those who receive offers believe (at Wave 1, prior to receiving the offer) they are less likely to work past age 62 or 65. As Lazear (1979) emphasized, employment contracts that lead workers to remain with the firm often have features (once mandatory retirement; now subtle pension incentives) that discourage workers from staying *too* long. Viewed from this perspective, those who do not expect to be working past age 62 are also likely to be workers with strong attachment to their employers.

Several differences between those who reject window offers and those who accept them are apparent. Those who accept window offers see layoffs as more likely, and wage growth less favorable, than those who reject them; and they see themselves as less likely to work beyond age 62. These differences are all in the expected direction: windows are accepted by workers who see the option of remaining with their employer as less valuable.

For those employed at Wave 1, HRS asked about their wage when they began working for their Wave 1 employers. Real wage growth per year with the Wave 1 employer is positively correlated with workers' expectation of future real wage growth, but is not related to either receiving or accepting a window offer. The wage-growth variable depends on respondents' recollection of their pay more than a decade ago, and so no doubt is not well measured. A verdict on the relationship between past wage growth and windows must wait for a more reliable measure of such growth.

Life Beyond the Window

Most previous analyses of early-out windows are based on payroll records of the employer offering the window. This means that little is known about what happens to workers who accept windows. Do they stop working altogether or take jobs with other employers? Do those who take new jobs work full time and earn about as much as on the job they left? Or do they move to "partial retirement" jobs with shorter hours and significantly lower pay? How do those who accept windows and "retire" characterize their retirement? These questions are important to employers interested in designing these programs.

To start answering these questions, Table 6 characterizes employment and retirement status at Wave 2 for those who accepted, rejected, or never received a window offer. Nearly half (45 percent) of those who accepted a window offer are employed at Wave 2. A significant fraction (13 percent of all those who accept windows, or nearly a third of those who are working) are self-employed. Half of those who accept windows characterize themselves as completely retired, while 28 percent say they are partially retired. As one would expect, those who accept window offers are less likely to be employed, and more likely to report themselves retired, than those never received such offers and those who rejected all early-out offers.

Among those who describe themselves as "completely retired" at Wave 2, those who accepted window offers report having a much more satisfactory retirement experience. Compared to those not offered windows, those who accept a window offer are much more likely to say they wanted to retire (rather than being forced to do so), that they are satisfied with their retire-

Table 6: Employment Status and Retirement Status at Wave 2 by Window Status

	Never Offered Window	(All) Offers Rejected	Offer Accepted
Employed	.69	.89	.45
Self-employed	.14	.01	.13
Completely retired	.18	.09	.51
Partially retired	.10	.03	.28
Among completely retired			
Wanted to retire	.46		.67
Forced to retire	.47		.19
Very satisfied w/retirement	.48		.70
Not at all satisfied w/retirement	.18		.03
Better than before	.44		.57
Worse than before	.27		.11
Among completely retired with no health limitations			
Wanted to retire	.75		.77
Forced to retire	.15		.11
Very satisfied w/retirement	.74		.75
Not at all satisfied w/retirement	.03		.00
Better than before	.65		.62
Worse than before	.05		.06

Source: Author's calculations using HRS data.

ment, and that they are better off than before retiring. However, the bottom panel of Table 6 reveals that this difference vanishes if we restrict our analysis to those with no health problem that limits their work. The negative overall descriptions of retirement among those who have never been offered a window is due to the fact that those who are in poor health fare less well in retirement, and that, in this age range (53–63, at Wave 2) those who retire without a window offer are likely to be in poorer health. Nonetheless, the lack of significant differences between healthy retirees who did and did not take window offers is hard to square with the "defenestration" view that workers who accept window offers often feel they have little choice in the matter and so are pushed through the window.

Table 7 compares the workweek and wages of those who are employed after accepting a window offer (from another employer) to those who rejected window offers. For those who reject a window offer, hours per week and inflation-adjusted hourly wages are (on average) just what they were when the window was offered. Among those who accept offers, however, those who return to work do so for somewhat shorter work weeks (11 hours per week) and substantially lower wages. While it is tempting to link the wage losses of those who accept window offers and then work elsewhere to

TABLE 7: Hours Worked and Wages, Before and After Window Offer

	(All) Offers Rejected	Offer Accepted
Window job		
Hours/week	42.10	43.25
	(7.66)	(8.91)
Weeks/year	49.89	49.57
	(5.55)	(6.87)
ln(wage/hour) mean	2.90	2.98*
	(.47)	(.50)
median	2.85	2.97
N	320	343
Wave 2 Job		
Hours/week	42.17	33.04*
	(8.62)	(15.50)
Weeks/year	49.92	45.72*
	(5.44)	(12.03)
ln(wage/hour) mean	2.90	2.45*
	(.45)	(.72)
median	2.88	2.25
N	266	124
Wave 2 window		
Hours/week	0.09	−10.99*
	(7.90)	(16.82)
Weeks/year	0.03	−4.03*
	(5.00)	(11.39)
ln(wage/hour) mean	−.02	−.53*
	(.37)	(.69)
median	−.00	−.50
N	262	124

Source: Author's calculations using HRS data.
Sample sizes are for ln(wage/hour); means of hours/week and weeks/year are based on slightly larger samples. * = significantly different (t ≥ 1.96) from the mean for "all offers rejected."

the tendency of window acceptors to become self-employed, we obtain almost the same wage loss when analysis is restricted to those whose Wave-2 job is working for someone else.

Multivariate Analyses

Three questions remain that are best answered with multivariate analyses. (1) Does the tendency for windows to be offered to advantaged workers with strong "permanent" attachment to the firm hold when various measures of advantage and attachment are considered simultaneously? (2) How important are the details of the window offer and the worker's expectations about where his/her current job is heading in explaining the decision of workers to accept the offer, once the characteristics of the jobs and workers are held constant? (3) How different are offer and acceptance rates for those who have already turned down one or more such offers?

The analyses here focus on windows offered between Wave 1 and Wave 2, and workers' responses to these offers. Above we noted that workers' expectations about layoffs, wage growth, and alternative jobs were strongly related to workers' decisions to accept window offers. These variables are first measured at Wave 1. Employer size and union status are not known for some employers.[15] These gaps and subtler problems with continuously measuring other time-varying variables make it difficult to include windows offered prior to Wave 1 in a formal analysis.

The first column of Table 8 shows the effect of worker and job characteristics on the probability of receiving a window offer between Wave 1 and Wave 2. As was true in the analysis of those who had *ever* received a window offer, the probability of receiving an offer over the two-year period between Wave 1 and Wave 2 is higher for males, for those with longer employer tenure, higher wages, and defined benefit pensions, and for unionized workers and (marginally) for those who work for larger firms.[16] What we learn from Table 8, then, is that these indicators of job attachment contribute individually to the probability of obtaining a window even when other factors are held constant.

Adding the number of window offers received *prior* to Wave 1 to this specification does not change the coefficients in Table 8 significantly, but its coefficient is strongly and significantly positive. As windows have become more common, so too has receiving several such offers ("refenestrations"). As workers become aware of the possibility that windows may not be a once-in-a-lifetime opportunity, structural modeling of the worker's decision becomes even more complicated.

The second column of Table 8 attempts to explain the decision to accept or reject windows offered between Wave 1 and Wave 2. Given the much smaller sample size, and the few differences between those who accept and reject offers in the earlier tables, one should approach this analysis with limited expectations. A few of the stronger results of the earlier tables are reversed, given Table 8's smaller sample and many control variables: those whose health limits their work are less likely to accept (though those in good health are less likely to do so, which makes sense); and those willing to accept risky jobs are less likely (in Table 8) to accept the window offer. On the other hand, those who expected at Wave 1 that their wages would increase in real terms were again less likely to accept the window offer, as were those who expected to work past age 62. The influence of the details of the

TABLE 8: Window Offers and Acceptances

Explanatory variable	Get Window Offer	Accept Window Offer
Male	.03	−.12
	(.01)	(.08)
Never married	−.04	−.08
	(.02)	(.16)
Married now	−.02	−.07
	(.01)	(.09)
Married, spouse working	.001	−.08
	(.01)	(.07)
Physical health ≥ good	.01	−.31
	(.01)	(.12)
Emotional health ≥ good	−.02	−.03
	(.01)	(.09)
Health limits work	−.004	−.26
	(.01)	(.13)
Years of schooling	.003	−.01
	(.002)	(.02)
Tenure (years)	.004	.004
	(.00)	(.004)
ln (wage/hour)	.05	.11
	(.01)	(.10)
Pension: DB	.02	.08
	(.01)	(.15)
Pension: DC	−.02	.03
	(.01)	(.18)
Pension: DB+DC	.04	.01
	(.01)	(.16)
Union contract	.03	.01
	(.01)	(.07)
Firm size ≥ 500	.01	−.05
	(.01)	(.08)
Financial horizon ≥ 5 Yrs	−.02	−.05
	(.01)	(.06)
Take risky job	.01	−.13
	(.01)	(.07)
How likely is layoff in next year (0–10)	.002	.01
	(.002)	(.01)
Expect real wage increase (+1,0,−1)	−.001	−.09
	(.01)	(.04)
Chances of finding equally good job (0–10)	−.00	−.01
	(.001)	(.01)
Chances of working past age 62 (0–10)	−.002	−.02
	(.001)	(.01)
Cash bonus/earnings		−.03
		(.09)
Temporary cash/earnings		−.40
		(.25)
Extra pension benefits/earnings		1.22
		(.53)

TABLE 8: *Continued*

Explanatory variable	Get Window Offer	Accept Window Offer
Pension credit: years		.02
		(.02)
Other incentives/earnings		.10
		(.13)
Temporary medical insurance		−.01
		(.16)
Permanent medical insurance		−.03
		(.13)
N	4324	307

Source: Author's calculations using HRS data.
Note: Also included in the regressions are variables whose coefficients are not reported in the table: race/ethnicity (2), wealth quartile (3), hours worked per week, weeks worked per year, industry (12), occupation (16).

offer seem less influential in this smaller sample, except for improved pension benefits.

When a variable which identifies those who had received and rejected window offers prior to Wave 1 is introduced, its coefficient was negative and moderately significant (−.142 (.073)). However, among those who had rejected an offer prior to Wave 1 but claimed they would have accepted a doubly generous one, there is no significant difference in accepting the offer between waves.

Conclusions

Early retirement windows offer, for a limited time, additional incentives (beyond those that might be included in a firm's pension plan) to retire. Their use has grown over time, and the size of the typical incentive is substantial. The Health and Retirement Study provides the first opportunity to study these early retirement windows with a representative sample of workers in the relevant age range. We confirm some important findings from earlier studies based on individual firms, and suggest several new conclusions:

1. Employers appear to be offering early-out windows more frequently in recent years. Receiving more than one offer has become fairly common, and workers who have received and rejected one such offer are more likely to get another, but less likely to accept it, than otherwise similar workers.

2. Roughly two-thirds of window offers are rejected. If windows not taken are less likely to be remembered than offers that actually triggered a departure, this two-thirds would be a lower bound for the true figure. The fact that most offers are rejected has two implications: (1) Workers may some-

times feel they have little choice but to accept an early-out offer, but this cannot be true of most offers; (2) Employers must make significantly more offers than they can expect to be accepted, raising the possibility that offers will be accepted by some workers the firm would rather keep, and be rejected by some that the firm would prefer had accepted.

3. Early-out windows tend to be offered to relatively advantaged workers who would otherwise have relatively permanent attachment to their firms.

4. The decision to accept windows is only weakly explained by the "usual suspects" — schooling, age, race, sex, industry, occupation — since they differ little between those who accept and those who reject offers. This should not be too surprising. Workers with more education have brighter alternatives than workers with less education if they accept the window (more pension benefits, higher wages if they work elsewhere) and also if they reject it (higher salary with current employer). Thus, such variables may have little influence on the decision to accept the window offer or remain with one's current employer.

5. The financial details of the offers do seem to influence workers' decisions to accept them. Those who accepted offers and those who rejected them had similar hourly wages but the accepted offers were more generous.

6. The amounts offered are substantial, even taking account of the fact that window recipients are relatively well paid. Those who rejected cash bonuses were on average rejecting offers of about $23,000, while rejected pension improvements averaged $4,000 per year. Accepted offers were higher still. Thus, if one sees early-retirement windows as unanticipated exogenous changes in the incentive to remain with an employer, and therefore as a particularly helpful experiment for assessing the impact of such incentives, the generosity of the offers reported by HRS respondents is encouraging: these amounts are large enough to be worth studying. On the other hand, half of the workers who reject one offer received another offer subsequently, so that offers after the first may not be strictly exogenous.

7. Roughly half the workers who accept early retirement windows do not retire altogether from the labor force. Moreover, the average "post-retirement" job represents substantial employment — on average, 30 hours per week — though hourly wages are significantly lower. These post-retirement jobs have important implications for modeling responses to such offers: the alternative to remaining with the firm is often to accept the early-retirement incentive and work elsewhere, so the fact that HRS allows the analyst to track such jobs gives it an advantage over data from individual firms' personnel files (which have better information on the window offer but no data on subsequent employment). For employers, the fact that those who accept window offers often work elsewhere raises the possibility that those who leave are those with the best alternative prospects, not those who are least productive on their current job.

The first two waves of the HRS give us a reasonably detailed picture of who receives window offers, but relatively limited samples for analyzing the decision to accept the offers, and for learning what happens thereafter to workers who accept them. As the fraction of the sample that received such offers grows over time, more detailed analyses of these issues will be possible.

The author is grateful to seminar participants at the HRS Early Results workshop, the Naval Postgraduate School, the University of Chicago, and the University of Michigan for comments on an earlier version of the work, and to Mel Stephens and Wei Li for research assistance.

Notes

1. One might still be concerned about how *firms* decide how generous the window offered to each worker should be. Moreover, in situations where firms make further offers to those who initially decline the offer, more generous offers might be correlated with characteristics that make workers unwilling to accept initial offers.

2. Lumsdaine, Stock, and Wise (1990) studied an unnamed Fortune 500 firm; Hogarth (1988) studied New York State employees; Mehay and Hogan (1998) studied responses of Navy and Air Force personnel.

3. For evidence on whether workers at larger firms have longer tenure with their employers, see Brown, Medoff, and Hamilton (1990); for evidence on unionization and tenure, see Freeman and Medoff (1984).

4. As a rule, offers other than the last have been rejected, because the offers come from the same employer, and accepting an offer leads to terminating one's employment. For respondents who received more than two offers prior to Wave 1, the outcome of the first and last offer was obtained from respondents, and I assume any offers between these were rejected. Similarly, for respondents who received more than two offers between Waves 1 and 2 I assume that offers between the first and last were rejected. Only 9 percent of all offers were inferred in this way to have been rejected.

5. For those reporting more than two offers at either wave, respondents were asked to date only the first and last. In constructing Table 1, I assumed that the year of any other offers was uniformly distributed between the known endpoints. Again, only 9 percent of the offers are affected by this assumption.

6. Offers received in 1992 could be reported either in Wave 1 or Wave 2, depending on whether they occurred before or after the Wave 1 interview. While respondents were reminded when the Wave 1 interview had occurred and asked in Wave 2 about offers since that interview, errors in recalling exactly when an offer occurred could lead to an offer received shortly after Wave 1 not being reported in Wave 2, or an offer shortly before Wave 1 being reported twice. In Wave 1, respondents were asked the year of the offer, while in Wave 2 month and year were obtained. Eleven respondents reported at both Wave 1 and Wave 2 accepting a window in the year of the Wave 1 interview (and for nine of these, they gave the *month* of the Wave I interview at Wave 2); six reported at Wave 1 that they had rejected a window that year, and reported at Wave 2 they had rejected an offer in the *month* of the Wave 1 interview. We deleted the Wave 2 reports of these windows, on the grounds that they very likely were re-reports of the same offer.

7. A survey by Hewitt Associates (Shalowitz 1992) does show a sharp increase in the number of *firms* offering windows in 1991–92 compared to the three preceding years, which is consistent with the message of Table 1.

8. Tabulations for earlier years suggest offers became more common during the late 1980s, too. However, reported acceptance rates are higher (averaging 43 percent, with no clear pattern) in 1985–88. This is consistent with poorer reporting of rejected offers in those years, so I am less confident that the apparent upward trend of offers in those years is real.

9. A few bonus amounts greater than two years salary were deleted as they appear to be outliers.

10. Amounts are missing for about 30 percent of those receiving these incentives, usually because respondents did not know the amount. Perhaps surprisingly, amounts were only slightly more likely to be missing for rejected offers (31 vs. 27 percent).

11. Earnings (measured at the end of job for jobs that ended before Wave 1, and at Wave 1 for ongoing jobs) were 8 percent higher for those who accepted windows than for those that rejected them.

12. For cash bonuses, the amounts relative to annual earnings are in line with the 3 to 12 months salary offered to those in the firm studied by Lumsdaine, Stock, and Wise (1990).

13. The firm size variable is available for those who are currently employed and received a window offer from their current employer, and for those who are not working but received an offer from their most recent employer. Size of employer was not asked in the sequence that deals with the employer before the current/last one.

14. For current hourly wages, I rejected values of ln (wage) less than 1 or greater than 6. A similar procedure was applied to wages on previous jobs, after inflating to $1992 using the CPI.

15. These variables were obtained for the current job of those working at Wave 1, and the last job of those who were not working, but not for previous jobs.

16. Birth cohort variables, not shown in Table 8, suggest a weak tendency for window offers to increase with age. Coefficients of occupation dummies showed no strong relationship to skill level.

References

Anderson, Patricia and Bruce Meyer. 1993. "Unemployment Insurance in the United States: Layoff Incentives and Cross Subsidies." *Journal of Labor Economics* 11, 1, part 2: 70–95.

Becker, Gary. 1993. *Human Capital: A Theoretical and Empirical Analysis with Special Reference to Education.* 3d edition: Chicago: University of Chicago Press.

Brechling, Frank. 1977. "The Incentive Effects of the Unemployment Insurance Tax." In Ronald Ehrenberg, ed., *Research in Labor Economics.* Vol. 1. Greenwich, JAI Press.

Brown, Charles, James Medoff, and James Hamilton. 1990. *Employers Large and Small.* Cambridge, Mass.: Harvard University Press.

Charles D. Spencer and Associates. 1992. "Survey of Early Retirement Incentives 1991: Components of Private, Public Employers' Offers." *Spencer's Research Reports* (April 24): 1–11.

Freeman, Richard and James Medoff. 1984. *What Do Unions Do?* New York: Basic Books.

Gustman, Alan L., Olivia S. Mitchell, and Thomas L. Steinmeier. 1994. "The Role of Pensions in the Labor Market: A Review of the Literature." *Industrial and Labor Relations Review* 47, 3: 417–38.

Gustman, Alan and Thomas Steinmeier. 1986. "A Structural Retirement Model." *Econometrica* 54, 3: 555–84.

Hogarth, Jeanne M. 1988. "Accepting an Early Retirement Bonus." *Journal of Human Resources* 23, 1: 21–33.

Juster, F. Thomas and Richard Suzman. 1995. "An Overview of the Health and Retirement Study." *Journal of Human Resources* 30 (Supplement): 57–56.

Lazear, Edward. 1979. "Why Is There Mandatory Retirement?" *Journal of Political Economy* 87, 6: 1261–84.

Lumsdaine, Robin L., James H. Stock, and David Wise. 1990. "Efficient Windows and Labor Force Reduction." *Journal of Public Economics* 43, 2: 131–51.

Mehay, Stephen and Paul Hogan. 1998. "The Effect of Separation Bonuses on Voluntary Quits: Evidence from the Military's Downsizing." *Southern Economic Journal* 65, 1: 127–39.

Oi, Walter. 1962. "Labor as a Quasi-Fixed Factor." *Journal of Political Economy* 70, 2: 538–55.

Shalowitz, Deborah. 1992. "Retirement Plans." *Business Insurance* (September): 3–4.

——. 1993. "Study Offers Window to Early Retirement." *Business Insurance* (October 18): 68.

Topel, Robert. 1983. "On Layoffs and Unemployment Insurance." *American Economic Review* 73, 4: 541–59.

Chapter 10
Retirement Expectations and Realizations: The Role of Health Shocks and Economic Factors

Debra Sabatini Dwyer and Jianting Hu

This chapter explores the relationship between people's expectations about retirement, their realizations of retirement, and the role of health shocks in this process. We look at how accurately people predict retirement and we examine the determinants of changes in retirement expectations. Expectations are made under uncertainty about future health, labor force status, household characteristics, and economic variables; therefore workers' plans must frequently be updated with new information. While many factors influence the decision to retire, we are particularly interested in the role of health shocks in people's decisions to alter their plans to retire.

Research to date has recognized the importance of understanding the relationship between health and retirement; however, until now, information about health, work, and economic wellbeing has been difficult to obtain in a single survey. The Health and Retirement Study (HRS) is the first national survey to combine comprehensive data on all of these areas. Nevertheless, much of the early HRS research used only the first wave of data, at which time many in the cohort were too young to retire. In this chapter we use new information on this group of people from both Waves 1 and 2, enabling us to observe this cohort moving into retirement. In what follows we first offer a brief discussion of the literature, and then discuss empirical models, data used in the analysis, results, and conclusions.

Motivation and Background

Never has the issue of longevity in the labor force been more important than it is today. By now it is common knowledge that our nation is aging and that the upcoming retirement of the baby-boomers is expected to put pressure on social welfare and insurance systems. The Social Security Trust Fund is currently operating at a surplus, but the fund is expected to be exhausted within about thirty years. As a result, bringing the system into actuarial balance is a subject of substantial policy interest. Proposals range from adjustments to a complete overhaul of the current "pay-as-you-go" system. As policy analysts, it is our job to determine the likely winners and losers of alternative proposals.

Several reform proposals being seriously considered recommend further increasing the normal retirement age (NRA) as well as increasing the early retirement age (ERA) — the earliest age one can begin receiving (reduced) social security old age insurance benefits. Raising the NRA is equivalent to a cut in benefits for those retiring before they reach the new NRA. In addition, if people respond by retiring later, this would raise revenue from payroll taxes. Raising the ERA would result in reduced benefit payments and increased revenues as well.

The justification for raising these ages rests on the fact that an increase in life expectancy lengthens the period during which social security benefits must be paid. Workers now have more time over which to choose between work and retirement. If people are living longer, the argument is that they can work longer and still enjoy a lengthy retirement. Nevertheless there is concern over the health of the labor force affected by such changes. Has medical technology improved longevity for those who are not very healthy? In other words, are people living longer with impairments? If so, it may be necessary to permit continued early retirement if they are troubled with health problems. Researchers have been unable to identify the extent of this problem until now. It is our goal, therefore, to examine the role of poor health in retirement planning and labor force exits.

The retirement age choice is one that is made over the working life cycle. However career choices and labor force commitments are made, the consequences of these decisions affect the timing of retirement. Regardless of the degree of planning, there is some uncertainty associated with the future propensity to afford leisure and desire work. Perhaps the largest source of uncertainty is associated with health and disability, or the ability to perform work. It is for this reason that we expect poor health to have quite a substantial impact on retirement. Bound et al. (1997), when looking at the effects of health on labor force transitions of older men and women using the first two waves of the HRS, find that poor health is a very strong predictor of labor force exits. Changes in health between the two waves have the biggest effect on labor force transitions. There were no economic controls in that research. Blau, Gilleskie, and Slusher (1997) focus on alternative measures of health and also conclude that health plays an important role in labor market transitions of older men.

When people report expectations about retirement, we assume this is the optimal choice given such factors as their current health, family, work, and economic status. This is consistent with the assumption prevalent in life-cycle retirement models, that individuals form rational long-range plans. If this is the case, and assuming preferences for work and leisure remain unchanged, then, *ceteris paribus*, any changes to expectations would be the result of changes to one or more of these factors. Consequently, those closer to retirement report more accurate expectations. Bernheim tests the rationality of retirement expectations in his research using the Retirement History Study (RHS). There he reports that individuals do not form expectations based on all information currently available, but they do respond rationally (in altering their expectations) to new information in the period directly preceding retirement. He also finds that while individuals do not use full information in forming expectations, the expectations are reliable indicators of actual retirement (Bernheim 1987, 1990). Honig uses the HRS and corroborate these conclusions (1996). Irelan (1977) uses the RHS as well and also finds that deviations from retirement expectations can be explained by unforeseen changes to retirement circumstances.

In the present study, we build on the work of Dwyer and Mitchell (1999) and follow expectations into retirement. The earlier research found that the two most important determinants of retirement expectations were health and access to health insurance. Magnitudes of the effects of economic factors were very small. It could not be determined whether health plays a much bigger role in the decision to retire than do economic factors (suggesting an inelastic price elasticity for leisure), or whether people in poor health have stronger preferences for retiring earlier (if they can afford to do so). This second interpretation of the Dwyer/Mitchell results is consistent with Bernheim's findings on the use of information in planning for retirement (1990). In the present study, we re-examine information used in planning for retirement, what drives changes to those plans, and who retires between Waves 1 and 2. The goal is to test for the rationality of expectations in the presence of heterogeneity among planners, as well as to examine the role of health shocks in changes to those expectations.

Research Questions and Hypotheses

We define retirement as complete withdrawal from the labor force. We hypothesize that during a planning period, using information available at that time, a worker selects an expected retirement age that maximizes utility over the remainder of his or her life. Expected retirement is influenced by potential labor earnings, income from pensions and social security, and preferences for leisure. Health status can also affect labor earnings and preferences for leisure. Of course, during the planning phase, full information on health and other factors is not available, so expectations regarding these future earnings and retirement income, non-labor income, and the value of non-market time, are all that can be used. As new information arrives, retirement expectations may be adjusted.

Actual retirement behavior can diverge from expectations for two reasons: new information becomes available after the plans are made (i.e. health shocks, early-out offers), or full information is not used in formulating expectations. In a model of changes to expectations, we would include changes to all of the factors that influence retirement. Some of those factors do not change much and theoretically should fall out of the model (future benefits). Labor earnings of older people and retirement income entitlements may be fairly well anticipated, though even here, learning may take place about pension plan rules and similar benefit entitlements. For this reason our model controls on earnings levels as well as on other non-labor income. We test to see if learning takes place by evaluating the effects of factors that do not change over time.

Econometric Modeling Issues

We use a two-period sequential model of the retirement decision-making process. The first question in this sequential process asks "Do you plan to retire by the second period?" and then, conditional on that response, the question is asked "Did you retire in the second period?" The two steps of the sequential process are characterized as follows:

$$EXP_1 = F(W_1, H_1, Z_1),$$
$$R_2 = G(W_2, \Delta W, H_2, \Delta H, Z_2 \mid EXP_1),$$

where

EXP_1 = expectations of retirement/work,
R_2 = retirement/work next period,
H_t = health status in period t,
W_t = vector of economic factors (income, assets, retirement income, health insurance),
Z_t = vector of other exogenous variables.

We assume that expectations are formed using the same variables as those that influence actual retirement—namely health and socioeconomic factors. The retirement model uses current information as well as changes from the first period, conditioning on expectations.

We test a number of hypotheses using this sequential model. First, we hypothesize that health shocks will significantly affect retirement in the second period, even after conditioning on expectations. Continuing health problems should not play a role on second-period retirement after conditioning on expectations. Likewise, labor income and future benefits are not expected to change, so we expect no effect on retirement in the second period after conditioning on expectations. This tests the rationality of expectations by checking to see if factors that have not changed were included in those expectations.

The sequential model assumes that the sequential steps are independent. In particular, we assume that expectations in the first period are independent of the outcome in the second period. To deal with the possibility of correlation across the equations we use a simultaneous multinomial logit model of work transitions. The corresponding schematic model is as follows:

$$WR2 \ = \ Q(W, \Delta W, H, \Delta H, Z),$$

where

$WR2$ = Labor force transition
     = 1 if expected to retire by the next period and did,
     = 2 if expected to retire by next period and did not,
     = 3 if did not expect to retire by next period and did,
     = 4 if did not expect to retire by next period and did not.

This models the probability of ending up in one of the four labor force transition cells.

Similar hypotheses are examined using both models. We expect health shocks, or a worsening of health in the second period, to increase the likelihood of retirement, regardless of which model we use and independent of the first period expectations. We expect changes in socioeconomic status to influence actual retirement as well, although, for the most part, we do not expect tremendous changes in most economic factors for older workers. Earnings tend to be stable and future retirement benefits are based on a lifetime of work. Early-out offers are expected to play a role. Factors that do not change should not substantially influence retirement in the second period, since we are conditioning on expectations from that period in the sequential model. If full information is used in forming expectations, then the groups should be homogeneous in the combined health and socioeconomic factors.

Data Description

The analysis uses the first two waves of the HRS; respondents in the first wave (1992) are between the ages of 51 and 61, and by Wave 2 (1994) they attained the ages of 53–63. We restrict the sample to age-eligible respondents who participated in both waves of the study, and who were either working, partially retired, or fully retired in the first wave.[1] Excluded are people who were disabled, unemployed, homemakers, and others who did not clearly fall into one of the work/retirement categories because of missing values. Our sample size is 5,902 individuals.

In the sequential model we have two dependent variables. The first is *EXP*1, which is a dichotomous variable that equals one if the respondent plans to retire by Wave 2. The second is a dichotomous indicator of retirement in Wave 2. In the multinomial Logit we define a categorical dependent variable that takes four values for the four possible outcomes as described above.

We use three measures of health status in all models. As a measure of functional capacity we use a self-report of the presence of work limitations. A self-report of overall general health measures disease and illness. These variables have proven to be complements rather than substitutes in retirement models (see Dwyer and Mitchell 1998). For each measure we include a change variable as well as a levels variable. We create indicators for whether the condition is reported in both Waves, or is a new problem in Wave 2. In addition we include a self-report of health in Wave 2 compared to Wave 1, which directly measures shocks to health status.[2]

Economic variables include net worth, household income, and future retirement income. Net worth is defined as assets minus debts. Assets include real estate, vehicles, businesses, IRAs, savings, inheritances, and trusts. Household income includes any labor earnings, pensions and retirement income, government transfers, rent, interest, and dividend income of any member of the household over the past year. Future retirement income includes both social security and pensions for retirement at ages 62 and 65.

Empirical Findings

Table 1 reports means and frequencies by expectations of retirement in Wave 1 and actual retirement in Wave 2. We separate those who expected to retire from those who did not, and report within-group differences. Almost three-quarters (74 percent) of the sample were working full time in both waves, and roughly 9 percent were retired in both waves; one-tenth moved from work to retirement. Of the 383 workers who planned to retire by Wave 2 (9 percent of Wave 1 workers), 173 fully retired (45 percent) and 41 partially retired (11 percent). Of the 4,565 who did not plan to retire, 8 percent did fully retire and 5 percent partially retired. Of most interest in this analysis are the 10 percent in the sample who changed retirement plans.

The biggest differences among Wave 2 retirees between those who planned retirement and those that did not are in changes in health status (those who did not plan to retire had a much higher prevalence rate of new work limitations), Wave 1 health insurance status, Wave 1 household income (those who planned retirement are better off), age, and sex. This suggests that information available at Wave 1 was used in planning for retirement, and what drove the change was a worsening of health. In fact, among those who planned to work, differences in economic variables are smaller.

In all cases, health status, defined here as having a problem that limits

TABLE 1: Means of Selected Variables by Expected Retirement Status

Variables	ALL N=4,947		Planned to Retire (EXP=1) N=383		Planned to Work (EXP=0) N=4,564	
	Retired	Working	Retired	Working	Retired	Working
Work limitations both waves[1]	0.11	0.04	0.10	0.06	0.11	0.04
Work limiting Wave 2 only[2]	0.30	0.06	0.19	0.07	0.36	0.06
Partner poor health W1	0.27	0.33	0.28	0.39	0.27	0.32
Health Ins. tied to work	0.67	0.67	0.76	0.68	0.62	0.67
Retiree health ins.	0.68	0.56	0.85	0.66	0.59	0.55
HH income ≥ $30,000	0.71	0.72	0.84	0.76	0.64	0.72
Social security benefit[3]	0.29	0.26	0.27	0.26	0.30	0.26
Pension	0.48	0.54	0.48	0.51	0.49	0.54
Early-out offer	0.05	0.01	0.10	0.01	0.05	0.01
High-school only	0.39	0.35	0.36	0.36	0.40	0.35
Some graduate work	0.13	0.13	0.17	0.12	0.11	0.13
Age	58.9	57.0	60.5	59.9	58.1	56.8
Female	0.52	0.47	0.41	0.45	0.58	0.47
White	0.75	0.76	0.77	0.71	0.74	0.76

Source: Authors' calculations; weighted tabulations of HRS gamma release, Waves 1 and 2.
Notes:
[1] The respondent reported the problem in both waves.
[2] The respondent reported the problem in wave 2 only.
[3] This variable = 1 if the expected annual benefit for retirement at age 65 is at least $20,000.

paid work a person can do, was worse among those who planned to retire between Waves 1 and 2.[3] Health was worse among all who actually retired by Wave 2. As expected, the aging process results in overall declines in health status, but the greatest deterioration was among retirees who did not plan to retire.

Table 2 reports the results from the sequential logit model. We condition on expectations status in Wave 1 and allow the slope coefficients to differ by that status. Not surprisingly, the presence of a work limitation significantly increased the probability of retirement in the second wave, particularly for those who did not plan to retire. In all models, a worsening of health, measured as a new work limitation between Waves 1 and 2, had a larger impact on retirement than did a persistent health problem.[4] Again, this is most apparent for those who did not plan to retire and then do. Those with a new work limitation in that group were 29 percent more likely to retire than those who did not, while those with a persistent one were only 18 percent more likely to do so. For those who expected to retire the corresponding figures were 43 percent and 30 percent respectively. The parameter estimates for health are larger in magnitude for those whose retirement represented a change in plans from Wave 1. This is not surprising, since poor health was a driving factor in forming the Wave 1 expectations that

TABLE 2: Logit Results of Wave 2 Retirement Status by Expectation Status

Variables	ALL N=4,947 Parameter Estimate	ALL N=4,947 Marginal Effect	Planned to Retire (EXP=1) N=383 Parameter Estimate	Planned to Retire (EXP=1) N=383 Marginal Effect	Planned to Work (EXP=0) N=4,564 Parameter Estimate	Planned to Work (EXP=0) N=4,564 Marginal Effect
Work limitations both waves	1.61** (0.18)	0.19	1.13** (0.45)	0.30	1.71** (0.20)	0.18
Work limiting Wave 2 only	2.19** (0.13)	0.30	1.45** (0.38)	0.43	2.43** (0.14)	0.29
Partner w/poor health W1	−0.13** (0.06)	−0.01	−0.17 (0.14)	−0.02	−0.15** (0.07)	−0.01
Health ins. tied to work	−0.16* (0.12)	−0.01	−0.14 (0.30)	−0.02	−0.22** (0.14)	−0.01
Retiree health ins.	0.67** (0.12)	0.04	1.42** (0.33)	0.08	0.37** (0.14)	0.04
HH income ≥ $30,000	0.21** (0.12)	0.01	0.37 (0.32)	0.03	0.05 (0.14)	0.01
Social security benefit	0.24** (0.11)	0.02	0.22 (0.26)	0.03	0.33** (0.13)	0.02
Pension	−0.27** (0.10)	−0.02	−0.36** (0.24)	−0.03	−0.21** (0.12)	−0.02
Early-out offer	1.84** (0.47)	0.06	2.44** (0.77)	0.13	1.76** (0.60)	0.06
High-school only	0.20** (0.11)	0.01	−0.12 (0.25)	0.03	0.25** (0.13)	0.01
Some graduate work	0.37** (0.16)	0.03	0.45* (0.35)	0.05	0.33** (0.20)	0.03
Age	0.21** (0.02)	0.01	0.12** (0.04)	0.03	0.14** (0.02)	0.01
Female	0.31** (0.10)	0.02	−0.20	0.03	0.55** (0.12)	0.01
White	−0.11 (0.12)	−0.01	0.25 (0.27)	−0.01	−0.04 (0.14)	−0.01
Goodness of fit stat	0.1096		0.1738		0.0859	

Notes: See Table 1. Standard errors in parentheses.
* Significant at the 0.1 level.
** Significant at the 0.05 level.

were already conditioned on. So for the group who planned to retire, a worsening of health only reinforced preferences toward earlier retirement but the health effect would have been bigger in the first step (the model of expectations; see Dwyer and Mitchell 1997).

Since poor health drove people out of the labor force, it is not surprising that the presence of a spouse in poor health worked the other way. If one partner was less likely to work, retirement became less affordable for the other.

TABLE 3: Multinomial Logit of Expected and Realized Retirement

| | Planned to Retire by W2 | | Didn't Plan to Retire by W2 | | | |
| | Not Retired | | Retired | | Not Retired | |
Variables	Parameter Estimate	Marginal Effect	Parameter Estimate	Marginal Effect	Parameter Estimate	Marginal Effect
Work limitations both waves	−0.86** (0.10)	−0.09	−0.80** (0.15)	−0.01	−0.30** (0.16)	−0.01
Work limiting Wave 2 only	−1.21** (0.07)	−0.12	−0.78** (0.11)	−0.01	−0.11 (0.15)	−0.01
Partner poor health W1	−0.15** (0.07)	−0.02	−0.08 (0.10)	−0.001	0.09 (0.08)	0.01
Health ins. tied to work	0.10** (0.07)	0.01	0.01 (0.10)	—	0.02 (0.09)	0.001
Retiree health ins.	−0.20** (0.07)	−0.03	−0.77** (0.12)	−0.01	−0.21** (0.09)	−0.01
HH income ≥ $30,000	−0.01 (0.07)	−0.002	−0.40** (0.11)	−0.01	−0.17** (0.09)	−0.01
Social security benefit	−0.17** (0.07)	−0.02	−0.02 (0.09)	—	0.01 (0.08)	—
Pension	0.12** (0.06)	0.02	0.17** (0.08)	0.002	0.07 (0.07)	0.004
Early-out offer	−0.86** (0.30)	0.15	−0.93** (0.36)	0.02	−0.34** (0.13)	−0.02
High-school only	−0.13** (0.06)	−0.02	−0.07 (0.09)	−0.001	−0.08 (0.08)	−0.004
Some graduate work	−0.17** (0.10)	−0.02	−0.17** (0.12)	−0.002	0.02 (0.12)	0.001
Age	0.13** (0.02)	0.02	0.46** (0.03)	0.01	0.36** (0.03)	0.02
Male	0.25** (0.06)	0.03	−0.03 (0.09)	—	0.03 (0.08)	0.002
White	0.05 (0.07)	0.01	0.12 (0.10)	0.001	0.25** (0.08)	0.01

Notes: See Table 1. Standard errors in parentheses.
—Value too close to 0 to report (<0.001).
* Significant at the 0.1 level.
** Significant at the 0.05 level.

Economic factors play a significant role in retirement by Wave 2, but more so for those who did not plan to retire. Variables include an indicator for Wave 1 household income of at least $30,000, social security, pensions, and the presence of health insurance.[5] People with higher household income and future social security benefits retired earlier. People paying into pension plans retired later. Early-out offers drove people out earlier. Access to retiree health insurance through the employer significantly increased the likelihood of retirement in all cases. This is Wave 1 information, since we use

Wave 1 health insurance status.[6] This implies that information about economic status is not fully accounted for when forming expectations, since pensions and retiree health insurance status are not likely to change much between the waves.

What these results suggest is that people form retirement expectations based on current health status and, to some extent, economic status. Health shocks play a big role in retirement for those who did not plan to retire. This makes sense, since Wave 1 health was conditioned by controlling for expectations. Among those who planned to retire, people more likely to do so were older, more educated, and in better economic shape than those who did not. For those who planned to continue working, those who did were younger, male, and healthier. Health played a bigger role than economic status in Wave 2 retirement for those who did not plan to retire.

Table 3 reports the results from the simultaneous model of expectations and realizations of retirement. The omitted category is those who planned to retire and did; that group was in the worst health. A respondent with a new work limitation was 12 percent less likely to be in the category of working after planning to retire, and 1 percent less likely to have not planned to retire at all. Those who planned to retire and did so were also more likely to have retiree health insurance, early-out offers, and not be within average education levels in the country.[7] The oldest respondents tended to fall into the category of retired in Wave 2 without having planned to do so.

Conclusion

One of the invaluable aspects of the Health and Retirement Study is its usefulness in understanding the relationship between people's expectations about retirement before the event actually arrives, and their actual subsequent retirement behavior. Defining retirement as complete withdrawal from the labor force, we hypothesized that health shocks would make plans deviate from realizations, while anticipated retirement-income benefits would provide little new information and so would have no impact on changes in plans. The empirical results show that those who planned to retire and did so were in worse health but in better economic shape. Overall, a tenth of the sample altered its retirement plans, and this change was associated with changes in own health status, particularly a move into poor health.

Appendix

In Wave 1 there were 6,960 age-eligible respondents in the Health and Retirement Study who met our criteria for work status (either working or retired). We exclude the unemployed, those on leave from jobs, disabled receiving transfers, and homemakers with little work experience. Similarly in Wave 2 we remove those who were unemployed, receiving disability transfers, or with missing values so that work status was unattainable. The resulting sample consists of 5,902 age-eligible respondents.

In addition to the variables created for each individual, we also created the same set of variables for those who had partners living in the same household, such as partner's health status and presence of work limitation.

Work Status/Retirement

Work status. We categorize respondents into three categories by wave: working, retired, or partially retired, using the self-reports of work status. This is not always clear, so we also use whether or not they were working for pay, how many hours they worked, and their self-report of retirement status. *Working*: means the respondent was working full time. *Retired*: means the respondent fully departed from the labor force. *Partially retired*: means the respondent was working part-time and considered him/herself partially retired.

Expected retirement age. For Wave 1 we use the age the person expected to fully retire from the labor force. If this was missing but available in Wave 2, we use the Wave 2 self-report (304 cases). In Wave 2 the question asked for the age he or she planned to retire — where retirement was defined by the respondent (so it could mean a switch to self-employment or partial employment). For this reason we do not extend the analysis to changes in retirement expectations between the two waves.

Health Measures

General Health Conditions. Change in health status between the two waves was defined as changes in *general health*: excellent, very good, good, fair, and poor; and *general health compared to last one or two years*: much better, somewhat better, same, somewhat worse, much worse.

Presence of Work Limitation. Change in the presence of work limitation between the two waves was defined as changes in impairments or health problems limiting the kind or amount of paid work.

Functional Limitations. Change in the number of functional limitations between the two waves was defined as a change in the *number of functional limitations*: to run or jog, to walk several blocks, to walk one block, to climb several stairs, to climb one stair, to lift 10 pounds, to stoop, kneel, or crouch, to reach or extend arms above shoulder level, and to pull or push large objects. Non-severe and severe functional limitations were defined as having some difficulties and severe difficulty performing each function.

Activities of Daily Living (ADL). Change in the number of ADLs between the two waves was defined as a change in the *number of activities of daily living:* to walk across a room, to sit for two hours, to get up from a chair, to get in or out of bed, to take a bath or shower, to eat, and and to dress. Non-severe and severe ADLs are defined as having some difficulties and severe difficulty to perform each function.

Instrumental Activities of Daily Living (IADL). Change in the number of IADLs between the two waves was defined as *number of instrumental activities daily living:* to pick up a dime from a table, to keep track of money or bill, and to make phone calls. Non-severe and severe IADLs was defined as having some difficulties and severe difficulty to perform each function.

Diagnostic Indicators. Having high blood pressure or hypertension and high cholesterol.

User of Medical Facilities. Change in using medical facilities between the two waves was defined as a change in staying in a hospital or a nursing home overnight, number of doctor visits, days of staying in bed due to illness or injury, and needing any professional nursing care at home in the past year.

Medical Conditions.[8] These included *mental health:* ever having emotional, nervous, or psychiatric problems, felt depressed in the past week, felt everything was an effort, restless sleep, felt unhappy, felt lonely, felt people were unfriendly, not enjoying life, felt sad, felt disliked, could not get going, poor appetite, felt listless, felt tired, felt not rested when woke up, felt depressed for weeks; *musculoskeletal conditions:* having arthritis or rheumatism, problems with back, feet and legs, and a fracture or broken bone; *head injuries and trauma:* having been unconscious due to a head injury; *respiratory and cardiovascular system conditions:* ever having chronic lung disease except asthma, ever having heart attack, coronary heart disease, angina, congestive heart failure, or others, currently having any angina or chest pains, any heart failure, seeing doctors for heart problems during the last 12 months, ever having a special test or treatment of heart, ever having heart surgery, ever having a stroke, and having asthma; *other conditions:* ever having diabetes or high blood sugar, ever having cancer or a malignant tumor of any kind except skin cancer, having kidney or bladder problems, stomach or intestinal ulcers.

Economic Variables

Household income. Measured as annual 1991 gross income. It includes all sources of household income. Past year labor earnings and pensions are asked of the respondent, partner/spouse, and other adult family members.

Private assets include household income from rent, interest, and dividends. Government transfers are also included.

Net worth. Real estate, vehicles, businesses, IRAs, savings, inheritances, trusts, minus debts reported in $1991 ($\times 10^{-4}$). Missing values, if any, were imputed by Juster and Suzman (1995).

Retiree health insurance. Self-report of having retiree health insurance in either of the waves.

Employer-provided health insurance. Self-report of having employer-provided health insurance in either wave.

Private pensions. The employer-provided pension plan descriptions are used to calculate annual pension benefits for retirement at age 65 for those who provided consent forms and information.

Estimated SS retirement benefits. An algorithm was devised for projecting social security old age benefits for retirement at age 65.

Early out offer. Respondent was offered an early retirement window.

The authors thank Benjamin Bridges, Olivia Mitchell, Jan Olson, Herbert Reff, and Chuck Slusher for helpful comments and/or data support. In addition they acknowledge Bernie Wixon and Denny Vaughan for their support.

Notes

1. Retirees are excluded from the multivariate analysis but useful for some of the descriptive analysis.

2. The HRS provides many health indicators to choose from, including reports of specific symptoms and conditions. Many of the questions were changed between the two waves, making them less useful in a transition model (ADLs, IADLs, and functional status variables). Dwyer and Mitchell (1998) show that the combined self-reports are exogenous good measures of overall health.

3. Models including several measures of health find the functional status variables to be most significant. Many of the specific symptoms are correlated with this measure causing multicollinearity. We exclude irrelevant variables to maximize degrees of freedom, given small sample sizes.

4. We would expect a health problem that existed in the first wave not to have a substantial impact on retirement in the second wave, since that was accounted for in the formation of the expectation, which is conditioned in. Because we do not control on the severity of the problem, it is possible for a condition to have existed but worsened in the second wave. For this reason we do not predict the effect of a persistent problem to be 0, as it is not, but smaller, as it is.

5. Wave 1 net worth is never significant so it is omitted.

6. Wave 2 economic status is endogenous.

7. They seem to be bimodal — low educated and in poor health, or highly educated and able to afford retirement.

8. We define a change in the two waves as whether or not the condition was present in both waves, Wave 1 only, Wave 2 only, or not at all.

References

Anderson, Kathy and Richard V. Burkhauser. 1985. "The Retirement-Health Nexus: A New Measure of an Old Puzzle." *Journal of Human Resources* 20: 315–30.

Bazzoli, Glora J., 1985. "The Early Retirement Decision: New Empirical Evidence on the Influence of Health." *Journal of Human Resources* 20: 215–34.

Bernheim, B. Douglas. 1987. "The Timing of Retirement: A Comparison of Expectations and Realizations." in: David A. Wise, ed., *The Economics of Aging*, Chicago: University of Chicago Press, 335–56.

——. 1990. "How Do the Elderly Form Expectations? An Analysis of Responses to New Information." in David A. Wise, ed., *Issues in the Economics of Aging*. Chicago: University of Chicago Press, 259–85.

Blau, David M., D. B. Gilleskie, and C. Slusher. 1997. "The Effect of Health on Employment Transitions of Older Men." Unpublished manuscript.

Bound, John. 1991. "Self-Reported Versus Objective Measures of Health in Retirement Models." *Journal of Human Resources* 26: 106–38.

Bound, John, M. Schoenbaum, T. Stinebrickner, and T. Waidmann. 1997. "Measuring the Effects of Health on Retirement Behavior." Unpublished manuscript, University of Michigan.

Dwyer, Debra Sabatini and Olivia S. Mitchell. 1999. "Health Shocks as Determinants of Retirement: Are Self-Rated Measures Endogenous?" *Journal of Health Economics* 18, 2: 173–93.

Gatti, Roberta. 1997. "Savings and Health Shocks." Unpublished manuscript. Howard University (November).

Honig, Marjorie. 1996. "Retirement Expectations: Differences by Race, Ethnicity, and Gender." *Gerontologist* 36 (3): 373–82.

Irelan, Lola M. 1977. "Almost 65: Baseline Data from the Retirement History Study." Research Report No. 49, Office of Research and Statistics, U.S. Social Security Administration. Washington, D.C.: Government Accounting Office.

Juster, F. Thomas and R. M. Suzman. 1995. "An Overview of the Health and Retirement Study." *Journal of Human Resources* 30 (Supplement): S7–56.

Rust, John and C. Phelan. 1997. "How Social Security and Medicare Affect Retirement Behavior in a World of Incomplete Markets." *Econometrica* 64, 4: 781–831.

Smith, James P. 1997. "The Changing Economic Circumstances of the Elderly: Income, Wealth, and Social Security." *Syracuse University Policy Brief*, No. 8.

Chapter 11
Planning for Health Care Needs in Retirement

Anna M. Rappaport

Support for health and long-term care expenses is vitally important to an understanding of retirement needs and resources. Among the challenges we face in this area, as a nation, is the fact that many people in the 55–64 age group have no satisfactory access to health care insurance and medical care coverage. In the past, employers were a major source of coverage supplementing Medicare, but over time they have gradually reduced their commitment to retiree health insurance. Changes in the private health care marketplace will also alter medical care and insurance options available to individuals and employers in the future. In addition, Medicare costs are projected to increase markedly as the baby boom generation ages, and the Medicare system will confront insolvency within the next decade.

Making the situation more complex is the fact that the elderly have high levels of out-of-pocket medical spending, making healthcare a major concern for the poor and nearly poor elderly. This is tied to the fact that healthcare needs rise with age, and many elderly are frail and require a wide range of help. This chapter examines how the elderly in the United States cope with healthcare problems at present, and it also evaluates several programs which help provide coverage among the older population. In doing so, we explore the roles of both employers and the government in providing medical care for the older population, and we discuss policy options for the future.

Health Care Costs and Utilization by Age

Utilization of health care services rises with age, a pattern confirmed by data on spending by consumer units for health care. Table 1 shows how medical spending varied with age in 1994 in the Consumer Expenditure Survey. At

TABLE 1: Average Consumer Expenditures for Health Care per Customer Unit (1994)

Age of Reference Person	Total ($)	Total Expenses ($)	Health Insurance ($)	Medical Services ($)	Drugs and Medical Supplies ($)
Under age 25	$ 505	2.7	$ 186	$ 218	$ 102
25–34	1,086	3.6	479	407	199
35–44	1,616	4.3	689	627	299
45–54	1,855	4.5	772	673	410
55–64	2,144	6.4	895	791	459
65–74	2,592	10.3	1,467	539	586
75 and over	2,787	14.4	1,496	639	653
Average for all ages	1,755	5.5	815	571	369

Source: U.S. Bureau of the Census (1996).

lower ages, healthcare costs are influenced by employer health coverage, whereas for people age 65 and over, healthcare costs reflect the availability and coverage of Medicare benefits and payments. The costs described in the table are in addition to what is paid for by taxes under Medicare and by what is financed by employers.

The evidence also demonstrates that older groups are more heavily female, the result of the fact that men suffer shorter life spans. Elderly females are also more likely to be widowed, whereas elderly males are much more likely to be married (see Weir and Willis, this volume).

Medical care costs for older persons are shared among Medicare, the individual, and employer plans. Employer costs are higher prior to Medicare eligibility, because Medicare pays much of the cost of retiree health after age 65. Average premiums for retiree health plans reported in a Mercer/Foster Higgins National Survey (1997) of employer-sponsored health plans were $5,000 per year for retirees younger than age 65 and about $1,900 per year for Medicare-eligible retirees.

Prescription drugs constitute a major source of out-of-pocket and employer spending for older persons. About half of Medicare beneficiaries living in the community (that is, not in nursing homes) reported that they had prescription drug coverage in 1994; the fraction reporting coverage is shown by age in Table 2. Sources of prescription drug insurance for those reporting coverage are shown in Table 3. Here we see that 59 percent report employer coverage, 29 percent report coverage from Medicaid, and 12 percent had Medigap coverage. Evidently, a major weakness of many Medigap plans is the lack of drug coverage.

Health care costs and utilization increase with age for adults. Total costs are quite difficult to measure, however, because cost information is typically

TABLE 2: Medicare Beneficiaries Having Prescription Drug Coverage by Age (1994)

Age Group	Percent Reporting Drug Coverage (%)
Under 65	62
65–74	54
75–84	47
85 and over	44

Source: Gross and Brangan (1997).

TABLE 3: Sources of Prescription Drug Coverage for Those Reporting Coverage (1997)

Source	Percent Reporting Source (%)
Medicaid	29
Employer plan	59
Medigap	12

Source: Gross and Brangan (1997).

maintained by payor rather than aggregated for a given individual or household. Differences in payment methods and payors also complicate the measurement of costs. For people covered by capitated plans, it is sometimes difficult to define what cost is beyond the premium. A capitated plan is one where the plan receives a set premium to provide health care rather than being reimbursed for services provided. The premium is the same regardless of what services are used. Utilization and underlying services provided vary greatly by individual. Premiums, of course, reflect an average cost for the covered group.

Another factor making it difficult to measure healthcare costs by age is that the charge for a hospital or physician service may vary greatly depending on who the payor is. Payors include Medicare, Medicaid systems, health plans, and individuals without coverage. Differences are due to differences in contracts between the payors and different providers. Table 4 shows estimated healthcare costs for the elderly by age group (Moon 1996). These estimates indicate that for Americans age 65 and over, out-of-pocket costs averaged 30 percent of income for those whose incomes were 150 percent of the poverty level or less. Costs increased by age both as a dollar amount and as a percentage of income. Females were also heavily represented among the poor, the nearly poor, and the very elderly. Out-of-pocket spending patterns by the elderly appear in Table 5. About half of spending is for Medicare Part B and supplement premiums and the balance is for cost-

TABLE 4: Health Costs for the Elderly by Demographic Group (1996)

Characteristics	Average Individu- alHealthcare Spending ($)*	Average Out-of-Pocket on Medicare Services ($)	Average Medicare Expenditures	Average Family Out-of-Pocket Costs as % of Family Income
Poverty Status				
Under 100%	1,921	298	5,894	30
100–150%	2,603	623	5,975	30
150–200%	2,716	683	5,014	26
200–400%	2,705	707	4,354	18
Over 400%	2,817	776	3,897	11
Age				
65–69	2,326	559	3,952	18
70–74	2,421	586	4,535	20
75–79	2,625	748	4,587	22
80–84	3,256	810	6,220	25
85+	3,412	637	7,132	25
Gender				
Male	2,491	633	4,383	18
Female	2,686	657	5,013	22
All elderly	*2,605*	*648*	*4,753*	*21*

Source: Moon (1996).
*Captures total out-of-pocket spending and spending on Medicare Part B premiums and private insurance premiums.

TABLE 5: Out-of-Pocket Spending for Health Care by the Elderly, by Type of Expense (1996)

Type of Spending	Type (%)
Private insurance premiums	31
Medicare Part B premiums	18
Medicare cost-sharing	25
Uncovered items*	26
Total	100
Average Out-of-Pocket Spending = $2,605	

Source: Moon, Kruntz, and Pounder (1996)
Note: Data are for the noninstitutionalized elderly population only.
*Medical care not covered by Medicare such as outpatient prescription drugs, eyeglasses and hearing aids.

TABLE 6: Annual Physician Contacts By Age and Sex

	1987	1990	1992	1994
Male	*4.6*	*4.7*	*5.1*	*5.2*
Under 5 years	6.7	7.2	7.1	7.0
5–14 years	3.4	3.3	3.5	3.5
15–44 years	3.3	3.4	3.7	3.7
45–64 years	5.5	5.6	6.1	6.3
65–74 years	8.1	8.0	9.2	10.1
75 years and over	9.2	10.0	12.2	11.6
Female	*6.0*	*6.1*	*6.6*	*6.7*
Under 5 years	6.7	6.5	6.7	6.5
5–14 years	3.1	3.2	3.3	3.3
15–44 years	5.8	6.0	6.2	6.2
45–64 years	7.2	7.1	8.2	8.3
65–74 years	8.6	9.0	10.1	10.5
75 years and over	10.0	10.2	12.1	13.4

Source: Centers for Disease Control and Prevention (1996–97).

TABLE 7: Respondent-Assessed Health Status by Age and Sex

	Fraction in Fair or Poor Health (%)			
	1987	*1990*	*1992*	*1994*
Male	*9.0*	*8.4*	*9.4*	*9.0*
Under 15 years	2.5	2.6	2.9	3.1
15–44 years	4.5	4.5	5.7	5.4
45–64 years	16.6	15.5	16.5	15.3
65–74 years	28.9	25.0	26.8	26.6
75 years and over	36.0	31.7	33.5	31.9
Female	*9.9*	*9.3*	*10.1*	*10.1*
Under 15 years	2.3	2.2	2.7	2.7
15–44 years	6.3	6.3	7.2	7.4
45–64 years	18.1	16.5	17.8	17.7
65–74 years	27.7	25.1	24.7	24.9
75 years and over	34.2	31.6	33.0	30.8

Source: Centers for Disease Control and Prevention (1996–97).

sharing and uncovered items. Prescription drugs can be a very costly item for persons requiring regular medication.

To help understand the relationship of spending to age, it is important to focus on utilization, which indicates how often a given type of service is utilized by age group. Gross and Branagan (1997) report age-specific rates

TABLE 8: Limitation of Activity Caused by Chronic Conditions by Age and Sex (%)

	Total with Limitation of Activity		Limited But Not in Major Activity		Limited in Amount or Kind of Major Activity		Unable to Carry on Major Activity	
	1990	1994	1990	1994	1990	1994	1990	1994
Male[1]	*12.9*	*14.3*	*3.8*	*4.2*	*4.7*	*5.3*	*4.4*	*4.8*
Under 15 years	5.5	7.6	1.4	1.8	3.6	5.0	0.5	0.8
15–44 years	8.4	10.1	2.3	2.8	3.5	3.9	2.7	3.4
45–64 years	21.4	21.3	4.7	4.6	6.6	6.9	10.1	9.9
65–74 years	34.0	34.7	13.0	13.3	8.4	8.5	12.7	12.8
75 years and over	38.8	40.7	20.3	21.6	10.2	10.2	8.3	8.9
Female[1]	*13.0*	*14.3*	*4.3*	*4.6*	*5.3*	*5.7*	*3.4*	*4.0*
Under 15 years	3.9	5.1	1.0	1.4	2.5	3.1	0.4	0.6
15–44 years	8.7	10.1	2.9	3.5	3.6	4.0	2.2	2.6
45–64 years	22.2	23.9	6.6	6.4	8.4	8.8	7.2	8.6
65–74 years	33.5	33.5	13.4	13.2	11.1	11.2	8.9	9.2
75 years and over	46.0	46.2	17.9	17.3	17.7	17.1	10.4	11.7

Source: Centers for Disease Control and Prevention (1996–97).
[1] Age adjusted.

of annual days of hospital care per 1,000 population. For example, the population average was 544 for all ages in 1995, but among those aged 65–74, the average hospitalization rate per year was 1,669 days, and for persons age 75 and over, it was 3,220 days annually. While the number of hospitalization days per 1,000 population has dropped steadily over time, it remains true that older people are hospitalized more often. Moreover, there has been an increase in the relative utilization at the very oldest ages. For example, people at ages 75+ use six times the average number of days of hospital care in 1995 as compared to the overall population, versus five times as much in 1980.

It is sometimes noted that physician contacts rise with age; this is confirmed in Table 6. Here we see that age and utilization of physicians is higher among the old, though the pattern is not as pronounced as for hospital days. The increase in physician contacts rises by 15 percent between age 65–74 to age 75+, whereas the number of hospital days approximately doubles between the two age groups. These data on healthcare utilization are consistent with other information on health status and activity limitations, which also paints a picture of declining health and increasing activity limitations with age. For instance, Table 7 shows changes in respondent-assessed health status by age between 1987 and 1994, while Table 8 shows activity limitations by age caused by chronic conditions. Respondents age 70+ are about 20 percent more likely to report fair or poor health when

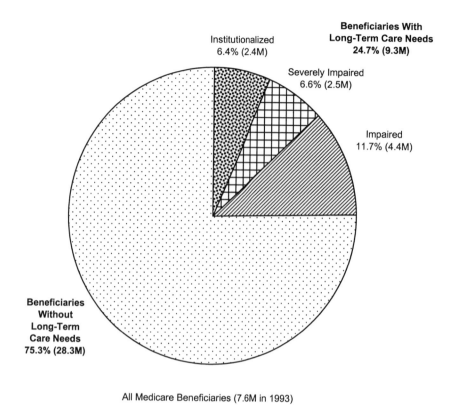

Figure 1. Distribution of Medicare beneficiaries by long-term care needs, 1993. "In-stitutionalized" means residing in a short- or long-term care facility. "Severely im-paired" and "impaired" refer to community-based beneficiaries with respectively three or more or one or two limitations in activities of daily living (ADLs) — bathing, dressing, walking, eating, toileting, or getting out of a chair. Source: Feder and Lambrew (1996).

compared to those age 65–74, and they report being in fair or poor health more than three times as often as the population as a whole. Elderly males report poor health slightly more often than elderly females, whereas among younger adults, females report poor health more often than males.

Long-term care needs also rise with age, where by long-term care we refer to nursing home usage. Figure 1 shows the distribution of Medicare benefi-ciaries by long-term care needs and indicates that 25 percent of this popula-tion had some type of long-term care needs in 1993. All of these data are consistent with rising needs and utilization with increasing age.

The Role of Employer Coverage in Providing Retiree Health Care Benefits

Larger employers in the United States have traditionally offered healthcare benefits to their retirees. Most often, a firm will impose a minimum age and years of service requirement for retiree health. Also, in many plans, retirees have had to share in the cost of the coverage. Retiree health coverage is important in retirement decisions, particularly for people retiring before age 65. One employer survey found that the average retirement age was 64 in organizations not offering retiree health coverage, versus 61 in those organizations that did offer retiree health (Mercer/Foster Higgins 1996).

Employers began to offer health care benefits during and after World War II, particularly in firms with unionized workforces. At that time, coverage for retirees was included in many plans without much consideration of the long-term cost consequences. At their inception, these plans were not particularly expensive, and the number of retirees was usually low. Of course, the demographic and economic consequences of population aging have changed all this today. Healthcare benefits for workers of all ages are now much more expensive, and cost considerations are a priority issue for businesses both large and small. As a result, healthcare benefits have been reduced recently, and coverage for active as well as retired employees is falling off (Table 9). Companies that were once large have downsized, and many of them have more retirees than they do active employees. While this is still unusual and not the norm, it is very common to have substantial numbers of retirees in mature organizations.

During the 1980s, private sector accounting standards for retirement-related benefits changed in important ways in the United States. Pension plan accounting standards changed first, and then retiree health benefits were included in the discussion about retirement benefit accounting. New rules were adopted for retiree health benefits accounting in Statement of Financial Accounting Standards Number 106, which for the first time treated retiree healthcare benefits like a pension benefit. Thus the anticipated costs of retiree health had to be recognized over the working lifetime of employees. These rule changes, together with increases in the costs of medical care and a number of demographic trends, produced costs which were a financial shock to many corporate managers. When these firms first assessed their retiree health costs and liabilities, many were forced to implement substantial changes in their benefit plans. These changes included limits on eligibility, benefit cuts, raising retiree contributions, and plan changes including the introduction of managed care (see Table 10). In some cases, retiree health benefits were discontinued, at least for future retirees or new entrants.

These upheavals in the accounting and medical marketplace produced a

TABLE 9: Employers Offering Retiree Health Coverage (%)

	1984	1991	1997
Midsize firms (200–999 workers)	51	44	33
Large firms (1,000–4,999 workers)	77	56	49
Jumbo firms (5,000+ workers)	91	72	66
Overall	67	46	37

Source: KPMG Peat Marwick (1996).

TABLE 10: Employer Cost Sharing for Retiree Health Insurance (%)

	Contribution Strategies for Retirees Under Age 65	Contribution Strategies for Medicare-Eligible Retirees
Employer pays all	20	27
Cost is shared	49	47
Retiree pays all	31	27

Source: Mercer/Foster Higgins (1997).

marked decline in health care coverage for both active and retired workers. This downward trend in coverage clearly contributed to the increase in the nation's uninsured population (EBRI 1997). For example, about 18 percent of Americans younger than age 65 had no health insurance in 1996, and the fraction of uninsured Americans under age 65 has been increasing over time. Much of this increase was due to the increase in uninsured children. Factors such as citizenship, employment, industry, firm size, income, race, age, and the number of children are important determinants of whether an individual has health insurance. For example, 44 percent of non-citizens under age 65 had no insurance, compared with 15 percent of citizens. Most uninsured workers were found in retail, service, or manufacturing industries, small private sector firms, or were young.

While most large U.S. employers do still offer healthcare coverage to retirees, those employers that do so have increased cost sharing and adopted several other measures to trim costs and control liabilities. Of employers offering plans, few pay the full cost for both pre-Medicare and post-Medicare retirees. Mazo, Rappaport and Schieber (1993) found that, over the years, companies have tightened eligibility for retiree health coverage using higher age and service requirements, and financial caps were placed on future retiree health obligations. In addition, managed care plans for retirees have grown increasingly popular. Therefore we conclude that employers have reduced their role in providing retiree health benefits, though they continue to play a significant role overall.

Retirees Lacking Employer Health Insurance Coverage

Retirees who do not have employer coverage are in a very different situation, depending on whether or not they are Medicare eligible. Medicare is currently made available to most Americans attaining the age of 65, and it is also provided to the severely disabled after a waiting period of 30 months. For those who are eligible, Medicare covers most hospital and physician care and a number of other services. However, the program does not presently cover prescription drugs, eye glasses, and hearing aids; various other services are also excluded. Medicare plans also typically require deductibles and co-payments. Despite these forms of co-insurance, Medicare covers a very substantial portion of older people's acute care medical costs. Many older persons also purchase so-called "Medigap" policies on the private marketplace, which provide supplemental coverage to fill in Medicare's gaps. Those who buy coverage when first eligible cannot legally be denied thereafter on the basis of health.

A very different situation prevails for a retiree or spouse who is not Medicare-eligible, since it is very costly for older people to purchase individually-sold health insurance coverage. Though some people can obtain this type of health insurance coverage, the policies generally require strict underwriting rules so that those in poor health either cannot get coverage or must pay very high prices. Some states offer special pools for the uninsured, or have mandates requiring insurance companies to cover anyone who applies. The 1996 Health Insurance Portability and Accountability Act (HIPAA) legislation limits pre-existing condition restrictions for persons who had prior coverage. It is unclear whether this will help early retirees or how much market there will be allowing them to buy individual coverage. However, the regulations permit charging a high price overall, and individuals buying coverage as HIPAA-eligibles are likely to pay a higher price for the coverage than those who buy underwritten individual coverage.

Healthy individuals have better options than those who are chronically ill. My own practice has shown that monthly premiums for health insurance by age vary between $330 and $465 per month for an individual in good health. These are premiums for a plan requiring a $250 deductible with 80 percent coinsurance and a $2,000,000 lifetime maximum (in 1998). Pre-existing conditions are not covered for 12 months.

Where Long-Term Care Fits In

Today, one-quarter of Medicare beneficiaries today require some type of long-term care support, as shown in Figure 1. Approximately 11 percent of the elderly age 65–74, 27 percent of those age 75–84, and 60 percent of the elderly over age 85 are disabled in some way and need help. There is a wide

TABLE 11: Monthly Premiums for an Individual in Good Health Purchasing
Insurance ($)*

Age	Male	Female
55	$370	$330
60	430	360
63	465	375

Source: Author's tabulations of unpublished data, William M. Mercer (1997).
* $250 deductible, 80 percent coinsurance, $2,000,000 lifetime maximum.

TABLE 12: Comparison of Supportive Housing Types

	Typical Number of Residents	Services	Cost per Month	Other
Board and care	2–200	Some ADL and IADL	$500–$3,000; many low-cost; half publicly supported	Most diverse in quality, size, and cost
Assisted living	15–100	ADL and IADL	$1,000–$3,000; typically private pay	Philosophy of independence promotes aging in place
Adult foster care	1–8	Some ADL and IADL	$600–$1,500; at least half publicly supported	Small, family-like
Continuing care retirement communities	100+, independent; 30+, assisted living; 30+, nursing home	Varies by buildings within the community	$900–$3,600 (varies by level of entrance fee); typically private pay	Independent is similar to congregate care; assisted living in CCRCs is similar to other assisted living
Congregate care	100+	Hotel-type services, such as meals and light housekeeping	$700–$1,500; typically private pay	Apartment buildings with some common services

Source: Hudson (1997).

variety of different needs for help, depending on the type and degree of disability. Generally, medical insurance and Medicare do not cover such help (other than medical services). Today, most such help is provided informally in the community by family and friends.

New housing options are also emerging which combine increasing levels of support with residential services. "Assisted living" options are emerging in many locations, a term that combines a residential environment and (depending on state regulation) supportive services. By 1996, 30 states had created an assisted living licensure category, passed legislation authorizing such a category, or covered assisted living as a Medicaid service (Mollica 1997). Table 12 compares five types of supportive housing. It shows a range of costs and services, providing much broader options than simply nursing homes or independent living.

The Managed Care Marketplace

The health care insurance marketplace has undergone substantial changes in recent years. Over the last decade, many employers have encouraged employees and retirees to choose managed care options. For example, the insured population in fee-for-service plans dropped from 59 percent in 1992 to 35 percent in 1995 (EBRI 1997: 243). Nevertheless, as the popularity of managed care options has grown, there has also been some backlash against the guidelines and practices that health maintenance organizations use to manage costs. Millenson (1997: 11) provides a perspective on this transition:

Not so many years ago, the managers of health maintenance organizations (HMOs) were regarded as wild-eyed socialists seeking to undermine fee-for-service medicine. Now, like aging sixties radicals who have traded in a peace sign for a profit-and-loss statement, HMO managers stand accused of acting like health care robber barons who skim off profits for themselves by scrimping on services for their members. Yet despite the heated rhetoric, some sixty million generally contented Americans were members of HMOs by the end of 1996. For better or worse, HMOs have become the tool that employers and (increasingly) Medicare and Medicaid have chosen for the nearly impossible task of attempting to ration care while keeping everyone happy.

While the HMOs have become a target for legislative action limiting their right to ration care, this has been limited to specific cases thus far. Maternity stays are an example (which usually does not affect the elderly), and federal legislation has mandated minimums for permitted maternity stays. More legislation is likely, as we shall see below.

Other developments also portend changes in the medical care insurance market. Several managed care companies had poor financial results in the late 1990s, as the costs of providing coverage to Medicare-eligible populations proved higher than expected. This industry, like many others, has had substantial consolidation in recent times, and there are relatively few important major players. It also appears that major HMOs may cut back their commitment to Medicare risk contracts. Under such contracts, an HMO is paid a predetermined amount that varies by geography, for providing care to Medicare patients. The plan generally offers a more generous program to the individual, and provides extra benefits over fee-for-service Medicare. Four major HMOs, namely Aetna, United Health Care, Oxford Health, and PacifiCare Health, have recognized problems linked to Medicare contracts by trimming new plan features in some way. For example, Aetna U.S. Healthcare withdrew from its Medicare HMO business in six states and selected counties, impacting 58,000 seniors (it will continue to operate in 16 states, covering just under a half million individuals). United HealthCare Corporation disclosed in mid-1998 that it would take a $900 million charge to reflect losses. Oxford Health and PacifiCare trimmed offerings and face continued troubles. Oxford's stock stood around 75 in 1997, falling to around 6 a year later as a result of its troubles. Each of these examples indicates that the healthcare marketplace is volatile and full of uncertainty.

As a result of these marketplace challenges, some of the previously generous Medicare HMO benefits have had to be trimmed. Some programs had previously offered extra benefits over Medicare, including prescription drugs, and in some cases, eyeglasses and dental care; now benefits have been reduced, and premiums added (Freudenheim 1997). These developments within the healthcare industry are also likely to impact employers sponsoring plans for actives and retirees, individuals purchasing coverage, and "Medicare+Choice" programs. In the case of Medicare+Choice programs, premiums charged to beneficiaries are likely to be higher and/or additional benefits beyond the minimum Medicare benefit are likely to be lower. At the same time, there is an increasing public backlash against managed care plans. Legislation and regulations are likely to restrict managed care plans from freedom to establish their own rules.

Policy Options

While numerous policy options are potentially available, the shape of health reform as it affects the elderly will be powerfully shaped by some recent key events. These include the Balanced Budget Act of 1997, health care proposals made by President Clinton in 1998, and changes anticipated in the health care marketplace.

The Balanced Budget Act of 1997

This Act provided for a number of changes to Medicare in order to help achieve a balanced budget by 2002. Cost reductions of $15 billion were partly offset by $10 billion in new preventive services. Several major changes were as follows:

Prospective payment systems expanded. Several areas were added to the prospective payment system, including hospital outpatient services, skilled nursing, home health, rehabilitation, and ambulance services. Under prospective payment, Medicare pays a flat fee based on diagnosis rather than reimbursing based on specific services provided. This shift will reduce the growth in these costs and bring them under much better control.

Part B premiums increased. Retirees currently pay for part of their Medicare benefits through premiums for Medicare B. Increasing such premiums shifts costs to retirees and reduces the tax-funded cost of the program.

New program provides for expanded choice. Under this program, called Medicare+Choice, Medicare will make a fixed payment to the plan which will then assume the risk. The types of plans under Medicare+Choice will include Coordinated Care Plans, private fee-for-service, and medical savings account plans. Prior to the Balanced Budget Act, HMOs could take risk under Medicare and such programs were increasing their market share, but other Medicare coverage was on a fee-for-service basis. These changes greatly expand the types of marketplace options available to individuals. It is anticipated that this program will shift many more beneficiaries into alternative programs. With the new options, there is to be a regular program permitting annual re-enrollment and providing beneficiaries information about all of the options. The Federal Employees' Health Benefits Program is supposed to be the model for this program.

Method changed for calculating the payment to risk programs. Under the prior law, payments to risk plans were based on the fees charged in the fee-for-service programs in the geographic area where the program was provided. This method of reimbursement produced excessive reimbursements in some areas, and very low reimbursements in others. In the areas with high reimbursements, there were very generous HMO offerings which included added benefits at no cost to the participant. In many areas with low reimbursements, there were no HMO offerings. The new method will gradually equalize payment, slow the rate of increase in payments, and increase the payments in low reimbursement areas.

Reduced reimbursement to health care providers. About half of the $115 billion savings in Medicare from the Balanced Budget Act changes is the result of changes in reimbursement to providers.

The Administration's Medicare Reform Proposals

Recent proposals to reform Medicare include plans to: (1) permit people age 62–64 to buy in at a cost of approximately $300 per month, with an added premium after age 65 to make up for costs over $300 per month per person, (2) extend COBRA to Medicare eligibility age for people terminating employment after age 55, and (3) permit the unemployed age 55 and over to buy into Medicare for approximately $400 per month per person. Though the details of these proposals have not yet emerged, it appears likely that the Republicans will oppose reforms of this type.

Potential Impact on the Poor

In the past, the Medicaid system has been a source of health care coverage of last resort for the poor. Medicaid systems, though they differ across states, provide for payment of Medicare Part B premiums; their benefits also help fill in for uncovered items, deductibles, and copayments for the poor. A danger that must be recognized is that changes in Medicare benefits put pressure on Medicaid payments, which may result in changes in Medicaid programs too. Currently Medicaid pays for about half of long-term care charges, and population aging will stress Medicaid at the same time that it puts pressure on Medicare. If benefits from both programs are cut, the poor may be much worse off.

Longer-Term Issues

Longer-term problems within the Medicare system remain, despite reforms enacted under the Balanced Budget Act of 1997. Out-of-pocket spending for medical care by the elderly is as high today as it was before Medicare was adopted in 1965. This implies continuing pressure to raise benefits. Yet projected tax allocations are inadequate in future years. In addition, the system is viewed as inefficient, when compared to managed care in the private sector. Another issue, not yet resolved, is that some people on Medicare purchase excessive coverage for the "gaps" in their insurance, while early retirees and spouses not yet eligible for Medicare without employer coverage have to pay a great deal for medical coverage. Often people cannot obtain satisfactory coverage if they are in poor health. These measures are exacerbated by demographic aging of the population.

In the near future, decisions will have to be made with regard to several policy issues, including the following:

Medicare Eligibility Ages

Currently, Medicare benefits are available at age 65. Social security eligibility ages in the future have already been modified, so that for persons born in 1960 and later, full benefits will be available at age 67. The higher age for full benefits is being gradually phased in. Earlier versions of the Balanced Budget Act would have aligned the Medicare eligibility age with the social security age. Such a change would have had a significant cost impact on employer plans, and presented additional problems of access to individuals without employer coverage. Life spans have clearly increased since the program was introduced in 1965, and this change seems logical in that light. Since this proposal, there has been a new proposal to reduce eligibility ages by permitting a voluntary buy-in prior to age 65. This entire area demands careful policy analyses.

Private sector options. Via the 1997 Balanced Budget Act, the government is now seeking to move retirees into private sector healthcare plans. At the same time, the healthcare industry is consolidating and having a difficult time remaining profitable. Reimbursement rates to capitated Medicare plans have been curtailed, while at the same time there is growing pressure to force plans to provide more services. Some have proposed legislating a "Patient's Bill of Rights," outlining access to treatment options and providers. All these changes challenge older people's access to care by potentially raising premiums.

Pre-65 coverage. Many Americans leave employment prior to age 65 without health coverage, either as a result of retirement, a move to self-employment, or a move to a job without coverage or the loss of a job. President Clinton's 1998 State of the Union Address proposed offering a Medicare buy-in to individuals who are 55 or over and do not have health insurance coverage. If such a buy-in were elected by those who are sicker — and, if enacted, this seems very likely — such a buy-in would impose additional costs on the Medicare program. A major problem with the plan is that it seems unlikely that the chronically ill and sicker among this group would be able to afford to pay for their own health care costs. This is a highly difficult issue, one that has been joined to the Medicare debate by the President's proposals.

Level of spending by beneficiaries. One method to reduce Medicare costs is to shift costs to beneficiaries, either through higher contributions or higher deductibles and copayments. Yet poor beneficiaries are already spending 30 percent of their income on out-of-pocket health care costs. Those whose income is four times the poverty level or greater are spending about 11 percent of their income. Cost shifting seems very harsh except for wealthier beneficiaries.

Options for Employer Plans

As has been demonstrated, employers' commitment to retiree health and to all kinds of career-based retirement benefits has fallen in the United States. This pattern may indicate that the social contract between employers and employees is gradually changing. Thus there are now few organizations where lifetime employment is expected, and benefit plans are changing in tandem. Specifically, employers have increasingly shied away from assuming open-ended risks in employee benefit plans. In light of uncertainty about Medicare, changes in medical technology, and life spans, the potential costs for retiree health are very uncertain. On the other hand, employers do not want long-term employees to feel vulnerable, and the lack of a marketplace where individuals can buy reasonably priced pre-65 health insurance has left many employers feeling that they have little choice but to take this risk. As a practical matter, HIPAA has not changed this situation. There is no real market for the employer to "insure" this risk on a long-term basis, so employers are bearing the risk. Where the risk is insured on a short-term basis, coverage availability is not guaranteed from year to year and the insurance is generally heavily experience rated.

Future legislation may powerfully change the dynamics of the situation.

For example, if a Medicare buy-in were available, it is possible that some employers would drop coverage or simply provide funds to help with the premium payment. Current law known as COBRA mandates that health insurance coverage continue for 18 or 36 months after a worker leaves his firm, depending on the reason for termination of coverage. If COBRA were modified to mandate longer coverage continuation to age 65, this would also change the dynamics from an employer perspective. One proposal, for instance, would mandate COBRA coverage and require that the premium charged would not exceed 125 percent of the average cost of the coverage. This amount would be a burden for many retirees, and employers would probably experience severe anti-selection with the people electing the coverage being either the relatively more affluent or those in poorer health. COBRA changes would mean that the employer had liability for a much larger group of people, since many people leave without enough service to be eligible as early retirees for retiree coverage. Future legislative proposals are likely to be highly controversial.

Another trend observed in the labor market is that employers feel it appropriate to shift responsibility for retirement wellbeing to the individual. The employers will still provide dollars and vehicles to help employees, but few will adopt the "we will take care of you" stance of the once entitlement-minded employers. This change in perspective explains the downward trend in retiree health coverage. It is paired with increased mobility, and such shifting employment patterns imply that fewer people will be eligible for these benefits as they reach age 65. This is the result of more employment in smaller firms and anticipated shorter durations of employment.

Employer support for health coverage is powerfully influenced by tax policy. Today health benefits can be provided on a tax-free basis to both active employees and retirees. A plan sponsor is not required to provide equal benefits to all employees or all retirees, and the plan can be designed to target groups in various ways. A change in the tax treatment of active or retiree health benefits could dramatically alter such benefit offerings. At this juncture it seems unlikely that tax reform will be enacted which will remove the preferential treatment of health benefits.

Conclusion

There remains substantial uncertainty over the issues that will influence future health care costs, health care insurance in the future — and particularly employer and government health care policy. Several predictions may nevertheless be offered. First, Medicare is unlikely to undergo one sweeping reform to reestablish its financial footing; rather it will experience multiple changes over a five to ten year period (if not longer). Second, it seems probable that employer commitment to health insurance will continue to decline through increases in cost sharing, redesign of plans, and perhaps, benefit cuts. For people needing health insurance coverage prior to age 65 (when they become Medicare eligible), changes in Medicare and/or COBRA could influence employer behavior to a great degree. For post-65 coverage, we expect to see a substantial shift to retiree premium plans, where the employer offers a reimbursement account for insurance premiums and the retiree is permitted a wide choice of insurance options at a group rate. Nevertheless, in the absence of legislative change, pre-65 health insurance access will continue to be available through many employer retiree healthcare plans. This makes it absolutely critical for people to recognize and assess likely high and rising costs of health care as they look ahead into retirement, and also to increase their savings to help insure they have health care coverage at older ages.

References

Board of Trustees of the Federal Hospital Insurance Program. *1997 Annual Report.* Washington, D.C.: U.S. Government Printing Office, 1997.

Centers for Disease Control and Prevention, National Center for Health Statistics, Division of Health Interview Statistics. 1996–97. "National Health Interview Survey." *Health* 180, 181, 197.

EBRI. 1997. *Databook on Employee Benefits.* 4th edition. Washington, D.C.: Employee Benefit Research Institute, 1997: 243.

Feder, Judith and Jeanne Lambrew. 1996. "Why Medicare Matters to People Who Need Long-Term Care." *Health Care Financing Review* 18, 2 (Winter): 99–112.

Freudenheim, Milt. 1997. "Medicare HMO's to Trim Benefits for the Elderly." *New York Times* (December 22): A1, A13.

Gross, David J. and Normandy Brangan. 1997. *Analysis of 1994 Medicare Current Beneficiary Survey.* Washington, D.C.: AARP Public Policy Institute, August.

Hudson, Robert. 1997. "Health Care and Housing Innovations: Integrating Delivery While Unbundling Costs." *Public Policy and Aging Report* 8, 2 (Spring): 13.

KPMG Peat Marwick. Various years. *Surveys of Employer-Sponsored Health Benefits.* Washington, D.C.: KPMG Peat Marwick.

Mazo, Judith, Anna M. Rappaport, and Sylvester J. Schieber. 1993. *Providing Health Care Benefits in Retirement.* Pension Research Council. Philadelphia: University of Pennsylvania Press.

Mercer/Foster Higgins. 1997. *National Survey of Employer-Sponsored Health Plans.* Washington, D.C.: Mercer/Foster Higgins, Inc.

Millenson, Michael L. 1997. *Demanding Medical Excellence: Doctors and Accountability in the Information Age.* Chicago: University of Chicago Press.

Mollica, Robert L. 1997. "Assisted Living: A New Model for Elders." *Public Policy and Aging Report* 8, 2 (Spring): 6.

Moon, Marilyn. 1996. "Restructuring Medicare's Cost Sharing." *Urban Institute Working Paper.* Washington, D.C.: Urban Institute, November.

Moon, Marilyn, Crystal Kuntz, and Laurie Pounder. 1996. "Protecting Low-Income Medicare Beneficiaries, the Commonwealth Fund." *Urban Institute Working Paper.* Washington, D.C.: Urban Institute, November.

U.S. Bureau of the Census. 1995a. "Consumer Expenditure of the United States." *Statistical Abstract of the United States, 1995*. Washington, D.C.: U.S. Government Printing Office.

U.S. Bureau of the Census. 1995b. "Marital Status of the Population." *Statistical Abstract of the United States, 1995*. Washington, D.C.: U.S. Government Printing Office.

Weir, David R. and Robert J. Willis. "Prospects for Widow Poverty." This volume.

Part III
Methodology and Data
Issues in Empirical
Retirement Research

Chapter 12
Evaluating Pension Entitlements

Alan L. Gustman, Olivia S. Mitchell,
Andrew A. Samwick, and Thomas L. Steinmeier

Pension plans are a prominent pillar of most countries' retirement systems. In the United States, pensions are offered by employers on a voluntary basis, usually on top of the government social security system. Today about two-thirds of U.S. households on the verge of retirement have some employer-based pension entitlement benefit.[1] Not only do employer-sponsored plans cover a large number of employees in the United States; they are also the vehicles for substantial wealth accumulation. Private and state/local pension system assets amount to several trillion dollars at present, and are projected to grow as the baby boom ages. Pensions will constitute a substantial portion of retirement wealth for the majority of older Americans for the foreseeable future.

The rapid growth in pensions has been followed with interest by policy-makers and researchers for several reasons. First, analysts concerned about poverty and income sufficiency acknowledge that pensions play a key role in wellbeing at older ages.[2] Second, researchers interested in modeling consumption, saving, retirement, and other aging-related behaviors understand that the special features of pension plans must be analyzed and incorporated into the next generation of behavioral models.[3] Finally, policy-makers concerned with social security policy recognize that any changes in government plans may have a powerful impact on employment-based pensions. For all these reasons, it is imperative to develop a better understanding of how pensions influence work and retirement, saving and consumption, and well-being in old age.

In the present chapter we describe how a new dataset on older Americans and their pensions will help address many of these issues. Specifically, we describe the creation of pension entitlement values needed for a range of research and policy questions using the Health and Retirement Study, a nationally representative survey on older Americans. After describing our methodology, we report on the resulting estimates and indicate how pension wealth varies by several key characteristics.

Methodological Overview[4]

Pension coverage rises with age and time on the job, such that well over half all U.S. workers in their 50s anticipate a future pension (Gustman et al., forthcoming). Most workers with pensions are covered by one of two main types of pension plans: defined benefit (DB) plans, or defined contribution (DC) plans. In a defined benefit pension, the benefit formula is specified by the plan sponsor, usually as a function of pay, years of service, and the worker's retirement age. After an initial vesting period (frequently 5 years), the worker gains a legal right to an eventual pension benefit at the plan's retirement age. A DB formula might, for example, grant an age-65 retiree a benefit worth 1.5 percent of final average pay multiplied by years of service; typically such plans will cap the amount of pay "counted," and will generally reduce the benefit amount for retirement prior to the so-called normal retirement age (age 65 in this example). Generally a DB plan will be financed by employer (pre-tax) contributions, though in some sectors, the worker will also pay into the plan. By contrast, a DC plan does not specify the retirement benefit; rather it determines how much will be contributed into the account each year the worker remains with the plan. Then the benefit payout is set at retirement, as a function of how much is accumulated in the worker's account — the result of lifelong contributions plus (or minus) investment earnings. Some plans have elements of both a DB and DC plan, and at some establishments workers have more than one plan — say, both a conventional DB pension and also a 401(k) defined contribution account (McGill et al. 1997).

Several different types of pension-related variables are of interest to policymakers and researchers focusing on the types of questions identified at the outset. One is *pension wealth*, which reflects the expected present value of pension benefits available to the respondent when he or she reaches a given retirement age. This measure is of most interest to analysts seeking to examine the adequacy of older Americans' retirement wealth accumulations, and perhaps to financial advisers seeking to counsel those making retirement plans. A second type of pension variable that interests analysts focused on labor market issues refers to the change in pension wealth when a worker delays retirement by one year. Termed the *pension accrual*, this pension metric is typically not a simple one, inasmuch as it varies with the worker's age, years of service, and pay, and it often is quite nonlinear. For instance, employees with a DB pension may find that an additional year of service is rewarded by greater retirement benefits up to the firm's early retirement age; after that point, the benefit accrual profile may level off—

and even become negative — if retirement is delayed further. Defined contribution pensions, by contrast, tend to reward delayed retirement more monotonically, inasmuch as they tend to be actuarially neutral with regard to the retirement age.

It has long been acknowledged that pensions contribute substantially to retirement wealth, and they also powerfully influence older workers' incentives to stay or leave the job. However, many previous studies have not been able to develop a rich and complete picture of the role of pensions, since these prior data usually fell short in several regards. One problem is that prior *worker-based* surveys have often been unable to capture detailed information on respondents' pensions. This is the case, for instance, for national Census and Current Population Survey files as well as some of the important longitudinal studies such as the Retirement History Survey.[5] This problem arises when individual workers are asked detailed questions regarding their company-provided pension plan rules, but unless they are nearing retirement the chance is remote that they have much knowledge of how their pension plan works (Mitchell 1988). Another problem is that although a few *firm-based* datasets are available containing high quality data on pensions, these datasets are not necessarily representative of the American workforce. This was a drawback of the Employee Benefit Survey, for instance, and other studies that rely on a single firm to model pension entitlements.[6] Finally, previous surveys have typically not combined good pension data on a nationally representative sample of workers nearing retirement. Even the old Retirement History Survey, extensively used by retirement researchers during the 1980's, did not contain good pension information, thus limiting the usefulness of that study for many purposes.

These shortcomings are rectified in several important ways by the new Health and Retirement Study (HRS), as described in Chapter 1. In what follows, we offer an overview of the steps involved in creating pension variables for the HRS dataset, and then go on to illustrate with concrete examples how pension wealth and pension accruals behave for a nationally representative sample of older Americans.

The HRS-Pension Provider Link

The Health and Retirement Study is a longitudinal database following a nationally representative sample of older Americans along with their spouses as they reach and then cross the retirement threshold. The original sample included 7,607 households about whom data were gathered on demographic factors, health, housing, family structure, work history and current employment, disability, retirement plans, net worth, income, and health and life insurance.[7] A total of 9,825 respondents were age 51 to 61 years of age in 1992, for the first wave of the study, and are termed the "age eligible" sample.

The same people, along with their spouses, were re-surveyed in 1994, 1996, and 1998, and follow-on funding will be requested through the year 2008 (and probably beyond).

The HRS included several questions in addition to the conventional sorts of social and economic questions typically asked in national surveys, for the benefit of researchers who seek better to understand the role of pensions in the retirement context.[8] Of particular interest to pension experts is the fact that HRS respondents who indicated that they had a pension from their current employer were asked the name and address of that employer. Subsequently, ISR interviewers contacted each named employer to obtain a copy of that firm's pension plan Summary Plan Description (SPD). If an employer did not send a pension SPD, publicly available pension records at the Department of Labor were searched and missing documents obtained where possible.[9] To preserve respondent confidentiality, in no case was the individual employee's name revealed to the firm, nor is the employer identification information made available to researchers.[10] In addition, pension SPDs were gathered for people having a pension from a past employer.[11]

A Synopsis of What the Pension Software Does

Evaluating workers' entitlements under these pension plans requires a multi-step method of attack. First, the plans were coded into a standard format called the Pension Provider Survey (PPS) and entered into a computer-readable file containing approximately 12,000 variables. Second, it was necessary to develop specialized computer software to manipulate these pension plan variables to determine pension entitlements for each individual worker (Curtain 1997).[12] After reading the pension variables coded for each plan, the PPS program converts these into systems of equations that represent the benefit formulas, vesting rules, retirement restrictions, and all other payment provisions for each pension plan. Next the program requests from the researcher a set of assumptions including (1) economic and demographic assumptions needed to compute future benefits, and (2) work and earning profiles for each respondent for whom pension entitlements will be created. These are then combined with the pension algorithms to produce a set of pension entitlement variables for each individual in each plan, in a standard format output data file. Finally, a researcher can link these pension entitlement files with other data on HRS respondents for analysis.[13]

An especially useful feature of the PPS software is that the researcher can specify a wide range of assumptions and input data, thus allowing a wide range of simulation scenarios. For instance, one can compute several types of retirement benefits permitted under a pension plan, including vested terminated payments, early and normal benefits, disability benefits, and others. The researcher can also compute benefits payable as of a particular quit age, or alternatively, the benefits payable as of all possible retirement ages. Benefit streams for each quit or retirement age until death are converted into an expected present value, discounting the future cash flows at a rate supplied by the user.[14]

For defined benefit (DB) plans, the employer-provided plan descriptions make it possible to calculate benefit amounts quite accurately. The asset value of the DB pension is therefore defined as the discounted value of the DB plan benefits from some retirement age until death, based on past earnings and years of service. In our analysis below, we express all values in 1992 dollars (even if the date of initial benefit receipt is some future date). For example, a 60-year-old worker who had been with his company for 20 years as of 1992 might be eligible to retire immediately. In that firm, though, the worker might not receive his full benefit since he had not attained the "normal" retirement age, i.e. age 65. If his benefit formula paid 2 percent of final earnings times years of service, his annual early retirement benefit (as of age 60) would then amount to 40 percent of his last earnings, reduced by an actuarial factor (e.g., 20 percent) in recognition of the fact that he would be receiving his benefit for a longer period of time. Should the worker wait to retire until age 65, the program would recognize that the retirement benefit formula would no longer require the early retirement penalty, and benefits that began at age 65 would be expressed in 1992 dollars when the worker was age 60.[15]

In each case, the specific pension plan rules are combined with the worker's individual past service and earnings to determine benefits he is currently entitled to. Benefits accrued by continued work would make use of projected service and earnings, extrapolating using a wage growth assumption provided by the researcher. Having computed a current as well as a future pension wealth, one would then difference them to compute the pension accrual with continued work. If the pension accrual with continued work is positive, it would be concluded that the pension plan rewards delayed retirement (conversely, some plans penalize deferred retirement).

Pension values for workers with defined contribution (DC) plans can also be computed with the help of the pension software. Computing the DC pension entitlement requires adding to the pension accumulation from the employer plus the employee contributions each year, crediting the accumulations with a real rate of interest. If employee contributions are mandatory, these are recorded in the pension SPD and used by the software. If voluntary contributions are allowed (e.g. to obtain employer matching funds), the software allows the user to specify what the worker will contribute.

Not only do HRS workers report current pensions — that is, a pension plan at their current place of employment — but there are also people in the HRS who indicate they are entitled to a pension based on a previous job.[16] In this instance, the pension software computes pension wealth for these "prior pensions" using similar inputs and in a similar output format.

One other issue has to do with the fact that some people have more than one pension plan on their current job, while others have a pension plan that has elements of both a defined benefit and a defined contribution pension. In the analysis below, we separately distinguish these cases from the simple DB and DC cases by listing them as combination plans.

Characteristics of Pension-Covered Respondents in the HRS

Key characteristics of HRS respondents with a pension plan document linked to their respondent records are recorded in Table 1. There are 2,396 age-eligible people for whom a pension link is available from their current job: of these 1,160 (48 percent) have a defined benefit plan, 499 (21 percent) have a defined contribution plan, and 737 (31 percent) have some sort of combination of pension plans. Of those who do not have a link to a current job pension plan, 1,082 people have matched "prior pensions" from previous jobs; some of these people are retired and receiving a benefit, while others are vested terminated workers entitled to a future pension. Overall, therefore, 35 percent of the age-eligible HRS sample have a pension document, and 6347 respondents have no pension document.[17] The huge number of prior pensions detected and collected for the survey respondents suggests that pensions acquired during middle age — before reaching age 60 — are important in financing retirement consumption.

Table 1 also shows how workers' nonpension wealth levels vary by pension plan type. (All dollar figures presented are in 1992 dollars throughout this paper.) Nonpension wealth includes net home equity, financial assets, own businesses, and Individual Retirement Accounts, but excludes pensions and social security wealth. The results show that people with both plan types on their current jobs have similar levels of nonpension wealth, about $131,000 at the median. Having had a pension previously is also associated with similar wealth levels. By contrast, people with no pension link have accumulated 23 percent less nonpension wealth, a median of $101,000, compared to their counterparts with a pension. This could imply that pension-covered jobs are more remunerative than those without, but may also suggest that workers with pensions are more likely to be savers outside their plans as well (Gustman and Steinmeier 1998).

Assumptions Used in Computing Pension Wealth

When computing pension wealth using the PPS program, two types of input files are required.[18] The first, called the parameter (INPARM) file, pertains to economic and other factors assumed to hold across all individuals in any given simulation run. These include the real interest and earnings growth rate, the rate of inflation and the extent to which pension benefits keep up with inflation after retirement, and several user-supplied social security vari-

TABLE 1: HRS Respondents With and Without a Pension Link

	Number	Mean Wealth ($000) Excluding Pensions	Median Wealth ($000) Exluding Pensions
Respondents with linked pension plan			
From current job			
DB pension	1160	$213	$131
DC pension	499	215	131
Combination plan	737	225	124
Total	2396	217	129
From previous job	1082	275	143
Respondents with no linked pension plan			
No pension link	6347	$279	$101

Source: Authors' calculations, 1992 HRS.
Notes: Having a linked pension indicates that a pension Summary Plan Description in the Pension Provider Survey is available for the HRS respondent. All figures other than sample size are weighted by HRS person weights.

ables including the level of the social security taxable earnings ceiling and its rate of change over time. In the analysis below, we adopt the long-term intermediate assumptions proposed by the Social Security Administration (Board of Trustees, 1995), consistent with our earlier work valuing social security wealth.[19] In particular, the cost of living is assumed to rise at 4 percent annually, earnings grow at 1 percent in real terms, and the real interest rate is set at 2.3 percent. In future work we will explore how sensitive our pension wealth computations are to the underlying economic assumptions, using the social security pessimistic and optimistic assumptions.[20]

PPS program options are also available concerning the quit age (or date) range, permitting the user to indicate at which age the worker is assumed to leave the firm. In the analysis here, we compute all pension wealth entitlements assuming retirement occurs at age 62.[21] The model in all cases assumes that after retirement, defined benefit pension benefits rise at half the rate of inflation. In addition, the PPS program caps the maximum pension benefit payable from a DB plan in 1992 at $112,200 per year assuming retirement at 65; this amount is actuarially reduced to $44,000 for a quit age of 55 following the rules for qualified pension plans described in McGill et al. (1997). Both caps are automatically indexed to the inflation rate in the program as specified in the law.[22]

A second type of input file required by the pension software program contains parameters set by the researcher pertaining to each participant (the INDATA file). For the present analysis, we take as given each worker's 1991 earnings (for his current job if working, or last earnings if not working), and then we project earnings forward as well as backward using a 5 percent nominal (1 percent real) real wage growth rate per year. In practice, the pension software permits users to explore other many options for allowing individual-specific wage growth rates in alternative simulations.

Some pension plans are integrated with social security, in that their contributions and/or their benefits are linked to the social security taxable earnings base or benefits received. For these plans, a social security algorithm was used that calculates benefit amounts for early and normal retirement ages, single and/or joint, etc. Therefore the computed pension benefits depend on each respondent's wage profile.[23]

Occasionally a worker in the HRS sample indicated that he or she had a pension plan from either a current or past job, but a pension document could not be obtained for that plan. This occurred when an employee refused to provide the name and address of the company, or if the pension plan document simply was unavailable. In the results discussed below, no pension entitlements were computed in the event of a missing pension. Rather, the pension-covered individual was simply excluded from the sample of people with a pension data link.[24]

The Process of Producing Pension Entitlement Estimates

The pension software[25] produces estimated pension entitlements with one participant per plan per line.[26] A household's total pension wealth, therefore, can be obtained by adding the entitlements across all plans covering the respondent and spouse. In what follows we focus on individuals rather than households to track specific wealth and accrual paths, but naturally a researcher can merge pensions using the household record IDs.

There are three types of simulation exercises that can be carried out with the PPS program; each run generates somewhat different output data files, useful for specific purposes (Curtin 1997). Runtype 1 produces pension entitlements tailored to individual quit dates for a given pension plan. It generates each worker's initial benefit amount, his pension benefit as a fraction of final earnings, and the expected present value of the lifetime pension benefit stream for that quit date. By contrast, Runtype 3 produces information on initial benefit amount for all possible quit dates within a range, and for a variety of benefit conditions (e.g., disability, early, normal, late retirement, etc.). This simulation also yields present values as of each quit date. Finally, Runtype 2 uses simulated participant data, running a given person through all plans for a range of quit dates. Below we report results derived from runs of various types, to illustrate how benefit levels and accruals are calculated for both hypothetical and real workers.[27]

Practically speaking, the PPS uses a two-step sequence. The first set of programs reads in the pension plan dataset and creates pension procedures based on these variables. One procedure is created for each plan, by reading the variables from each coded pension document using a variable dictionary supplied with the software. The second set of programs incorporates these procedures into code that calculates pension entitlements, when combined with economic assumptions and information on the pension-covered workers. This second step can be re-run using alternative economic input parameters and data on workers, so that users may flexibly simulate pension entitlements under a wide range of circumstances. It is in this second stage of the program that users select the desired run type, whether only respondent or respondent and spouse benefits are to be modeled, whether annuities or present values will be generated, and so forth. To illustrate some of the types of information generated by the software, we next turn to a summary of results from two specific simulations.

Levels of Pension Wealth in the HRS

Many analysts using the HRS require a comprehensive measure of pension wealth to include as an empirical control variable in analysis of a range of behaviors from consumption, to saving, to *inter vivos* transfers, to bequests. Others seek to understand how the distribution of wealth varies by household characteristics, and will similarly need a measure of pension wealth to include as a component of the overall distribution. Experts interested in the adequacy of retirement wealth need a good measure of expected pension income to determine whether people seem to be saving enough, and if not, why not.

To satisfy these purposes, we have generated a measure of the present value of pension benefits using the long-term intermediate social security assumptions described above. Results appear in Table 2, which is constructed to correspond to categories of respondents described in Table 1.[28]

The top panel of Table 2 reports the present value of expected pension benefits for all HRS respondents with a linked pension on their current job. One finding is that the median worker in our sample covered by a DC pension appears to have accumulated less pension wealth than the median DB-covered employee. This is not surprising, given the relative newness of DC pensions, and the shorter time most employees have contributed to these plans. Another finding is that mean pension wealth values exceed medians. For those with a DB plan quitting work at age 62, for instance, mean pension wealth totals $114,000 while median wealth is a third lower at $75,000. The pattern is similar for those having combination plans. Pension wealth for DC-covered workers has a means of $48,000 and a median half that amount at $24,000. The fact that pension wealth is skewed is evident in the small bottom-to-top quartile ratio.

Focusing on the next segment of Table 2, here we report both current and previous pension plan entitlements for workers having a current job-linked pension; thus prior pensions are included as well. Here, not surprisingly, the net present value of pension wealth rises, since additional "old

TABLE 2: Pension Wealth Levels ($000) for HRS Respondents With Pension Link
(with SSA Intermediate Assumptions)

	Mean	Median	Std. Dev	25th %-ile	75th %-ile
Pension wealth for repondents with linked pension from current job					
Current plan only					
DB only	$114	$75	$125	$31	$152
DC only	48	24	61	9	62
Combination	129	77	190	35	164
Total	105	61	142	24	135
All pension plans (in PPS)					
Pension wealth, DB only	120	79	132	33	164
Pension wealth, DC only	56	28	87	10	75
Pension wealth, comb	136	82	193	37	168
Total	112	68	149	26	144
Pension Wealth for respondents having a linked pension from prior job only					
Pension wealth	107	47	137	102	164
Pension wealth for respondents with any linked pension					
Pension wealth	110	62	145	21	151

Source: Authors' calculations, 1992 HRS, using version 6.0 of the PPS software.
Notes: Having a linked pension indicates that a Pension Summary Plan Description in the Pension Provider Survey is available for the HRS respondent. All figures other than sample size are weighted by HRS person weights and assume retirement is at age 62.

plans" are added in. But for older workers with a pension plan on their current jobs, their "old" pension wealth is not enormous, worth around 5 percent of total pension wealth.

The second panel of Table 2 depicts pension wealth for respondents who only have a linked pension from a previous job, but no current plan. It is interesting to see that mean pension wealth for this group totals about $107 thousand, or about 5 percent lower than people with linked pensions on their current jobs; however, the median is 31 percent lower. In any event, the fact that median pension wealth from a prior plan is around $47,000 underscores the importance of gathering previous pension information over time to not "lose" major components of people's pension entitlements.

The final panel of Table 2 uses the most inclusive definition of "having a pension link," that is, counting people with either a current or a past pension (or both). Mean (median) pension accumulations of $110,000 ($62,000) are similar to those accumulated on the current job ($105,000 and $61,000 respectively).[29]

In sum, the results suggest that pension accumulations for older workers on their current jobs are substantial, totaling around $75,000 for the average covered worker with a DB, and about $24,000 for those with a DC plan only. Overall, the median pension entitlement for any worker with a pension link on his current job stood at $68,000 in present value. Pensions earned on previous jobs are also quantitatively important for older workers, boosting median total pension entitlements to around $79,000 (for the DB case) and $28,000 (for the DC case). Respondents with only a prior pension had a median pension entitlement of $47,000.

Pension Accruals in the HRS

Researchers concerned with pensions also seek to understand how plan wealth changes for a worker considering whether to remain employed an additional year or retire immediately. Accordingly, we have computed pension accruals for the sample, defined as the difference between a worker's pension wealth if he worked another year and then stopped work, as compared to leaving now and investing the contributions at the real interest rate. All figures are given in 1992 dollars.

One way to understand how plan accrual profiles work is to focus on a single illustrative pension plan. To this end, we develop a hypothetical 40-year old worker with earnings equal to the HRS average in 1992. This annual earnings level is then extrapolated forward and backward from 1992 using the real 1 percent wage growth rate assumed throughout the analysis. The average age at hire in the HRS sample was about 38, so the hypothetical worker is assumed to have joined the 1992 employer at that age and remained at that job until retirement. We then simulate how this worker's pension entitlement would change through time in the given pension plan; the plan was selected to illustrate some of the interesting features peculiar to actual defined benefit pensions.[30]

The results of this exercise appear in Figure 1. The jagged or spiked line, which is read using the right-hand scale, refers to the change in the hypothetical worker's DB pension wealth as he moves up in seniority with the firm. The first spike, at age 42, occurs with vesting, at which point the worker gains a legal right to an eventual retirement benefit. It will be noted that the present value of vesting in the plan is only a few thousand dollars. Accruals over the next decade are virtually nil, and the next spike coincides with the company's early retirement age at 54.[31] In that year, the worker's DB pension accrual is approximately $40,000. Subsequent accruals are small but positive until the worker reaches age 62, at which time he becomes eligible for a more generous benefit formula. After this age, pension accruals for continued work are negative. This type of pattern is not uncommon in defined benefit plans where the firm wants to encourage older workers to leave.[32]

The second line of Figure 1, plotted against the left scale, reflects the level of pension wealth to which the worker is entitled as his length of service with the firm increases. The sharp spike in the accrual at 54 is reflected in the

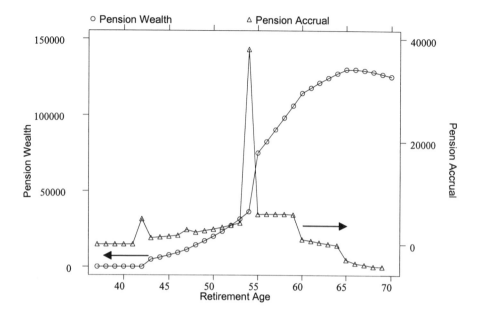

Figure 1. Illustrative defined benefit plan: pension accrual and wealth profiles for a hypothetical individual. Source: Authors' calculations.

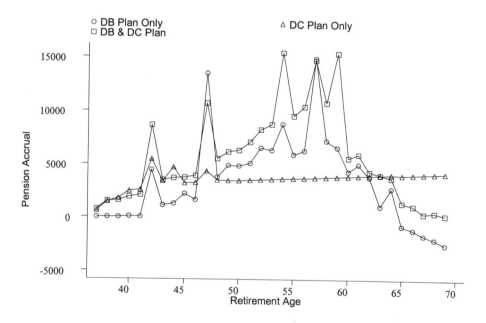

Figure 2. Cross-pension average: pension wealth profiles for a hypothetical individual. Source: Authors' calculations.

TABLE 3: Current Job Pension Accruals as Fraction of Last Wage: HRS Respondents With Pension Link (Using SSA Intermediate Assumptions)

	Current DB Only		Current DC Only		Combination	
Age	N	Median (%)	N	Median (%)	N	Median (%)
50	67	18.38	26	9.72	53	18.28
51	118	15.27	40	7.46	101	21.92
52	144	19.34	51	5.92	60	18.17
53	131	16.36	64	10.23	94	20.29
54	113	23.42	43	5.92	65	30.22
55	87	14.16	62	9.21	65	21.69
56	128	14.69	49	10.76	65	22.53
57	96	13.36	39	10.76	63	24.66
58	75	13.29	44	10.23	54	22.35
59	75	16.02	39	7.16	57	23.38
60	87	11.53	28	5.63	42	13.53
61	39	7.93	14	n.a.	18	n.a.
Total		15.81		8.80		21.26

Notes: See Table 2. n.a. = not available for N ≤ 20.

upward shift in the total pension level function at age 55, with the slope of the function flattening thereafter with age.

Next, we put the same hypothetical worker with HRS-average earnings and service through the entire set of plans covering HRS respondents on their current jobs; the results are displayed in Figure 2. Once again, the worker is aged from 40 to age 70, so as to depict differences in accrual patterns by plan type. The cross-pension plan averages reveal that DB plans, as a group, present a spiked profile, with accruals rising sharply at vesting, and after ten years of service. Pension accruals again rise sharply for early retirement which varies in this sample from age 55 to 60. After the normal retirement date, which for these plans ranges between age 60 and 65, workers typically pay a penalty through a declining and eventually negative pension accrual. By sharp contrast, the accrual profile for defined contribution pension plans confirms that there is a smooth accrual path with virtually no retirement inducement. Combination plans look more like DB than DC plans.

To determine whether and how these observations on simulated workers generalize to *actual* workers, we have carried out the same simulations using actual pension accruals for the HRS respondents covered by these plans. Here we focus only on plan accruals for current plans, computing the changes in pension wealth as retirement is deferred. Table 3 shows that DB and combination plans behave fairly similarly overall, with a pronounced early retirement peak around the mid-50s, and another, smaller hump for workers reaching their late 50s. DC plan accruals are relatively flat for this population, as a result of the fact that contributions are accounting for the change in plan value with age.[33] In sum, pension accruals are large and highly nonlinear for DB as well as combination plans, but are small and quite linear for DC pensions. Analysts interested in ways that pensions influence retirement saving patterns will clearly need to pay close attention to these differential incentives.

Conclusion

Designers of the Health and Retirement Study sought to collect data and make available to researchers the best possible estimates of pension wealth and pension accruals. The goal of this chapter is to introduce users to this valuable new information on pension wealth levels and pension accruals, and to describe baseline information about these data. These variables are available to researchers (with some restrictions) through the University of Michigan's Institute for Social Research. It is anticipated that many — perhaps most — HRS researchers will find the pension entitlement variables created here sufficient for their analytic purposes. A handful of users will, however, seek to conduct their own simulations, perhaps changing economic assumptions or computing pension entitlements for different retirement ages or different retirement circumstances than the ones developed here. This should now be possible with the information provided in Curtin (1997) and the pension files provided.

In any event, we are certain that the evidence here will only whet researchers' appetite for new pension knowledge. The richness of the pension plan information in the HRS is unsurpassed by any other public or private nationally representative data source. Further, the fact that the HRS respondents (and spouses) are being resurveyed every two years makes the longitudinal study an invaluable information base with which to track work and retirement patterns, saving and consumption profiles, and the paths of wealth and wellbeing in old age.

Gustman and Steinmeier are grateful for research support from the Pension and Welfare Benefit Administration of the U.S. Department of Labor, and the Bureau of Labor Statistics. All four authors acknowledge research support from the National Institute on Aging. Mitchell also acknowledges research assistance from the University of Pennsylvania's Aging Research Center and the Pension Research Council. Charlie Brown, Jody Lamkin, Bob Petticolas, and Mel Stephens provided invaluable help at several stages of the project, and Gary Fields provided helpful suggestions. Opinions remain solely those of the authors.

Notes

1. For a discussion of pension coverage statistics in the population at large see Hinz and Turner (1998), Gustman et al. (forthcoming), and Kennickell and Sunden (1997).

2. For instance see Levine, Mitchell, and Moore (this volume).

3. Gustman and Mitchell (1992) and Lumsdaine and Mitchell (forthcoming) review a range of behavioral models in which pensions play a key role.

4. This section draws on Gustman et al. (forthcoming).

5. Two recent exceptions are the Survey of Consumer Finances and the Mature Women survey associated with the National Longitudinal Survey.

6. For a review of data sources on pensions see Gustman and Mitchell (1992) and Lumsdaine and Mitchell (forthcoming).

7. Interested researchers are invited to examine the HRS website located at www.umich.edu/~hrswww.

8. In addition, administrative data on respondents' earnings and benefits histories were collected in collaboration with the Social Security Administration. Access to rounded SSA information, and the employer data, is restricted to a limited set of users who must have their research and data security plans approved by the ISR, and who maintain the strictest confidentiality regarding HRS respondents.

9. A pension provider could also have been a multiemployer (joint labor-management) plan.

10. The research is supported by a cooperative agreement between the NIA and the University of Michigan with additional funding from the Social Security Administration, the U.S. DOL (Pension and Welfare Benefit Administration), and the U.S. Department of Health and Human Services (Assistant Secretary for Planning and Evaluation). Two other national surveys have also collected pension plan descriptions from employers besides the HRS, namely the Survey of Consumer Finances (SCF) and the National Longitudinal Survey of Mature Women (NLS-MW). The HRS, however, is the only large nationally representative study of Americans on the verge of retirement.

11. As pointed out in Gustman et al. (forthcoming), pension documents could be matched proportionally more highly for employees of large firms, and also for those covered by a defined benefit rather than a defined contribution plan. For example, a worker who reported having a DB or combination plan and worked at a company with more than 500 employees had a 77 percent chance of a pension match. Someone covered by a DC plan only, but in an equivalent sized company, had two-thirds chance of a pension link. A worker with a DB or combination plan, employed at a firm with 24–99 employees, had only a 52 percent chance of having his employer plan document linked with his case, while a person with only a DC plan in the same size firm had a probability of only 32 percent.

12. The original version of the software was written by Richard Curtin at the University of Michigan's ISR; it was subsequently updated by Robert Petticolas and Jody Lamkin with input from Mel Stephens, Thomas Steinmeier, and Andrew Samwick.

13. Access to the data is restricted to preserve respondent confidentiality. The conditions under which researchers may obtain restricted files are described at www.umich.edu/~hrswww.

14. Survival probabilities for future cash flows are taken from data kindly supplied by Felicitie Bell in the Social Security Administration's Office of the Actuary. A comparison of these data with the 1990 Vital Statistics figures shows that lower survival rates in the latter datasource would have resulted in lower pension wealth figures than those reported here. For summary statistics from these mortality data see Gustman et al. (forthcoming). Users of this software program should be aware that the survival rates and pension wealth variables calculated from them reflect population averages by sex and birth cohort; they are not available by race and income.

15. The pension software program correctly computes the present discounted

value of retirement benefits from retirement on by inflation, mortality, and a real discount rate. The issue is more complex if the worker terminates his employment prior to retirement and some time passes before he receives his first benefit. As of the present writing, the pension value from 1992 to the commencement of the benefit stream is discounted by inflation and a real discount rate, but not by mortality. This should have a relatively unimportant impact on simulated magnitudes given here, and a future version of the program should be able to incorporate this change.

16. This excludes people who indicate they have received a lump sum from a prior job's pension.

17. Some in the latter group could, of course, have a pension but they may have refused to permit the HRS to contact their employer, or no pension-matched SPD may have been found. In the future it is likely that obtaining pension SPDs will grow increasingly difficult, inasmuch as pension plans are no longer required to furnish their SPDs to the U.S. Department of Labor. This no doubt saves costs, but it also makes future analysis of company-sponsored pension plans much more difficult.

18. For an extensive discussion of each input file and variable description see Curtin as adapted (1997).

19. See Mitchell, Olson, and Steinmeier (this volume) and Gustman et al. (forthcoming).

20. The social security assumptions (%) for the three cases are as follows:

	Optimistic	Intermediate	Pessimistic
CPI change	3.0	4.0	5.0
Real wage growth	1.5	1.0	0.5
Real interest rate	3.0	2.3	1.5

For further discussion of these assumptions see Advisory Council (1997).

21. All entitlements are computed as of 1992 when Wave 1 of the HRS was fielded. In future work we will examine alternative retirement ages as well.

22. There are two aspects of inflation that the user has control over. The first is the cost of living adjustment (COLA) on the pension, which we set to half of observed inflation. This conforms to evidence in Gustman and Steinmeier (1994). This value is used for any DB plan that does not specify explicitly what its COLA rate was (the default does not override plan-provided information). The second is whether the nominal dollar amounts specified in the plan are indexed to inflation. For example, if the plan had a formula promising 1.5 percent of pay up to $40,000 and 1.25 percent of pay above that, we grow the $40,000 with inflation when computing benefit entitlements for retirement after 1992. The user is permitted to set this switch in the pension software, and in this paper we set the switch to index actual plan features if these are reported.

23. It should be noted that for the present paper we use earnings profiles derived for each individual, but we do not use the administrative records described in Mitchell, Olson, and Steinmeier (this volume).

24. Other analysts will devise their own hot-deck or imputation program to fill in missing values for these respondents. Since the choice of imputation routine will depend on each user's particular problem, we have chosen not to fill in missing data.

25. See Curtain (1997) for a full discussion of run and output options.

26. If a respondent has more than one plan, the INDATA file must enter each person as many times as he or she has pension plans.

27. We have generated an output database using the assumptions spelled out in the Data Appendix available to users interested in understanding more about the structure of the output database.

28. These results are the output of Runtype 1; see Curtin (1997).

29. To determine how sensitive these results are to the underlying economic assumptions used in creating the present values, we will simulate pension entitlements using the optimistic and the pessimistic SSA assumptions. These results show that results are not affected materially. This is because the optimistic scenario has a higher real wage growth rate which tends to increase benefits, but also uses a higher real interest rate which tends to decrease the present value of these streams.

30. The analysis assumes that DC plans requiring employee payments averaged 8.36 percent in annual employee contributions (the sample average), and DC assets earn 2.3 percent annual real returns.

31. Note that the spike in the accrual profile occurs at the age before pension wealth increases. In the case of vesting, the worker is first entitled to benefits if work continues until age 43 (five years after hire). Thus, the opportunity cost of leaving the firm at age 42 is high. Similarly, the plan's early retirement age is 55, so that there are strong disincentives to leave just prior to that age. This is reflected in the graph by a spike at age 54.

32. Such patterns have also been confirmed in earlier analysis of defined benefit pension accruals; see for instance the studies reviewed in Gustman, Mitchell, and Steinmeier (1994).

33. In this analysis all worker assets in DC plans are assumed to grow at 2.3 percent annually (equivalent to a 6.3 percent nominal rate) and then are discounted back to the computation date at the same real rate.

References

Advisory Council. 1996. *Report of the 1994–1996 Advisory Council on Social Security.* 2 vols. Washington, D.C.: Social Security Administration.

Board of Trustees. *Annual Report of the Board of Trustees.* Social Security Administration (SSA), Washington, D.C.: U.S. Government Printing Office. Various years.

Curtin, Richard T. 1997. "Pension Estimation Program Documentation." April. Modified for use with PCs by Jody Lamkin. Documentation updated by C. Brown and M. Stephens, Survey Research Center, University of Michigan.

Gustman, Alan L. and Olivia S. Mitchell. 1992. "Pensions and the U.S. Labor Market." In Zvi Bodie and Alicia H. Munnell, eds., *Pensions and the Economy: Sources, Uses, and Limitations of Data.* Pension Research Council. Philadelphia: University of Pennsylvania Press: 39–87.

Gustman, Alan G., Olivia S. Mitchell, Andrew A. Samwick, and Thomas L. Steinmeier. Forthcoming. "Pension and Social Security Wealth in the Health and Retirement Study." In Robert Willis, ed., *Wealth, Work, and Health: Innovations in Survey Measurement in the Social Sciences.* Ann Arbor: University of Michigan Press.

Gustman, Alan S., Olivia S. Mitchell, and Thomas Steinmeier. 1994. "The Role of Pensions in the Labor Market." *Industrial and Labor Relations Review* 47, 3: 417–38.

Gustman, Alan G. and Thomas L. Steinmeier. 1994. "Cost of Living Adjustments in Pensions." In Olivia S. Mitchell, ed. *As the Workforce Ages.* Ithaca, N.Y.: ILR Press.

———. 1998. "Effects of Pensions on Savings: Analysis with Data from the Health and Retirement Study." Paper presented at the Carnegie-Rochester Conference Series on Public Policy, Rochester, N.Y., April.

Hinz, Richard P. and John A. Turner. 1998. "Pension Coverage Initiatives: Why Don't Workers Participate?" In Olivia S. Mitchell and Sylvester Schieber, eds., *Living with Defined Contribution Pensions: Remaking Responsibility for Retirement.* Pension Research Council. Philadelphia: University of Pennsylvania Press. 17–37.

Kennickell, Arthur B. and Annika E. Sunden. October 1997. "Pensions, Social Security, and the Distribution of Wealth." Working paper, Board of Governors of the Federal Reserve System.

Levine, Phillip B., Olivia S. Mitchell, and James F. Moore. "Women on the Verge of Retirement: Predictors of Retiree Wellbeing." This volume.

Lumsdaine, Robin and Olivia S. Mitchell. forthcoming. "Retirement." In Orley Ashenfelter and David Card, eds., *Handbook of Labor Economics*. Amsterdam: North Holland.

McGill, Dan, Kyle Brown, John Haley, and Sylvester Schieber. 1997. *Fundamentals of Private Pensions*. 7th edition. Pension Research Council. Philadelphia: University of Pennsylvania Press.

Mitchell, Olivia S. 1988. "Worker Knowledge of Pension Provisions." *Journal of Labor Economics* 6 (January): 21–39.

Mitchell, Olivia S. and James F. Moore. 1998. "Can Americans Afford to Retire? New Evidence on Retirement Saving Adequacy." *Journal of Risk and Insurance*, 65, 3: 371–400.

Mitchell, Olivia S., Jan Olson, and Thomas L. Steinmeier. "Social Security Earnings and Projected Benefits." This volume.

Moore, James F. and Olivia S. Mitchell. "Projected Retirement Wealth and Saving Adequacy." This volume.

Chapter 13
Social Security Earnings and Projected Benefits

Olivia S. Mitchell, Jan Olson,
and Thomas L. Steinmeier

Researchers seeking to trace out patterns of retirement wealth in the United States recognize the key role played by social security benefits in older persons' portfolios. However, until recently it has been virtually impossible to obtain good information on expected benefits for a nationally representative sample of Americans, since household surveys do not typically elicit good quality information on this important source of wealth. This gap has recently been rectified with the linking of social security administrative records to the Health and Retirement Study. These administrative records constitute a very special dataset created for analysts working with the HRS under restricted access conditions. In this chapter we describe how we created this dataset and how it can be linked with the HRS. Examples of research using the files include Dwyer and Hu (this volume), Mitchell, Moore, and Phillips (this volume), and Moore and Mitchell (this volume).

An Overview of the Issues

When linking social security administrative records to respondent files collected under the HRS, it was necessary to make a number of decisions regarding particular variables and the assumptions needed to generate them. In this chapter we provide two levels of explanations regarding our rationale for, and definitions of, constructed employment, earnings, and social security wealth variables. First, we offer a description in conceptual terms, and then in an appendix provide more technical detail.

The file we have created is called the Summary Earnings and Projected Benefits File, or SEPBF for short. It contains information derived for respondents of the 1992 Health and Retirement Survey who authorized the University of Michigan's Institute for Social Research to obtain and link administrative records for them from the Social Security Administration. We emphasize that the SEPBF and all derived variables contained therein are intended for research purposes only, and the files are accessible only to registered users of the Health and Retirement Study. The dataset may be linked only with HRS files containing no geographic detail below the Census Division level, in order to preserve respondent confidentiality.[1]

The SEPBF contains three types of variables, aimed at meeting specific data needs of the research community working with the HRS. First, HRS researchers require summary measures of labor market attachment, often useful in modeling retirement and saving patterns. Second, researchers often need information on aggregate earnings, since they are measures of interest in their own right and are also of use in assessing respondents' retirement saving. Third, researchers are interested in social security wealth when studying retirement behavior and preparedness for retirement. In the context of the HRS, it is useful to have measures of social security wealth as of a common year — here taken to be 1992 — for comparability purposes with other wealth measures obtained at that interview date.

Measures of each type of variable presented in this study are those for respondents of the first wave of the HRS who authorized the release of earnings and benefit data to the University of Michigan's Institute for Social Research. Further, for the present study, only files for non-disabled HRS Wave 1 respondents and spouses (surveyed in 1992) were included in tabulations provided.[2] Here we explain in general terms the why and how of deriving these key earnings and projected benefits measures. Additional technical details appear in Appendix A for the interested reader.

Employment Summary Measures

A range of employment summary measures was created derived from administrative records supplied by the Social Security Administration (SSA), in accordance with agreements signed between the Institute for Social Research (ISR) at the University of Michigan and the SSA. Of the HRS survey respondents asked to sign a permission form in 1992 allowing access to their earnings and benefit records at SSA, some 75 percent complied with the request. ISR provided identifiers to SSA, and individual earnings records were obtained for cases with matching identifiers. A final match rate of 66 percent of the entire Wave 1 HRS sample was obtained.[3] If no permission was obtained, or if a match could not be generated, no employment variables were generated in the SEPB file for that case ID.

In Table 1 we summarize results for several of the labor market variables reported in the SEPBF. The sample included in this table covers individuals not in receipt of disability benefits from social security as of 1991, and with nonzero earnings at some point in their careers.[4] One summary measure indicates how many years a respondent's record showed zero covered earnings by decade of age from age 20–29, 30–39, . . . to age 80–89 (see variables 44–50 in Appendix B). Only the years 1951 through 1991, inclusive, are used in this computation. If the respondent's current age was part way through a decade at the time of the HRS survey, only the relevant years "at risk" are included in the count. Thus, for instance, a 52-year-old respondent would have a value of at most 3 years in the column pertaining to the number of years with zero covered earnings from age 50 to 59.

Descriptive statistics on this variable by sex and marital status appear in Table 1 for respondents who had had some positive covered earnings over their lifetimes.[5] Here we see that men with at least some nonzero earnings in the HRS cohort devoted 80–90 percent of their potential work years to covered employment, whereas women with nonzero earnings devoted about half the time to covered jobs during their twenties and thirties, with the fraction rising to 60–80 percent thereafter. The fraction of time spent in covered employment varies with marital status: more married than nonmarried men were in covered employment all their lives, whereas more nonmarried than married women were in covered jobs. Specifically, among married men, only 10–15 percent of the prime-age years (20–59) were spent without earnings, while for married women the fraction of zero-earnings years topped 50 percent during the childrearing years. Nonmarried women have lower numbers of zero years, but their fractions still stand at 40 percent during the childrearing period (these women were not married in 1992 but some had been married previously).

Another way to measure respondents' length of time working under the social security system measures total quarters of coverage (QCs), or the number of quarters an individual worked in jobs covered by social security rules. Specific numbers of quarters of coverage (QCs) are needed for establishing eligibility for social security benefits; persons reaching age 62 after 1990, for instance, must have 40 quarters of coverage to be insured for social security retirement benefits. Historically, QCs referred to earnings in a calendar quarter, but more recently one quarter of coverage has been credited for a specified amount of earnings. For example, in 1992, a worker was entitled to a quarter of coverage for each $570 in earnings in covered employment, up to 4 per year; that figure is indexed over time (SSA 1992, Table 2.A.7). For the SEPB datafile, quarters of coverage requirements in the past were computed by the ANYPIA software program. This is a computer program prepared by the Office of the Actuary, Social Security Administration, that incorporates current as well as historical social security rules relevant to HRS respondents (Office of the Actuary 1995).

The SEPBF reports total quarters of coverage for each individual, as well as quarters of coverage over each two-year period from 1982 through 1991. Table 1 summarizes the total number of quarters reported in covered em-

TABLE 1: Covered Employment Measures in the Summary Earnings and Projected Benefits File

	Mean	Std. Dev
Fraction of years with zero reported earnings by decade (%)		
Married men		
20–29	15.43	24.80
30–39	10.16	24.84
40–49	12.44	27.63
50–59	12.06	25.66
Married women		
20–29	52.44	33.12
30–39	52.96	37.61
40–49	39.42	39.85
50–59	28.68	34.60
Nonnmarried men		
20–29	15.62	24.99
30–39	13.91	27.58
40–49	20.88	33.14
50–59	20.53	32.14
Nonmarried women		
20–29	47.67	34.71
30–39	39.95	37.41
40–49	29.30	37.39
50–59	20.33	31.29
Covered employment: quarters of coverage (QC) and total years		
Married men		
Total QC's (#)	125.00	34.90
QC 1982–83(#)	7.40	2.73
QC 1984–85(#)	6.90	2.78
QC 1986–87(#)	6.71	2.78
QC 1988–89(#)	6.69	2.79
QC 1990–91(#)	6.60	32.85
Yrs. cov. employment, 20–50	26.20	6.37
Married women		
Total QC's (#)	71.65	41.88
QC 1982–83(#)	4.50	3.78
QC 1984–85(#)	4.62	3.71
QC 1986–87(#)	4.78	3.70
QC 1988–89(#)	4.81	3.70
QC 1990–91(#)	4.72	3.73
Yrs. cov. employment, 20–50	15.52	8.48
Nonmarried men		
Total QC's (#)	114.71	38.42
QC 1982–83(#)	5.83	3.32
QC 1984–85(#)	5.90	3.36
QC 1986–87(#)	5.90	3.29
QC 1988–89(#)	5.79	3.37
QC 1990–91(#)	5.75	3.38
Yrs. cov. employment, 20–50	24.96	6.95

TABLE 1: *Continued*

	Mean	*Std. Dev*
Nonmarried women		
Total QC's (#)	85.11	44.43
QC 1982–83(#)	5.40	3.55
QC 1984–85(#)	5.48	3.49
QC 1986–87(#)	5.64	3.46
QC 1988–89(#)	5.76	3.38
QC 1990–91(#)	5.74	3.41
Yrs. cov. employment, 20–50	18.31	8.67
Disability insured as of 12/91 (%)		
Married men	84	
Married women	59	
Nonmarried men	75	
Nonmarried women	72	

Source: Authors' calculations.
Notes: Number of observations reported as Sample 2 in Appendix Table 3. All tabulations weighted by HRS sample weights.

ployment; the number of covered quarters by two-year pairs between 1982–1991, and our computation of the total number of years in covered employment between the ages of 20 and 50. As before, these employment variables indicate that married men had the highest numbers of years in covered employment between age 20 and 50 (26 years) as well as total quarters in covered employment (125) compared to nonmarried men (25 years, 115 quarters) as well as married and nonmarried women (16 years, 72 quarters; 18 years and 85 quarters respectively). Both men and women averaged 5–7 quarters of coverage within the last several pairs of years leading up to the HRS survey.

Also included in the SEPBF is an indicator of each respondent's eligibility status for the Social Security Disability Insurance program as of year-end 1991. Most married men (84 percent) and nonmarried men (75 percent) were eligible for SSDI based on their own work record, whereas fewer married women (59 percent) and nonmarried women (72 percent) were eligible. As is clarified below, any HRS respondents in receipt of disability insurance payments at the time of the survey have no social security retirement benefits computed in the EPBF (but their earnings and employment are shown).[6] Individuals receiving DI benefits are therefore excluded from computations in Table 1.[7]

Computation of Summary Earnings Data

As described above, QCs measure the work attachment requirement for social security insured status. Once eligible, retiree benefit amounts are based on the respondent's average long-term covered earnings. Specifically, the number of years in the averaging period equals the number of full calendar years after 1950 (or, if later, after age 21) and up to the year in which the worker attains age 62, becomes disabled, or dies—generally minus 5 "dropout" years. For most HRS respondents, the result is 35 years. For the SEPBF, the Average Indexed Monthly Earnings (AIME) amount was computed using the ANYPIA program (Office of the Actuary 1995).

To compute the respondent's current AIME (that is, based on earnings through 1991), the algorithm used covered earnings from 1951 to 1991, recorded up to the taxable maximum earnings ceiling in the administrative records file supplied by the Social Security Administration.[8] The ANYPIA program then indexes earnings up to age 60 by economy-wide average wage increases; for example, earnings in 1951 were inflated by a factor of almost 9 to convert them to 1992 dollars. Subsequently the respondent's highest indexed earnings are averaged after eliminating the requisite number of dropout years (see below for a more detailed discussion). This computation yields the respondent's current AIME amount, in $1992. Zero earnings years—including imputed future zeros—are included as necessary in the AIME calculation.[9]

Two other AIME measures were also created (but not retained in the EPBF), namely the AIME that the respondent would have had at the early, and also at the normal, retirement age. Because some HRS respondents (and their spouses) were not old enough to be eligible to receive social security retirement benefits in 1992, it was necessary to project earnings forward in order to determine what these potential AIME amounts might be if they did work to the social security entitlement ages. Each nondisabled respondent's earnings were therefore projected to age 62, which is the earliest age he or she could file for retired worker benefits under social security rules, and also to that respondent's normal retirement age. This normal retirement age is age 65 for older members of the sample, but has been raised to age 67 for those born in 1960 or later, with gradual increases for ages in between. We projected earnings for each person using a weighted average of his or her own earnings over the past five years, corrected for inflation. (Further details appear in Appendix A.)

These earnings calculations may be summarized in several ways. Table 2 describes respondents' average annual real taxable earnings by decade of life, computed beginning at age 20–29, and running to age 50–59. For each decade of age, average earnings are computed only to the social security taxable maximum, and only over the years in which the individual had nonzero earnings. Table 2 indicates that average annual taxable earnings while age 50–59 stood at approximately $27,700 for married men, with nonmarried men averaging about $20,500, nonmarried women about $14,700, and married women about $10,600.[10]

TABLE 2: Earnings Measures in the Summary Earnings and Projected Benefits File

	Mean	Std. Dev
I. Average annual real taxable earnings by decade of life ($)		
Married men		
20–29	14544	5974
30–39	23929	9280
40–49	28823	14095
50–59	27692	18084
Married women		
20–29	6566	5412
30–39	7407	7625
40–49	10484	10145
50–59	10578	12170
Nonmarried men		
20–29	12551	6334
30–39	20538	10282
40–49	22070	14755
50–59	20476	17869
Nonmarried women		
20–29	6450	5556
30–39	9613	8532
40–49	13511	11491
50–59	14692	13639
II. Average indexed monthly earnings ($)		
Married men	1992	858
Married women	641	585
Nonmarried men	1567	895
Nonmarried women	838	703

Source: Authors' calculations.
Notes: Number of observations reported as Sample 2 in Appendix Table 3. In Panel I earnings are included only up to the Social Security taxable maximum earnings and averages computed only over those with at least one nonzero earnings year using years over which there were postive earnings. For the group age 50–59, average earnings are computed only over relevant years. In Panel II zero years of earnings are included in AIME formula as relevant; see text.

Table 2 also replicates the computation representing respondents' current AIME amounts, which as noted earlier include zero earnings years as necessary in the calculation. Married men's AIME averages $1,990, with nonmarried men close behind at about $1,570; married women's lower earnings and fewer years of covered employment no doubt contributed to the lower average AIME of about $640, while nonmarried women are higher at about $840. Additional information is also provided in the EPBF file regarding the twenty lowest earnings years in the AIME average, arranged in ascending order. These variables are included primarily to allow analysts to update the AIME using survey-reported earnings for 1992 and later. In addition, analysts wishing to compute alternative AIME figures may use these lowest earnings years to recompute AIME values for other retirement dates (Office of the Actuary 1995; Myers 1993).

Social Security Benefit Measures

Social security wealth variables are available in the SEPBF for respondents where the AIME could be computed and who were not currently receiving Social Security Disability Insurance (SSDI).[11] This was accomplished using the ANYPIA algorithm described above, which combines the respondent's AIME with the relevant formula to obtain that person's primary insurance amount, or PIA. The PIA is the monthly amount payable to a retired worker who begins to receive benefits at the normal retirement age (currently, age 65) or to a disabled worker who has never received a retirement benefit reduced for age. The 1992 formula is as follows (the "bend points" are indexed over time):

$$\text{PIA} = 90\% \text{ of AIME up to } \$387$$
$$\text{plus } 32\% \text{ of excess up to } \$2333$$
$$\text{plus } 15\% \text{ of any excess above that.}$$

If a respondent was not eligible to receive social security benefits based on quarters of coverage through December 1991, the PIA and all social security wealth variables were set to zero (along with the spouse benefits if there was no spouse). Spouse benefits were also set to zero if the respondent had no covered earnings, and in addition the spouse was also ineligible for benefits due to an insufficient earnings record.

Having computed the respondent's PIA, we then derived the social security benefits he or she and his or her spouse (if any) could receive at the retirement ages under consideration. The rules for benefit determination specify that the PIA is the retirement benefit at the normal retirement age. Workers can also receive early retirement benefits (assuming eligibility) at age 62; under the law, early retirees receive a benefit equal to the PIA reduced by 5/9 of 1 percent or 1/180 per month of entitlement before age 65. The normal retirement benefit computations take into account the fact that the full PIA has been payable at age 65 but the normal retirement age will be gradually moved up in the future.

In addition to computing the retired worker benefits, we also derived spouse benefits if the HRS respondent had a spouse and if sufficient data were available with which to compute these. Each member of a married couple is entitled to receive social security benefits based on his or her own earnings record, and based on the spouse's earnings record if such benefits would be higher. (Spouse benefits are generally equal to 50 percent of the worker's PIA.) Specifically, dual entitlement arises if the woman's (man's) benefit computed on her (his) own earnings record is lower than that computed as a spouse. In this instance, at retirement she (he) will be dually entitled with a benefit reflecting her (his) own entitlement, plus an additional amount taking her (him) to the level she (he) is entitled to as a spouse.

To illustrate this point, suppose that a woman is married to a man who is eligible for retired worker benefits from social security based on his own work record. The wife in this case can receive 50 percent of his PIA as a spouse benefit if she were age 65 at retirement; if she were 62–64, her spouse benefit would be reduced by a monthly amount which comes to 8⅓ percent per year she was under age 65. For the EPBF complete computation, we also compute the benefits she would be entitled to based on her own work history. The computer algorithm inquires which calculation is higher, and associates with the wife the higher of the two benefit amounts. Users of the EPBF file should note that the constructed spouse variables do not distinguish between respondents projected to receive only spouse benefits, and those projected to be dually entitled.[12]

For currently married persons, the ANYPIA code was also used to project survivor benefits under social security rules. If an eligible worker dies, the surviving widow/er can receive up to 100 percent of the deceased worker's PIA; such benefits, reduced for early retirement, can begin as early as age 60. Remarriage after age 60 does not result in the loss of benefits.

For nonmarried persons, eligibility for survivor or other auxiliary benefits could not be determined. In the social security program, persons who were divorced after 10 or more years of marriage are entitled to divorced spouse or survivor benefits. Widow(er)s are entitled to survivor benefits. Persons who are separated but not formally divorced are generally considered to be married in the program. But because the HRS did not obtain social security numbers from surviving divorced former spouses in the HRS, it was not possible to compute spouse benefits to which HRS divorced or separated individuals might be entitled. Users of this database should therefore be alert to the possibility that social security benefits derived for divorced or separated persons will be understated. Likewise benefits computed for persons widowed at the time of the survey recognize only prospective payments based on their own record as workers, since we cannot compute widow/er benefits to which an HRS widowed individual might be entitled. Evidence suggests the results will underestimate social security benefits and wealth of many widows and divorced women.[13]

Having computed these various social security benefit amounts, the question arises as to the best way to summarize their value to the retiree. In the EPBF file we have adopted the concept of social security wealth for this purpose, which simply refers to the present value of the social security benefit payable in the form of an annuity from retirement until death. Benefit values after retirement are multiplied by survival probabilities from that age forward, and discounted to 1992 by multiplying by the conditional probability of being alive at that retirement age, given that he or she is alive at his current age in 1992.

The social security wealth computation is straightforward for the case of a nonmarried respondent leaving the workforce at age 62. Mathematically, we simply sum annual benefit amounts payable from age 62 on, multiplied by the survival probability at each age, and divide by an appropriate discount rate. Age-specific mortality rates by birth cohort were supplied by the Office of the Actuary at the Social Security Administration; for the discount rate we use the interest rate profile consistent with the intermediate set of assumptions chosen by the Social Security Trustees (Board of Trustees 1995). A similar wealth value can be computed assuming the worker retires at the normal retirement age, by using the AIME and PIA computed as of that age.

Computing social security wealth for married respondents is somewhat more complex, since the system pays different benefit amounts depending on the couple's mortality experience. As long as both members of a couple survive, retired worker and/or spouse benefits can be paid. However, when one of the members of the couple dies, the other may receive a survivor benefit if it exceeds the survivor's own retired-worker benefit.[14] Hence the derivation of social security wealth here requires that the present value computation incorporate retiree, along with possibly spouse and survivor benefits, weighted by the probability of the different outcomes obtaining. Here too, the interest rate profile used is the one consistent with the intermediate set of assumptions chosen by the Social Security Trustees.

An overview of the resulting social security wealth variables is provided in Table 3. Here we report descriptive statistics on each respondent's Primary Insurance Amount, computed in 1992 when the HRS was first fielded, based on the respondent's earnings to date, and also two projected PIA amounts using earnings projected to the early retirement age and to the normal retirement age (variables 6–8). For married men, the PIA based on earnings to 1992 totaled approximately $800, rising to $882 with earnings to the normal retirement age; levels for unmarried men were, respectively, about $680 and $750. Women's PIAs are lower, rising to $420 and $520 at the normal retirement age for married and nonmarried women respectively.

We also computed three total social security wealth variables. One reflects HRS respondents' entitlements as of 1992 ("current"), filling in future years of earnings to age 62 with zeros. The other two social security wealth values are based on the benefits receivable if the respondent continued to work until the early retirement age, and also if he or she worked until the normal retirement age. These values are given as social security wealth variables in the second panel of Table 3. These present values amount to about $170,000–180,000 for married men and women working until their normal retirement age, much more than double the values for unmarried men and women. The fact that married persons' social security wealth is larger reflects the fact that social security retirement benefits are payable to both members of an eligible couple, as well as survivor benefits if one of the members of the couple should die. By contrast, because of data limitations, the social security wealth computation for a nonmarried individual does not include any survivor or divorced spouse benefit, though as noted above, perhaps as many as three-quarters of the widows may receive a survivor benefit over their lifetimes.

A clearer idea of the separate computations that are incorporated into a married couple's security wealth figure is also available from Table 3. For different retirement ages, we report the expected present value of social security retirement benefits that an eligible respondent and spouse can collect based on his/her own earnings records, the spouse's earnings records (if any), and as a survivor based on his/her partner's earnings record (if applicable). Thus for example, the wealth value for married men's "respondent" benefits as of the normal retirement age totaled approximately $89,000, with the spouse's benefit on her own account totaling $28,000; the figures are roughly reversed when the married women are the unit of analysis.[15]

These social security wealth variables will be reasonable representations of the expected future value of benefit payments in most cases, but the reader should recall that our projections may be low for separated, divorced, and widowed older persons, as discussed above. Another important factor to be alert to is the point that estimated benefits and social security wealth are also likely to be low for those respondents having had social security disability benefits in their past. This is because during such periods, SSA protects against the loss of or the reduction in the amount of retirement insurance benefits, by providing that the period during which the person is disabled will generally be excluded from determining either retirement benefits or social security wealth.[16]

As a final note, researchers should note that some respondents were already receiving social security retirement benefits when the HRS was launched. Data derived from social security benefit records for those respondents were not used in computing the AIME, PIA, and wealth variables described here. Nor have the projected benefit amounts discussed here been compared directly with those obtained from social security benefit records. These tasks remain for future research.

Conclusion

Researchers exploring older Americans' preparedness for retirement require information on earnings, labor market attachment, and social security benefits. To better understand the factors affecting both the retirement decision and wellbeing in old age, we have linked administrative records on earnings and benefits from Social Security Administration data with respondent files in the HRS. Other analysts will find the summary measures con-

TABLE 3: Social Security Measures in the Summary Earnings and Projected Benefits File

	Mean	Std. Dev
Respondent's average primary insurance amount (1992$)		
Married men based on		
Earnings through 1991	808	277
Earnings to early ret. age	866	295
Earnings to normal ret. age	882	304
Married women based on		
Earnings through 1991	337	268
Earnings to early ret. age	396	298
Earnings to normal ret. age	423	316
Nonmarried men based on		
Earnings through 1991	677	306
Earnings to early ret. age	732	335
Earnings to normal ret. age	754	347
Nonmarried women based on		
Earnings through 1991	419	291
Earnings to early ret. age	487	320
Earnings to normal ret. age	518	337
Social security wealth (present value, 1992$)		
Married men (couple's benefits)		
As of 1992	148198	47263
As of early ret. age	161641	47559
As of normal ret. age	175457	50818
Married women (couple's benefits)		
As of 1992	161780	51001
As of early ret. age	170994	50003
As of normal ret. age	187650	55284
Nonmarried men*		
Current	67777	31436
As of early ret. age	72942	33383
As of normal ret. age	75761	34643
Nonmarried women*		
As of 1992	50678	35826
As of early ret. age	58474	38265
As of normal ret. age	64644	41749
Components of social security wealth for married men (present value, 1992$)		
Based on earnings through 1991		
Respondent's own	80804	30351
Respondent's spouse	486	3268
Respondent's surv. sps.	902	3197
Spouse's own	19258	26207
Spouse's spouse	14709	15776
Spouse's surv. sps.	32039	14602

TABLE 3: *Continued*

	Mean	*Std. Dev*
Earnings to early retirement age		
Respondent's own	85832	31275
Respondent's spouse	646	3897
Respondent's surv. sps.	1383	3936
Spouse's own	26507	31511
Spouse's spouse	14197	16696
Spouse's surv. sps.	33077	16435
Earnings to normal retirement age		
Respondent's own	88808	32346
Respondent's spouse	729	4242
Respondent's surv. sps.	1852	5144
Spouse's own	27854	34906
Spouse's spouse	14923	17419
Spouse's surv. sps.	41291	21566
Components of social security wealth for married women		
Earnings through 1991		
Respondent's own	22535	28754
Respondent's spouse	16344	16803
Respondent's surv. sps.	34719	17723
Spouse's own	86565	33902
Spouse's spouse	682	3896
Spouse's surv. sps.	936	3033
Earnings to early retirement age		
Respondent's own	27373	32588
Respondent's spouse	15941	17513
Respondent's surv. sps.	35757	18372
Spouse's own	89923	33693
Spouse's spouse	778	4311
Spouse's surv. sps.	1220	3626
Earnings to normal retirement age		
Respondent's own	28613	35933
Respondent's spouse	16931	18194
Respondent's surv. sps.	43451	22374
Spouse's own	96150	37963
Spouse's spouse	785	4276
Spouse's surv. sps.	1721	4914

Source: See Table 1.

Notes: Number of observations reported as Sample 3 in Appendix Table 3.

* Wealth values for nonmarried persons are based on respondent's own earnings records, and underestimate benefits available as survivors (for widows/ers) and divorced spouses (if the marriage lasted 10 years prior to divorce); see text.

tained in the Summary Earnings and Projected Benefits File to be of substantial use in measuring old-age wealth, models of retirement and health, and for policy analysis. While an average user may use these created variables as they appear in the file (subject to restricted access conditions), more sophisticated analysts will be able to devise their own algorithms to derive alternate outcomes.

The authors gratefully acknowledge the helpful assistance and comments of Benjamin Bridges, Tim Cheney, Gary Fields, David Howell, Mike Leonesio, and Larry Smith, and research support from Texas Tech, the Wharton School, and the University of Michigan. Programming assistance was furnished under a National Institute on Aging Grant to the University of Michigan's Institute for Survey Research. Opinions are solely those of the authors and do not represent the views of the institutions with which they are affiliated.

Appendix A: Algorithms and Assumptions Used in the Creating the SEPBF

This Appendix is intended to provide additional technical details on how the EPBF dataset was constructed. An idea of the SEPBF layout may help the general reader understand the nature of variables created, in concert with the detailed variable list supplied in Appendix B. Briefly, the SEPBF contains one record for each individual in the HRS from whom a valid permission form was obtained, and who had nonzero earnings at some point in his/her career. Each person in the file is identified by a case ID that matches the same variable in the HRS records and is the variable for linking these records to the HRS data set.[17] For individuals who were married at the time of the HRS interview, there is also a spouse ID, which is the HRS case ID of the record of the spouse. This variable has a value of 0 if there is no spouse, and a value of 99999 if there was a spouse but the spouse does not have a record in the main HRS data set.[18] In addition to the case ID variables noted above, the other variables in the record are grouped into three categories and discussed in turn. These three sets of variables are (1) labor market attachment variables, (2) earnings aggregates, and (3) measures of family social security wealth.

Labor Market Attachment Variables

The SEPB dataset contains three groups of variables measuring labor market attachment. As shown in Appendix B, variables 44 to 50 indicate the number of years by age decade that the individual reported zero earnings. These decades are the same decades used in calculating the average earnings by decade, and the same limitations apply. Specifically, only the years between 1951 and 1991, inclusive, are included. This means, for example, that an individual who is 56 years old in 1992 and who had four years of nonzero earnings and two years of zero earnings in the 1986–1991 time period will have a value of two assigned to variable 47. (Data in Table 1 correct for the fact that the number of potential years of work in some age intervals varies by respondent age.)

A second variable indicates the respondent's total quarters of coverage (or credits) as of year-end 1991. This is needed to establish whether the individual is presently insured under the old-age retirement program, or whether he or she may become insured on the basis of future work. The respondent's total quarters of coverage at the end of 1991 appear in variable 30. For workers attaining age 62 in 1991 or later, 40 quarters of coverage are required to be eligible for old age benefits when they retire. Researchers can update the total quarters of coverage after 1991 using the work status and earnings figures available in the HRS surveys in 1992 and later. An individual received one quarter of coverage up to a maximum of four quarters per year for each $570 of earnings in 1992. This $570 amount is adjusted annually according to the average annual earnings index.

A third group of variables is useful for establishing whether the individual is currently insured under the disability insurance program. Whether the individual was currently insured at the end of 1991 is given by variable 31. In most cases, the individual is required to be fully insured and have 20 quarters of coverage or credits) in the previous 10 years (40 quarters or credits) to be disability insured. Variables 32–36 can be used to update the disability insurance status at two-year intervals for the following ten years, again using work status and earnings figures from the household HRS surveys in 1992 and later. For example, if an individual had 3 quarters of coverage in 1982–1983 and 18 quarters of coverage in the period 1982–1991, and if the household survey indicates that the individual had 8 quarters of coverage in 1992 and 1993, then we can infer that the individual had 23 quarters during 1984–1993 (18 plus 8 minus 3), making him or her disability insured at the end of 1993.

A final entry in the labor market variable group indicates whether the individual was receiving social security disability insurance benefits as of December 1991. This is variable 4, taking a value of 1 if the individual was receiving disability benefits as of December 1991 and a value of 0 if he or she was not on disability at that time. Unlike most of the other variables in this file, this variable comes not from the summary earnings record but from the benefits record. If the individual was collecting social security disability as of December 1991, all variables described in the next two sections (average monthly earnings, primary insurance amount, social security wealth, etc.) are set to -9. This is because the algorithms that are used to calculate these variables for the dataset are appropriate only for old-age benefits for persons without prior entitlement to disability benefits. Spouses of workers receiving social security disability insurance benefits are included if they are age-eligible respondents in their own right.

Earnings Summary Variables

Variables 37 to 43 in the SEPB file provide the average real taxable earnings by decade of life. These decades are age decades, not calendar decades, and run from ages 20–29 to ages 80–89. For each decade, the average is calculated using only the years in which the individual had positive earnings; years in which there were no earnings are excluded from the average. Further, these are real earnings, which means that each annual earnings amount is indexed to 1992 using the consumer price index (CPI-U). The indexing is done prior to averaging. The user is reminded that no annual earnings are available in the social security records before 1951 or after 1991. Further, only taxable earnings up to the maximum amount subject to social security taxes are available in these records, and zeros appear in the record for respondents too young to have worked the full decade.

Projected Social Security Retirement Benefit Variables

Social security benefits for HRS respondents are calculated in three stages. First, the Average Monthly Indexed Earnings (AIME) amount is calculated for everyone, using the number of years of earnings as specified in the social security law. If a respondent does not have enough positive years of earnings, zeros are filled in for the remaining years. Next, the Primary Insurance Amount (PIA) is calculated from average monthly earnings using a formula that depends on when the individual turns age 62. Finally, an adjustment factor reflecting early or late retirement is applied to the PIA to determine the benefit amount, as required.

Variable 5 in Appendix B lists the calculated AIME amount based on earnings through 1991, rounded to the nearest $10; for this computation zeros are filled in for years between 1991 and the year the respondent turns age 62. This AIME figure is calculated by a program created by the Social Security Administration called ANYPIA, that incorporates the many changes that Congress has made in social security law over the years (Office of the Actuary 1995).

For the AIME computation, earnings before the age of 60 are indexed upward to age 60 by a factor calculated from SSA's average annual wage series. Earnings after age 60 enter the average on an unindexed basis. In general, for persons without current or prior disability, the number of computation years equals the years after 1950 (or age 21 if later) to age 62, excluding 5 "dropout" years. For HRS respondents who turned 60 in 1992 and before, earnings before age 60 are indexed according to the average annual wage series, and the high 35 years are averaged. For respondents who turn 60 after 1992, the indexing amount was not known in 1992. For these individuals, earnings are indexed to 1992, and the high 35 years are averaged (including zero earnings years, if any).[19]

The SEPBF also contains the variables necessary to update the AIME amount based on earnings in 1992 and subsequent years as reported in the household surveys, at least for those individuals who attained age 62 in 1979 and after, and are thus governed by the indexed earnings formula (SSA, Table 2.A8). Variables 51 to 70 contain the lowest 20 years of earnings in the AIME computation, arranged from the lowest year and in ascending order. The amounts reported are indexed (and not nominal) amounts, meaning that they are indexed to age 60 if the earnings were before age 60 and the individual had reached 60 by 1992, or if the individual was under age 60 in 1992, they are indexed to 1992. The indexing rules are the same as those that are applied in computing the average indexed monthly earnings figure itself. Note that these variables may contain a number of zero amounts, which signifies that the individual thus far had positive earnings for fewer than the number of computation years. Also, this entire set of 20 variables is set equal to zero if the individual reached age 62 before 1979, in which case the monthly earnings were figured using unindexed earnings rather than indexed earnings.

To illustrate the updating process, suppose that we obtain a 1992 earnings figure from the household survey, and we want to see how this affects the AIME. First, the earnings amount is indexed to age 60 or 1992, as appropriate. Then the indexed amount is compared to the low year in the average (the figure in variable 51). If the new amount is less, then the 1992 earnings do not affect the AIME. If it is greater, then the difference, divided by 35 (or the number of computation years), is added to the AIME (variable 5). This is equivalent to substituting the 1992 figure for the low indexed amount in the average. For additional years of earnings after 1992, the process is repeated. The fact that the 20 lowest indexed earnings years are reported implies that, based on future observed earnings in the household survey, the AIME figure can be updated at least through the year 2011.

Next come estimated primary insurance amounts (PIA), reported in variables 6–8. The PIA in variable 6 is based on earnings though 1991 and the AIME reported in variable 5. If the individual was 62 or older in 1991, the amount in variable 7 is the same as in variable 6. Otherwise, the PIA in variable 7 is based on projected earnings through age 61, with the projection method discussed later in this section. Variable 8 is similar to variable 7, except that earnings are projected through the year immediately before the normal retirement age. In calculating variable 8, it is assumed that the individual applies for benefits at the normal retirement age.

The PIA calculation is done by the ANYPIA program. The formula applied to the AIME figure is determined by the year the individual attains 62.[20] Those individuals who turn age 62 in or after 1978 have their PIA calculated using an AIME that depends on the year they turn 62 (variable 5). For instance, the formula for individuals who turn 62 in 1986 is 90 percent of the first $297 of average indexed monthly earnings, 32 percent of the next $1493, and 15 percent of anything beyond that. These "bend points" are indexed to the national average annual wage level, but there are always just three segments in the formula. As before, this formula gives the primary insurance amount for the year the individual turns 62, and the resulting amount is indexed upward every year by the cost of living index.

For individuals who attain 62 in or before 1992, the bend points are known (e.g. SSA 1995, Table 2.A.11), and the PIA indexed to 1992 is reported in variable 6. For individuals who attain 62 after 1992, the AIME is indexed to age 60 (if necessary) and the bend points are indexed to age 62, both using the increases in the national average annual wage index projected by the Social Security Administration. The PIA is calculated using the projected formula applied to the projected average indexed earnings, giving a PIA value that would apply to the year the individual turned 62. The resulting amount is then deflated to 1992 using the projected increases in the consumer price index. This gives the value of the primary insurance amount in 1992 dollars and is thus comparable to the amounts calculated for individuals who reach 62 in or before 1992. The assumptions used to forecast the national average annual wage and the consumer price index are the "intermediate" assumptions offered by the Office of the Actuary of the Social Security Administration and are reported in Appendix Table 1.[21]

As mentioned before, the primary insurance amount in variable 6 is calculated solely on the basis of the earnings in years up to and including 1991 (with zeros filled in to age 62 as necessary). The amounts in variables 7 and 8 project future earnings up to the year before the retirement age (early for variable 7 and normal for variable 8) in cases where the individual was under that age in 1991. The method of projecting these future earnings adopted for the present purposes is to compute for each HRS respondent a weighted average of his or her own recent earnings and to project these earnings into future years.

More specifically, earnings in the five-year period 1987–1991 are indexed to 1991 levels using the National Average Wage Index of the Social Security Administration. The indexed wages are then averaged, with the 1987 through 1991 single-year earnings given weights of 1, 2, 3, 4, and 5, respectively. This procedure thus places more weight on more recent earnings. This weighted average is then indexed upward to each year up to and including the year before the individual reaches the early (for variable 7) or normal (for variable 8) retirement age, using the National Average Wage Index found in Appendix Table 1. The resulting wage series is then used to calculate a primary insurance amount in exactly the same way as before, and the resulting values appear as variables 7 and 8.

APPENDIX TABLE 1: Economic Assumptions, Trustees' Report

Year	% Change in Ave. Annual Covered Pay	% Change in CPI	Ave. Annual Interest Rate (%)
1993	1.3	2.8	6.1
1994	3.5	2.5	7.1
1995	4	3.1	7.7
1996	4.1	3.2	7.6
1997	4.3	3.3	7.6
1998	4.1	3.4	7.4
1999	4.2	3.5	7.2
2000	4.5	3.7	7.1
2001	4.7	3.9	7
2002	4.8	4	6.9
2003	4.9	4	6.7
2004–9	5.1	4	6.5
2010	5.1	4	6.3
2020+	5	4	6.3

Source: Board of Trustees (1995), Table II.D1.

This procedure gives reasonable results for individuals with a steady work history who are planning to work at least until age 62. However, data users must be alert to the fact that there are several cases where it may not give good results. For instance, if a woman has an intermittent work history, her earnings in the last five years may give only a very noisy indication as to her work intentions for the future years. In such a case, it is probably difficult to produce an algorithm which will give accurate projections of the course of her future earnings. Another case where the algorithm is susceptible to error is if the individual has retired within the last year or two. The trouble here is that it is difficult to know whether the fact that there are no earnings in the last year or two signifies a permanent retirement or a temporary interruption of employment. Thus, users are cautioned that, particularly for respondents with intermittent work histories and individuals who may have recently retired, the projected primary insurance amount and the projected social security wealth variables should be regarded as being subject to substantial potential errors.

Computed Social Security Wealth Variables

As described above, we have computed social security wealth several different ways for the SEPB dataset. Our intention was to make these variables as comparable as possible, in conceptual terms, to the other measures of wealth reported in the HRS. Three versions of social security wealth appear in the SEPBF. The first (variable 9 in Appendix B) is the expected present value of benefits already accrued by the respondent, based on his covered earnings up to and including 1991. (This computation assumes the person would have no covered earnings between 1992 and the year he turns age 62; a zero is entered if the person would not be eligible for benefits based on this work record). The second and third wealth variables (positions 16 and 23) represent the expected present value of benefits based on a respondent's projected earnings if he/she was younger than age 62 at the time of the survey, up to the year before attaining the early or normal retirement age. These projections, described in the previous section, are carried out for all individuals and for both spouses of a married couple (with caveats to be explained below). In the case of a married couple, if one spouse was at or over the retirement age and the other was under it, the projection is done only for the spouse who was under the retirement age, and the full earnings through 1991 are used for the older spouse.

Social security wealth calculations depend on a number of assumptions. One set of assumptions has to do with mortality, since the calculation multiplies the expected benefit for each year times the probability that the individual will live to collect it. In the next section we discuss the specific mortality tables used in creating the SEPB file. In all cases, social security wealth calculations are discounted back to the respondent's age in 1992, taking into account the conditional survival probability of the person living to that future age, given his/her current age. Another set of assumptions has to do with the expected future paths of wages, prices, and interest rates. Needless to say, there are differing opinions of the likely future course of these variables, but we have chosen to evaluate the social security wealth on the basis of the "intermediate" assumptions supplied by the Board of Trustees of the Federal Old-Age and Survivors Insurance and Disability Insurance Trust Funds (Board of Trustees 1995, p. 56).[22]

The wealth calculations were handled as follows. For each nonmarried respondent, we consider each year beginning with the year 1992. For each member of a married couple, benefits are computed for each spouse separately; here we consider each year beginning with either age 60 (which is the youngest age a married individual could collect surviving spouse benefits) or the year 1992, whichever is later. For married persons, two calculations are undertaken, depending on whether the spouse is or is not projected to be still living; we weight each calculation by the probabilities (as calculated from the mortality tables) that the individual is still living and the spouse is either living or not, respectively. For every year in which the spouse is still living, the approach was to first ask whether that spouse is age 62 or older. If he or she was under 62 years old, that individual may only receive benefits based on his or her own earnings record. If the spouse is 62 years old or older, then we compared the benefits the retiring individual could receive on the basis of his or her own earnings with the amount that he or she could receive as a spouse based on the spouse's earnings. The individual would then be assigned the higher benefit amount.[23]

To determine the benefits that would be available on the basis of a respondent's own earnings history, the PIA in nominal dollars is calculated by the ANYPIA program on the basis of the earnings history. For persons older than the retirement age in 1992, we assume that they became entitled (that is, they were eligible and applied to receive benefits) in the first year that at least some benefits would have been received, but in no case later than the normal retirement age that would apply to their birth cohort. For individuals younger than the retirement age, we assume that they will first become entitled at the early retirement age of 62 (for variables 9 and 16), and at the normal retirement age (for variable 23), assuming they have sufficient quarters of coverage to be entitled to receive benefits.[24] The benefit amount is then the product of the primary insurance amount times any reduction or augmentation factor that depends on the person's age of retirement.[25]

In addition to benefits to which a respondent might be entitled on his or her own record, a married respondent might also be entitled to benefits as a spouse of a retired worker. Where possible, the SEPB file reports these spouse benefits, calculated based on the other partner's earnings record as of the previous year by the ANYPIA program for married couples.[26] The basic spouse benefit is 50 percent of the husband's (or wife's, as relevant) PIA. A reduction factor is then applied which is determined by when the individual would have first started collecting spouse benefits. The reduction factor, calculated monthly, totals 8.33 percentage points for each year before age 65 that the individual first collects spouse benefits; that is, the benefit is reduced by 25/36 of one percent multiplied by the number of months preceding age 65. This reduction factor is scheduled to be modified when the normal retirement age increases from its present level of 65. The spouse benefit is then 50 percent of the partner's PIA multiplied by the spouse reduction factor.[27] For married respondents, therefore, the EPBF reports a total benefit due the individual as *either* the benefit based on his/her own earnings record, or the spouse benefit based on the spouse's earnings record, whichever is higher. (As noted above, in dual entitlement cases, benefits are classified in the EPBF as spouse benefits or survivor benefits as relevant; increasing numbers of women are dually entitled over time).

If the worker is deceased, a widow/er may be eligible both for survivor benefits based on the earnings record of the deceased and for retired-worker benefits based on his or her own record. If the widow(er) is entitled to both, he or she is dually entitled and receives a full benefit based on his or her own record plus a partial benefit based on the deceased spouse's record. The amount of the partial benefit is the difference between the widow/er's own retired-worker benefit and the amount to which he or she is entitled as a widow/er. Because the benefit amount received in this case is equal to the higher, surviving spouse benefit, the variable is identified in Appendix B as the "surviving spouse benefit." The calculations based on the individual's own benefits are exactly the same as in the previous situation.

Unlike other social security retirement benefits, surviving spouse benefits may begin as early as age 60.[28] For the surviving spouse calculations (variables 12, 19, and 25), there is an additional problem: these benefits may depend on when the partner died. Hence, a separate calculation is made for each possible year of death between 1992 and the year immediately before the year for which the benefits are being calculated, and the weights on the calculated amounts are proportional to the partner's mortality probability in the successive years.

For each possible year in which the retired-worker partner could have died, the calculations require several steps. First, the worker's PIA is calculated based on his/her earnings record up to the year immediately prior to death. Note that if the age at death was younger than 62, these calculations differ from the regular old-age calculations because there are fewer years in the calculation of average indexed monthly earnings. Next, if the worker was eligible for any delayed retirement credits, these are added to the primary insurance amount. If the worker died before the spouse turned 65, the PIA is subject to a reduction of 5.7 percent (not 5.7 percentage points) for each year the spouse collects survivor benefits before age 65. Again, the calculation of this reduction is modified when the normal retirement age rises above its current value of 65. Finally, if the spouse had applied for benefits, the surviving spouse benefit would be subject to a limitation that it should not be any larger than the amount payable to the worker had he/she still been alive (as long as this restriction does not lower the benefit below 82.5 percent of the worker's primary insurance amount).

In overview, then, for every year that a member of a married couple could collect benefits, the person is modeled as receiving either (a) benefits based on his or her own earnings record or spouse benefits (conditional on the partner being alive), or (b) benefits based on his or her own earnings record or surviving spouse benefits (conditional on the partner being deceased). As noted, those modeled as dually entitled are shown as spouse or survivor beneficiaries. Data for the partner are computed similarly. Finally, the amounts are weighted by the probabilities that the two partners will be individually and/or jointly alive, and the amounts of the two partners are added. These calculations are carried out in nominal terms of the year the benefits are to be collected, and projected using the "intermediate" assumptions regarding wage growth and consumer price index growth.[29]

To form a wealth measure, future benefits are discounted according to the interest rate in the set of "intermediate" assumptions (Appendix Table 1), and the discounted amounts summed for all the years that either member of the couple might collect benefits. The wealth measure for unmarried individuals is similar, except that there is no partner, no spouse benefit, and no surviving spouse benefit. The wealth is simply the discounted value of the future benefits based on the individual's own earnings history. All values are reported as of the respondent's current age in 1992, discounted using conditional survival probabilities based on the respondent's current age.[30]

In the case of married couples, there are additional components for each of these social security wealth variables (variables 10–15, 17–22, and 24–29; these variables are set to zero for nonmarried respondents). One set of variables represents the expected present value of components of social security wealth that the respondent could collect, and others represent the expected present value of components that his or her spouse could collect. Each set of three is comprised of (a) benefits that the individual could collect on his/her own earnings record, (b) spouse benefits that the individual could collect on the basis of the partner's record, and (c) surviving spouse benefits that the individual could collect on the basis of the partner's record if that partner died.

For example, if the wife has a PIA substantially greater than twice her husband's, and if she is younger than her husband, then it is likely that variables 10, 13, 14, and 15 in her record would have positive amounts, and variables 11 and 12 would contain zeros. This is because she will collect benefits on her own account but never on her husband's account, while the husband will be dually entitled with the larger amounts received as spouse benefits and surviving spouse benefits rather than benefits based on his own account. However, since the older husband reaches retirement age before she does, he will collect benefits for a few years on his own account until she applies and he is able to collect spouse benefits. The same figures will appear on the husband's record, but the pairs of three variables will be reversed. That is, variables 10–12 will refer to benefits he is expected to collect, and variables 13–15 will refer to variables she is expected to collect.

These component quantities can be combined in different ways for different purposes. For example, if the interest is in an individual's lifetime retirement benefits, then the appropriate combination would be the sum of variables 10–12 (or alternatively variables 17–19 or 24–26). This will give the total expected value of the social security benefits that that individual is expected to collect. Alternatively, if a researcher were instead interested in retirement incentives, then variable 10 should be combined with variables 14 and 15 to give the total expected benefits based on the individual's own earnings history, assuming no change in spouse labor force behavior.[31]

The SEPBF data user should be aware that in a minority of cases the social security wealth variables computed for the SEPB file are subject to potentially severe measurement problems. The instances involve individuals who were single at the time of the HRS survey but who were separated or previously married. For such individuals, the social security wealth just described is necessarily based on their own earnings records in the SEPBF. However, if the individual is a widow or widower, his or her actual social security benefits might in reality be higher if they are computed based on the deceased spouse's record.[32] Alternatively, if the individual had been divorced from a marriage that lasted for 10 or more years, the individual might be eligible for benefits based on the former spouse's earnings record. Persons who are separated but not legally divorced are generally considered to be still married for purposes of the program. In none of these cases were the relevant records for former spouses obtained from the Social Security Administration. In fact, until someone files for benefits, the Social Security Administration does not necessarily know that any two people are linked.

A different measurement problem arises for persons married in 1992 who might divorce, in that spouse's benefits are only payable to married persons who had been married at least 10 years by the time of the divorce. Our computations for elements of social security wealth available to members of a couple assuming that they remain married at least 10 years.

Eventually, it will be possible to fine-tune these wealth measures for separated, divorced, and widowed individuals once they begin collecting benefits. For now, all that can be done is to calculate the wealth based on the respondent's own record and to note there may be understatement of benefits for widows or widowers, and for divorced people who previously were married for a decade or more.[33]

Mortality Data

Mortality statistics used in calculating wealth variables are taken from the Social Security Administration's actuarial projections.[34] These projections contain, among other things, the estimated probability of survival, by sex, for each year of age up to 120 and for each birth cohort from 1900 to 1980; this time span includes all cohorts of interest for purposes of the HRS.

Summary statistics from these mortality data, reported in Appendix Table 2, indicate very strong trends in increasing life expectancy over time. The most dramatic increases in life expectancy are those at birth, but a large part of this increase comes from reduced infant mortality, which is clearly not relevant for the HRS respondents. Even so, there are projected to be nontrivial increases in life expectancy at age 25 and, perhaps more importantly, at age 65, and it is clear that the percentage of individuals living to very old ages (age 85 or 100) is going to grow very rapidly in the coming years, given recent mortality trends.

The SEPBF user should be aware that these mortality statistics, and the social security wealth variables calculated from them, are population averages by sex and birth cohort. These mortality data are not available separately by race, and they also do not reflect any individual differences which might make individuals perceive their own mortality probabilities to be either higher or lower. Vital Statistics mortality probabilities are calculated separately by race, but they are not projected into the future, and they are available only to age 85. Given the increasing percentage of the population,

APPENDIX TABLE 2: Changes in Longevity over Time

	Birth Cohort								
	1900	1910	1920	1930	1940	1950	1960	1970	1980
Life expectancy									
At birth: men	52.0	56.7	62.3	66.6	69.7	72.3	73.4	74.8	76.2
women	58.8	64.4	70.2	73.9	76.8	79.4	80.4	81.7	82.9
At age 25: men	68.8	70.7	72.8	74.4	75.8	76.6	77.1	77.8	78.4
women	75.1	77.8	79.5	80.6	81.6	82.5	83.2	83.8	84.4
At age 65: men	79.0	79.8	80.8	81.4	81.9	82.3	82.8	83.2	83.6
women	83.5	84.4	84.9	85.4	85.8	86.2	86.7	87.1	87.5
Survival rates									
Birth to 65: men	46.7	52.4	60.2	66.8	72.2	75.6	77.1	79.0	80.7
women	57.8	65.3	72.7	77.7	81.5	84.6	85.9	87.2	88.4
Birth to 85: men	11.0	14.1	18.6	22.3	25.6	28.3	30.3	32.5	34.6
women	25.5	31.3	36.7	40.5	43.8	47.0	49.1	51.2	53.1
Birth to 100: men	0.2	0.3	0.5	0.7	1.0	1.3	1.7	2.0	2.5
women	1.3	1.8	2.5	3.2	4.1	5.1	6.0	7.1	8.2

Source: Authors' calculations using data supplied by the Office of the Actuary, Social Security Administration.

particularly women, who survive past 85, this last limitation is a matter of concern.

Our decision to employ mortality statistics furnished by the Social Security Administration is therefore a compromise. Neither these figures nor those supplied by Vital Statistics reflect all the variables observable by individuals that might plausibly affect individuals' estimates of their own mortality probabilities. Among such factors are people's current health status, including the presence and severity of disease, family income levels, and whether they participate in any activities or occupations which elevate the mortality risk. The construction of such individual-specific mortality tables would be a research program in itself, not one which we undertake here. Hence it should be understood that the social security wealth variables reported in the EPBF are approximations. Users exploring differences in social security wealth arising from mortality probabilities that differ according to factors other than age and sex should derive their own social security wealth variables.

Hot Deck Procedures

The social security variables just described are calculated for each 1992 HRS respondent for whom the HRS received an earnings record from the Social

Security Administration. That is, there is a one-to-one correspondence between respondents' records in the SEPBF and the earnings summary file supplied by the SSA to the Health and Retirement Study. All of the variables except the couple's social security wealth amounts can be calculated from the respondent's own earnings record, and it does not matter whether the record for the spouse is present, or for that matter even whether the individual has a spouse.

The situation is different for a married couple's social security wealth variables, since in this case it is necessary to have a record for the spouse as well. For some 1356 out of 4077 married HRS sample couples, the social security file contains a record for one spouse but not for the other.[35] This could have occurred either because the spouse did not grant permission to access the earnings record, or because a valid match to the earnings record could not be found at the Social Security Administration. In these cases, for the missing spouse record, we substituted an actual earnings record from another respondent with the same sex and similar levels of earnings and labor force attachment.[36] This procedure is known as "hot-decking" in the survey literature. We emphasize that in such cases, there is only one record in the summary social security variables file; we did not create a record for the "hot-decked" or missing spouse's earnings history. Rather, this hot deck record was used only to impute the family social security wealth variables for the respondent for whom we did receive a social security earnings record. (It will be recalled that respondents surveyed by the HRS, who were outside the HRS age range of 51–61 in 1992, appear in the HRS by virtue of being married to age-eligible spouses. The observations in the tables are for age-eligible respondents, though family social security wealth computations include benefit estimates for age-ineligible spouses).

For the hot deck procedure, we relied on all the earning records received from the Social Security Administration. Each non-missing record was assigned to a single cell in a five-way classification table, based on the information the respondent gave in the household survey. The table was chosen to reflect the five variables that we believed were closely associated with different levels of average monthly earnings and, therefore, potential benefit amounts. These five variables are: sex (male or female), work status at the time of the 1992 interview (working or not working), 12 categories of age in 1992, 26 categories of annual earnings, and 6 categories of observed work experience.[37] For individuals who were working at the time of the 1992 interview, annual earnings are taken as the reported earnings for the calendar year 1991, while if the individual was not working at the time of the 1992 interview, annual earnings are calculated from the wage (which could be given as an amount per hour, per week, per month, or annual) in the last job. Total observed experience is the sum of the tenures in the current job in 1992 (if employed at the time), the last job (if not employed at the time), and up to three previous jobs that lasted for more than 5 years.[38]

APPENDIX TABLE 3: Sample Sizes in the Summary Earnings and Projected Benefits File

	N
Sample 1: Entire SEPB file	*8257*
Sample 2: Sample 1 minus age ineligible minus those in receipt of SSDI in 1991	*5999*
Married	4606
Men	2326
Women	2280
Nonmarried	1393
Men	413
Women	980
Sample 3: Sample 2 minus married respondents where spouse not interviewed in HRS or spouse in current receipt of SSDI	*5728*
Married	4335
Men	2217
Women	2118
Nonmarried (same as sample 1)	

Source: Authors' calculations.

The rationale for the earnings and experience variables is fairly clear: since the average monthly earnings figure in the social security calculations depends on the average earnings and the number of years the individuals have been in covered employment, it is important to take this information into account when matching. Age is important in considering whether a given number of years of experience represents a large or moderate percentage of the number of years of eventual experience when the individual retires. Also, sex is important if it is likely that participation patterns vary considerably between men and women, even for those with similar earnings. Finally, it probably makes a considerable difference, especially for the projected wealth variable, whether the individual is or is not currently working. The projected earnings of a married woman who has worked in the past but who is not currently working may well be quite different from those of a married woman with a same average earnings but who is continuing to work.

With all available earnings records grouped into this five-way table, the records were then randomized within each cell of the table. Since there are 7,488 potential cells in the table, and we have 8,394 earnings records, each cell has on average a little more than one record. Then, when we have an individual with a social security earnings record but no matched record for the spouse, we select a "donor" HRS household file to construct the gender, 1992 work status, wage, and experience variables for the spouse, and use a randomly chosen record from the same age-gender-work status-wage-experience cell to represent the spouse's missing record. When necessary, the wage, experience, and/or age cells are broadened until a match is found. Again, this matched record is used only to construct measures of family social security wealth for those individuals for whom we do have an actual earnings record.

Appendix B: Variables in the Summary Earnings and Projected Benefits File (SEPBF)

Variable Number	Beginning Column	Variable Name
1	1	Case ID
2	6	Spouse ID (=0 if no spouse, =99999 if no HRS data record for spouse)
3	11	Hot deck ID (=0 if not married or spouse has social security record, =99999 if spouse was not interviewed)
4	16	Disability insurance benefits code (=1 in benefit receipt, =0 else)
5[a]	17	Average indexed monthly earnings ($)
6[a]	22	Primary insurance amount, earnings to 1991 ($)
7[a]	27	Projected primary insurance amount, earnings to age 62 ($)
8[a]	32	Projected primary insurance amount, earnings to NRA ($)
9[b]	37	Current individual or couple social security wealth ($)
10[b]	43	Respondent's own benefit ($)
11[b]	49	Respondent's spouse benefit ($ including dual)
12[b]	55	Respondent's surviving spouse benefit ($ including dual)
13[b]	61	Spouse's own benefit ($)
14[b]	67	Spouse's spouse benefit ($ including dual)
15[b]	73	Spouse's surviving spouse benefit ($ including dual)
16[b]	79	Projected individual/couple social security wealth; age 62 ($)
17[b]	85	Respondent's own benefit ($)
18[b]	91	Respondent's spouse benefit ($ including dual)
19[b]	97	Respondent's surviving spouse benefit ($ including dual)
20[b]	103	Spouse's own benefit ($)
21[b]	109	Spouse's spouse benefit ($ including dual)
22[b]	115	Spouse's surviving spouse benefit ($ including dual)
23[b]	121	Projected individual/couple social security wealth; NRA ($)
24[b]	127	Respondent's own benefit ($)
25[b]	133	Respondent's spouse benefit ($ including dual)
26[b]	139	Respondent's surviving spouse benefit ($ including dual)
27[b]	145	Spouse's own benefit ($)
28[b]	151	Spouse's spouse benefit ($ including dual)
29[b]	157	Spouse's surviving spouse benefit ($ including dual)
30	163	Total quarters of coverage (through 1991)
31	166	Social security disability insurance status in 1991 (=1 disability insured, =0 not)
32	167	Number of nonzero quarters of coverage 1982–83
33	168	Number of nonzero quarters of coverage 1984–85
34	169	Number of nonzero quarters of coverage 1986–87
35	170	Number of nonzero quarters of coverage 1988–89
36	171	Number of nonzero quarters of coverage 1990–91

Variable Number	Beginning Column	Variable Name
37[c]	172	Aver. taxable real earnings, age 20–29 ($)
38[c]	178	Aver. taxable real earnings, age 30–39 ($)
39[c]	184	Aver. taxable real earnings, age 40–49 ($)
40[c]	190	Aver. taxable real earnings, age 50–59 ($)
41[c]	196	Aver. taxable real earnings, age 60–69 ($)
42[c]	202	Aver. taxable real earnings, age 70–79 ($)
43[c]	208	Aver. taxable real earnings, age 80–89 ($)
44[c]	214	Zero earnings years, age 20–29
45[c]	216	Zero earnings years, age 30–39
46[c]	218	Zero earnings years, age 40–49
47[c]	220	Zero earnings years, age 50–59
48[c]	222	Zero earnings years, age 60–69
49[c]	224	Zero earnings years, age 70–79
50[c]	226	Zero earnings years, age 80–89
51[d]	228	Lowest earnings year in AIME average
52[d]	234	Next lowest earnings year in AIME average
53[d]	240	Third lowest earnings year in AIME average
—	—	
70[d]	342	20th lowest earnings year in AIME average

Notes: Respondents who declined permission to link HRS and administrative records have no EPBF record; see text. Variables 5–8 rounded to nearest $10, variables 37–43 rounded to nearest $100. Variables 9–29 hotdecked as required.
[a] Values based on respondent's own earnings record; =0 if none; =−9 if worker (or spouse) receiving DI in 1991.
[b] Includes earnings only to maximum social security taxable earnings; =−9 if the respondent (or spouse) receiving DI in 1991; =0 if respondent not eligible for benefits or eligibility is unknown (e.g. for current widows); =0 for spouse benefits where spouse could not be interviewed in the HRS.
[c] Excludes years before 1951 and after 1991.
[d] =−9 if respondent receiving DI.

Notes

1. The SEPBF is a restricted file; conditions under which users may access the data are described at www.umich.edu/~hrswww. Email questions regarding the SEPB and HRS datasets should be directed to hrsquest@umich.edu. Readers interested in more detailed information about social security rules may consult the References for citations or the SSA website (www.ssa.gov/).

2. In later releases, additional consent forms were obtained and added to the file; as of this writing the SEPB file has not been amended to include these cases.

3. These figures refer to the HRS Wave 1 respondents. In Waves 2 and thereafter additional respondents supplied permission forms, but these respondents have not yet been included in the SEPB dataset supplied with this release of the SEPB file.

4. Respondents with no positive covered earnings were excluded from the initial SEPB file; in later versions people who had no covered earnings records were added to the file. Some people with zero recorded earnings never worked for pay, while others probably worked in noncovered jobs. The types of jobs remaining uncovered

have diminished over time, but most often would include government (e.g. federal, state, and local), agricultural, and nonprofit employment.

5. Tabulations in Table 1 are weighted by HRS sample weights. Some HRS respondents do not have covered earnings reported in the administrative records, since their jobs were not covered by social security in times past. For a discussion of covered and uncovered jobs see Myers (1993).

6. As noted below, disability benefits are not included in the SEPB file.

7. DI recipients are identified (variable 4, Appendix B, is set to 1) and they have a missing value code (-9) inserted in lieu of social security benefit amounts in the social security benefit fields (variables 9–29 in Appendix B). In this way, DI recipients can be distinguished from those ineligible for benefits due to insufficient quarters of coverage; those not eligible to receive social security benefits have a 0 in their benefits variable fields (variables 9–29). If a DI recipient was married, no benefit is computed for that person's spouse either, and a missing data value (-9) appears in variables 9–29.

8. In 1992 this maximum was an annual $55,500; for historical amounts, see SSA (1995).

9. Users should note that the respondents' consent agreements allowed the provision only of records to date, and annual earnings before 1951 are not available in electronic form at SSA. HRS study data can be used for updating earnings in 1992 and later years.

10. Earnings while age 50–59 are averaged only over possible work years in Table 2.

11. Retirees may also qualify for other benefits including disability and Medicare payments, among others, but these are not the focus of the present analysis.

12. This refers to the variable 10–29 series described in Appendix B. So for instance, if a spouse's dual entitlement benefit is higher than the benefit she could receive based on her own earnings record, the larger benefit is entered in her husband's variable 14 (Appendix B) and a zero is entered in his variable 13. In her record (assuming she is included in the SEPB file), the values of her variables would be compatible with those appearing in her husband's file (i.e., her variable 11 equals his variable 14, and her variable 10 equals his variable 13).

13. Estimates from the Survey of Income and Program Participation (SIPP) linked to SSA benefit data show that a large majority of aged widows receive benefits based on their husbands' earnings records. An internal SSA study found that 77.6 percent of aged widows in 1990 who were receiving social security benefits received benefits based wholly or partially on the deceased husbands' earnings record. This suggests that SEPBF-computed benefits data for nonmarried women will underestimate the eventual benefits that many of these women will receive, since we do not have deceased spouses' earnings records linked to the file. For divorced women the in-house study suggested that approximately 30 percent of divorcees received social security benefits either wholly or partially based on the (deceased) former husbands' earnings records. This suggests that the understatement of likely benefits may be less serious for divorced than currently widowed women.

14. Under current social security rules, persons receiving survivor's benefits are sometimes entitled to retired-worker benefits on their own record, and to higher survivor benefits based on their spouse's record. As noted above in the discussion of spouse benefits, these dually entitled beneficiaries are classified in the SEPBF simply as spouse or survivor beneficiaries.

15. The higher benefit values reported for male as compared to female HRS respondents in Table 3 reflect the fact that HRS age-eligible male respondents are somewhat older on average, as compared to HRS women respondents.

16. For each of these cases and for current disability insurance beneficiaries, the

SEPBF total social security wealth variables may be modified using social security benefit files in conjunction with the earnings records.

17. As noted earlier, the SEPBF may not, in general, be linked to HRS data containing geographic detail below the Census Division level.

18. This might occur if, for example, that spouse did not participate in the survey, or if he/she did not consent to have social security administrative data appended to his or her file. In this case social security projected wealth variables are imputed using the hot deck procedure described below.

19. The average earnings computation for workers who attained age 62 prior to 1978 is computed slightly differently (see SSA, various years, or www.ssa.gov/).

20. Special rules apply if the individual turned 62 before 1979 (see SSA, various years). What is reported in variable 6 is the primary insurance amount as of 1992, reflecting the cost of living increases since the individual first became eligible.

21. The consumer price index is the CPI-W, or the index for urban wage earners and clerical workers.

22. The 1995 report was the latest year available at the time that these wealth variables were calculated.

23. In generating variables 16 and 23, the individual is assumed to begin collecting benefits when he or she first applies for social security benefits. This is held to be the early retirement age for variable 16 and the normal retirement age for variable 23. In addition, the individual cannot collect spouse benefits until the spouse has applied as well, in accordance with the rules (Myers 1993).

24. If a respondent was not entitled to social security benefits based on his own work record as of his age in 1992 his social security wealth benefit variable 10 would be set to zero; similarly for benefits based on work until age 62 (in which case variable 17 would be set to zero), and until the normal retirement age (and variable 24 would be zero).

25. Normally, the benefit would be subject to the earnings test, which may reduce benefits for those continuing to earn after receipt of benefits. The potential benefit may also be increased because of the delayed retirement credit if the individual has worked after the normal retirement age and lost some benefits to the earnings test. The earnings test does not apply after 70 years of age. Here, earnings are imputed only before 1992 or if the individual is under the retirement age; benefits are calculated only on or after 1992 and if the individual is above the retirement age. As a result the wealth program assumes no earnings in years after the individual becomes eligible for that benefit.

26. The data user should understand that there are some cases where spouse benefits for HRS respondents married at the time of the 1992 survey could not be computed based on the married parties' earnings records; see below for hot deck and missing data treatment.

27. In reality this benefit would be subject to earnings tests, both one based on the individual's own work and also one based on the work of the partner (since the individual cannot collect benefits in any month the partner does not also collect benefits). However, the wealth program assumes no work past the retirement age as indicated in the previous footnote.

28. Variable 9 assumes no projected earnings and the widow/er applies for benefits at age 60 (or immediately, if she/he is older than age 60). For variables 16 and 23 the widow/er is assumed to continue his/her employment status until, respectively, the early or the normal retirement age, before applying for these benefits.

29. If an individual was not eligible for own retirement benefits, his/her own worker benefits would be set to zero. In a married couple, if either spouse was receiving DI in 1991, the wealth variables for both spouses are set to -1 and the AIME and PIA are set to zero. As long as both partners were not receiving DI, and if either

partner would be projected to be eligible for benefits by the early or normal retirement age, the relevant wealth variables are positive.

30. As noted, this will probably underestimate wealth for potentially three-quarters of the currently widowed women, and some unknown fraction of divorced women, inasmuch as we do not have their former spouse's earnings records.

31. Depending on whether the individual gives full weight to benefits that the spouse will collect after the death of the individual, the researcher may want to alter the relative weights of variable 15 and perhaps variable 14 in the sum.

32. As noted earlier, three-quarters of aged widows with benefits received survivor benefits based on their deceased husbands' earnings records (unpublished SSA estimate).

33. Widows age 60–61 who were already receiving benefits in the HRS are handled like other widows in the survey; their social security wealth was calculated on the basis of their own earnings even if they were already receiving benefits as widows.

34. Felicitie Bell in the SSA's Office of the Actuary kindly supplied these data. The survival rates given in the SSA data (Table 5) are higher than those reported in the 1990 Vital Statistics tables. This implies that social security wealth figures calculated on the basis of the survival rates in the Vital Statistics tables would have been lower than the wealth figures reported here.

35. Some of those without an earnings record had never worked for pay in covered employment. Of the 1356 spouses without social security records for instance, 614 were women.

36. If there were no records which matched exactly the five categories, adjacent cells were searched until a match was found. Adjacent earnings cells were searched first, followed by adjacent age cells and adjacent experience cells. In no case was it necessary to vary earnings, age, and experience by more than one category to find a match. Also, in no case was a male record substituted for a female or vice versa, or a record for someone not working in 1992 substituted for someone working or vice versa. Note that it was possible to substitute a disabled beneficiary's record when the other hot deck criteria were met.

37. The age categories used were five years in width for ages between 25 and 74. Individuals 24 years old and younger were grouped into a single category, as were people 75 years and older. The earnings categories are $2,000 wide between $0 and $24,000, $3,000 wide up to $42,000, $4,000 wide up to $50,000, $5,000 wide up to $60,000 and $10,000 wide up to $100,000. Earnings over $100,000 were grouped into a single cell, since this is considerably above the social security taxable maximum. The experience categories are 0–5, 6–10, 11–20, 21–30, 31–40, and 41+ years.

38. The HRS did not ask respondents directly about the total number of years they had been employed in all jobs, so experience must be proxied by the total experience in jobs reported in the survey.

References

Ballantyne, Harry C. 1984. "Present Policies and Methods Regarding the Long-Term Adjustment of Benefits." *Social Security Bulletin* 47, 10 (October).

Board of Trustees of the Federal Old-Age and Survivors Insurance and Disability Insurance Trust Funds. 1995. *1995 Annual Report*. Washington, D.C.: U.S. Government Printing Office.

Bondar, Joseph. 1995. "How to Compute a Retired-Worker Benefit." *Social Security Bulletin* 58, 1 (Spring).

Dwyer, Debra Sabatini and Jiangting Hu. "Retirement Expectations and Realizations: The Role of Health Shocks and Economic Factors." This volume.

Fields, Gary S. and Olivia S. Mitchell. 1984. *Retirement, Pensions, and Social Security.* Cambridge, Mass.: MIT Press, 1984.

Gustman, Alan L. and Olivia S. Mitchell. 1992. "Pensions and the Labor Market: Behavior and Data Requirements." In Zvi Bodie and Alicia H. Munnell, eds. *Pensions and the Sources, Uses, and Limitations of Data Economy: Need for Good Data.* Pension Research Council. Philadelphia: University of Pennsylvania Press, 1992: 39–87.

Gustman, Alan. L. and Thomas L. Steinmeier. 1986. "A Structural Retirement Model." *Econometrica* 54, 3 (May): 555–84.

Gustman, Alan, Olivia S. Mitchell, and Thomas Steinmeier. 1995. "Retirement Research Using the Health and Retirement Study." *Journal of Human Resources* 30 (Supplement): S57–83.

Hurd, Michael D. 1990a. "The Joint Retirement Decision Of Husbands And Wives." In David A. Wise, ed., *Issues in the Economics of Aging.* Chicago: University of Chicago Press, 231–54.

——. 1990b. "Research on the Elderly: Economic Status, Retirement, and Consumption and Saving." *Journal of Economic Literature* 28, 2 (June): 565–637.

Leonesio, Michael. 1993. "Social Security and Older Workers." *Social Security Bulletin* 56, 2 (Summer).

Lingg, Barbara A. 1990. "Women Beneficiaries Aged 62 or Older, 1960–88." *Social Security Bulletin* 53, 7 (July). (For updated data, see Tables 5.A14 and 5.A15 in the *Annual Statistical Supplement, 1995* to the *Social Security Bulletin.*)

Mitchell, Olivia S. 1991. "Social Security Reforms and Poverty Among Dual-Earner Couples." *Journal of Population Economics* 4: 281–93.

Mitchell, Olivia S., James F. Moore, and John W. Phillips. "Explaining Retirement Saving Shortfalls." This volume.

Moore, James F. and Olivia S. Mitchell. "Projected Retirement Wealth and Savings Adequacy." This volume.

Myers, Robert. 1993. *Social Security.* Pension Research Council. Philadelphia: University of Pennsylvania Press.

Nelson, William J., Jr. 1994. "Disability Trends in the United States: A National and Regional Perspective." *Social Security Bulletin* 57, 3 (Fall).

Office of the Actuary, Social Security Administration. *Users Guide for PIA Calculation Program, Version 1995.1*, U.S. Department of Health and Human Services, Publication #11–11501, 1995.

Pozzebon, Silvana and Olivia S. Mitchell. 1989. "Married Women's Retirement Behavior." *Journal of Population Economics* 2, 1: 301–53.

Quinn, Joseph F., Richard V. Burkhauser and Daniel A. Myers. 1990. *Passing the Torch: The Influence of Economic Incentives on Work and Retirement.* Kalamazoo, Mich.: W.E. Upjohn Institute.

Social Security Administration (SSA). Various years. *Annual Statistical Supplement to the Social Security Bulletin*, U.S. Department of Health and Human Services. Washington, D.C.: U.S. Govt. Printing Office.

"Social Security Programs in the United States." 1993. *Social Security Bulletin*, 56, 4 (Winter).

Steuerle, C. Eugene and Jon M. Bakija. 1994. *Retooling Social Security for the 21st Century.* Washington, D.C.: Urban Institute.

Thompson, Lawrence H. 1983. "The Social Security Reform Debate." *Journal of Economic Literature* 21, 4 (December): 1425–67.

U.S. Department of Health and Human Services. 1987. *SSA's Retirement History Survey: Compilation of Reports.* September. Washington, D.C.: U.S. Government Printing Office.

Contributors

John Ameriks is a PhD candidate in the Department of Economics at Columbia University and a senior research associate in the Strategic Research unit at TIAA-CREF. He is completing his doctoral dissertation on the subject of individual asset allocation behavior in designated retirement accounts. Previously, Mr. Ameriks was a research associate at Economists Incorporated. He received the BA from Stanford University and the MA and M. Phil. from Columbia University.

Charles Brown is Professor of Economics and Research Scientist at the Survey Research Center at the University of Michigan. His research interests include a diverse set of topics in labor economics, such as compensating differentials, equal-opportunity programs, unions and productivity, minimum wage laws, employer size and wages, the accuracy of survey data, and offers of early retirement windows. Previously, Dr. Brown taught at the Department of Economics at the University of Maryland. He received the AB and MA from Boston College, and the PhD from Harvard University.

Robert L. Clark is Professor of Business Management and Economics at North Carolina State University. His research interests include how firms use employee benefits to achieve personnel objectives, government regulation of employee benefit programs, international employee benefits, retirement policies, and the economic response to population aging. He is a member of the American Economic Association, the Gerontological Society of America, the International Union for Scientific Study of Population, and the National Academy of Social Insurance. Dr. Clark earned a BA from Millsaps College and MA and PhD degrees from Duke University.

Debra Sabatini Dwyer is an Assistant Professor at the SUNY-Stonybrook Department of Economics. Her research interests include aging, health and work, disability policy, and measurement error in survey data. Previously, she did postdoctoral research at the Center for Policy Research at Syracuse University. Dr. Dwyer received the MS and PhD in Labor Economics from Cornell University.

Gordon P. Goodfellow is a senior associate of Research and Information Center at Watson Wyatt Worldwide, where he has specialized in the analysis of social security policy and private defined contribution plans. Previously, he worked with the Office of the Assistant Secretary for Planning and Evaluation as a senior policy analyst and project manager of the Panel Study of Income Dynamics.

Alan L. Gustman is Loren M. Berry Professor of Economics at Dartmouth College. His areas of research are labor economics and the economics of aging. He is a Research Associate at the National Bureau of Economic Research and a member of the National Academy of Social Insurance. Dr. Gustman serves on advisory panels to the University of Michigan for the design of its Health and Retirement Survey and to the Bureau of Labor Statistics for its National Longitudinal Survey. From 1976 to 1977 he served as Special Assistant for Economic Affairs for the U.S. Department of Labor. He holds a BA from City College of New York and a PhD in economics from University of Michigan.

P. Brett Hammond is Manager of Corporate Projects at the Teachers Insurance Annuity Association-College Retirement Equities Fund (TIAA-CREF). His research publications are in the areas of pensions, higher education, science and technology, finance, and health policy. Dr. Hammond received the bachelor's degree in economics and politics from the University of California, Santa Cruz and the PhD in public policy from MIT.

Marjorie Honig is Professor of Economics at Hunter College and the Graduate School of CUNY. Her research interests focus on issues related to the economics of aging, with emphasis on individual retirement decisions and the roles of social security and employer pensions. Her current research examines workers' expectations regarding retirement income and the timing of retirement. She is a member of the Advisory Board for the Brookdale Foundation National Fellowship Program and is an advisor to the International Longevity Center of the Mount Sinai Medical Center. Dr. Honig received the PhD in economics from Columbia University.

Jianting Hu is Economist at the Social Security Administration. His research interests include social security and disability issues, and econometrics. He received the PhD in economics from New York University.

Phillip B. Levine is Associate Professor of Economics at Wellesley College. His research interests focus on policy-relevant topics including unemployment insurance, welfare policy, and the effects of demographic change in labor markets. Dr. Levine is a faculty research fellow at the National Bureau of Economic Research. He has served as a senior economist at the White House Council of Economic Advisers on issues relating to the labor market, education, and welfare policy. Dr. Levine received the BS from Cornell University and the PhD from Princeton University.

Olivia S. Mitchell is the International Foundation of Employee Benefit Plans Professor of Insurance and Risk Management, and Executive Director of the Pension Research Council, of the Wharton School at the University of Pennsylvania. Her research interests include the economics of retirement and benefits, social security and pensions, and public as well as private insurance. Dr. Mitchell is also a Research Associate at the National Bureau of Economic Research and she serves on the Steering Committee for the University of Michigan's HRS/AHEAD projects, funded by the National Institute on Aging. Her previous academic positions included a faculty appointment at Cornell University and visiting scholar at Harvard University. Dr. Mitchell received the BS in economics from Harvard University, and the PhD in economics from the University of Wisconsin.

James F. Moore is a PhD candidate in the Department of Insurance and Risk Management at the Wharton School of the University of Pennsylvania. His research interests include retirement saving behavior, securitization of insurance risk, innovation in insurance and securities markets. Previously, Mr. Moore was a pension consultant with William M. Mercer, Inc. He received the BS in Applied Mathematics and Economics from Brown University.

Jan Olson is Social Science Analyst at the Office of Research, Evaluation, and Statistics of the Social Security Administration. Her research interests include retirement and income security. Dr. Olson received the PhD from Cornell University.

John W. Phillips is an economist at the Social Security Administration. Previously he was a Postdoctoral Fellow at the Population Studies Center, University of Pennsylvania. His research interests include labor economics and public finance. Previously, Dr. Phillips taught at Syracuse University. He received the BA and PhD in economics from Syracuse University.

Joseph F. Quinn is Professor of Economics at Boston College. His research focuses on the economics of aging, with emphasis on the economic status of the elderly, the determinants of individual retirement decisions, and patterns of labor force withdrawal among older Americans. Professor Quinn is a founding member of the National Academy of Social Insurance, and serves on the Board of Governors of the Foundation for International Studies on Social Security, the (Massachusetts) Governor's Council on Economic Growth and Technology, the Executive Board of the Gordon Public Policy Center at Brandeis University, and the Editorial Board of the Review of Income and Wealth. He recently co-chaired (with Olivia Mitchell of the Wharton School) the Technical Panel on Trends and Issues in Retirement Saving for the 1995–96 Social Security Advisory Council. Professor Quinn received his undergraduate education at Amherst College and the PhD in economics from MIT.

Anna M. Rappaport, FSA, is Managing Director of William M. Mercer, Incorporated specializing in strategy for retirement benefits. Her areas of interest include demographics and the aging society, and the impact of retirement systems on women. Currently Ms. Rappaport is serving as President of the Society of Actuaries. She is a Board member of the Pension Research Council, a member of the National Academy of Social Insurance, a member of the American Academy of Actuaries, and a member of the Chicago Network. She is Fellow of the Society of Actuaries and she has an MBA from the University of Chicago.

Andrew A. Samwick is Assistant Professor of economics at Dartmouth College and a faculty research fellow of the National Bureau of Economic Research. His research interests include saving, portfolio choice, executive compensation, taxation, social security, and pensions. Dr. Samwick received the BA from Harvard University and PhD from MIT.

Sylvester J. Schieber is the Director of Watson Wyatt Worldwide's Research and Information Center in Washington. He specializes in the analysis of public and private retirement policy and health policy issues. He has been responsible for the development of a number of special ongoing survey programs at Watson Wyatt focusing on these issues. Previously, Dr. Schieber worked as Research Director of the Employee Benefits Research Institute and also held positions at the Social Security Administration. Dr. Schieber serves on Watson Wyatt's Board of Directors and was a member of the 1994–95 Social Security Advisory Council. Dr. Schieber received the PhD in economics from the University of Notre Dame.

Thomas L. Steinmeier is Professor of Economics at Texas Tech University. His research interests include the estimation of improved models of retirement and asset accumulation, and an exploration of methods to blend data from household surveys with administrative records on pensions and social security. Dr. Steinmeier is currently a co-principal investigator at the Study of Health, Retirement and Aging. Previously, he taught at Dartmouth College. Dr. Steinmeier received the PhD from Yale University.

Mark J. Warshawsky is Director of Strategic Research for TIAA-CREF. His research has focused on pension and retiree health benefit plans, individual annuities and life insurance, asset allocation behavior, national health expenditures, corporate finance, and securities markets. Prior to joining TIAA-CREF, he was a Senior Economist at the Internal Revenue Service and at the Federal Reserve Board. Dr. Warshawsky received the PhD in economics from Harvard University.

Drew Warwick is Research Associate at Watson Wyatt Worldwide's Research and Information Center. Mr. Warwick specializes in retirement policy issues and the relationship between retirement investment decisions and defined contribution plans. Previously Mr. Warwick was an economist in the Office of Employment Projections, Bureau of Labor Statistics, where he did research relating to forecasting employment demand for financial industries and occupations. Mr. Warwick received his MA in Monetary Economics from Georgia State University.

David R. Weir is Research Associate at Harris School of Public Policy and Visiting Associate Professor of Economics at the University of Chicago. His areas of interest include economics of aging and health including insurance, evaluation of medical interventions, and design of public policy. Dr. Weir received the BA in History from University of Michigan and the PhD in economics from Stanford University.

Robert J. Willis is Professor of Economics at the University of Michigan. He is also a faculty member of the Survey Research Center at the Institute for Social Research and the Population Studies Center. His research interests include labor economics, economic demography and economic development. Dr. Willis has been elected to the Board of Directors of Population Association of America, has served on advisory boards of the Panel Study of Income Dynamics, the High School and Beyond Survey, and the Health and Retirement Study. He was recently appointed as representative to the Census Advisory Board by the American Economic Association. Dr. Willis received the PhD from the University of Washington.

Index

The Pension Research Council

The Pension Research Council of the Wharton School at the University of Pennsylvania is an organization committed to generating debate on key policy issues affecting pensions and other employee benefits. The Council sponsors interdisciplinary research on the entire range of private and social retirement security and related benefit plans in the United States and around the world. It seeks to broaden understanding of these complex arrangements through basic research into their economic, social, legal, actuarial, and financial foundations. Members of the Advisory Board of the Council, appointed by the Dean of the Wharton School, are leaders in the employee benefits field, and they recognize the essential role of social security and other public sector income maintenance programs while sharing a desire to strengthen private sector approaches to economic security.

Executive Director

Olivia S. Mitchell, *International Foundation of Employee Benefit Plans Professor*, Department of Insurance and Risk Management, The Wharton School, University of Pennsylvania, Philadelphia.

Senior Partners

AARP
Actuarial Sciences Associates, Inc.
JRT Research, Ltd.
Morgan Stanley & Co., Inc.
Mutual of America Life Insurance Company
Price Waterhouse LLP
State Street Corporation
Watson Wyatt Worldwide
William M. Mercer Companies, Inc.

Institutional Members

Buck Consultants, Inc.
Employee Benefit Research Institute
Ford Motor Company
Hay/Huggins Company, Inc.
Instituto Cultural de Seguridade Social
Investment Company Institute
John Hancock Mutual Life Insurance Company
J.P. Morgan Investment Management Inc.
KPMG Peat Marwick LLP
Loomis, Sayles & Company, L.P.
Merck & Co., Inc.
Metropolitan Life Insurance Company
New York Life Insurance Company
The Principal Financial Group
The Prudential Foundation
The Segal Company
TIAA-CREF
ULLICO
VALIC

Advisory Board

Vincent Amoroso, F.S.A., *Principal*, Deloitte & Touche, Washington, DC
David S. Blitzstein, *Director*, United Food & Commercial Workers International Union, Washington, DC
Marshall Blume, *Howard Butcher Professor of Finance and Director, Rodney L. White Center for Financial Research*, The Wharton School, Philadelphia, PA
Zvi Bodie, *Professor of Finance*, Boston University, Boston, MA
Christopher M. Bone, Chief Actuary, Actuarial Sciences Associates, Inc., Somerset, NJ
Michael S. Gordon, Esq., Law Offices of Michael S. Gordon, Washington, DC
P. Brett Hammond, *Manager of Corporate Projects*, TIAA-CREF, New York, NY
Judith F. Mazo, *Senior Vice President and Director of Research*, The Segal Company, Washington, DC
Alicia H. Munnell, *Peter F. Drucker Chair in Management Sciences*, School of Management, Boston College, MA
Robert J. Myers, F.S.A., *International Consultant on Social Security*, Silver Spring, MD
Richard Prosten, *Director*, Washington Office, Amalgamated Life Insurance/Amalgamated Bank of New York, Washington, DC

Anna M. Rappaport, F.S.A., *Managing Director*, William M. Mercer, Inc., Chicago, IL

Jerry S. Rosenbloom, *Frederick H. Ecker Professor of Insurance and Risk Management*, The Wharton School, Philadelphia, PA

Sylvester J. Schieber, *Vice President and Director of Research and Information Center*, Watson Wyatt Worldwide, Washington, DC

Richard B. Stanger, *National Director*, Employee Benefits Services, Price Waterhouse LLP, New York, NY

Marc M. Twinney, Jr., F.S.A., *Consultant*, Bloomfield Hills, MI

Michael Useem, *Professor of Management and Sociology*, The Wharton School, Philadelphia, PA

Jack L. VanDerhei, *Associate Professor of Risk and Insurance*, Temple University, Philadelphia, PA

Paul H. Wenz, F.S.A., *Second Vice President and Actuary*, The Principal Financial Group, Des Moines, IA

Stephen Zeldes, *Benjamin Rosen Professor of Economics and Finance*, Columbia University, New York, NY

Recent Pension Research Council Publications

Fundamentals of Private Pensions. Dan M. McGill, Kyle N. Brown, John J. Haley and Sylvester Schieber. Seventh edition. 1996.

The Future of Pensions in the United States. Ray Schmitt, ed. 1993.

Living with Defined Contribution Pensions. Olivia S. Mitchell and Sylvester J. Schieber, eds. 1998

Pension Mathematics with Numerical Illustrations. Howard E. Winklevoss. Second edition. 1993.

Pensions and the Economy: Sources, Uses, and Limitations of Data. Zvi Bodie and Alicia H. Munnell, eds. 1992.

Positioning Pensions for the Twenty-First Century. Michael S. Gordon, Olivia S. Mitchell, and Marc M. Twinney, eds. 1997.

Prospects for Social Security Reform. Olivia S. Mitchell, Robert J. Myers, and Howard Young, eds. 1999.

Providing Health Care Benefits in Retirement. Judith F. Mazo, Anna M. Rappaport and Sylvester J. Schieber, eds. 1994.

Securing Employer-Based Pensions: An International Perspective. Zvi Bodie, Olivia S. Mitchell, and John A. Turner. 1996.

Social Security. Robert J. Myers. Fourth edition. 1993.

Available from the University of Pennsylvania Press:
telephone 800/445-9880, fax 410/516-6998.
More information about the Pension Research Council is
available at the web site:
http://prc.wharton.upenn.edu/prc/prc.html